memory and vision

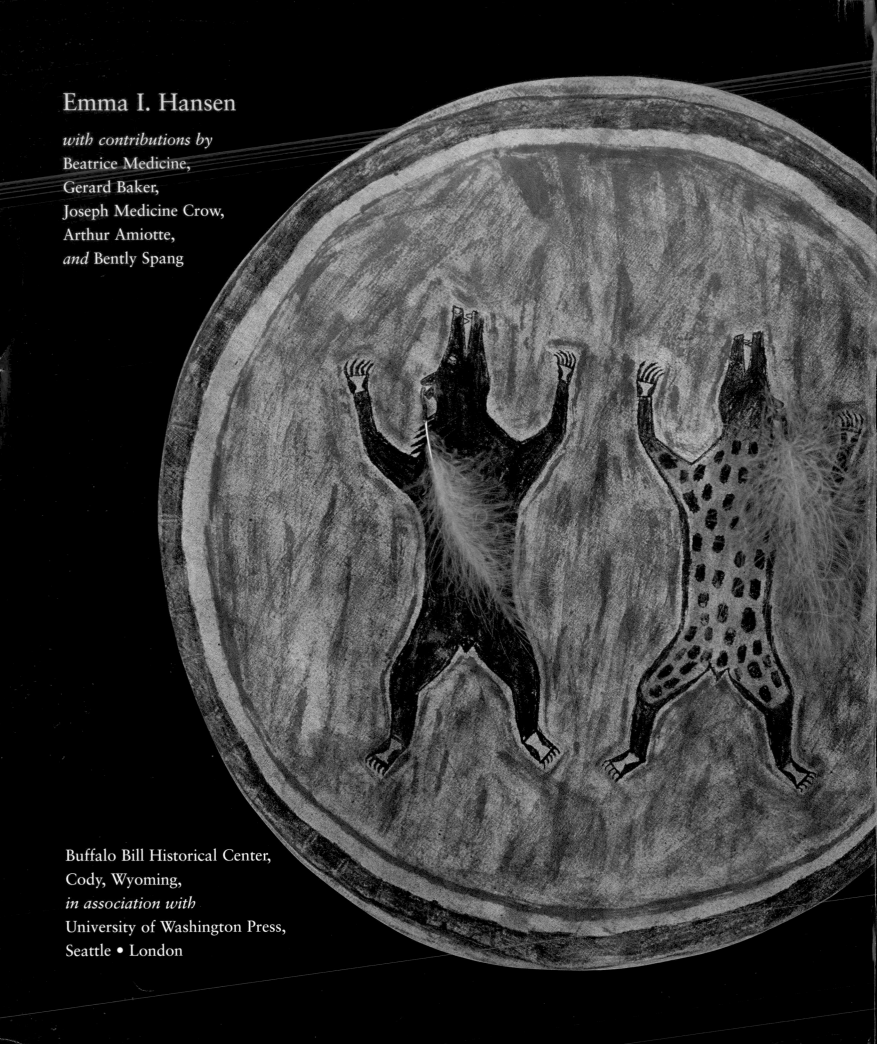

Emma I. Hansen

with contributions by
Beatrice Medicine,
Gerard Baker,
Joseph Medicine Crow,
Arthur Amiotte,
and Bently Spang

Buffalo Bill Historical Center,
Cody, Wyoming,
in association with
University of Washington Press,
Seattle • London

ARTS, CULTURES, AND LIVES OF PLAINS INDIAN PEOPLE

memory and vision

Editorial services and project management by Suzanne G. Fox, Red Bird Publishing, Inc., Bozeman, Montana
Designed by Carol Beehler, Bethesda, Maryland

Printed in Singapore

Buffalo Bill Historical Center
720 Sheridan Avenue
Cody, Wyoming 82414-3428
www.bbhc.org

University of Washington Press
P.O. Box 50096
Seattle, Washington 98145-5096
www.washington.edu/uwpress

Library of Congress Cataloging-in-Publication Data

Hansen, Emma I.
Memory and vision : arts, cultures, and lives of Plains Indian peoples /
Emma I. Hansen ; with contributions by Beatrice Medicine ... [et al.].
    p. cm.
Includes bibliographical references and index.
  ISBN-13: 978-0-295-98579-4 (hardback : alk. paper)
  ISBN-10: 0-295-98579-8 (hardback : alk. paper)
  ISBN-13: 978-0-295-98580-0 (pbk. : alk. paper)
  ISBN-10: 0-295-98580-1 (pbk. : alk. paper)
  1. Indians of North America—Great Plains—History.
  2. Indians of North America—Material culture—Great Plains.
  3. Indians of North America—Great Plains—Social life and customs.
  I. Medicine, Beatrice.
  II. Buffalo Bill Historical Center.
  III. Title.
  E78.G73H346 2007
  978.00497—dc22
                    2007037375

Photo Credits
All photographs of Buffalo Bill Historical Center objects are by Chris Gimmeson, except for these:

Buffalo Bill Historical Center: NA.202.296 Buffalo Robe, p. 73; NA.702.31 Painted Hide, p. 99; NA.202.839 Buffalo Robe, p. 103; NA.205.14A/B Eagle Feather Bonnet and Trailer, P.166; NA.204.5 Ghost Dance Shirt, p. 207; NA.106.245 Storage Bag, p. 243; 9.76 *Coyote Legend*, p. 253.

Sean Campbell: NA.202.294 Robe, p. 72; NA.202.81 Dress Yoke, p. 84; NA.108.13 Shield Cover, p. 109; NA.108.15 Shield Cover, p. 141; 16.77 *Drama on the Plains*, p. 254; NA.202.1007 shirt, p. 280; NA.302.102 *Banner*, p. 283; 8.02 *Buffalo Medicine Keeper*, p. 286.

Devendra Shrikhande: NA.504.234 Pipe Bag, p. 39; 27.78.22 Ledger Drawing, p. 108; 40.70.2 Ledger Drawing, p. 120; 27.78.3 Ledger Drawing, p. 138.

Lucille Warters: NA.504.131 Pipe Bag, p. 37; NA.202.914 Man's Moccasins, p. 107; NA.502.4 Horse Dance Stick, p. 160; NA.403.86 Martingale, p. 178; NA.202.193 Jacket, p. 226; 7.94 *Crow Indian Parade Rider*, p. 271; 9.96 *Star Blanket*, p. 287.

Cover: Child's Toy Tipi Cover, Tsistsistas (Cheyenne), Montana, ca. 1890; tanned hide, glass beads, pigment, dyed porcupine quills, sinew, wool cloth; 34 ½ x 60 inches. From the Collection of Richard Larremore Livermore given by his granddaughter Ann Livermore Houston NA.507.123

Foreword • 6

Preface • 9

1 People of the Plains • 13

2 Land of Many Gifts • 49
Women's Roles • 94
BEATRICE MEDICINE

3 Buffalo and the People • 99
The Buffalo as Part of the Mandan-Hidatsa Way of Life • 146
GERARD BAKER

4 Honor and Celebration • 149
Crow Tribal Leaders • 198
JOSEPH MEDICINE CROW

5 Adversity and Renewal • 203
A New and Different Life on a Small Part of a Very Old Place • 246
ARTHUR AMIOTTE

6 Our People Today • 253
A Cheyenne in Cyber Space • 294
BENTLY SPANG

The Authors • 298

Bibliography • 301

Index • 306

The marvelous book you are holding, *Memory and Vision: Arts, Cultures and Lives of Plains Indian People,* is the culmination of several years of dedicated scholarly work inspired by the completion of the award-winning reinterpretation of the Plains Indian Museum at the Buffalo Bill Historical Center in 2000. The authors set out to provide the cultural and historical contexts for the outstanding collections of Native American art in the Plains Indian Museum, and I believe you will agree that they succeeded beyond all expectations.

The authors are all Plains Indian scholars and tribal members. Emma I. Hansen, Pawnee and Curator of the Plains Indian Museum; Arthur Amiotte, Oglala Lakota artist and educator; Gerard Baker, Hidatsa and Superintendent of Mount Rushmore National Memorial; Joseph Medicine Crow, Crow Tribal Historian; Beatrice Medicine, Lakota anthropologist from the Standing Rock Reservation (sadly, recently deceased); and Bently Spang, Northern Cheyenne artist. What makes that fact important is that, like the exhibitions in the Plains Indian Museum, the authors provide contexts for Native American life based upon their expertise, scholarly research, and individual insights. Their voices give the book a gravitas and authority that would very likely not be possible otherwise.

The images that support this interpretation of Plains Native arts and cultures are from the collections of the Plains Indian Museum and the Whitney Gallery of Western Art here at the Buffalo Bill Historical Center. The book is also illustrated with historical photographs from the McCracken Research Library as well as contemporary photography. As with the voices and interpretations of the authors, these images clearly show the daily lives, struggles, and triumphs of the Plains Indian people.

It is important to note that this fine publication would not have been possible without the financial and emotional support of Margo Grant Walsh, who is both a member of our Board of Trustees and a member of the Plains Indian Museum Advisory Board. Margo, please accept our heartfelt thanks for your contributions, continuous encouragement, and patience.

Thanks also to the University of Washington Press, first, for believing in the project, and then for doing so much to make it a reality. Without the skills and dedication of such a staff, even the best ideas and images would not become the reality of ink on paper that can engage you with those ideas and images.

As one of the world's premier museums of the American West, the Buffalo Bill Historical Center is proud to offer visitors and scholars alike unparalleled collections, interpretation, and publications. With the appearance of this book, anyone interested in the arts, lives, and cultures of the Plains Indian people can continue to enjoy the entrancing stories conveyed in the Plains Indian Museum, and the richness and variety of our collections. We're pleased to offer it to you, and trust you will be pleased as well.

ROBERT E. SHIMP, PH.D.
Executive Director
Buffalo Bill Historical Center

As curator over the last fifteen years, I have been fortunate to care for and interpret the collection of the Plains Indian Museum of the Buffalo Bill Historical Center in Cody, Wyoming. The collection itself is remarkable, comprised of culturally significant and often spectacularly beautiful examples of Plains Indian artistry dating from the middle of the nineteenth century to the present. Unlike the ethnographic assemblages of large North American and European natural history museums of the late eighteenth and early nineteenth centuries, the Plains Indian Museum's collection originated with the Northern Plains clothing and accouterments of Native American performers in Buffalo Bill's Wild West shows that toured from 1883 to 1913. Over the years, it has developed through the acquisitions of major private collections and, more recently, works representing the creative output of contemporary Plains Native artists.

Taken as a whole, the collection manifests the artistic abilities and vibrant creativity of Native people of the Great Plains over almost two hundred years. Beyond their exceptional artistic excellence, works of the collection also are powerful expressions of the cultures, values, historical experiences, and contemporary lives of the people who created them. During the period represented by the collection, Plains Native peoples adapted to the Plains environment and created diverse cultural traditions, thrived as free buffalo hunters of the region, and, finally, struggled with and eventually survived the difficult reservation experiences of the late 1800s and early 1900s to build new lives for their families. Memory, both collective and individual, and vision have played powerful roles throughout these experiences, assisting people in maintaining cultural identities,

Blackfeet Camp and Ceremony
Montana, ca. 1905
Photograph by Roland Reed (1864–1934)
P.43.72

in understanding the spiritual underpinnings of tribal traditions, and in shaping the future. Among Plains Indian and other Native peoples, art, memory, and vision are essentially interwoven, each reinforcing and providing the foundation for the other.

This book follows the interpretive approach of the museum's exhibitions to present the historical and cultural contexts during which the works were created, as told through the voices of Plains Indian individuals such as Pretty Shield, Iron Teeth, Plenty Coups, Luther Standing Bear, and others who wrote of their experiences or told them to early twentieth century researchers. Other voices are those of contemporary Native scholars and writers. This publication is not a definitive work on any one Plains society, but rather an attempt to convey the diversity of tribal cultures and historical experiences that are often generalized when considering Native peoples of this region. The essays written by Plains tribal members who are artists and scholars—Arthur Amiotte, Gerard Baker, Beatrice Medicine, Joseph Medicine Crow, and Bently Spang—also contribute to the diverse voices represented in the book.

Since 1976, the museum has benefited from the guidance and support of the Plains Indian Museum Advisory Board of tribal artists, educators, historians, community leaders, and other interested individuals. Current Advisory Board members are Arthur Amiotte, Mary Gooch Armour, Strawn Cathcart, Robert D. Coe II, Adeline Fox, Garrett E. Goggles, Marilyn C. Hudson, Joann Jundt, Joseph Medicine Crow, Harold Ramser, Jr., Betty Lou Sheerin, Harriet Stuart Spencer, Darwin J. St. Clair, Jr., Curly Bear Wagner, and Margo Grant Walsh. Oglala Lakota artist Arthur Amiotte and Crow historian Joseph Medicine Crow, who are both founding members of the Advisory Board, each contributed essays to this publication. The late renowned Cherokee artist and educator Lloyd New was instrumental in the formation of the Advisory Board and over many years provided beneficial counsel and advice. He always reminded museum staff and Advisory Board members of the importance of interpreting contemporary Native American arts and considering the future education role of this institution, particularly for Indian people. Advisory Board member and past chair Margaret S. Coe, whom we lost in 2006, will be remembered for her role as a strong and dignified advocate for the Plains Indian Museum. Margo Grant Walsh is also deserving of special recognition because it is due to her continuing generosity and support that the book has become a reality. Margo Grant Walsh is the daughter of Alfred Grant, Pembina Band, Turtle Mountain Tribe, Chippewa Nation. Through my tenure as curator, members of the Board of Trustees of the Buffalo Bill Historical Center also have been consistently supportive of this publication and other Plains Indian Museum projects.

This publication has benefited immeasurably from the work of other staff members of the Buffalo Bill Historical Center. Rebecca S. West, Curatorial

Assistant of the Plains Indian Museum, has steadfastly contributed to the details of producing this book, as she has with many past museum endeavors. In addition to managing the logistics of moving and photographing our diverse collection, she researched and wrote caption text and assisted in the overall review of the finished work. As a member of our small department, she also managed many daily activities and programs of the museum, ensuring that I would have the necessary time to devote to this project.

The photography of the objects, completed by Buffalo Bill Historical Center Photographer Chris Gimmeson, reveals the individual beauty of works selected for this book. Throughout the project, she has striven to understand the significance of the materials and produce images that demonstrate their artistic qualities. The selection of paintings and sculptures from the Whitney Gallery of Western Art, one of the five museums of the Buffalo Bill Historical Center, was assisted by Sarah Boehme, former curator of the Whitney Gallery, who generously provided collections information and her expertise about these works. Anne Marie Shriver, who currently is the Historical Center's web content developer, continued her support for Plains Indian Museum programs through assisting with many aspects of the book. Ann Marie Donoghue and Elizabeth Holmes of the Historical Center's registration department and Gary Miller and Connie Vunk of collections also assisted in record-keeping and moving collection objects for photography. Mary Robinson and Linda Clark of the Historical Center's McCracken Research Library helped out by efficiently providing research materials and historical photographs for the book.

Appreciation should also be given to Pat Soden, Director of the University of Washington Press, as well his staff in the cooperative publication of this book.

Finally, I wish to acknowledge the friendship, assistance, and support of many Northern Plains people who have contributed to my knowledge of their cultural histories and provided guidance and advice during the years I have lived in Wyoming. ✦

EMMA I. HANSEN
Curator, Plains Indian Museum
Cody, Wyoming
May, 2006

People of the Plains

East of my grandmother's house the sun rises out of the plain. Once in his life a man ought to concentrate his mind upon the remembered earth, I believe. He ought to give himself up to a particular landscape in his experience, to look at it from as many angles as he can, to wonder about it, to dwell upon it. He ought to imagine that he touches it with his hands at every season and listen to the sounds that are made upon it. He ought to imagine the creatures there and all the faintest motions of the wind. He ought to recollect the glare of noon and all the colors of the dawn and dusk.

—N. SCOTT MOMADAY[1]

Memories of the Land

Even now, when automobiles and interstate highways make traveling across the North American Plains relatively fast and comfortable, the journey still offers one considerable time to reflect on the landscape and its connections to those who came before us. These long stretches of flat grasslands, rolling prairies, and mountain foothills provide seemingly endless opportunities for the traveler to wonder about what the journey was like for Plains Indian ancestors who lived in and traveled these vast expanses, on foot and on horseback. Along ancient trails east of the Rocky Mountains or through the valleys of the Arkansas, Platte, Missouri, and Saskatchewan Rivers, many places give pause and allow one to imagine an earlier time when Native families migrated each year to hunt or gather food, to trade, or to join relations for annual ceremonies. As they moved with their horses and dogs dragging tipi poles and travois packed with their lodges, foods, household goods, clothing, and personal belongings, the people would have felt anticipation and excitement. Men traveled ahead, looking for herds of buffalo or signs of danger, and the women and boys managed the families' horses. Mothers and grandmothers carried babies in cradles on horseback or on travois. Older children managed the camp dogs or helped in other ways.

Crossing rivers and streams or stopping along the way, one wonders if these ancestors passed this way or stopped in these places or stayed for periods of time. When visiting a buffalo jump, where layers of skulls and bones show that it was

"Spotted Fawn"–Cheyenne Girl of 13
Northern Cheyenne Reservation, Montana, ca. 1890
Photograph by L.A. Huffman (1854–1931)
P.100.3575

used for generations, or an ancient village or renowned sacred site, one feels a renewed connection to these ancestors. Native American people may think about these matters from time to time, not because we are living in the past as people outside the cultures might believe, but because of a deeply felt respect for and a desire to understand our cultural histories and the generations who came before us, and to carry the lessons of the ancestral past into our current and future lives.

To early Euro-American travelers and settlers, the Great Plains appeared foreign and dangerous, a largely uninhabited land destined to be possessed and conquered. Nineteenth–century travelers and people living east of the Mississippi called the region the "Great American Desert," believing it largely hostile to cultivation.[2] Conversely, Thomas Jefferson, who sent the Lewis and Clark expedition westward in 1804–06, viewed the American West, including the Great Plains, as an "agrarian Eden," a chosen country suitable for territorial expansion and colonization by Euro-Americans.[3]

Since the earliest Euro-American exploration of the West, the concept of dominating the land and conquering its Native people through establishing military forts and civilian settlements has underpinned countless histories and works of fiction in both print and film. Underlying this viewpoint is the popular notion that the Plains region was a vast pristine wilderness ready to be discovered, explored and developed into farms, ranches, towns, and, more recently, national parks and recreation areas.[4]

For Native people of the Plains, however, the land was home. They explored, studied, and understood the varied landscapes, the resources, and spiritual features that provided the foundations for cultural beliefs and traditions. Although sometimes interrupted by historical circumstances, these ancestors strived to pass on their knowledge of the land, its resources, and its meaning to their children and grandchildren. A majority of Plains tribal members now travel and live away from their reservations and traditional homelands, but for many there remains this significant connection to the land.

The Great Plains region, stretching from the foothills of the Rocky Mountains in the west to the Mississippi River in the east and from the Saskatchewan River in Canada to the Rio Grande in the south, is a difficult and harsh environment, with frequent droughts, sudden spring thunderstorms, blinding snowstorms, and climates that vary from hot summer days to cold, dry winter nights. The landscape is diverse, with flat to rolling grasslands, terraced stream valleys, isolated mountain areas, and intermountain basins. For Native people of the Plains, however, the land also harbored tall grass prairies with abundant herds of buffalo and other grazing animals and fertile river valleys that supported farming traditions.

Francisco Vásquez de Coronado described his encounters with Apachean buffalo hunters as he and his Spanish army crossed the Southern Plains in 1541.[5]

Living in buffalo hide tipis, the hunters traveled in small family groups. Their dogs served as pack animals, dragging tipi poles and travois loaded with belongings as they traveled to puebloan villages in eastern New Mexico, where they traded hides, meat, and salt for corn and other vegetables, turquoise, shell ornaments, and obsidian.

The Coronado expedition also traveled to present-day central Kansas, where they met the people of Quivira, considered by archaeologists and tribal historians to be the ancestors of the Wichita who were following another well-established way of life on the Plains based upon farming and hunting.[6] Over a thousand years ago, Plains village farmers such as the Wichita had established villages along the Missouri, Platte, Republican, and Arkansas Rivers and smaller streams. By the 1700s, these Plains farmers and hunters were identified as the Hidatsa, Mandan, and Arikara of the Missouri River region of present North Dakota, the Pawnee, Omaha, Ponca, Kansa (Kaw), and Otoe of the Central Plains region of present Nebraska and northern Kansas, and the Osage and the Wichita of the Southern Plains, including what is now southern Kansas, Oklahoma, and Texas.

Living in large villages of grass houses in the Southern Plains or mat-covered lodges and earth lodges in the Central and Northern Plains, the women of these

Buffalo Grazing the Big Open, Northern Montana, 1880
Photograph by L.A. Huffman (1854–1931)
P.100.3622

*Woman and Children Traveling
with Horse and Travois*
Northern Plains, nineteenth century
Vincent Mercaldo Collection P.71.1071

tribes tilled gardens along the fertile river bottoms, raising several varieties of corn, beans, squash, and sunflowers.[7] When crops were plentiful, the surplus was traded to hunting groups of the western grasslands. Once or twice a year, in the summer and sometimes the winter, the people traveled into the prairies for extended buffalo hunts. Like other buffalo hunters, they lived in buffalo hide tipis; when they moved, their dogs carried their belongings on packs and travois. Women collected berries, nuts, and seeds, dug nutritious tubers, and gathered other plants for medicines. The people supplemented these foods by hunting deer, elk, mountain sheep, and antelope. The buffalo, of course, from which the necessities of life were produced, was of primary economic and spiritual importance to Plains Indian people—an importance that continues symbolically to this day.

Other buffalo-hunting tribes living in the Northern Plains of present Wyoming, Montana, Alberta, and Saskatchewan include the Blackfoot, Crow, Assiniboine, and Gros Ventre. In the mid–seventeenth century, Plains tribes acquired horses from Spanish settlements in the southwest and firearms from French and English traders in the north. Horses allowed the people already living in the Plains to travel greater distances to hunt and trade, and to transport larger tipis and more belongings. This additional trade also brought European goods besides firearms—metal knives, kettles, glass beads, cloth, needles, and other items. The availability of the buffalo, opportunity for trade, and displacement from traditional homelands created by Euro-American settlements attracted other

The young Piegan girl stands outside her own small painted lodge. Plains Indian girls often had their own lodges, made just like full-sized ones, with which they practiced women's responsibilities of transporting, putting up, and furnishing family homes.

cultural groups to the Plains from the Great Lakes and other regions. As the Cheyenne, Arapaho, Kiowa, Comanche, and Sioux became firmly established in their historical territories during the seventeenth and early eighteenth centuries, the buffalo-hunting way of life made possible by the horse flourished for only 100 to 150 years. The timeless image of the Lakota, Cheyenne, or Comanche warrior on horseback, however, survives and often symbolizes all Native Americans in popular imagination.

CHEYENNE BOY
#45

The significance of the land to Native people of the Plains has been expressed in oral and artistic traditions. During the 1830s, the Crow leader Arapooish, or Rotten Belly, described the land of the Crow in his address to Robert Campbell of the Rocky Mountain Fur Company.

The Crow country is a good country. The Great Spirit has put it exactly in the right place; while you are in it you fare well; whenever you go out of it, whichever way you travel, you will fare worse.

If you go to the south, there you have to wander over great barren plains; the water is warm and bad and you meet with fever and ague.

To the north it is cold; the winters are long and bitter and there is no grass; you cannot keep horses there, but must travel with dogs. What is a country without horses?

On the Columbia they are poor and dirty, paddle about in canoes and eat fish. Their teeth are worn out; they are always taking fish bones out of their mouths. Fish is poor food.

To the east they dwell in villages; they live well, but they drink the muddy waters of the Missouri—that is bad. A Crow's dog would not drink such water.

About the forks of the Missouri is a fine country; good water, good grass, plenty of buffalo. In summer it is almost a good as the Crow country, but in winter it is cold; the grass is gone and there is no salt weed for the horses.

The Crow country is exactly in the right place. It has snowy mountains and sunny plains, all kinds of climates and good things for every season. When the summer heats scorch the prairies, you can draw up under the mountains, where the air is sweet and cool, the grass fresh, and the bright streams come tumbling out of the snow banks. There you can hunt the elk, the deer and the antelope when their skins are fit for dressing; there you will find plenty of white bears and mountain sheep.

In the autumn when your horses are fat and strong from the mountain pastures you can go down into the plains and hunt the buffalo, or trap beaver on the streams. And when the winter comes on, you can take shelter in the woody bottoms along the rivers; where you find buffalo meat for yourselves and cottonwood bark for your horses or you may winter in the Wind River valley, where there is salt weed in abundance.

The Crow country is exactly in the right place. Everything good is to be found there. There is no country like Crow country.[8]

This connection to the land endures. Marilyn Hudson of the Hidatsa expressed it in 2005 as she described the Fort Berthold Reservation, homeland of the Hidatsa, Mandan, and Arikara (Three Affiliated Tribes) in northern North Dakota along the Missouri River, prior to its flooding after the construction of Garrison Dam.[9] She described this place as "land which no longer exists, but a place in time to which I, and others of my generation, am irrevocably tied spiritually and physically."[10]

It is the land of our birth and the land of our fathers and their fathers before them. It is the land which nourished and sustained the Mandan, Hidatsa and Arikara people from a time well before Columbus to the twentieth century.

The Mandan origin story of the universe describes quite well the land on which we lived. A ball of mud is divided between Lone Man and First Creator. They first created a river as a dividing point. First Creator took the west side and Lone Man took the east side. First Creator made the mountains, hills, coulees, running streams on the west side of the river. Lone Man made mostly flat land with lakes and ponds on the east side. Then they created the four-leggeds, the swimmers of the waters, and those that crawl over the creation, the winged beings of the skies and finally the two-leggeds. The west side of the Missouri River is rugged and hilly with badlands suited to cattle ranching. The east side has rich, level soil well suited to fields and farming.[11]

Sacred Places

Native people venerate certain places on the Great Plains as inherently sacred sites from which their ancestors and cultural knowledge, beliefs, and traditions originated. Other locations where significant events occurred are sanctified as important to tribal histories and patrimonies. The strong spiritual bond of Plains Native people to their lands has arisen through longstanding residence and a sense of place reflected in language, oral traditions, and ceremonies going back hundreds or thousands of years. It has been reinforced by struggles to retain and protect homelands and the cultural histories and sacred ceremonies associated with them.

For traditional Plains Indian people, this reverence for the land expands beyond the physical environment and its earthly components to its associated spiritual relationship to the universe as a whole. Blackfeet tribal member Curly Bear Wagner has described this reverence:

> Everything is important to our people. We respect everything that the Creator has given to us. We respect it because everything out there is living—the sun, the moon, the stars, the clouds, the sky, the mountains, the trees, the rocks, the grass, the water—all those things are living. They are all related and we are part of that relationship. The Creator gave us these things for our survival. So, therefore, we respect these things he has given to us. We honor these things. He has given us the roots, the herbs, the plants, the trees for healing purposes. He has taught us how to go up into the mountains and fast, to call upon him to show us how to use these different things he has given to us for our survival. Everything out there was important for our survival as a people. This is what we call our way of life. And even today these things are important for our survival, not only the Indians', but all people's survival.[12]

In *God is Red*, Dakota author Vine Deloria, Jr. wrote that sacred sites are "places of overwhelming Holiness where the Higher Powers, on their own initiative, have revealed Themselves to human beings." He continues, "This tradition tells us that there are places of unquestionable, inherent sacredness on this earth, sites that are holy in and of themselves."[13] Deloria states that Indian people have many more sacred places in North American than do non-Indians "because of our considerably longer tenure on this continent and that these sites are

Petroglyph in Bighorn Basin of Wyoming
Photograph by Michael T. Bies, 1991

"sanctified each time ceremonies are held and prayers offered."[14] In another writing, he described the role of sacred places in Native American spiritual life:

> From time immemorial, Indian tribal Holy Men have gone into the high places, lakes, and isolated sanctuaries to pray, receive guidance from the Spirits, and train younger people in the ceremonies that constitute the spiritual life of the tribal community. In these ceremonies, medicine men represented the whole web of cosmic life in the continuing search for balance and harmony.[15]

For most Native people, a sacred place is one where the Creator or other spiritual beings communicate with those on earth. These places often consist of monumental or unusual physical features such as mountains, waterfalls, springs, or bluffs. Deloria noted that it is at these sites that people must perform ceremonies to preserve the universe and all its elements and that they "must perform certain ceremonies at specific times and places in order that the sun may continue to shine, the earth prosper, and the stars remain in the heavens."[16]

In 1921, the ethnologist Melvin R. Gilmore wrote, "Each of the nations and tribes of Indians had certain places within its own domain which they regarded as sacred, and to which they accordingly paid becoming reverence. These places were sometimes water-springs, sometimes peculiar hills, sometimes caves, sometimes rocky precipices, sometimes dark, wooded bluffs."[17] He went on to discuss five sacred places of the Pawnee located in their traditional homelands of Nebraska and northwestern Kansas, in particular the site known as *Pahuk* or *Pahaku*.[18]

In 1914, Gilmore had traveled through the Pawnee homelands with White Eagle, an elder and chief of the Skidi band of the Pawnee, accompanied by a younger man, Charles Knife Chief, who served as interpreter. Despite the fact that the Pawnee had been removed from their homelands to northern Oklahoma in 1874–75 to make way for Euro-American colonization, White Eagle easily recalled the location of the sacred places and associated traditions.[19]

Pahuk is a prominent bluff heavily wooded with cedar trees, in a bend of the Platte River north of Cedar Bluffs in eastern Nebraska where, many years before, the Pawnee had learned how to build their medicine lodges and gained other tribal knowledge about healing and medicines from the *rahrurahki*, the powerful animals who lived at this place. White Eagle told Gilmore that when the Pawnee lived in a village on the Platte a long time before, a father sacrificed his son to *Tirawahat*, "the one above." The animals took pity and brought the young man back to life, and each taught him his particular knowledge and accompanying rituals. From that time on, Pawnee elders and medicine men visited this place and made offerings to gain their own knowledge.

Pahuk, which is now on private land, is on the National Register of Historic Sites. For the Pawnee, *Pahuk* and other sacred sites, village locations, and burial grounds in Nebraska and Kansas have deep and continuing significance despite

Pretty Shell and Pretty Beads in
Doorway of Tipi
Crow Reservation, Montana, 1903–1925
Dr. William and Anna Petzoldt Collection
PN.95.113

their removal from these homelands more than 130 years ago. In 1994, a group of tribal elders including descendants of Knife Chief made a formal visit to Nebraska, stopping at *Pahuk* and other places important to Pawnee cultural traditions and talking with Nebraska residents about their history.[20] Over the years, other tribal visits have occurred as Pawnee people strive to understand and pass on their tribal memories of their homelands to their children and grandchildren.

The Kiowa trace their origins to the Yellowstone Lake region of the Northern Plains. As N. Scott Momaday recounted in *The Way to Rainy Mountain*, the Kiowa story was one of a long migration that took them south to present-day Oklahoma and Texas. It was through this migration journey that their cultural traditions were established.

> The great adventure of the Kiowas was a going forth into the heart of the continent. They began a long migration from the headwaters of the Yellowstone River eastward to the Black Hills and south to the Wichita Mountains. Along the way they acquired horses, the religion of the Plains, a love and possession of the open land. Their nomadic soul was set free. In alliance with the Comanches they held dominion in the Southern Plains for a hundred years. In the course of that long migration they had come of age as a people. They had conceived a good idea of themselves; they had dared to imagine and determine who they were.[21]

Kiowa people today often travel to the Northern Plains land of their origins to attend the annual Crow Fair at Crow Agency, Montana, for hand games with the Crow people, or to tour the Yellowstone region which is called in Kiowa *Tung Sa'u Dah*, meaning "hot water," or "the place of hot water." Elders on these trips often refer to their origins in a retelling of their own migration story and are able to recall place names for both the Black Hills and Yellowstone region.[22]

Throughout the Plains, carved or painted images on rock, known as petroglyphs and pictographs, are located near rivers and streams, along cliff facings, on rock outcroppings, and in caves. Consisting of symbolic figures and images of animals, humans, and powerful spiritual beings with horns or wings, these rock images hold deep significance to Native people. Producing such images would have been arduous. Petroglyphs consisted of images which were incised, carved, or scratched into rock surfaces. Pictographs were painted images created with mineral pigments often mixed with organic binders such as fat or grease.

Since the first recordings and documentation by Euro-American travelers on the Plains, there have been attempts to analyze petroglyphs and pictographs as well as to categorize them by archaeological or art historical styles. Native elders and spiritual leaders, however, interpret the images based upon ancient traditional understandings.

George Bird Grinnell described a site known as Painted Rocks on the Northern Cheyenne Reservation in Montana, which the people described as mysterious because the images appeared on the rocks "without anyone having painted them." In the early 1900s during Grinnell's fieldwork, Painted Rocks was remembered by Cheyenne warriors as a place to pray for success in battles and to leave offerings.[23]

Petroglyphs and pictographic images can also be found in several places in the Wind River and Bighorn and Pryor Mountains of Wyoming and Montana, in some cases in caves and along high cliffs that can be reached only by climbing narrow ledges. Native people of the region both historically and contemporaneously have had enormous spiritual respect and reverence for these images as well as traditional knowledge and beliefs about them. The Eastern Shoshone of the Wind River Reservation of Wyoming, and the Crow of Montana, both with centuries of residence in the region, say that the images were created by spirits rather than their own tribal members. The Northern Arapaho who were settled on the Wind River Reservation with the Eastern Shoshone in 1878, but who traveled throughout the Rocky Mountain region in the eighteenth and nineteenth centuries, also express an interest and reverence for these images.[24]

At Legend Rock, which is located along a small stream near Thermopolis in central Wyoming, several petroglyphs of deer, elk, buffalo, mountain sheep, bear, mountain lion, antelope, dogs, rabbit, turtle, birds, and people have been dated by archaeologists from 500 to 1,700 A.D. Castle Gardens, also in central Wyoming, is a group of sandstone outcroppings which the wind has eroded into unusual formations, reminiscent of the towers of castles. This site is marked with numerous images identified as "shield-bearing warriors, as well as shields."[25] The images were created by incising the smoothed sandstone, and then painting it with different pigments. Similar paintings of shield-bearing warriors can be found at Pictograph Cave near Billings, Montana.

In the Northern Plains, other sacred sites revered and respected by Native people can be found in secluded remote high places where young men seek visions, grounds where annual sun dances and other ceremonies take place, areas where plants are collected for medicines and spiritual uses, and sites where individual prayer and offerings are made.

Rising above the Great Plains along the Wyoming and South Dakota border are a circle of mountains known *Paha Sapa*, the Black Hills. For the Lakota, Dakota, Cheyenne, Arapaho, Nakota, Arikara, Hidatsa, Ponca, Kiowa, and Mandan, the Black Hills of the Northern Plains are pre-eminent sacred lands. Lakota spiritual leader Pete Catches said of the Black Hills,

> To the Indian spiritual way of life, the Black Hills is the center of the Lakota people. There, ages ago, before Columbus traveled over the sea, seven spirits came to the Black Hills. They selected, that area, the beginning of sacredness to the Lakota people. Each spirit brought a gift to the Lakota people. . . . Our people that have passed on, their spirits are contained in the Black Hills. This is why it is the center of the universe, and this is why it is sacred to the Oglala Sioux. In this life and the life hereafter, the two are together.[26]

Medicine Wheel
Big Horn Mountains, Wyoming, 1986
Photograph by Richard Collier
Wyoming State Historic Preservation Office

Within *Paha Sapa* are many sacred places, including Bear Butte, Harney Peak, Wind Cave, Buffalo Gap, and Bear Lodge (Devil's Tower). Bear Butte, *Mato Paha*, in South Dakota is a monumental butte on the Northern Plains and a high holy place, visited by many generations of Lakota and Cheyenne for peace and solitude and to induce spiritual reflections through vision quests. Rising above the prairie 4,426 feet, Bear Butte has been the site of Sun Dances and other ceremonies as well as councils and gatherings, vision quests, sweat lodges, and prayers. For the Cheyenne, Bear Butte is the source of the four sacred arrows brought to the people by the prophet Sweet Medicine. For the Lakota, Bear Butte is where the original instructions of life were given to the people.

The highest point in the Black Hills and one of the most sacred to the Lakota is Harney Peak. Here, the holy man Black Elk had his famous vision and referred to the mountain as the "center of the world." As he described to John Neihardt, "There, when I was young, the spirits took me in my vision to the center of the earth and showed me all the good things in the sacred hoop of the world."[27]

Another ancient site in Wyoming, the Bighorn Medicine Wheel, has been the subject of much research and speculation concerning its origins while remaining an important focus of Native American spiritual life. The Medicine Wheel is built on a peak of the Bighorn Mountains at an elevation of 9,642 feet and consists of a stone circle almost ninety feet in diameter. Twenty-eight spokes radiate from a central stone cairn with six smaller stone cairns along the periphery. The largest of dozens of such formations in the Northern Plains, this medicine wheel represents thousands of years of Native American culture. For the Crow, Cheyenne, Lakota, Arapaho, and Shoshone, the Medicine Wheel is a holy place, a site of vision quests and peace talks where offerings of thanks are given and important ceremonies continue to be conducted. "For more than a millennium, the Wheel has been a place for fasting and vision quests, a place for prayer and ritual," says Crow tribal elder and leader of the Medicine Wheel Alliance John Hill.[28] Bill Tallbull from the Northern Cheyenne, who was active in preserving the Medicine Wheel for Native American spiritual activities, described its significance:

> To the Indigenous Peoples of North America, the archaeological sites on North American soil are not "archaeological" sites. They are sites where our relatives lived and carried out their lives. Sacred sites such as the Medicine Wheel are no different. To Native Americans they are living cultural sites from which help comes when "The People" needed or need help. They were/are places where tribal peoples went in times of famine and sickness, in periods of long drought when animals would leave, or in more current times when tribes are being torn apart by politics, alcohol, or other abuses.
>
> The men make a pledge to go and vision quest at these places, seeking help. As we leave to go to these sites, our every breath is a prayer. We follow the path to the sites; observing a protocol that has been in place for thousands of years. The Native American approaching these sites must stop four times from the beginning of his or her journey to arrival at the site. A trip to a Sacred Site was/is not done just for curiosity, but only after much preparation and seeking.
>
> Many Blessings have come to "The Peoples" in this way. Many tribes have received covenants (bundles) from these sites. Some Tribes still carry the bundles that were received from a certain mountain or site. These are considered no different than the covenants given Moses or the traditional law that went with it.[29]

Bear Lodge, known to non-Indians as Devil's Tower, is a monumental and unique geological feature of the Northern Plains that figures prominently in tribal oral traditions. A large, solitary butte in northeastern Wyoming some 865 feet high from base to summit, Bear Lodge was a sacred site where men went to fast and pray and seek supernatural blessings. It was named "Devil's Tower" in 1875 by a scientific team escorted by Colonel Richard I. Dodge. Native people prefer the name "Bear Lodge" ("Grey Horn Butte" for the Lakota), however, as it continues to be a place for meditation, Sun Dances, and prayer.

The Crow, Arapaho, Blackfeet, Cheyenne, Lakota, Kiowa, and Arikara all have traditions related to the formation of Bear Lodge. One Arikara version relates how a girl and her brothers escaped from their sister, who had turned into a bear, by standing on a rock that rose into the sky. As the bear clawed up the rock trying to reach the siblings, it left deep furrows, the distinctive markings of Bear Lodge. The boys and their sister became the cluster of seven stars of the Pleiades.

> Then that is what happened: then they went upward that way. Then they became stars. They are the ones. The little star is the girl; the others are the six. These are the ones that are clustered.
>
> And there where the rock was—where the rock was—there was a horde of bears [going around]. There were many bears there. And where the bear sister had jumped up and bumped the rock, it was slightly slanted.[30]

The Sweetgrass Hills, a region of volcanic buttes just south of the Canadian border in northern Montana, is a place for fasting, sweat lodge ceremonies, and vision quests for the Blackfeet, Gros Ventre, Salish, Kootenai, Chippewa Cree, and Assiniboine people. Rich in plants and animals such as elk and moose, and situated over a major aquifer, this area has been continuously used by Native people for religious practices for centuries. The Sweetgrass Hills are near other significant sacred sites, including Writing-on-Stone in Alberta, Canada, and Chief Mountain in Glacier National Park. The Blackfeet and other people continue to go into the hills to gather sweetgrass and other roots and plants for food and medicines. Wagner describes the significance of this area to the Blackfeet:

> Our people camped outside of the hills because of the land, the sacredness of the land. . . . The women would go in there and gather roots. Or, they go up there and they fast or they hunt and they gather sweet pine or sweet grass and they come out. In that way, the spirits are connecting with our people in there. The water source, the water, is very important, the hills themselves are very important to the environment. . . . They are all part of the sacredness of that area and the land around them.[31]

For the Native people of the Great Plains, the last half of the nineteenth century was marked by conflicts and assaults on traditional ways of life. The buffalo, the people's homelands, and the freedom to travel were lost. Descendants of those who suffered these struggles and losses remember and memorialize the sites where they took place—among them Sand Creek in eastern Colorado, Marias River in Montana, the Washita River in Oklahoma, and Wounded Knee in South Dakota—which have become sanctified because of the people's sacrifices. According to Deloria, "Every society needs these kinds of sacred places because they help to instill a sense of social cohesion in the people and remind them of the passage of generations that have brought them to the present. A society that cannot remember and honor its past is in peril of losing its soul."[32] "Each

Bear Lodge (Devil's Tower)
Photograph by Emma I. Hansen, 2000

tribe has a responsibility to protect its sacred sites," says Gordon Yellowman, Sr., of the Southern Cheyenne and Arapaho.[33]

Despite valiant efforts, the Hidatsa, Mandan, and Arikara were not able to prevent their North Dakota homelands from being flooded when Garrison Dam was built in 1947. When the tribes were notified in 1944 that Congress had passed the Flood Control Act authorizing the construction of the dam, Marilyn Hudson related, "This news was a punch that took the breath away and broke the hearts of the people. It was just beyond belief that their beloved lands would be flooded." A 1945 Tribal Resolution opposing the construction of the dam reads, "the cemeteries of our forefathers will be destroyed and with it all our memories and kind remembrances of the burial places that have been held sacred for all; the lands of the Indians were inherent property from time immemorial and in no sense given to them by any human power arriving from somewhere else."[34]

The next six or seven years would be marked by intense opposition to the dam as negotiations began with the federal government. Men and women who wanted nothing more to do but live peacefully on their land and tend their cattle, horses, and fields suddenly found themselves in a tragic struggle for their very existence. Leaders emerged from the bottomlands and from the prairies and from the buttes to take their place in this battle. Several who had gone away to early government boarding schools, such as Hampton Institute, Carlisle Indian Industrial School and Haskell Institute, found themselves preparing documents of defense, and served as interpreters for the traditional tribal leaders. Lines of defense included the right of original occupancy; the sanctity of treaties; provisions of the Louisiana Purchase; the Dawes Act, which provided for allotments of lands; wardship theories; trust status of Indian land; lack of Congressional power to condemn tribal land; certificates of competency; sovereignty; and humane treatment of citizens. They were the generation of my parents who bore the full brunt of this terrible blow. Today's tribal leaders identify this time as the second most traumatic event in the history of their people; the 1837 smallpox epidemic, which killed ninety percent of the Mandan and Hidatsa populations in the upper Missouri River villages, being the first.[35]

"My ancestors said prayers and suffered themselves for my generation," Calvin Grinnell said of these struggles. "Their prayers carried me into the twenty-first century. It is my responsibility to pray and suffer and take care of sacred bundles so future generations may live."[36] Protecting sacred lands, once naturally safe because of their isolation, has become more challenging as commercial enterprises, recreational activities, and tourism have moved into even the most remote parts of the Plains. Legal action, compromise, and negotiation are the contemporary means of protecting sacred homelands.

As tribes were confined to reservations in the late nineteenth century, missionaries and government agents worked together to banish traditional religious practices. In 1883, the Bureau of Indian Affairs outlawed the Sun Dance and other Native traditional ceremonies and participation was punished by withholding rations or imprisonment. In 1890, Lakota adherents of the Ghost Dance religion were massacred at Wounded Knee and practitioners of other tribes were arrested. Although many rituals were discontinued, Native traditionalists tried to hold on to their spiritual practices by conducting ceremonies in secret or changing their ceremonial calendar to conform to national and Christian holidays. Small groups of Native people sometimes were able to travel to isolated sacred sites to renew their traditions without official notice.

In 1934 under the Indian Reorganization Act (ten years after Indian people were granted American citizenship in 1924), this prohibition was lifted and Indian people were legally allowed to practice their religions. Ceremonies once again openly took place under the direction of elders who remembered old tribal ways. Although some Indian people had moved away from tribal traditions, since the 1960s Native spirituality and ceremonies have experienced incredible renewal. Urban Indians have returned to their homelands to find the vital link that ties them to their tribal past, and people living on reservations have found new faith in traditional beliefs.

Serious stumbling blocks to Native religious freedom persisted into the 1970s, as Native American Church members were prosecuted for the ritual use of peyote and Native people had conflicts with federal officials over access to sacred sites for ceremonial use. In 1978, under the American Indian Religious Freedom Act, Congress recognized its obligation "to protect and preserve for American Indians their inherent right of freedom to believe, express, and exercise the traditional religions of the American Indian, Eskimo, Aleut, and Native Hawaiians, including but not limited to access to sites, use and possession of sacred objects, and the freedom of worship through ceremonial and traditional rights." This act, however, has failed to clarify the religious use of sacred sites on public lands. According to John Echohawk, executive directive of the Native American Rights Fund,

> American Indian tribes, Native Hawaiians and Alaska Natives and all world religions share a unifying dependence upon sacred sites. Worship at sacred sites is a basic attribute of religion itself. However, when thinking of sacred sites, most Americans think only of well-known Middle Eastern sites familiar to the Judeo-Christian tradition such as the Mecca, the Wailing Wall, Mount Sinai or Bethlehem. Unfortunately, the laws of the United States overlook that our own landscape is dotted with equally important American Indian religious sites that have served as cornerstones for indigenous religions since time immemorial.[37]

With the signing by President William Clinton in 1996 of an executive order preserving American Indian sacred sites, there is some hope that these areas will be preserved and protected for future generations. In 1993, the Sweetgrass Hills, located on Bureau of Land Management and privately owned lands, were listed as one of the Eleven Most Endangered Historic Sites in the Nation by the National Trust for Historic Preservation because of plans for gold exploration there. Under pressure from a coalition of Blackfeet people, ranchers, and environmentalists, the development of the hills and surrounding lands has been postponed for the immediate future.[38]

The connection of Plains Indian peoples to their homelands, created and reinforced through generations of residency, is fundamental to the origination of tribal cultures, arts, beliefs, values, and traditions that define and bind the people together. Some of these unifying essentials, such as the close spiritual relationship with the buffalo, reverence and respect for elements of the earth and sky, and recognition of the importance of kinship, are shared and recognized by all Plains Indian peoples, although they are expressed in varying ways through oral traditions, ceremonies, and songs. Other attributes, such as languages, tribal histories and experiences, spiritual practices, and cultural arts, identify and define a people more specifically as Lakota, Cheyenne, Crow, Arapaho, Kiowa, Pawnee, or other tribal group. A few of these beliefs and practices central to the formation and continuation of Plains Indian or, more specifically, tribal identities, deserve closer scrutiny.

Pipes and Calumets: Messages to the Heavens

> Before talking of holy things, we prepare ourselves by offerings. If only two are to talk together, one will fill his pipe and hand it to the other, who will light it and offer it to the sky and earth. Then they will smoke together, and after smoking they will be ready to talk of holy things.
>
> Mato-Kuwapi (Chased By Bears), Santee-Yanktonai Dakota[39]

Ceremonial pipes have played a pre-eminent role in the lives of Native peoples of the Plains. As a means of prayer, pipes have been used to give thanks, to establish new relationships and seal agreements, to mark significant passages of ceremonial life, and to begin important expeditions. Considered one of the earliest forms of spiritual expression among North American Indians, the ritual use of tobacco was widespread throughout the continent. Tobacco was believed to be a gift from the supernatural powers to men, and the act of smoking considered a message or prayer to the heavens.

The sacred pipe was a gift to the Lakota from the White Buffalo Calf Woman. Black Elk described this gift:

> Then she presented the pipe to the chief. It was an ordinary pipe but there was a calf carved in one side and there were twelve eagle feathers tied on with a grass that never breaks. She said, "Behold this, for you shall multiply with this and a good nation you shall be. You shall get nothing but good from this pipe, so I want it to be in the hands of a good man, and the good shall have the privilege of seeing it, but the bad shall not have the privilege of seeing it." The pipe is still in the possession of the Sioux.[40]

After the original pipe was given to the Lakota people, two other types of pipes were made: one with an **L**-shaped bowl which was used primarily for ceremonies, and the other with the bowl in a **T**-shape.[41]

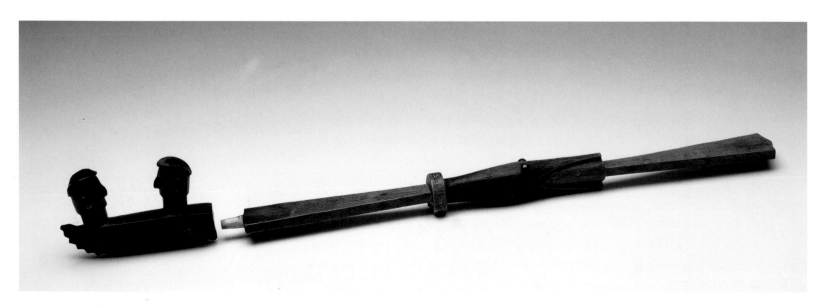

CHIEF
ROCKY BEAR
SIOUX

Pipes were used in times of war and times of peace. A leader of a war expedition carried a pipe as a symbol of his leadership and his responsibilities for his party. During ceremonies, the pipe was smoked to ask for protection and success and to seek guidance on the expedition. Pipe ceremonies also took place to establish alliances between different tribal peoples and in councils before important deliberations. During the late eighteenth through nineteenth centuries, Euro-American traders and government officials often presented metal pipe tomahawks to Indian leaders as symbols of their authority.

Calumets were decorated pipestems which were not actually used in smoking. Usually made from ash and decorated with owl, eagle, and duck feathers, with bands of tanned hide and horsehair streamers, the end of the stem was covered with the stretched head, neck, and breast of a mallard duck. Such calumets were used in ceremonies to ensure peace or in adoption rituals. Among the Omaha, the *wáwa*—"to sing for someone" ceremony—was held to bring about peace, with one man ritually adopting another from a different clan or tribe. During the songs of the ceremony, the calumets were danced and waved over the head of a child selected by the man being adopted. In this ceremony, both the

Calumets

Omaha, Nebraska, ca. 1875
Wood, pigments, duck and woodpecker heads, deer hide, wool cloth, duck, owl, and eagle feathers, horsehair, blackbird bill, corn stalks, yarn; 34⅜ inches
Gift of Mr. and Mrs. Richard A. Pohrt
NA.502.195.1-.2

Calumets are powerful ceremonial pipes. They were never smoked, but instead were displayed and moved during ceremonies conducted to establish peaceful relations between unrelated groups.

child and the man became ritual sons to the "father." This ceremony also involved an exchange of gifts.[42]

Although pipe bowls were made from bone, pottery, steatite, shale, limestone, and other materials, among people of the Plains catlinite, also called pipestone, has been most widely used. Quarried at a site in southwestern Minnesota now known as the Pipestone National Monument, this distinctive red stone is named for the artist George Catlin, who in 1836 was the first Euro-American to document the site. The name "catlinite" was given to the stone by the scientist Dr. Charles Thomas Jackson, who first analyzed samples of the mineral that Catlin had provided.

Members of tribal groups from throughout the plains and prairies visited the site to quarry pipestone, even though it was in the territory of the Eastern Sioux. According to Catlin,

> At an ancient time the Great Spirit, in the form of a large bird, stood upon the wall of rock and called all the tribes around him, and breaking out a piece of the red stone formed it into a pipe and smoked it, the smoke rolling out over the whole multitude. He then told his children that this red stone was their flesh, that they were made from it, that they must all smoke to him through it, that they must use it for nothing but pipes; and as it belonged alike to all the tribes, the ground was sacred, and no weapons must be used or brought upon it.[43]

The carved stems of the pipes were made of wood and decorated with porcupine quillwork and beadwork, as well as feathers. Men made their own pipes,

Pipe Bowl
Lakota (Sioux), Northern Plains, ca. 1880
Pipestone (catlinite); 9⅝ x 5⅛ inches
NA.504.220

Many Lakota stories tell of Iktomi, the trickster, and his misadventures. The scene on this pipe bowl represents Iktomi climbing away from a snake, whose body is coiled around the bowl.

Pipe Bag
Lakota (Sioux), Northern Plains, ca. 1885
Tanned deer hide, cotton cloth, tin cones, dyed porcupine quills;
5 ⅝ x 4 ⅛ inches
Dr. Robert L. Anderson Collection NA.504.281

This pipe bag, collected from Sitting Bull during his imprisonment at Fort Randall, features a buffalo on one side and an elk on another, both done in dyed porcupine quillwork.

Pipe Bag
Lakota (Sioux), Northern Plains, ca. 1881
Tanned deer hide, glass beads, pigment; 32 ¼ x 5 ¾ inches
Dr. Robert L. Anderson Collection NA.504.104

Sitting Bull and his followers were imprisoned at Fort Randall along the Missouri River in Dakota Territory in 1881–1883 after their return from Canada. During that time, he traded items to the post trader, D.L. Pratt, including this beaded pipe bag.

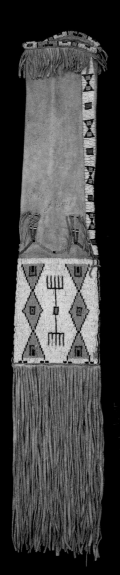

Pipe Bag
Lakota (Sioux), Northern Plains, ca. 1885
Tanned deer hide, glass beads, canvas, rawhide, dyed porcupine quills;
35 x 6 inches
Chandler-Pohrt Collection, Gift of Mr. and Mrs. Harold R. Tate NA.504.227

A warrior on horseback wearing a long eagle-feather bonnet is depicted on this bag together with a name, "Kiyuka." Pictographic figures such as this were characteristic of early reservation Lakota beadwork.

Lakota (Sioux), Northern Plains, ca. 1885
Tanned deer hide, glass beads, dyed porcupine quills, tin cones, dyed horsehair; 39 ½ x 6 ⅞ inches
Adolf Spohr Collection, Gift of Larry Sheerin NA.504.131

The beading of this pipe bag from the early reservation period features images a buffalo on one side and a horse on another—both fundamental to the lives of nineteenth-century Plains Indian people.

Pipe Bag
Lakota (Sioux), Northern
Plains, ca. 1885
Tanned deer hide, glass
beads, dyed porcupine
quills; 23 ¼ x 7 ¾ inches
Bequest of Adele K.
Willoughby NA.504.147

Pipe Bag
Hinono'ei (Arapaho), Oklahoma,
ca. 1890
Tanned deer hide, glass beads, porcu-
pine quills, brass bells, eagle feathers,
pigment; 36 x 9 ½ inches
Chandler-Pohrt Collection, Gift of Mr.
William D. Weiss NA.504.305

The beadwork images on both sides of
this Southern Arapaho pipe bag are
associated with the symbolism of the
Ghost Dance and elements of the
earth and sky. They include human figures (holding a pipe on one side and a
plant stalk on the other), the crescent
moon, birds, and turtle.

Pipe Bag
Tsistsistas (Cheyenne),
Northern Plains,
ca. 1875
Tanned deer hide,
glass beads;
37 x 6 ⅜ inches
Chandler-Pohrt
Collection NA.504.245

Pipe Bag
Apsáalooke (Crow), Montana,
ca. 1885
Tanned deer hide, glass
beads, wool cloth;
17 x 6 ¾ inches
Adolf Spohr Collection, Gift
of Larry Sheerin NA.504.11

Pipe Bag
Lakota (Sioux), South Dakota.
ca. 1895
Tanned deer hide, glass
beads, dyed porcupine quills;
39 ¾ x 8 ¾ inches
Gift of Corliss C. and
Audrienne H. Moseley
NA.504.111

The beading of this pipe bag
depicts two human hands
and American flags. During
the early reservation period
of about 1880–1920, the
American flag was a common
motif in Lakota beadwork.

37

and women dressed the stems. Women also made pipe bags of hide with painted, beaded, and quilted designs that were used to store the pipe, with the bowl separated from the stem.

Pipes continue to have a significant role in contemporary Plains spiritual life. Curly Bear Wagner has said,

> The pipe is one of our most sacred instruments of our people. We were guided by the pipe. We use it in all our ceremonies, the pipe. To us the bowl of the pipe is made of stone and to us that represents the earth. The stem of the pipe is made of wood and so, to us, that represents all the different things on the earth. When we smoke the pipe, the smoke that goes out of the pipe, that's our prayers going up to the Creator because the smoke is like a spirit. You see it for a minute and then it disappears.[44]

Crow Tobacco Society

An essential component of Crow cultural identity is the story of their long migration from the Great Lakes region, which took place over several generations, until their final arrival in their Northern Plains homelands in southern Montana and northern Wyoming. This migration involved a separation from their Hidatsa relatives, who remained in the Upper Missouri River region of North Dakota, and a transition from a farming and hunting tradition to one primarily based on buffalo hunting. Intrinsically linked to this migration is the establishment of the Crow Tobacco Society, which is based upon the planting of sacred tobacco seeds and ceremonial adoptions. According to tradition, it is the Crow Tobacco Society that defined and ensured the continuance and well-being of the Crow as a great people.

Historically, the Crow recognized three political divisions in their tribe: the Mountain Crows, the largest group, who were located primarily in the Yellowstone valley; the River Crows, who were centered north of the Yellowstone River; and the Kicked In The Bellies, a subgroup of the Mountain Crows who spent most of the year near the Shoshone River on the south side of the Bighorn Mountain range. According to tradition, the ancestral people of the Crow and Hidatsa once lived east of their historical location, most likely in the Great Lakes region. They began their movement west in search of buffalo, stopping in the area of Devil's Lake in northeastern North Dakota. These people had two leaders who were brothers, No Vitals (No Intestines, in some references) and Red Scout, each with their own followers. The group following No Vitals called themselves Apsáalooke, which translates as "Children of the Large Beaked Bird," incorrectly translated as Crow by early Europeans. They also called themselves, as they still do, *Bíiluuke*, meaning "Our Side." In 1932, tribal historian Joe Medicine Crow consulted an elder named Cold Wind about the story of the migration and origin of the Crow and Hidatsa.

OPPOSITE, LEFT: **Pipe Bag**
Northern Plains, ca 1850
Tanned deer hide, glass pony beads, porcupine quills; 37 x 6½ inches
Museum Purchase from a special fund provided by Silas Cathcart, Peter Kriendler and William D. Weiss NA.504.158

OPPOSITE, CENTER: **Pipe Bag**
Amoskapi Pikuni (Blackfeet), 1890
Tanned deer hide, glass beads; 35⅝ x 6½ inches
Chandler-Pohrt Collection, Gift of the Pilot Foundation NA.504.234

OPPOSITE, RIGHT: **Pipe Bag**
Amoskapi Pikuni (Blackfeet), Montana, ca. 1880
Tanned deer hide, glass beads; 30⅝ x 6⅜ inches
Museum purchase from a special fund provided by Silas Cathcart, Peter Kriendler and William D. Weiss NA.504.159

Cold Wind continued that, on the way, these migrants stopped for some time at Sacred Waters (Devil's Lake in northeastern North Dakota). . . . Here on the shores of this lake, two chiefs No Vitals and Red Scout—fasted and sought the Great Spirit's guidance on their perilous journey. Red Scout received an ear of corn and was told to settle down and plant the seeds for his sustenance. No Vitals received a pod of seeds and was told to go west to the high mountains and plant the seeds there. These seeds were sacred, and the proper way to use them would be revealed to the people when they got there someday. The Great Spirit promised No Vitals that his people would someday increase in numbers, become powerful and rich and own a large good, and beautiful land![45]

According to Medicine Crow, by the turn of the seventeenth century, the people had reached the Missouri River region, where they settled near the Mandan in an earth lodge village at the confluence of the Knife and Missouri Rivers. Oral traditions recount that a disagreement over the sharing of meat caused the group under No Vitals to leave and began the long journey that eventually took them to their Wyoming and Montana homelands.

Tobacco Society Blanket
Apsáalooke (Crow), Northern Plains, ca. 1860
Wool cloth, red-winged blackbird, pinon jay, common nighthawk and hawk feathers, deer hide, glass beads; 49⅜ x 68 inches
Adolf Spohr Collection, Gift of Larry Sheerin
NA.205.6

This blanket was worn during the ceremonies of the Crow Tobacco Society. The ceremony was held every spring, when members of the Tobacco Society planted sacred tobacco seeds and adopted new members. At its origin in the 1700s, when the Crow people separated from their Hidatsa relatives, Tobacco Society leaders prophesied that as long as they performed this ceremony, the Crow would remain a great people. The Tobacco Society continues to be an important part of Crow life.

Tobacco Society Ceremony and Field
Crow Reservation, Montana, 1903–1925
Dr. William and Anna Petzoldt Collection
PN.95.78

Women of the Tobacco Society follow in a procession at the tobacco fields.

Thus, one spring morning there was hurried activity in the village. Large dogs and tamed wolves were harnessed to travois. As relatives bade farewell, No Vitals and about four hundred tribal members faced westward and left. Thus began perhaps one of the longest and most dramatic migrations of any Indian tribe, covering thousands of miles over rough and rugged terrain through intense winters and torrid summers, and consisting of about one hundred years of wandering. . . . When the wandering tribe finally arrived in this area of present southern Montana and northern Wyoming, the people were still pedestrians. No Vitals, who led the exodus around the turn of the seventeenth century, had been succeeded as head chief by his protégé, Running Coyote. He was entrusted with the care of the sacred seeds given to Chief No Vitals at the Sacred Waters.[46]

The ceremonies associated with the Crow Tobacco Society, during which members re-enact the tribe's separation from the Hidatsa and its movement onto the Plains, reinforce the message of the migration story. Members of the Tobacco Society believe that the ritual planting and harvesting of *Nicotiana mutivalvis*, a rare variety of tobacco spiritually identified with the stars, fulfills the vision and mission undertaken by No Vitals.[47] In the early 1900s, the ethnologist Robert Lowie was able to identify about thirty chapters of the Tobacco Society among the Crow, each with distinctive characteristics, including the Blackbirds who wore blankets on which skins of birds were tied.[48] The Crow warrior Two Leggings described his adoption into the Tobacco Society:

> The melting snow came, followed by the grass-growing season. My wife and I packed our belongings and traveled to the Mountain Crows where Sees the Living Bull had moved. After waiting one day I picketed my white horse, loaded with presents, by my tipi door. Then I invited my medicine father for a smoke. When he came I told him that the presents and horse were his. I asked him to adopt me during a Tobacco Dance which I had heard would be held in three days. Calling him father, I said that although he had showed me many things I still had not received what I wanted most. I asked him to give me or make me one of his medicines so I could bring back more horses and scalps.
>
> The next morning the Mountain Crows broke camp and went down Elk River to meet the River Crows for the planting of the tobacco. On the way Sees the Living Bull and I struck camp with them in the mountains. We traveled no farther because the River Crows joined us there. During the celebration of the tobacco planting Sees the Living Bull adopted me. I was very happy. Now he could not refuse me.[49]

The Tobacco Society was historically the "central set of ceremonies and rituals of the Crow people," according to McCleary. He noted that No Vitals saw the seeds of the Crow's sacred tobacco as stars and believed the seeds were a gift from the stars as well as the stars themselves.[50] Although the tobacco seeds have not been planted in recent years, Crow Tobacco Society members continue to hold adoption ceremonies and day-long gatherings through which their tribal origins are remembered and re-enacted.

Recording History: Lone Dog's Winter Count

The Sioux, Kiowa, and other Plains people pictorially chronicled their band and family histories through winter counts—calendars of memorable events recorded by drawings representative of each year. The winter counts served as mnemonic devices which, combined with oral histories, helped the people to remember and preserve their past.

The Sioux considered a year to be the period that occurred from first snowfall to first snowfall. Each band or extended family group (*tiospaye* in Lakota) had a designated winter count keeper. This person was responsible for consulting with a council of tribal elders to select a particular event for which the year would be named and then for adding a drawing that represented that event to the winter count. The selected event would not necessarily be the most significant for the year, but would be the most memorable. Each year's name served as a reference that could be consulted to chronicle the order of the years. Band and family members were able to recall the year by referencing the name of the year and its corresponding events as it was recorded in the winter count.

Traditionally, only men served as winter count keepers, although in later

years family winter counts sometimes passed on to women. This position of winter count keeper was often passed down through generations of a single family. In 1879, American Horse, an Oglala Lakota living on Pine Ridge Reservation, related that his grandfather had begun his winter count that was continued by his father, and himself.[51] Winter counts are usually identified by the name of the last keeper.

Traditionally, winter counts were drawn with pigments on tanned buffalo hides, in much the same way as men recorded important events and significant deeds of their own individual histories. Over time, they could be copied many times as more space was needed or when a new keeper began his work. Therefore, there could be differences among copies, reflecting each keeper's individual artistic style.

During the late nineteenth century, muslin and paper were being used for copying winter counts. Also, in later years, written words accompanied the drawings on winter counts on muslin and paper. As interest in winter counts developed among ethnographers and other collectors visiting the reservations, the objects were also reproduced for sale, although these were most often painted on buffalo hides, which collectors preferred.

Lone Dog's Winter Count
Dakota (Sioux), 1800–1871
Copy made for the Missionary Education
Movement, early 1900s
Muslin, paint; 36 ⅝ x 60 ⅝ inches
NA.702.5

A winter count is a record of tribal history. Each year, the keeper of the count added one symbol, representing a memorable event from that year. Winter counts were originally painted on buffalo robes and were often maintained through several generations and shared with other tribal members.

Lone Dog was a Yanktonai winter count keeper who lived in Montana Territory near Fort Peck, Montana. His winter count was first described by Garrick Mallery in 1877. His information and understanding on the winter count did not come from Lone Dog himself, but from a Lieutenant High Reed who made a copy of the winter count and obtained interpretations of its symbols from Sioux people at Fort Sully, Dakota Territory.[52]

Several copies of Lone Dog's winter count in buffalo hide and muslin are now in museum and private collections. The Plains Indian Museum's version was reproduced on cloth in the early 1900s by the Missionary Education Movement of New York City. This Christian religious organization had assembled examples of Indian-made clothing and other materials for educational purposes, including the reproduction of the winter count.

In his analysis of Sioux winter counts, Mallery based his designation of specific years on a well-known and widely reported event, the Leonid meteor storm of November 12, 1833. He tied this event to the year designated on winter counts as "The Year the Stars Fell." On Lone Dog's winter count, "The Stars Fell" is drawn as a moon in black with numerous red stars. Mallery noted that other winter counts referred to this year as "storm of stars winter" or "plenty-stars-winter." Accepting this designation, Lone Dog's winter count is a chronicle beginning in the year 1800–1801, the year that thirty Lakota were killed by the Crow. This event is indicated by thirty parallel black lines in three columns. The winter count ends in 1870–1871, the year the Hunkpapa had a battle with the Crow in which fourteen Hunkpapa and twenty-nine Crow were killed. The Crow fortification is shown as a round circle surrounded by warriors with bullets flying. According to Mallery, this is the first instance in the winter count in which any warfare or killing is portrayed where guns explicitly appear to be used, rather than arrows or lances, although the Dakota had actually begun using firearms several years earlier.[53] The winter count is read counterclockwise from the center outward.[54]

Some events may have had significance only to Lone Dog's people, although others had much broader importance. For example, the year 1801–1802 is named "Many Died of Smallpox" (symbolized by the head and body of a man covered with red spots referring to the smallpox pandemic that devastated the Ponca, Otoe, Iowa, Arikara, Mandan, Crow, and Sioux).[55] Other deadly diseases for Native Americans were recorded, including whooping cough in 1813–1814 (shown by a blast of air coughed from a human figure), and measles in 1818–1819, during which "The measles broke out and many died" (depicted as a human figure covered with red spots). In 1869–1870, an eclipse of the sun that occurred on August 7, 1869, was depicted on Lone Dog's and other winter counts. The sun in the drawing is painted black, while the stars are shown in red.

Other chronicled events demonstrated nineteenth–century changes and adaptations in tribal life. In 1818–1819, La Framboise, a Canadian trader, built a post using dry timber. The dryness of the wood is shown by a dead tree near the post. In 1868–1869, Texas cattle were brought into the country, symbolized by a drawing of a horned and spotted bull.

For Plains Indian people, winter counts reinforced oral traditions as a way of recalling group histories by individual tribal members. The visual images in winter counts also helped to preserve those histories for future generations.

Plains Indian elders of earlier centuries obviously realized it was important to preserve and pass on such histories, traditions, and values as elements of the entire fabric of cultural life through a continual oral retelling as well as visual recording and interpretation through art. At times when the very survival of Plains Native peoples was threatened by the destructive forces of the late nineteenth and early twentieth centuries, perhaps this effort to uphold cultural traditions and protect tribal memories seemed futile. Indeed, much knowledge was lost as elders passed and their descendants were forced to learn new ways of life. However, while some histories and memories survive within communities, others were recorded by Native and other scholars and writers, and, as complementary resources, these records provide insights into past lives of Plains Indian people. As tribal arts were collected and preserved by museums and private individuals as representative material remnants of past lives, artists within communities continued to express their heritages in traditional and innovative ways. The memories, cultural histories, and arts, taken together, continue to be important to Native people as they strive to gain control over their lands, the education of their children, traditional religious practices, and the interpretation of their own lives.

1. N. Scott Momaday, *The Way to Rainy Mountain* (Albuquerque: University of New Mexico Press, 1969), p. 83.

2. The idea that the West constituted primarily a desert has been attributed to Major Stephen H. Long of the U.S. Army Engineers who traveled the Missouri River in 1819 and the Platte River region in 1820 and characterized the area as "unfit for cultivation and uninhabitable by a people, depending upon agriculture," despite his meeting with Pawnee, Otoe, and Omaha people who had farmed this region for centuries. In 1805, William Clark had earlier characterized the Upper Missouri region in the same way, followed by Zebulon Pike in 1806 who compared the Central Plains to the deserts of Africa. See Edwin James, "Account of an expedition from Pittsburgh to the Rocky Mountains, Performed in the Years 1829, 1820, under the command of Major S. H. Long," *Early Western Travels, 1748–1846* (Cleveland: Arthur H. Clark Company, 1905); Zebulon Montgomery Pike, *The Expeditions of Zebulon Montgomery Pike to headwaters of the Mississippi River through Louisiana Territory, and in New Spain, during the years 1805–1807* (Minneapolis: Ross & Haines, 1965), p. 8; Carolyn Gilman, *Lewis and Clark: Across the Divide* (Washington, D.C.: Smithsonian Books, 2003), p. 31.

3. Gilman, *Lewis and Clark,* pp.57–58.

4. For a discussion of the relationship of Plains Indian people to Yellowstone National Park and how it has been interpreted, see Peter Nabokov and Lawrence Loendorf, *American Indians and Yellowstone National Park: A Documentary Overview* (Yellowstone National Park: National Park Service, 2002) and *Restoring a Presence: American Indians and Yellowstone National Park* (Norman: University of Oklahoma Press, 2004).

5. George Parker Winship, "The Coronado Expedition, 1540–1542," *14th Annual Report of Bureau of American Ethnology, 1892–1893* (Washington, D.C: Smithsonian Institution, 1896), pp. 527–529.

6. Raymond J. DeMallie and John C. Ewers, "History of Ethnological and Ethnohistorical Research," *Handbook of North American Indians*, Vol. 13, Part I (Plains) (Washington, D.C.: Smithsonian Institution, 2001), p. 23.

7. For a description of horticultural traditions on the Northern Plains, see Gilbert Wilson, "Agriculture of the Hidatsa Indians; An Indian Interpretation," *University of Minnesota Studies in the Social Sciences*, 9, Minneapolis, reprinted as *Buffalo Bird Woman's Garden: Agriculture of the Hidatsa Indians (*St. Paul: Minnesota Historical Society Press, 1987).

8. Arapooish, a Crow chief to Mr. Robert Campbell of the Rocky Mountain Fur Company, as recounted by Washington Irving, in *The Adventures of Captain Bonneville, U.S.A., in the Rocky Mountains and the Far West* (1837; reprint, Norman: University of Oklahoma Press, 1961), pp. 164–165.

9. In 1936, the Hidatsa, Mandan, and Arikara developed a governing constitution and adopted the formal name of the "Three Affiliated Tribes of the Fort Berthold Indian Reservation" under the Indian Reorganization Act of 1934. See Mary Jane Schneider, "Three Affiliated Tribes," *Handbook of North American Indians* (Washington, D.C.: Smithsonian Institution, 2001), pp. 391–398. Construction of Garrison Dam, begun in 1947 under the Flood Contract Act (Public Law 78-534) of 1944, resulted in the flooding of the homelands of the Three Affiliated Tribes.

10. Marilyn Hudson, "'We Are Not Here to Sell Our Land': The Mandan, Hidatsa, and Arikara People and the Flood Control Act of 1944," presentation at Plains Indian Museum Seminar, Buffalo Bill Historical Center, October 1, 2005.

11. Ibid.

12. Curly Bear Wagner, interview with author, January 20, 2000.

13. Vine Deloria, Jr. in *God is Red: A Native View of Religion* (Golden, Colorado: Fulcrum Publishing, 1994), p. 272.

14. Ibid, p. 275.

15. Vine Deloria, Jr., "Sacred Lands," *Winds of Change* 8 (4), 1991, p. 31.

16. Deloria, *God is Red,* p. 275.

17. Melvin R. Gilmore, *Prairie Smoke* (New York: Columbia University Press, 1929), pp. 16–17.

18. Ibid., pp. 19–20. Also see, Don Cunningham, "Pahuk Place," *NEBRASKA land* (June 1985), pp. 27–31.

19. Melvin Gilmore, "The Legend of Pahuk," *Nebraska State Historical Society,* 1914, MS 231 Series 1, Folder 1 and "Trip with White Eagle Determining Pawnee Sites, August 27–29, 1914," *Nebraska State Historical Society;* Douglas R. Parks and Waldo R. Wedel, "Pawnee Geography: Historical and Sacred," *Great Plains Quarterly* 5, no. 3 (Summer 1985), pp. 153–155.

20. This visit was reported in a story by Shari Buchta, "Tribal Elders to Visit Sites in Nebraska," in *The Fremont Tribune*, June 8, 1994, pp. A1–2.

21. Momaday, *The Way to Rainy Mountain*, p. 4.

22. Nabokov and Loendorf, *American Indians and Yellowstone National Park*, pp. 58–61.

23. George Bird Grinnell, *The Cheyenne Indians: Their History and Ways of Life*, Vol. 2 (New Haven: Yale University Press, 1923), pp. 96, 148.

24. Julie E. Francis and Lawrence L. Loendorf, *Ancient Visions: Petroglyphs and Pictographs of the Wind River and Bighorn Country, Wyoming and*

Montana (Salt Lake City: The University of Utah Press, 2002), pp. 16–18.

25. Ibid, p. 138.

26. Quoted in Mario Gonzalez, "The Black Hills: The Sacred Land of the Lakota and *Tsistsistas*," *Cultural Survival Quarterly*, Winter, 1996, p. 67.

27. John G. Neihardt, *Black Elk Speaks: Being the Life Story of a Holy Man of the Oglala Sioux* (Lincoln: University of Nebraska, 1932; reprint 1979), pp. 43–44, 271.

28. John Hill Sr., "The Medicine Wheel of Wyoming," presentation at Plains Indian Museum Seminar, Buffalo Bill Historical Center, September 14, 2000.

29. David Hurst Thomas, *Exploring Ancient Native America: An Archaeological Guide* (New York: Macmillan, 1994), p. 238.

30. Douglas R. Parks, *Traditional Narratives of the Arikara Indians* (Lincoln and London: University of Nebraska Press, 1991), Vol. 4, p. 736.

31. Wagner interview, October, 1999.

32. Deloria, *God is Red*, p. 272.

33. Gordon Yellowman, Sr., "Noaha-Vose--Hoxehe?Eohe?E," presentation at Plains Indian Museum Seminar, September 15, 2000.

34. Hudson, "'We Are Not Here to Sell Our Land.'"

35. Ibid. In 1992, Congress enacted legislation acknowledging that the United States government did not justly compensate the tribes at Fort Berthold Reservations when it acquired their lands and, subsequently, awarded the tribe $5.1 million, approximately $33 an acre, to pay for the land and relocation and reconstruction costs. For more information on this case, see Paul VanDevelder, *Coyote Warrior: One Man, Three Tribes and the Trial That Forged a Nation* (Boston: Little, Brown and Company, 2004).

36. Calvin Grinnell, "The Oral Tradition of the Mandan and Hidatsa on Lewis and Clark," presentation at Plains Indian Museum Seminar, October 3, 2003.

37. John Echohawk, "Justice," *Native American Rights Fund Newsletter*, Winter, 1997, p. 2.

38. For more information on the struggle to protect the Sweetgrass Hills, see Jane Brown Gillette, "Sweetgrass Saga," *Historic Preservation* (September–October 1994), 28–33, 90–92, and Andrew Gulliford, *Sacred Objects and Sacred Places: Preserving Tribal Traditions* (Boulder: University Press of Colorado), pp. 159–254.

39. Frances Densmore, "Teton Sioux Music," *Bulletin of American Ethnology* 61 (Washington, D.C: Smithsonian Institution, 1918), pp. 95–96.

40. Black Elk, *The Sixth Grandfather: Black Elk's Teachings Given to John C. Neihardt*, Raymond J. DeMallie, ed. (Lincoln and London: University of Nebraska Press, 1989), pp. 283–284.

41. William K. Powers, *Oglala Religion* (Lincoln and London: University of Nebraska Press, 1975), p. 86.

42. Alice C. Fletcher and Francis La Flesche, "A Study of Omaha Indian Music," *Archaeological and Ethnological Papers of the Peabody Museum* 1(5) (Cambridge, Mass.: Harvard University, 1893; reprint, Lincoln: University of Nebraska Press, 1994); Margo P. Liberty, W. Raymond Wood, and Lee Irwin, "Omaha," *Handbook of North American Indians*, p. 409.

43. George Catlin, *Indian Art in Pipestone: George Catlin's Portfolio in the British Museum*, John C. Ewers, ed. (Washington, D.C.: Smithsonian Institution Press, 1979), p. 20. Also see, George Catlin, *Letters and Notes on the Manners, Customs, and condition of the North American Indians*, Vol. 1 (London, 1844; reprint, New York: Dover, 1973), pp. 169, 175, 205–206.)

44. Curly Bear Wagner, interview with author, January 20, 2000.

45. See Timothy P. McCleary, *The Stars We Know: Crow Indian Astronomy and Lifeways* (Prospect Heights, Illinois: Waveland Press, Inc., 1997), p. 16.

46. Joseph Medicine Crow, *From The Heart Of The Crow Country; The Crow Indians' Own Stories* (New York: Orion Books, 1992), p. 19.

47. Ibid, p. 20, 22–23.

48. Frederick E. Hoxie, *Parading Through History: The Making of the Crow Nation in America 1805–1935* (Cambridge, United Kingdom: Cambridge University Press, 1995), p. 40.

49. Robert H. Lowie, *The Crow Indians* (Lincoln and London: University of Nebraska Press 1983), pp. 174, 276.

50. Peter Nabokov, *Two Leggings: The Making of a Crow Warrior* (New York: Thomas Y. Crowell, Publishers, 1964), pp. 143–144.

51. McCleary, *The Stars We Know*, p. 18.

52. Garrick Mallery, "Picture Writing of the American Indians," *10th Annual Report of the Bureau of Ethnology for 1888–89* (Washington, D.C.: Smithsonian Institution, 1893), pp. 3–822; (reprint, New York: Dover Publications 1972), p. 269.

53. Garrick Mallery, "A Calendar of the Dakota Nation," *Bulletin of the United States Geological and Geographical Survey of the Territories*, Vol. 3, No. 1. (Washington, D.C.: U.S. Government Printing Office, 1877), pp. 3–25.

54. See Mallery, "Picture Writing of the American Indians," pp. 273–287, for an explication of all symbols of Lone Dog's Winter Count.

55. See Russell Thornton, *American Indian Holocaust and Survival: A Population History Since 1492* (Norman: University of Oklahoma Press, 1987), pp. 91–92 for a description of the effects of the 1801–1802 smallpox epidemic that spread throughout the central and northern Plains.

*War, killing meat, and bringing it into camp, horse-
stealing, and taking care of horses, gave our men
plenty of hard work; and they had to be in shape
to fight at any time, day or night. We women had
our children to care for, meat to cook and to dry,
robes to dress, skins to tan, clothes, lodges, and
moccasins to make. Besides these things we not
only pitched the lodges, but took them down and
packed the horses and the travois, when we moved
camp; yes, and we gathered the wood for our fires,
too. We were busy, especially when we were going
to move. I loved to move, even after I was a married woman with children to take care of. Moving
made me happy.*

—PRETTY SHIELD[1]

2 Land of Many Gifts

In 1931, when the Crow woman Pretty Shield was interviewed at the age of sev-
enty-four by Frank B. Linderman, her major responsibility was caring for her
grandchildren who were growing up in a world in rapid transition. She worried
about how the grandchildren would turn out, saying, "They have only me, an
old woman, to guide them, and plenty of others to lead them into bad ways. The
young do not listen to the old ones now, as they used to when I was young. I
worry about this, sometimes."[2]

Pretty Shield was pleased to relate her life as a girl, a young woman, and as
the wife of the warrior Goes Ahead, during the time when the Crow traveled the
Northern Plains as buffalo hunters. She was, however, reluctant to talk about
Crow life after the buffalo were gone and the people were moved to the reservation. When asked about this time she said, "There is nothing to tell, because we
did nothing. There were no buffalo."[3] The narrative of her pre-reservation life
provides a lively account of the significant roles of Crow women within tribal
economies and familial, societal, and spiritual realms of tribal life.

In contrast to the published remembrances of Pretty Shield, the roles of
women within nineteenth century Plains Indian cultures has not often been so
well-documented in historical and ethnographic sources nor completely understood by outside observers. The Plains environment could be difficult and harsh,
but it also provided many gifts to the people who lived there—abundant resources
in the buffalo and other game and plant foods available to sustain productive

Dolls
Lakota (Sioux)
Northern Plains, ca. 1910
Tanned deer hide, glass beads, tin cones, horse
hair, tin cones, porcupine quills; woman:
21 x 9⅛ inches; man: 22 x 8⅞ inches
Irving H. "Larry" Larom Collection
NA.507.7 A/B

Mother and Child—Apsaroke, 1908
Crow Reservation, Montana, 1908
Photograph by Edward S. Curtis (1806 1952)

lives and rich cultural traditions. All family members had meaningful and essential contributions and roles to carry out in this way of life.

Nineteenth–century Christian missionaries to Plains tribes, in particular, had difficulty in understanding the hard-working Plains Indian women. John Dunbar, who was a Presbyterian missionary to the Pawnee from 1831 to 1849, described his first impression of the daily work of Pawnee women in the following way:

The Pawnee women are very laborious. I am inclined to think they perform more hard labor than any other woman on this continent, be they white, black or red. It is rare, they are seen idle. When a Pawnee woman has nothing to do she seems to be out of her element. They dress the skins for the tent covers, which is done with no small labor, sew them together, and fit them for the tents—make all the robes, which are many, both for their own use and the market—cut and bring all the wood on their backs—make all the fires—do all the cooking of course—dry all the meat—dig the ground—plant—hoe and gather all the corn, of which they raise in abundance, as they also do of beans and pumpkins—cut the timber, and build all their dwellings, both fixed and movable—set up and take down the portable tents—bridle and unbridle, saddle and unsaddle, pack and unpack all the horses—make all their moccasins, mats, bags, bowls, mortars, etc. etc. . . . Since the ground has thawed, they have bestowed some hundreds of days of hard labor in digging Indian potatoes. A woman does not succeed in digging more than a peck, laboring diligently from sunrise till sunset. Soon after light, I have seen droves of the women and girls with their hoes and axes on their shoulders, starting off to their day's work. . . . Their women are mere slaves.[4]

This characterization of Plains Indian women as "slaves," "chattel," or "drudges" was commonly found in nineteenth-century journals and letters by Christian missionaries, Euro-American travelers, traders, and government representatives. Contemporary researchers have associated this denigration of Native women and their work by early outside observers with Euro-American biases concerning manual labor and the proper role of women, as well as an inability to communicate directly with the women.[5] In the case of the Pawnee, Dunbar failed to recognize that women did exercise power as owners of their own homes in which their husbands, unmarried children, and married daughters with husbands and children lived. In addition to their economic contributions from gardening and gathering plants, creating homes, and producing meals, clothing, household goods, and other necessities, Pawnee women—especially elders—cared for and guided children and were influential in ceremonial and social areas of cultural life.

The practical contributions of Plains Indian men—hunting for buffalo and other game and warfare and defense of the people—on the surface were considered more glorious and highly honored than the work of women. Indeed, the skills of hunters and their courage in battle and war deeds were commemorated through oral and cultural traditions, paintings on hide, muslin, and paper, and winter counts. However, women also were accorded respect for their work and accomplishments. Speaking of the lives of Dakota women, Ella Deloria said:

A woman caring for children and doing all the work around the house thought herself no worse off than her husband who was compelled to risk his life continuously, hunting and remaining ever on guard against enemy attacks on his family.[6]

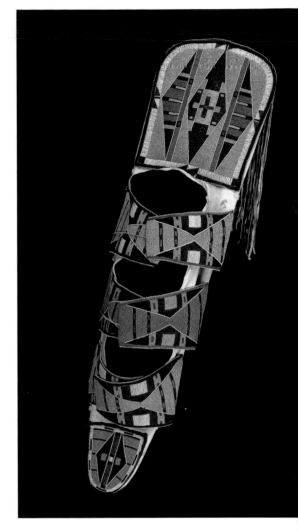

Cradle
Apsáalooke (Crow), Montana, ca. 1900
Tanned deer hide, glass beads, wool cloth;
59 x 11 inches
The Catherine Bradford Collection,
Gift of The Coe Foundation NA.111.6

Typically a gift from female relatives, a cradle provided comfort, safety, and a clear view of the world for the baby within. The baby would have been held securely in this beautifully beaded Crow cradle with the wide straps, which were laced together in the front.

Among the Crow, Pawnee, Dakota, and other Plains peoples, the division of labor between men's work and women's work in practical terms was neither absolute nor inflexible. Although men were generally in charge of hunting and defense and women were primarily responsible for the home, food preparation, and rearing children—and either could be ridiculed for crossing the boundaries established through this division of labor—both men and women were also sometimes involved in each other's work. Men assisted in cutting wood, slicing meat or preparing corn for drying, and spending time with children. Acquiring such skills as food preparation or repairing clothing and moccasins served men well when they traveled on their own. Women also were known to support and assist in hunting and warfare.[7]

Nourishing the People: Plant Gathering and Gardening

In the variable environments of the Plains region, women collected an abundance of plants for foods and medicines and various other uses. The starchy tuber from the prairie turnip or Indian breadroot (*Psoralea esculenta*) was probably the most important food plant gathered in the Plains. Collected by Lewis and Clark and first scientifically described by Frederick Pursh in 1814 in *Flora Americae Septentrionalis*, this plant has also been called the "prairie potato," "white apple" by Lewis and Clark, or in French the *pomme blanche* or *pomme de terre*, and *Timpsula* by the Lakota.

Prairie turnips grew throughout the Plains on well-drained hillsides—particularly in Montana, the Dakotas, Kansas, Nebraska, and Missouri—and were col-

Two Moon's Children
Northern Cheyenne Reservation, 1879
Photograph by L.A. Huffman (1854–1931)
P.100.3581

Burden Basket
Nueta (Mandan), Upper Missouri River Region, ca. 1860
Willow, box elder bark, tanned hide; 7 x 11¾ inches
Chandler-Pohrt Collection, Gift of Mr. William D. Weiss NA.106.183

Mandan, Hidatsa, and Arikara women made baskets such as this one to carry corn and other garden produce from their gardens to their villages and for collecting wild plant foods. Basket-making was a sacred art that only a few women possessed the skills and rights to pursue.

OPPOSITE: *"Pretty Nose," Cheyenne Girl*
Northern Cheyenne Reservation, Montana, 1879
Photograph by L.A. Huffman (1854–1931)
P.100.3574

lected in large quantities by women in late spring through early summer using their digging sticks to break through the hard ground. The tuber parts of the plant, which grow about four inches below the ground, have been used for food and traded in the Great Plains for centuries. Women prepared the tubers by peeling the heavy brown rinds. They were eaten fresh, boiled in soups with meat and other vegetables, or dried for later use. Prairie turnips were often braided together by their stems into bundles that could be stored in lodges or underground caches and easily transported when the people traveled. Ground into flour, prairie turnips could also be used to thicken soups or made into a pudding flavored with berries.

The nutritional value of prairie turnips is similar to that of white potatoes. Prairie turnips sustained people through difficult times, when the buffalo and other game were scarce or when the gardens of the farming tribes had failed to provide sufficient crops because of drought, insect infestation, or destruction during enemy raids. On April 29, 1844, John Dunbar recorded such a time of

Northern Cheyenne Women Gathering Wood
Northern Cheyenne Reservation, Montana, early 1900s
Photograph by Mrs. George Bird "Elizabeth" Grinnell P.37.8

Two women are gathering small pieces of firewood along a hillside while one woman tends a baby. Women often collected plant foods, gathered firewood, and completed other duties together. Such cooperation helped lighten women's daily workloads and provided time for socializing.

scarcity for the Pawnee, in which they dug "hundreds of bushels" of the plant along the low sandy bottomlands of the Loup Fork.[8] John Ewers has also cited a similar desperate circumstance for the Yankton Sioux living in the vicinity of Fort Union in 1856 when they relied on prairie turnips to survive a period of scarce game. Ewers noted that such times have been recorded in Sioux winter counts.[9]

On tribal hunts, bands sometimes deliberately passed through areas where the women could gather large quantities of prairie turnips. Dried surplus prairie turnips were later traded to other tribal groups. According to Ewers, the economic importance of the prairie turnip and the woman's digging stick used to collect them is reinforced in oral traditions, the Sun Dance, and other ceremonies among the Blackfeet and other Plains Native people, noting that, "Among several Plains tribes, the humble digging stick came to be recognized as a symbol of great importance of women's contributions to their tribal cultures."[10]

Women also gathered other tubers and roots such as groundnuts and Jerusalem artichokes, bitterroot, spring shoots from cattails and ragweed, ground plums, wild onions, lamb's quarters, and seeds and nuts. Wild plums, chokecherries, buffalo berries, and other fruits were gathered in the summer and fall months, to be eaten fresh or dried and stored for winter use. Many of the women's activities related to providing and preparing food for their families were determined by their knowledge of the seasons and an understanding of the locations and growing habits of the plants. Crow tribal member Louella Johnson described the seasonal cycle thus:

> The first things that come up would be bitterroot. These are the roots that come up first. Shortly following that would be the turnips. They come up probably the last, oh, the early part of July. Then the berries start ripening in the summer. Those would be the chokecherries, the plums, the buffalo berries, and grapes. Grapes are a little further towards fall and also the buffalo berries are good after the first frost. So, during the summer probably the first ones would be the chokecherries and the June berries. Some people call them Saskatoon, some people call them service berries. They have many names, but those are the first berries that are ripe.[11]

As groups of women left their camps and villages to collect berries and other wild foods, these excursions sometimes provided opportunities for young men to approach young women in whom they were interested.

> It was . . . a common thing for a young man to help his sweetheart pick June berries. A young man might send word to his sweetheart by some female relative of his own saying, "That young man says that when you want to go for June berries, he wants to go along with you!" Or else he watched when she came out of the lodge to start berrying. For it was not our custom for a young man to talk openly with a young woman.[12]

Some of the berries were mixed with dried and roasted meat and fat to make pemmican, a nutritious food that men carried when they traveled. Other berries were made into dried cakes for later use and stored in tanned hide bags or parfleches. The process involved pounding and crushing the berries with a stone hammer or maul, forming the pulp into balls, and drying them in the sun. Buffalo Bird Woman, a Hidatsa elder, described the making of chokecherry cakes:

> We pounded the chokecherries on the stone mortar in the lodge or out on the floor of the corn stage. We did not like to do so out on the ground outside the lodge on account of the dust that got in the cherries.
>
> Two or three cherries were laid on the stone and struck smartly, then two or three more. When enough pulp had accumulated it was taken up in the woman's hand and made into a ball, and then squeezed out in lumps thru the first finger and thumb of the right hand by pushing with the left thumb in to the right palm.
>
> These lumps we dried on the corn stage on a skin. On warm days they dried in three days' time. But if the weather was damp and chilly, it might take 5 or 6 days. They were ready, when a lump broke dry clear thru. If the lump was put away while still soft inside, it spoiled and smelled bad.[13]

A woman learned about the uses, locations, and preparations of these plant foods from childhood because this knowledge would serve her and her family throughout her life. Pretty Shield described the labor of using a digging stick to pry prairie turnips from hard sun-dried ground when she was a young girl, but also the gratification of learning this essential skill.

> We were camped on Big river. It was summer and I was seven years old. I, with two other little girls, was digging turnips, using a very sharp digger made from the limb of a choke-cherry tree. The sun was hot. You have seen the heat dancing above the grass on the plains? Well, the heat was dancing that day, and even the birds were thirsty for water. . . . The turnips were plentiful, but hard to dig because the ground was so dry; and besides we were too little to have great strength. . . .
>
> One day in the moon when the berries began to turn red [July] I went with five other girls to the turnips that grew so plentifully between The-two-creeks [Davis and Thompson]. We were afoot, running races, and singing all the way to the place where the turnips grew. Then we began a race to see who could dig the most turnips, and became quiet as sleeping babies, each girl working hard to beat the others.[14]

Like her own mother and grandmother, Pretty Shield passed on her knowledge of plant foods to her youngest granddaughter, Alma Hogan Snell. Because her own mother had died when Snell was a year and a half old, she lived with her grandmother and learned the traditional ways of doing things. She has carried the knowledge of plants and their uses for foods and medicines throughout her life and passed this knowledge on to younger generations.

Mashed berries made into berry cakes
Crow Reservation, Montana, 1903–1925
Photograph by Reverend W.A. Petzoldt, D.D.
(1872–1960)
Dr. William and Anna Petzoldt Collection,
Gift of Genevieve Petzoldt Fitzgerald PN.95Ī.176

Berry cakes lie out to dry in the sun, while a Crow
woman forms more cakes from berries that have
been pounded and crushed into pulp. Once thor-
oughly dried, berry cakes would be stored in hide
bags for later use.

She [Pretty Shield] said, "The earth is like our mother because it gives us food like a mother provides food from her breast." She respected it. I remember she'd say that when the farmers first came, they "cut into the face" of the earth—*iisáduukaxik*. It's like a wound there, and it hurt her.

When I was with Grandma and all the old ladies that used to go and dig turnips, I'd watch them, and I noticed that they *did* care. They all did the same thing. They had a routine about it. They didn't just go carelessly around; they did these things patiently and correctly, and they were just right at home there. They would dig the roots with their sticks; then they would replace the soil and tamp it down just like nobody had bothered it. They always said Aho [thank you] to the Creator, and if there were any wild seeds, they would scatter them about for more turnips to grown in another year. So I always do that now.[15]

The Mandan, Hidatsa, and Arikara, Pawnee, Omaha, Otoe, Ponca, and Wichita gathered plants for food, but the women of these tribes also raised crops along fertile river bottomlands. By the early 1700s, the economies of the Cheyenne and Crow had gone from being primarily horticultural and buffalo hunting to being supported by seasonal migration in pursuit of the buffalo herds. Just as the Crow had moved from present-day North Dakota to their homelands in Montana and Wyoming, the Cheyenne migrated from the Great Lakes region through the Black Hills. The development of their buffalo hunting traditions were well remembered by elders in the late nineteenth to early twentieth centuries. Iron Teeth, a Northern Cheyenne woman who was ninety-two years old

Feast Bowl
Santee Dakota (Eastern Sioux), Eastern Plains, ca. 1870
Ash burl wood, tanned leather; 6 x 14¼ inches
NA.106.159

Using burls of ash and maple, men—and sometimes women—carved large bowls for serving utensils and for food bowls for honored guests at formal meals. Eastern Dakota people often carved images of animals and spirits along the rims of their bowls. The image of Eya, the spirit of gluttony, is carved on the rim of this bowl.

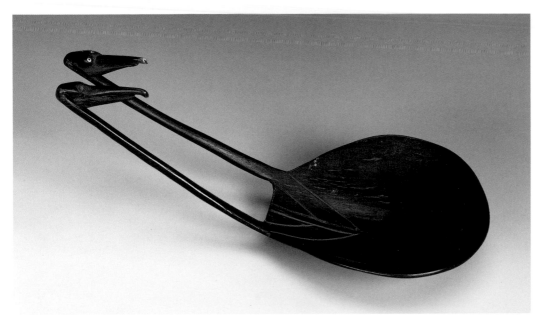

when she was interviewed by Dr. Thomas B. Marquis in 1926, experienced firsthand the transitions in the lives of her people.

> Ninety-two years ago, I was born in the Black Hills country. The time of my birth was in
> the moon when the berries are ripe, in the last part of the summer. My father was a
> Cheyenne Indian, my mother was a Sioux. My parents brought up their family as members
> of the Cheyenne tribe. Our people traveled over the whole country between the Elk River
> and Mexico. . . .

We planted corn every year when I was a little girl in the Black Hills. With sharpened sticks we punched holes in the ground, dropped in the grains of corn, then went hunting all summer. When the grass died we returned and gathered the crops. . . . We learned of vegetable foods growing wild. We gathered wild turnips, wild sweet potatoes and other root foods. We found out the best place for berries.[16]

For the Mandan, Hidatsa, Arikara, Pawnee, and Wichita, who remained horticulturalists throughout the nineteenth century and beyond, corn was the essential food, the mother to all the people that provided sustenance from generation to generation. Mother Corn was a central theme in tribal traditions, fundamental to the creation of the people themselves. According to Wichita traditions, at creation, the Wichita men were given the bow and arrow and taught to hunt buffalo and the women were provided an ear of corn and taught how to cultivate, harvest, and use it for food. For the Arikara, Corn Woman conferred the gift of corn on the people and taught them the ways that it was prepared and cooked. Among the Mandan, the growing of corn was associated with the formation of the earth lodge villages and the cultivation of associated crops—beans, squash, and sunflowers.

The Corn People were living under the ground by a lake. One day some of the people saw an opening reaching up to the land above, and there was a vine growing in this hole. They asked the Fox to climb up and see this land. He climbed up, but, when he stuck his nose out, he got only a brief look at the beautiful land above because Sun burned his nose.

Then they asked Elk to go up and dig the hole larger with his horns. He made the hole large so the people could get through. The people started up following the vine. They came up continuously for four days, but on the last day a woman heavy with child broke the vine and ended the migration forever. All these people had been raising the corn on this land beneath the earth.

There were four leaders in the group that reached the earth. They were three brothers and a sister. Their names were Good Furred Robe, Cornhusk Earrings, Uses His Head for Rattle, and a sister named Waving Corn Stalk. Good Furred Robe began to lay out the villages and the fields. He laid out the lodges in rows like the rows of corn, and he assigned the garden plots to each family. Then he distributed the corn, beans, squash, and sunflower seeds to each family.[17]

The Hidatsa learned about growing corn from the Mandan. According to tradition, the Hidatsa had lived near Devil's Lake in North Dakota before migrating west, where they met the Mandan at the mouth of the Heart River. In 1804 Lewis and Clark met the Hidatsa living in three villages at the mouth of the Knife River, and the Mandan in two villages nearby on the Missouri. Both the Mandan and Hidatsa were nearly annihilated by the smallpox epidemic of 1837–1838 and the few hundred survivors joined together in one village known as Like-a-Fishhook at a bend of the Missouri River near Fort Berthold. They

Set of Utensils
Lakota (Sioux), Northern Plains, 1881–1883
Horn, thread and glass beads; 9 ⅜ x 1 inches,
6 ¾ x 1 ¼ inches, 7 ½ x 1 ⅛ inches,
8 x 1 ¼ inches
Dr. Robert A. Anderson Collection
NA.106.311A–D

Sitting Bull traded these forks, knife, and spoon
to Mr. D.L. Pratt, Sr., the post trader at Fort
Randall, South Dakota during his imprisonment
there from 1881–1883. The utensils were carved
of horn following a Euro-American style, but
one of the forks is decorated with beads.

were joined there by the Arikara in 1862. All three tribes shared a fundamental dependence upon and reverence for corn, which together with other crops cultivated by women sustained the people.

> One day a war party, I think of ten men, wandered west to the Missouri River. They saw on the other side a village of earth lodges like their own. It was a village of the Mandans. The villagers saw the Hidatsas, but like them, feared to cross over, lest the strangers prove to be enemies.
>
> It was autumn, and the Missouri River was running low so that an arrow could be shot from shore to shore. The Mandans parched some ears of ripe corn with the grain on the cob; they broke the ears in pieces, thrust the pieces on the points of arrows, and shot them across the river. "Eat!" they said, whether by voice or signs, I do not know. The word for "eat" is the same in the Hidatsa and Mandan languages.
>
> The warriors ate of the parched corn, and liked it. They returned to their village and said, "We have found a people living by the Missouri River who have a strange kind of grain, which we ate and found good!" The tribe was not much interested and made no effort to seek the Mandans, fearing, besides, that they might not be friendly.
>
> However, a few years later, a war party of the Hidatsas crossed the Missouri and visited the Mandans at their village near Bird Beak Hill. The Mandan chief took an ear of yellow corn, broke it in two, and gave half to the Hidatsas. This half-ear the Hidatsas took home, for seed; and soon every family was planting yellow corn.[18]

Plains Native women were skilled horticulturists who grew several varieties of corn, beans, and squash, as well as sunflowers and melons. They traditionally planted their gardens in fertile river bottomlands where the soil was soft and could be easily worked and where the plants would be resistant to drought.

Pawnee women cultivated at least ten varieties of corn, seven of pumpkins and squashes, and eight of beans.[19] The Mandan grew seven varieties of corn and several of beans and squash.[20]

Buffalo Bird Woman listed nine varieties of corn that were grown in Like-a-Fishhook village, each of which was planted separately to keep the strains pure. There were also five varieties of beans and several types of squash, classified according to their size and shape. Initially using digging sticks, hoes made from buffalo shoulder bones lashed to wooden handles, and rakes formed of wood or deer antlers, and later, as they became available through trade, metal hoes, the women worked their gardens daily during the planting season. Sunflowers were planted in the spring as soon as the ice in the Missouri River broke and the ground could be worked. Corn was then cultivated in rows interspersed by squash and beans.

> We Hidatsa women were early risers in the planting season; it was my habit to be up before sunrise, while the air was cool, for we thought this was the best time for garden work. Planting corn by hand was slow work; but by ten o'clock the morning's work was done, and I was tired and ready to go home for my breakfast and rest; we did not eat before going into the field. I usually went to the field every morning in the planting season, if the weather was fine. Sometimes I went out again a little before sunset and planted; but this was not usual.[21]

Ceremonies, ritual songs, prayers, and feasts sanctified each step of the planting, growing, and harvesting seasons under the spiritual direction of those who held special powers and sacred bundles related to the cultivation of gardens. Feasting and celebrations took place after harvests with people invited to share in the offerings from the fresh garden produce.

For Hidatsa women, the growing of corn and the other crops in their gardens had deep spiritual connections. Women guarded their young and tender corn plants from the magpies, crows, and gophers that could destroy the crop, and sometimes made scarecrows to frighten away the birds. A platform was often built in the garden where girls and young women of the household sat and sang as they watched out for threats to the growing plants.

> We cared for our corn in those days as we would care for a child; for we Indian people loved our gardens, just as a mother loves her children; and we thought that our growing corn liked to hear us sing, just as children like to hear their mother sing to them.[22]

Hidatsa women prepared foods from the fresh vegetables or preserved them for later use. Sunflower seeds were roasted and ground into meal which was mixed with other vegetables in a soup or rolled into balls to be eaten when traveling. Corn, squash, and beans were eaten fresh or dried and stored, with the surplus sometimes traded to the Lakota, Cheyenne, and other non-horticultural people.

Creating a Home

Native women of the Plains were primarily responsible for building and maintaining their homes and creating the household goods and furnishings for their tipis, grass houses, and earth lodges. Women were expected to have the skills and knowledge to produce the tipi decorations and liners, buffalo robes, storage bags, parfleches, baskets, and other belongings and those with exceptional abilities and expertise were greatly admired and called upon for guidance.

When bands settled in new locations, women were in charge of putting up the tipis and bringing in and placing all the furnishings in their proper places. When it was time to move camp again, women took down and packed tipis, bedding, clothing, food, and other household items onto the travois and were in

Moving camp
Crow Reservation, Montana , 1903–1925
Photograph by Reverend W.A. Petzoldt, D.D. (1872–1960)
Dr. William and Anna Petzoldt Collection, Gift of Genevieve Petzoldt Fitzgerald PN.95.52

Women are mounted on their horses that, packed with parfleches and other bags, are pulling tipi poles as they move to a new location.

charge of moving all the household goods and children, leaving the men free to look for potential threats and defend the group if necessary. When the group traveled, men rode ahead of the women, children, and elders, ever vigilant about any potential danger and ready to protect the others. Pretty Shield described the excitement of the Crow people when they moved to a new village location.

> A crier would ride through the village telling the people to be ready to move in the morning. In every lodge the children's eyes would begin to shine. Men would sit up to listen, women would go to their doors to hear where the next village would be set up, and then there would be glad talking until it was time to go to sleep. Long before the sun came the fires would be going in every lodge, the horses, hundreds of them, would come thundering in, and then everybody was very busy. Down would come the lodges, packs would be made, travois loaded. Ho! Away we would go, following the men, to some new camping ground, with our children playing around us. It was good hard work to get things packed up, and moving; and it was hard, fast work to get them in shape again, after we camped. But in between these times we rested on our traveling horses. Yes, and we women visited while we traveled. There was plenty of room on the plains then, so that many could ride abreast if they wished to. There was always danger of attack by our enemies so that far ahead, on both sides, and behind us, there were our wolves who guarded us against surprise as we traveled. The men were ever watching these wolves, and we women constantly watched the men.[23]

Case
Tsistsistas (Cheyenne), Northern Plains, ca. 1860
Rawhide, pigments, cotton thread, sinew; 15 x 12 ¾ inches
Gift of Mr. Nick Eggenhofer NA.106.8

Women sometimes used rawhide cases such as this to store medicines derived from plants to treat headaches, pains, and other ailments.

Iron Teeth also described the excitement of the people, particularly of the children when they traveled. Women watched the children, who were helping with horses or dogs, playing, or riding on the travois.

> Our children used to ride in woven willow baskets swung between the travois poles, when we were traveling. They would often climb out, play along the way, then climb back in again and go to sleep. . . . I always watched closely any basket where my children might be riding. Even when no danger was apparent, as I rode the horse that dragged their basket poles I enjoyed looking back and exchanging glances with exactly the right number of pairs of sparkling black eyes peeping up at me. One day a pair of eyes was missing! I jumped from my working animal, mounted a led one, and hurried back along the line of travelers. My fright was changed to joy when I found my missing girl asleep with another woman's children in their basket.[24]

Once the people arrived at their destination, women unpacked their travois, put up their lodges, and brought in their belongings as quickly as possible. Alma Hogan Snell recounted what her grandmother, Pretty Shield, told her about the process.

They put up those lodge poles and they might just put up about four, the main ones, and then put their buffalo robes in there in case that they didn't finish pitching the lodge, at least they will have that protection from the outside. Then, afterwards, they would slip in the poles and stretch it out. If they were to stay there for awhile then they would get the pegs and put them in there and stretch it to where it would be more permanent. They were the ones who brought in the bedding, the clothes, the parfleches, and everything and place them in the right places in the lodge. They were the ones who went out and looked for wood. She [Pretty Shield] said, "We didn't only pitch the lodge, we gathered wood so that we can make fire right away, so that the water would get hot by the time we get things done, and we're ready to put things into that."[25]

Snell described Pretty Shield as "a good lodge maker."[26] Pretty Shield recalled for her granddaughter the care with which she prepared, pieced together and sewed buffalo hides for a tipi. The old buffalo hide lodges had particular spiritual significance for the Crow.

The lodges would be a sanctuary. It actually is a place of refuge. It protects you. It means so much more. I think it means more than a house, actually. It has the animal structure to it, the buffalo animal structure to it that protects us even from other animals that could invade the lodge. You could wrap up in a buffalo robe and stay still. The smell of the buffalo is so overwhelming and yet the hide is so tough. My grandmother says it protected them from many things, the buffalo.[27]

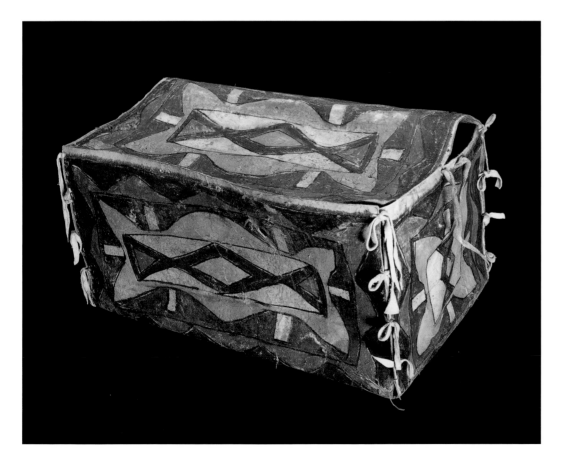

Box
Lakota (Sioux), Northern Plains, ca. 1890
Rawhide, pigments, tanned deer hide;
16 ½ x 9 ½ x 8 ¾ inches
Irving H. "Larry" Larom Collection NA.106.11

Lakota women made painted rawhide boxes for storing and transporting clothing and other items. This box is made from a single piece of rawhide folded and laced together at the seams with thongs of tanned hide.

Horticultural people such as the Mandan, Arikara, and Hidatsa also lived in tipis when they followed the buffalo herds on their summer and winter hunts. During the rest of the year, they lived in villages of closely packed earth lodges on high terraces overlooking river channels, where both firewood and water would be readily available. The earth lodges of a village, sometimes consisting of a few hundred households, surrounded a central open area where ceremonies and dances were held.

Groups of women built earth lodges under the direction of the owner. The lodges were circular structures thirty to sixty feet in diameter, sunk into the ground and built over a central support of four large timbers. Covered with earth over a wooden framework, the earth lodges had fireplaces in the center with smoke holes above. Covered wooden walkways provided entrance to the lodge. Women were closely identified with their earth lodges and had ownership in the furnishings and domestic equipment used in the lodges and gardens.

The building of the lodges was a sacred undertaking. During the notching of the four center poles of Mandan earth lodges, a female elder would be called upon to sing and ask for blessings for the inhabitants of the lodge.[28] Buffalo Bird Woman related, "We said the four posts were alive and we prayed always and made offerings. . . . . We thought the house to be sacred and the posts upheld it."[29] "We thought the earth lodge was alive and had a spirit like a human body, and that its front was like a face, with the door for mouth."[30] Contemporary Hidatsa people like Calvin Grinnell continue to have a fascination and respect for the earth lodge and traditional way of life that it symbolized.

Our ancestral homes where our people thrived were in villages made up of earth lodges. These were built along the Missouri River, these villages, and there's evidence of that— archaeological evidence of that. The earth lodge had a central fireplace, four posts that held up the main beams, and were about forty to fifty feet in diameter, which not only served as a living quarters, but also they kept their best ponies in there the winter months so they wouldn't lose them. This was a very energy efficient dwelling in that it remained cool in the summer and warm in the winter. It retained heat. These sorts of homes were well suited for the harsh winters that North Dakota is known for and we have short summers, of course.

They were unique. Our people thought that they had a spirit, that there was life to everything and that there should be respect given to people's homes, to people's living quarters, because they were made out of natural things. The trees provided the logs, the four post logs and then of course the rest of the structure and the earth and then the rocks for the fire, the ground that they sat upon.

Everything was natural. Then, the spirit imbued upon it by the people living in there. There was a respect for a person's way of life, a person's individuality and entire families who lived in these earth lodges, earth households.[31]

The Art of Women

The art of Plains Indian women, created for their homes, family members, and gift-giving, reflected the shared tribal values of industry, generosity, humility, and hospitality. Women who possessed these virtues were greatly admired and sought out by younger women and girls for advice and guidance.

> How I loved to watch Kills-good pack her things to move camp. The painting on her parfleches was brighter, her bags whiter, than those of any other Crow woman; and, ah, she had so many pretty things. Besides, I thought her favorite horse, a proud pinto, was far and away the best horse in the Crow tribe. And yet Kills-good was not proud. Instead, she was kindly and so soft-spoken that all the people loved her.[32]

Women took great care and pride in furnishing their tipis and earth lodges with functional, yet often finely decorated, parfleches and other rawhide trunks and bags, soft tanned buffalo robes, backrests made of slender peeled willow sticks laced together, bowls made from rawhide or carved from wood, carved wood or horn spoons, and hide bags made from tanned hide and decorated in

Green hides showing geometric design for parfleches
Crow Reservation, Montana
Photograph by William H. Rau (1855–1920)
Dr. William and Anna Petzoldt Collection,
Gift of Genevieve Petzoldt Fitzgerald
PN.95.299

Women first staked out raw hides and painted geometric designs on them while they were still wet. Then they cut out the patterns from which rawhide cases would be formed. The finished parfleches were stiff but durable storage and carrying cases.

LEFT: **Parfleche**
Tsistsistas (Cheyenne), Plains,
ca. 1890
Rawhide, pigments; 25 ½ x 15 ½ inches
Chandler-Pohrt Collection,
Gift of Mr. William D. Weiss NA.106.148

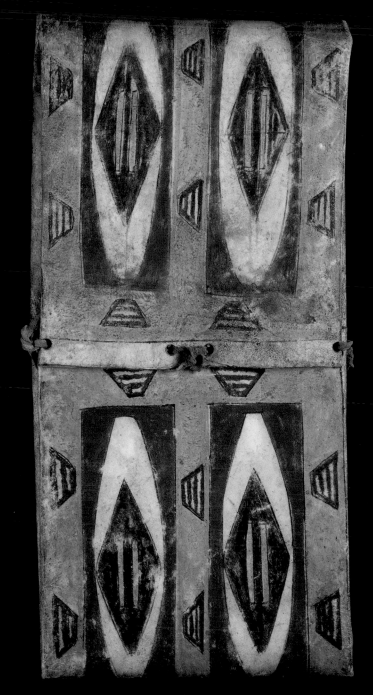

Parfleches
Lakota (Sioux), Northern Plains,
ca. 1885–1890
Rawhide, pigments; 26 ¾ x 12 ½ inches
Gift of Irving H. "Larry" Larom Estate
NA.106.234.1-.2

Made of stiff rawhide, parfleches were usually made in pairs to be carried on horses
or travois or stored in lodges. Clothing,
dried meat and other foods, and household
utensils were stored in parfleches.

porcupine quillwork, beadwork, or natural pigments. Household objects such as these were transportable, functional, and practical, yet also carved, painted, quilled, beaded, and embellished to reflect distinctive cultural traditions. Because of these qualities, Plains Indian material culture has been characterized as possessing "an aesthetic of mobility."[33] As Euro-American trade items became available in the Plains in the early nineteenth century, iron pots and kettles, metal knives, wool blankets, and other tools and household items were added to this assemblage of necessities, although many people preferred the older, more traditional creations.

Hides of buffalo, deer, elk, and other animals were the raw materials from which women created tipis, parfleches and other bags, clothing, moccasins and leggings, and painted robes. Rawhide containers made from buffalo hide were used for storage and transportation of food, clothes, and household goods. Made in sets of two, parfleches were hung by hide loops in tipis and earth lodges and tied to horses or packed on travois for travel.

The use of parfleches by Plains Indian people was recorded in French journals as early as 1700. The word "parfleche" is thought to derive from the French word *parer*, meaning "to parry," and *fleche*, meaning "arrow," with the term referring originally to a shield or body armor of rawhide made by some tribes of the Northwest. In time the term became a more generalized name for rawhide and the distinctive envelope-shaped case made of rawhide.[34]

Women made parfleches and other rawhide bags to accommodate the shapes and sizes of the objects they held, such as the cylinders which protected feather bonnets. The common shape was an envelope made from an oblong section of hide with the long sides folded inward and the short sides folded to meet in the middle. Women painted the vibrant geometric designs of the parfleches when the hides were staked out to dry and before they were cut. Some early parfleches were decorated with intricate incised designs made by carving the surface of the hides.

After buffalo became scarce and the tribes were settled on reservations in the late nineteenth century, women made parfleches and other rawhide bags from the hides of domestic cattle. By this time, manufactured containers were available for daily life, so parfleches were primarily made for gift-giving. Alma Hogan Snell recalls the use of parfleches when she was a girl.

> The parfleches are our suitcases, you might say, because I have seen them put clothes in there. I have seen them put even dry meat in there. When they put clothes in there, they usually added a little sweet grass in there and then the next item, whatever it is. And then, tie them up right and then put them against the wall.[35]

Women worked long hours cleaning, scraping, tanning, and softening buffalo hides that would serve as warm sleeping and wearing robes. Buffalo Bird Woman described this process of coating the rawhide with a mixture of boiled backbone

Cylinder Cases
Apsáalooke (Crow), Montana, ca. 1885
Rawhide, tanned deer hide, pigments;
53 x 5 ½ x 4 ¼ inches
Chandler-Pohrt Collection, Gift of PacifiCorp
Foundation NA.106.595.1-.2

sinew, brains, and sage. "After drying it for several days, she soaked it, fleshed it, wrung it out, and scraped it again. She stretched it on a frame, rubbed it with a rough stone for several hours, and drew it over a rope many times. Only then was it ready to be painted or embroidered with dyed quillwork."[36]

Alma Hogan Snell remembered that Pretty Shield tanned hides that were used for warmth in her small reservation home. Sometimes, Pretty Shield had all of her granddaughters involved in the process, each pulling and stretching the hide to make it soft, or she would continue to work the buffalo hide alone until it was soft. "I have seen her take that robe and go against her knee in a fold and roll that fold and keep rolling it until it got soft. Then, she'd go to another spot. That robe I know very well because I slept in it. I slept in the robe with her."[37]

After buffalo robes were tanned, women could paint them using natural

Buffalo Robe

Hidatsa, Upper Missouri River Region, ca. 1850
Tanned buffalo hide and fur, pigments;
71 x 46 inches NA.202.295

Both men and women painted on hides, but their styles were distinctive. While men's art was representational, women's was geometric, using color and patterns revealed to them in dreams and passed on as gifts from one generation to another. The design of this robe, known as the "box and border," was painted only by women and is thought to symbolize the internal organs of the buffalo showing its internal structure.

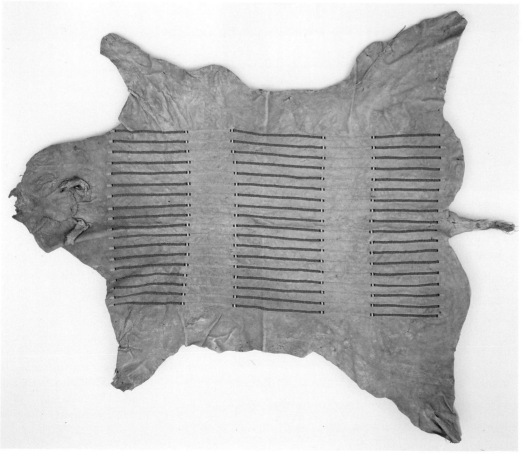

Robe

Lakota (Sioux), Northern Plains, ca. 1890
Tanned hide, glass beads; 56 ¼ x 28 ¾ inches
Gift of Mr. and Mrs. Royal B. Hassrick
NA.202.294

The pattern of horizontal stripes on this child's robe is an older Northern Plains design that was used by many groups. The earlier robes featured this pattern in paint and quillwork, while on the later ones, the pattern was executed in beadwork.

Buffalo Robe
Lakota (Sioux), Northern Plains, ca. 1870
Tanned buffalo hide and fur, pigments;
105 ⅛ x 64 ½ inches
Gift of Mr. and Mrs. Royal B. Hassrick
NA.202.296

pigments or decorate them with porcupine quillwork or beadwork. Painting on hides is an ancient means of expression for Plains Indian people, described in the journals of the expedition of Francisco Vásquez de Coronado.[38] Natural pigments were produced from the earth and plants of the region, including ochre, hematite for red, charcoal for black, lake algae for green, buffalo gallstones for yellow, and blue clays. Ground into fine powders, the pigments were mixed with water and thin glue made from boiled hide scrapings, which helped the paint to hold its colors. Pretty Shield remembered that she had boiled buffalo hooves into a jelly to mix with the powdered pigments and dried this mixture and cut it into squares. Later, she mixed water or grease with this substance to produce the colors for hide painting.[39] Commercial pigments became available through Euro-American traders during the eighteenth century and were widely used by Plains

Indian people by the end of the nineteenth century. Paints were applied using reed brushes and porous pieces of buffalo bone which had been sharpened for drawing fine lines or rounded for applying paint to larger areas. Women tended to paint geometric designs on buffalo robes, while men painted their accomplishments in hunting and warfare in pictographic representations.

As wool blankets became available through European and American trading posts during the mid-nineteenth centuries, they were used like buffalo robes for bedding and outer clothing. Wearing blankets were decorated with strips of porcupine quillwork or beadwork created in tribally distinctive designs.

The use of porcupine quillwork as a means of embellishing buffalo robes, bags, tipi liners and decorations, moccasins, ornaments, and clothing was another ancient tradition on the Plains. Geometric and floral designs were created by flattening and dying the hollow quills from porcupines and then wrapping or sewing them with sinew on hide. Porcupine quillwork was more widely used by peoples of the Central and Northern Plains, while painting with natural pigments prevailed in the Southern Plains. Split bird quills and plant fibers were also used in designs in much the same way as porcupine quills. Traditionally, the quills were dyed with natural plant dyes, but once Euro-American trade materials became available, other more vibrant colors were created from boiling quills with strips of brightly dyed blankets and aniline dyes.

By the middle of the nineteenth centuries, small glass beads became widely available and the creation of quillwork by Plains peoples declined except among the Lakota and the Mandan, Arikara, and Hidatsa, who continued to produce this work into the twentieth century. The latter particularly favored the vivid red, yellow, orange and violet dyes they obtained from the Fort Berthold traders for blanket strips and decorations on men's clothing, pipe bags, and other materials.

Although Plains Indian women began doing beadwork on hide products in earnest in the middle of the nineteenth century, the manufacture of beads from natural materials was an age-old tradition, evidenced by small stone and bone beads found in archaeological sites dating to more than 10,000 years ago. Prior to the arrival of glass trade beads, many natural materials were used to make beads, including shells, stones, wood, and seeds. European glass beads began to appear on the Plains by the early 1800s, brought by Euro-American traders and travelers such as Lewis and Clark. The earliest glass beads used were known as pony beads. At three to four millimeters in diameter, these were larger than the later seed beads and came in limited range of colors, primarily black, white, and blue. The early beaded designs on leggings, men's shirts, moccasins, women's dresses, pipe bags, and saddle blankets were sometimes combined with quillwork and tended to be relatively simple, consisting primarily of broad bands and blocks of single colors and basic squares, triangles, and rectangles. The smaller

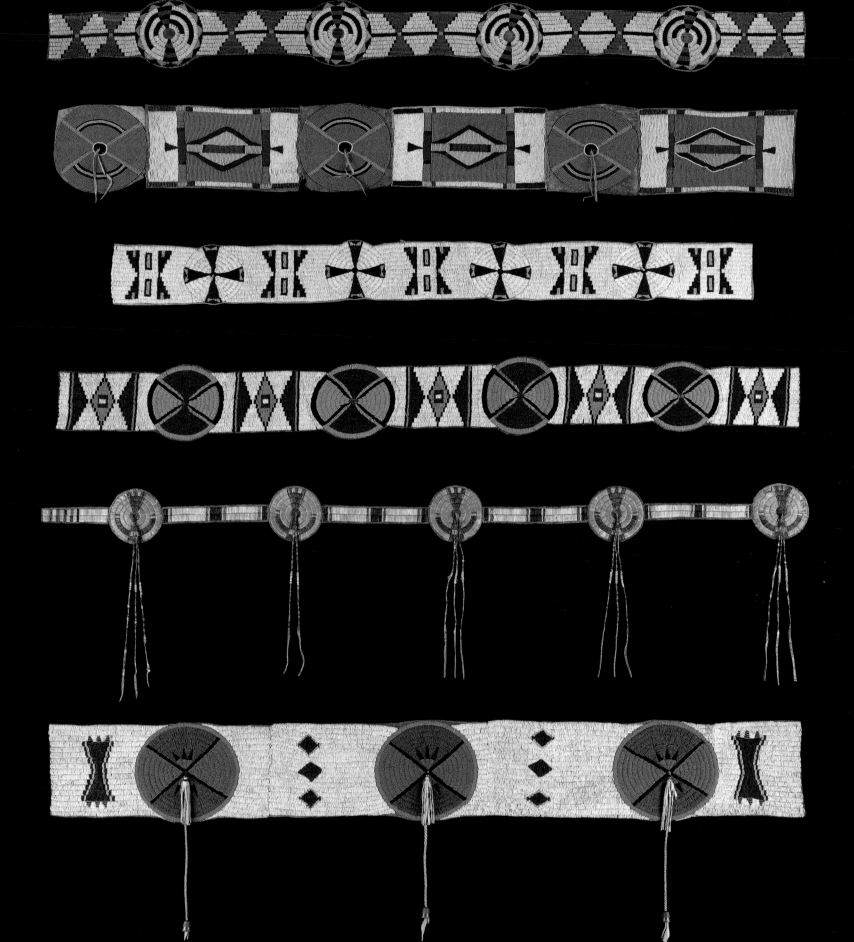

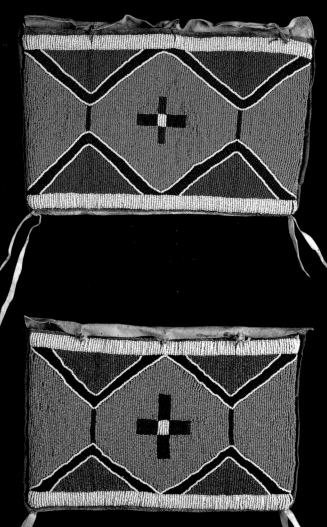

Storage Bags
Amoskapi Pikuni (Blackfeet), Montana,
ca. 1890
Tanned deer hide, glass beads, wool
cloth; 17 ⅝ x 13 inches
Adolf Spohr Collection, Gift of Larry
Sheerin NA.106.21A/B

Storage bags such as these are sometimes called "possible bags" because they
were used to store every possible thing.
Made in pairs of soft tanned hide, they
were decorated with painting, beadwork,
or porcupine quillwork in culturally specific designs.

Storage Bags
Apsáalooke (Crow), Montana, ca. 1890
Tanned deer hide, glass beads;
10 ¼ x 6 ¾ inches
Gift of Mr. & Mrs. J. Whitney King, Jr.
NA.106.54A/B

By the beginning of the early reservation
period around 1880, Northern Plains
women embellished entire fronts of storage bags in beadwork. Thus the bags also
served as decorations in the lodges, or
were tied on saddles.

glass seed beads (approximately one-half to two millimeters in diameter) became more readily available on the Plains around 1850 through long-established trading networks and at centers of trade such as the Mandan, Hidatsa, and Arikara village of the upper Missouri River, where they were obtained in exchange for hides, surplus foods, and other items. These beads were manufactured in a wider variety of colors and, because of their size, could be combined in more intricate geometric designs than pony beads.

By this time, women began incorporating beads into their works. Initially sewn with deer and other animal sinew and later with cotton thread, beads decorated storage bags and other lodge furnishings, moccasins, clothing, and other materials. The sinew came from the tendon along the backbone of a deer, bison, or other animal which had been cut off in strips and dried. A section of the sinew would be torn off, dampened, and smoothed for sewing or wrapping or twisted to make bow strings or ropes. Alma Hogan Snell recalled watching Pretty Shield sewing with sinew.

> She would take it [the sinew] and she would roll it in her mouth and she would roll it on her leg so that it made nice thread and then she would put it in her needle. Usually, I would see her work on moccasins more than anything else and she would sew with that. It didn't last long. After she got through with one strip then she would have to go over it again and thread another one.[40]

A great deal of a woman's time was spent in creating clothing, moccasins, bags, and accessories for herself and her family. Using her skills in tanning hides of deer and other animals and her artistry in painting, quillwork, and beadwork, she was able to produce functional but beautiful and culturally meaningful items for everyday use and special ceremonial occasions. Among some peoples, in particular the Kiowa, Plains Apache, Comanche, and Cheyenne of the Southern Plains, the fine processing of the hides themselves was the significant work. Dresses, leggings, shirts, and moccasins of the Southern Plains were examples of simple elegance, with modest beadwork centered upon single motifs or narrow bands along hems and sleeves, highlighted by painting and long fringes. Northern Plains people such as the Lakota preferred more heavily beaded materials, particularly by the end of the nineteenth century. As seed beads became widely available, the diversity of tribal styles and designs greatly increased. These artistic styles became markers of ethnic identity which seemed to intensify as tribal traditions, and indeed the peoples themselves, were threatened with extinction during the last part of the nineteenth century.

In much the same way that men were honored and recognized for their abilities in hunting and warfare, Plains Indian women were admired for their creative skills. Although all women were expected to have skills in hide tanning and other basic arts, some women who were particularly talented in a specific decorative

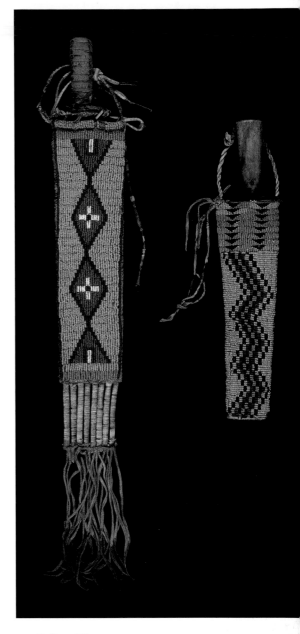

LEFT: **Knife and Case**
Lakota (Sioux), Northern Plains, 1881–1883
Tanned deer hide, glass beads, dyed porcupine quills; 19 ¼ x 3 ⅛ inches NA.102.89A/B

RIGHT: **Knife and Case**
Lakota (Sioux), Northern Plains, 1881-1883
Tanned deer hide, glass beads, dyed porcupine quills, tin cones; 9 ¼ x 2 ¾ inches
NA.102.90A/B

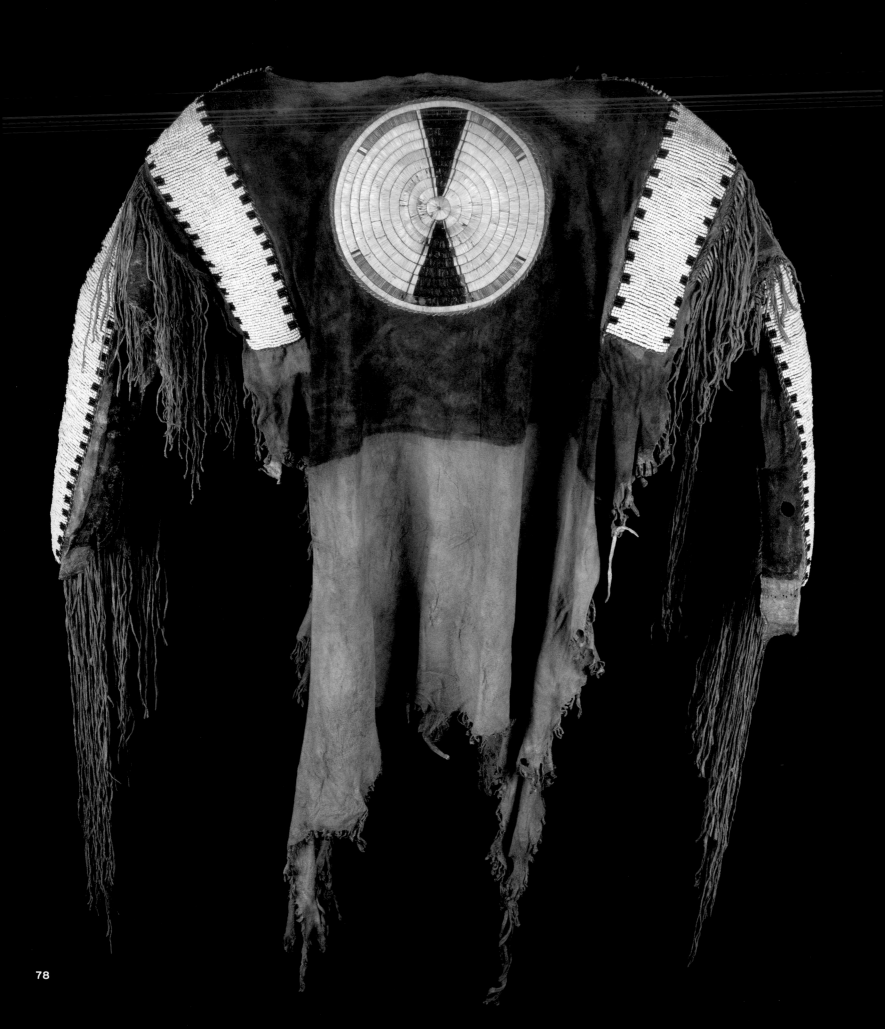

Shirt
Upper Missouri region, Montana or North
Dakota, 1830–1850
Deer hide, buffalo hide, porcupine quills,
pigment, glass pony beads; 27 ½ x 21⅛ inches
Chandler-Pohrt Collection, Gift of William D.
Weiss NA.202.348

This shirt is an example of traditional hide and
quill working, but the woman who made it was
also experimenting with a new material–
Venetian glass "pony beads." In the early nineteenth century, Plains Native peoples could
trade with Euro-Americans at posts and forts
along the Upper Missouri River, exchanging
buffalo hides and furs for European-made
goods such as red stroud cloth, mirrors, and
glass beads, which they incorporated into traditional designs.

LEFT: **Shirt**
Sahnish (Arikara), North Dakota, ca. 1885
Tanned deer hide, dyed porcupine quills,
ermine hide and fur, wool cloth;
27 ½ x 48 inches
Gift of Hope Williams Read in memory of Barry
Williams NA.202.199

Arikara, Mandan, and Hidatsa women of the
Fort Berthold Reservation continued to apply
quillwork to men's shirts, pipe bags, and other
items long after beadwork became prevalent
on the Northern Plains. They tended to use
dyes available from the reservation trading
post to create bright oranges, reds, violets, and
yellows in their quillwork.

Woman Using Smoother in Applying
Porcupine Quills
Northern Cheyenne Reservation,
Montana, ca. 1902
Photograph by Mrs. George Bird
"Elizabeth" Grinnell
Gift of Mr. Nick Eggenhofer P.62.1.33

Moccasins

Lakota (Sioux), Northern Plains, ca. 1885
Tanned deer hide, dyed porcupine quills, cotton cloth, horse hair, tin cones, glass beads, rawhide; 10 3/8 x 3 3/4 inches
Gift of Mr. and Mrs. Irving H. Larom NA.202.6

Everyday moccasins have little or no decoration. Pairs with elaborate decoration were worn for special occasions and rites of passage. These moccasins combine porcupine quillwork with glass beads, cloth, and tin cones in the design.

Moccasins

Eastern Dakota (Eastern Sioux),
Eastern Plains, ca. 1885
Tanned deer hide, rawhide, cloth, dyed porcupine quills; 9 x 3 3/4 inches
Chandler-Pohrt Collection NA.202.462

Dress

Tsistsistas (Cheyenne), Oklahoma, ca. 1890
Tanned deer hide, cowrie shells, glass beads,
tine cones, pigment; 52 x 30¼ inches
Chandler-Pohrt Collection, Gift of Mr. William D.
Weiss NA.202.446

The cowrie shells embellishing the yoke of this
formal Southern Cheyenne dress originated in
the Indian and South Pacific Oceans. They
arrived on the Plains via the ancient interconti-
nental trade network. Long after manufactured
trade goods were available, seashells remained
popular clothing decorations. This dress is decorated in yellow pigment on the top which was
common among the Cheyenne, Arapaho, and
Kiowa of the Southern Plains. It also features
red pigment along the bottom, and bands of
beadwork.

LEFT: **Dress**
So-soreh (Shoshone), Wyoming
or Idaho, ca. 1880
Tanned mountain sheep hide
and fur, glass beads, wool cloth,
pigment; 54 x 64 inches
NA.202.872

This dress was made from two
hides, with the animal's tail
incorporated into the design of
the bodice with its surrounding
bands of beadwork.

OPPOSITE: **Girl's Dress**
Apsáalooke (Crow), Montana
ca. 1885
Wool cloth, muslin, imitation
elk teeth, rawhide;
21 ¾ x 13 ¾ inches
Irving H. "Larry" Larom
Collection NA.202.39

Children of the Plains wore
smaller versions of adult clothing, such as this dress of trade
cloth decorated with imitation
elk teeth carved of bone

Dress Yoke
Gaigwa (Kiowa), ca. 1920
Tanned deer hide, elk teeth, glass beads, pigments, cloth; 22 ¾ x 35 ½ inches
Gift of William D. Owsley NA.202.81

Kiowa women of the Southern Plains wore dresses of soft tanned deer hides with long fringes at the skirt and sleeves. This dress top is painted in yellow pigments and decorated with beaded strips and appliqué and elk teeth, greatly prized throughout the Plains. The number of teeth applied to a dress symbolized a woman's husband's prowness as a hunter and provider; thus, the dress signified a family of means.

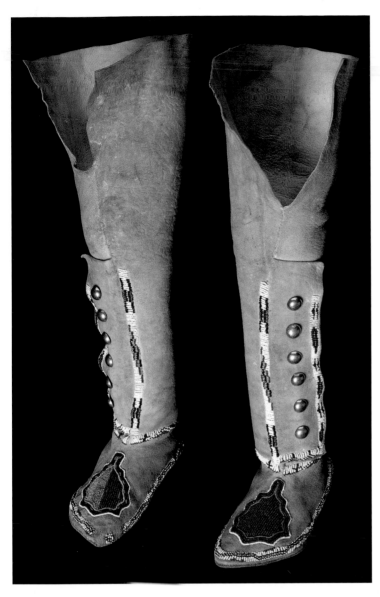

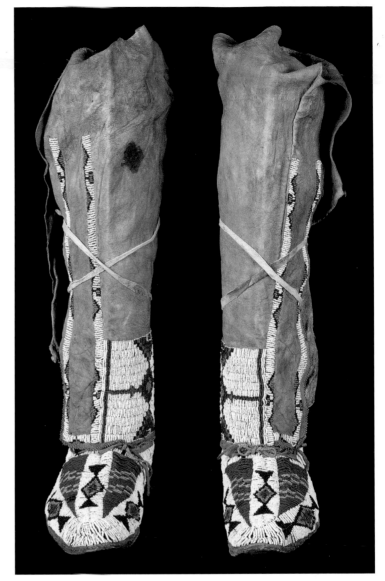

ABOVE LEFT: **Woman's Moccasins**
Gaigwa (Kiowa), Oklahoma, ca. 1890
Tanned deer hide, rawhide, pigment,
glass beads, silver; 16 ½ x 7 ⅛ inches
Chandler-Pohrt Collection NA.202.469

Kiowa women, like other women of the
Southern Plains, wore high moccasins,
leggings with folded tops. These moccasins or boots are painted in yellow pigments and embellished with beadwork
trim and a single leaf design on each
toe.

LEFT: **Moccasins**
Amoskapi Pikuni (Blackfeet), Montana,
ca. 1885
Tanned deer hide, glass beads, wool
cloth; 10 ¼ x 3 ½ inches
Adolf Spohr Collection, Gift of Larry
Sheerin NA.202.21

ABOVE: **Woman's Moccasins**
Hinono'ei (Arapaho), Oklahoma, ca. 1885
Tanned hide, rawhide, glass beads, pig-
ment; 16 ½ x 9 ¾ inches
Chandler-Pohrt Collection, Gift of the
Pilot Foundation NA.202.824

medium were called upon to produce specialized items with gifts provided in payment. Cheyenne, Arapaho, and Lakota women who excelled in beadwork or porcupine quillwork belonged to special societies or guilds in which membership was limited to women of high moral character. Only women of these societies had the rights to make the decorations for sacred tipis or tipi liners. Before learning to do quillwork, Blackfoot women were required to undergo special initiations to ensure that they would not go blind nor be harmed by doing this finely detailed work.[41]

Women treasured their hide scrapers and workbags of tools. Some of these items were passed from mothers to daughters in much the same way as were knowledge and skills. Some also had other sentimental significance.

This hide scraper I have is made from the horn of an elk my husband killed, just after we were married. He cut off the smaller prongs and polished this main shaft. The Indian men of the old times commonly made this kind of present to their young wives. Besides using them in tanning, the women made marks on them to keep tracks of the ages of their children. The five rows of notches on this one are the age-records of my five children. Each year I have added a notch to each row, for the living ones. Any time, I can count up the notches and know the age of any of my children. Throughout 72 years it has always been a part of my most precious pack. There were times when I had not much else. I was carry-

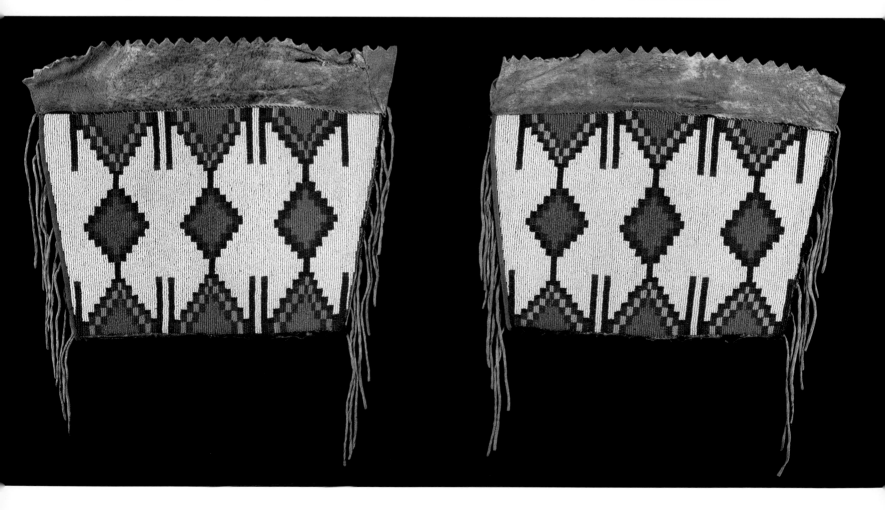

Moccasins

Meskwaki, Tama, Iowa, ca. 1880
Tanned deer hide, glass beads;
10 ¼ x 8 ⅞ Inches
Chandler-Pohrt Collection, Gift of the
Pilot Foundation NA.202.448

The designs of these moccasins are characteristic of the Prairie style of beadwork, which developed as Native people from the Eastern Woodlands and Great Lakes regions, including the Meskwaki, Delaware, Winnebago, and Potawatomie, were relocated west to the prairies of Nebraska, Iowa, Kansas, and Oklahoma. As they were settled in lands near resident groups such as the Pawnee, Oto, Osage, Ponca, and Omaha, a new beadwork style synthesizing these diverse traditions emerged that featured curvilinear and geometric designs executed in bright colors.

ing it in my hands when my husband was killed on upper Powder River. It was tied to my saddle while we were in flight from Oklahoma. It was in my little pack when we broke out from the Fort Robinson prison. It never has been lost. Different white people have offered me money for it. I am very poor, but such money does not tempt me. When I die, this gift from my husband will be buried with me.

This sheath knife scabbard was also made for me by my husband, soon after we were married. Since then, every day it has dangled from my belt. It is not for sale. Red Ripe was the only husband I ever had. I am the only wife he ever had. Through 50 years I have been his widow. I could not sell anything he made and gave to me.[42]

Lives of Children

Turtle Lung Woman told me many things, including how I was to live and conduct myself according to the Lakota code of conduct. She knew the laws and lived them, so in many ways, it was easier to learn from her. She spoke to me, told me stories, and through her own actions, she demonstrated how I was to live and conduct myself as a Lakota woman. The way she spoke was important. I listened carefully to her Lakota words. An important word she used over and over was wótakuye, which referred to the way I was related to those around me.

—Delphine Red Shirt[43]

Children of Plains Indian tribes learned their future roles in life through play and learning from adult examples and through guidance and counsel of older family members. Children naturally embodied the hope for the future and represented the continuation of cultural traditions, the family, and the tribe. In the intimate setting of a Plains Indian village, responsibilities of child rearing and teaching were supported by the shared values of the community and an extended kinship system that tied individuals together through descent, marriage, and spiritual or social affiliations.

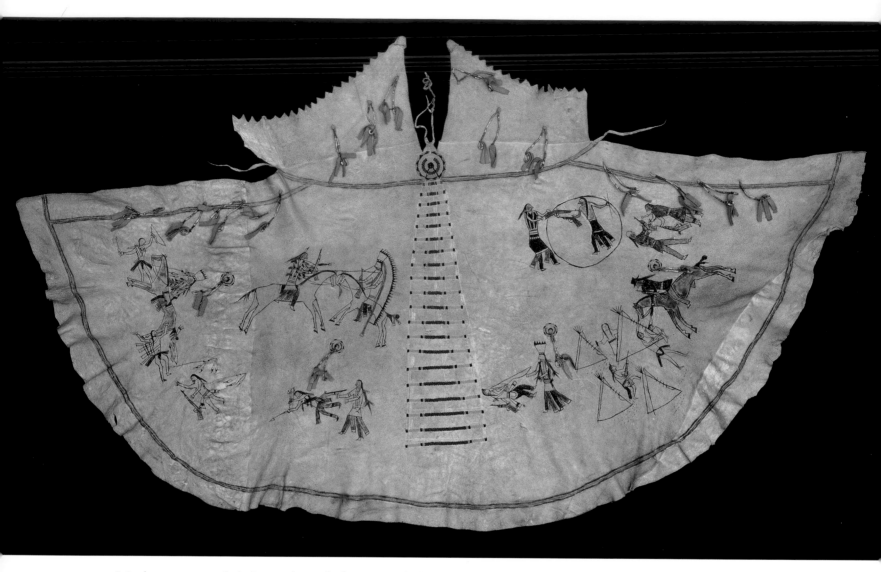

Mothers wrapped their newborn babies in soft deerskin blankets to keep them warm. They could then be carried on the mothers' backs in hides or wool blankets. When the baby was a few months old, they were tightly wrapped and laced into cradles. The creation of a beautifully decorated cradle in anticipation of a baby's birth was a powerful expression of family love and symbolic of the practical and spiritual importance of children. Such cradles provided safe and secure places for babies when families traveled or when mothers and other female relatives were working, and children often spent much of their first two years in cradles.

Among the Wichita of the Southern Plains, the making of the cradle was shared by both the mother's and father's relations and represented the joining of the two families, with a grandmother or other female elder guiding the gathering of materials, design, and construction of the cradle. Among other Plains peoples, a grandmother or aunt took on the responsibility of making a cradle following a culturally specific design. Such cradles were often passed on in families. Among

Child's Tipi Cover
Tsistsistas (Cheyenne), Montana, ca. 1890
Tanned hide, glass beads, pigment, dyed porcupine quills, sinew, wool cloth; 34 ½ x 60 inches
From the Collection of Richard Larremore Livermore given by his granddaughter Ann Livermore Houston NA.507.123

With pictographic art of men on horseback, tipi villages, and warfare scenes, this child's tipi cover is made in a similar fashion to full-size Cheyenne tipis. Younger girls learned the adult women's responsibilities of putting up and maintaining tipis by playing with such smaller versions.

the Lakota, "The cradle board was made by a sister of the father. It was an object of art if it was well made, with the leather portion elaborately decorated with the finest quillwork or beadwork. Sometimes the wood frame was decorated as well."[44] The creation of a cradle was a spiritual endeavor accompanied by prayers, blessings, and thanks for the newborn and for the materials from which it would be fashioned.

The importance of children was reflected in the public celebrations of significant events in a child's life, such as when he received a name, when a child's ears were pierced, at a girl's first menstrual cycle, or when a boy undertook a vision quest. Through play, imitation of adult activities, and formal instruction, children learned the adult responsibilities of men and women and the skills needed to sustain life in hunting, defense, gathering of foods, and horticulture. They also received spiritual instruction from grandparents and other elders.

Young boys were taught by fathers and other male relatives to make bows and arrows and encouraged to practice hunting, beginning with small animals around their village. When a boy brought home his first game, this important milestone was celebrated as his mother cooked and shared the meat with as many people as possible.

From an early age, girls were taught by their mothers and grandmothers to make moccasins, clothing, and lodge covers and to help in preparing food, carrying water, and other daily work. They often played with miniature tipis and dolls, which prepared them for their roles as adult women and mothers.

Our dolls were made by tying a stuffed buckskin head on the end of a forked stick. Such a doll had hair glued to the head, beads for eyes, and a face painted on the buckskin. The

ABOVE. **Doll**
Lakota (Sioux), South Dakota, ca. 1890
Tanned deer hide, canvas, pigment, cowrie and dentalium shells, glass beads, horse hair; 17 ⅜ x 9 inches
Chandler-Pohrt Collection, Gift of Mr. William D. Weiss NA.507.64

Grandmothers often made dolls dressed in clothing reflecting tribal styles for little girls. This doll wears a hide dress decorated with beadwork and cowrie shells, beaded moccasins, and a necklace made of dentalium shells, echoing the clothing and ornaments worn by adult women.

LEFT: **Toy Cradle and Doll**
Apsáalooke (Crow), Montana, ca. 1885
Canvas, wool cloth, glass beads, tanned deer hide, wood; 20 ¾ x 6 ¼ inches
Adolf Spohr Collection, Gift of Larry Sheerin NA.507.3

LAND OF MANY GIFTS

was buffalo hair. The clothing was of beaded and fringed buckskin. We girls built play-house tepees for ourselves and our dolls. We would hang little pieces of meat out upon bushes and play like we were drying meat, the same as our mothers did at the home lodges. Sometimes we would play at moving camp. The boys would come with willow baskets. Everything would be put into the baskets and then the boys would drag them to wherever we might want to go. We would ride stick horses. The doll might ride on a stick horse beside the play-mother, or it might be carried on her back.[45]

As girls matured, they were given the tools they would need to produce clothing and household furnishings needed for their families. Lone Woman recalls that "In time, Turtle Long Woman was given a small bag with sinew, an awl, and a needle in it, and she learned how to make moccasins. This occurred around puberty, when she was expected to practice skills like tanning and quill-work, even making moccasins during her *i náthi,* when she was in the midst of her menses. Until then, she was free as a young girl to play."[46] A girl's first achievement, such as the creation of a garment, a bag, or a pair of moccasins, would be celebrated through a feast and a presentation of gifts.

Grandmothers played a significant role in rearing children and provided spiritual and practical guidance. They cared for children, made them toys and beautiful clothing following the designs of adult clothing, and were significant sources of cultural knowledge and wisdom which they passed on through instruction, stories, and games. It was through the wisdom of such grandmothers and other elders that children learned about life and their heritage as Plains Indian people. ✸

TOP: **Cradle**
Tsistsistas (Cheyenne), Montana, ca. 1890
Tanned deer hide, wood, glass beads, wool and cotton cloth, brass tacks, 26 x 10 inches
Adolf Spohr Collection, Gift of Mr. Larry Sheerin NA.111.2

The making of a beautifully decorated cradle signified the welcoming of a baby into the family. Under the supervision of one woman, family members contributed to the process. Carried on a mother's back or propped up in camp while the mother and female relatives worked, a cradle allowed a baby to see his family and everything that was going on around him.

LOWER LEFT: **Toy Cradle**
Apsáalooke (Crow), Montana, ca. 1895–1900
Tanned hide, wool cloth, glass beads;
25 ½ x 7 ½ inches
In memory of Frank O. Horton and Henriette S. Horton NA.507.98

LOWER RIGHT: **Toy Cradle**
Gaigwa (Kiowa), Oklahoma, ca. 1885
Tanned deer hide, wood, glass beads, brass tacks, cloth; 15 ½ x 5 inches
Gift of Richard W. Leche NA.507.1

1. Frank B. Linderman, *Red Mother: The Life Story of Pretty-Shield, Medicine Woman of the Crows* (Rathway New Jersey: The John Day Company, 1932; reprint, *Pretty-Shield; Medicine Woman of the Crows* (Lincoln: University of Nebraska Press, 1972), p. 134.

2. Ibid., p. 23.

3. Ibid., p. 10.

4. John Dunbar and Samuel Allis, "Letters Concerning the Presbyterian Mission in the Pawnee Country, Near Bellevue, Nebraska, 1821–1849," *Collections of the Kansas State Historical Society, 1915–1918*, Vol. 14, Topeka, p. 611.

5. Katherine Weist, "Beasts of Burden and Menial Slaves: Nineteenth Century Observation of Northern Plains Indian Women," in Patricia Albers and Beatrice Medicine, *The Hidden Half: Studies of Plains Indian Women* (Washington, D.C.: University Press of America, Inc., 1983), pp. 38–41.

6. Ella Deloria, *Speaking of Indians* (New York: Friendship Press, 1944), p. 24.

7. The role of Plains Indian warrior women has been addressed by Beatrice Medicine in "'Warrior Women'—Sex Role Alternatives for Plains Indian Women," in Albers and Medicine, *The Hidden Half*, pp. 267–280; and John C. Ewers, "Women's Roles in Plains Indian Warfare," *Plains Indian History and Culture: Essays on Continuity and Change* (Norman: University of Oklahoma Press, 1997), pp. 191–204.

8. Dunbar and Allis, "Letters Concerning the Presbyterian Mission," p. 664.

9. John C. Ewers, "The Humble Digging Stick: Symbol of Women's Contributions to Plains Indian Culture," presentation at the Plains Indian Museum Seminar, Buffalo Bill Historical Center, September 28, 1996.

10. Ibid.

11. Louella Johnson, interview with author, January 21, 2000, Lodge Grass Montana.

12. Buffalo Bird Woman in Carolyn Gilman and Mary Jane Schneider, *The Way to Independence: Memories of a Hidatsa Indian Family, 1840–1920* (St. Paul: Minnesota Historical Society, 1987), p. 65.

13. Ibid. The corn stage was a raised platform on which Hidatsa women spread corn to dry.

14. Linderman, *Pretty-Shield*, pp. 71–72, p. 103.

15. Alma Hogan Snell, *Grandmother's Grandchild: My Crow Indian Life*, Becky Matthews, ed. (Lincoln and London: University of Nebraska Press, 2000), pp. 35–36.

16. Thomas B. Marquis, "Iron Teeth, A Cheyenne Old Woman," *Cheyenne and Sioux: The Reminiscences of Four Indians and a White Soldier* (Stockton, California: University of the Pacific, 1973 p. 52, pp. 54–55.

17. From a story told by Scattercorn, a Mandan woman, in Alfred W. Bowers, *Mandan Social and Ceremonial Organization* (Moscow, Idaho: University of Idaho Press, 1991), pp. 194–195.

18. Gilbert Wilson, "Agriculture of the Hidatsa Indians; An Indian Interpretation," *University of Minnesota Studies in the Social Sciences*, 9, Minneapolis, reprinted as *Buffalo Bird Woman's Garden: Agriculture of the Hidatsa Indians* (St. Paul: Minnesota Historical Society Press, 1987), pp. 6–7.

19. For a description of the varieties of corn, beans, and squash grown by Pawnee women, see Gene Weltfish, *The Lost Universe: Pawnee Life and Culture* (Lincoln: University of Nebraska Press, 1965), pp. 119–123.

20. George F. Will and George E. Hyde, *Corn Among the Indians of the Upper Missouri* (Lincoln: University of Nebraska Press, 1964), p. 204.

21. Buffalo Bird Woman in Wilson, *Buffalo Bird Woman's Garden*, p. 23.

22. Buffalo Bird Woman in Wilson, *Buffalo Bird Woman's Garden*, p. 27.

23. Linderman, *Pretty Shield*, p. 22.

24. Marquis, *Cheyenne and Sioux*, p. 62

25. Alma Hogan Snell, interview with author, January 22, 2000.

26. Ibid.

27. Ibid.

28. J. Raymond Wood and Lee Irwin, "Mandan," *Handbook of North American Indians. Plains Volume*, Raymond J. Demallie, ed. (Washington D.C.: Smithsonian Institution, 2001), Volume 13, Part 1, p. 352.

29. Gilman and Schneider, *The Way to Independence*, p. 18.

30. Gilbert L. Wilson, *Waheenee: An Indian Girl's Story: Told by Herself to Gilbert L. Wilson* (St. Paul, Minnesota: Webb Publishing Company, 1927; reprint, Lincoln and London; University of Nebraska Press, 1981), p. 45.

31. Calvin Grinnell, interview with author, December 13, 2000.

32. Linderman, *Pretty Shield*, p. 34.

33. Ralph T. Coe, *Sacred Circles: Two Thousand Years of North American Indian Art* (Kansas City: Nelson Gallery Foundation, 1977), p. 161.

34. Barbara A. Hail, *Hau, Kóla!* (Providence, R.I.: Haffenreffer Museum of Anthropology, 1980), p. 209.

35. Snell interview with author.

36. Gilman and Schneider, *The Way to Independence*, p. 43.

37. Snell interview with author.

38. George Parker Winship, "The Coronado Expedition, 1540–1542," *14th Annual Report of Bureau of American Ethnology, 1892–93*, p 404.

39. Linderman, *Pretty Shield*, pp. 135–136.

40. Snell interview with author.

41. See Mary Jane Schneider, "Women's Work: An Examination of the Women's Roles in Plains Indian Arts and Crafts," Albers and Medicine, *The Hidden Half*, p. 112, and Hail, *Hau, Kóla!*, 1981, p. 47.

42. Marquis, *Iron Teeth*, p. 80. Royal Hassrick noted that among the Sioux, the markings on the handles of elk horn scrapers indicate the accomplishments of a woman in tanning hides or making tipis. See Royal Hassrick., *The Sioux* (Norman: University of Oklahoma Press, 1969), p. 42.

43. Delphine Red Shirt, *Turtle Lung Woman's Granddaughter* (Lincoln and London: University of Nebraska Press), p. 73. In this book, Red Shirt recounts the remembrances of her mother Lone Woman about her life and the life of her mother's grandmother, Turtle Lung Woman.

44. Ibid, p. 116.

45. Marquis, *Iron Teeth*, p. 56.

46. Red Shirt, *Turtle Lung Woman's Grandmother*, pp. 122–123.

Women's Roles

BEATRICE MEDICINE

Indian Nations of the Northern Plains have endured much adulation as the "noble savage" as well as many stereotypes. This attitude seems augmented by the reference to them as "warrior" societies. This imaginary distinction has sublimated the contributions of Indian women to the point where such terms as "drudge," "slave," "whore," and "squaw" have been used by the dominant society. The latter term still resonates in some parts of the country, as evidenced by the current opposition to the naming of places, creeks, and mountains with this word.

Some historical accounts have claimed that women had such low status, they were traded for horses. From an indigenous viewpoint, these offerings indicated that the man was worthy of a woman, as they assured the family that their daughter would be betrothed to a successful warrior hunter and horse raider.

Even the magnificent courting robes of buffalo skins were painted with designs that indicated such heroic deeds as rescuing a friend in battle, among other signs to show male status. These metaphors showed the importance of the achievements of men, just as future paintings on the nuptial tipi would indicate the honor of the occupants, and as the tipi liners and such women's work as notches on fleshing tools revealed the industry of women. Male and female roles complemented one another in social and economic endeavors.

Furthermore, the blanketing of the Plains Indians covered the varied and vibrant cultures of lifeways and worldviews of each nation. By considering gender roles in the context of these societies, we may better understand and appreciate the similarities and differences of adaptation to a similar ecological background.

Varied lifeways (culture) and ethos (world views) were articulated in each nation. Commonalities in the Plains culture area were nomadism, women's sodalities, portable

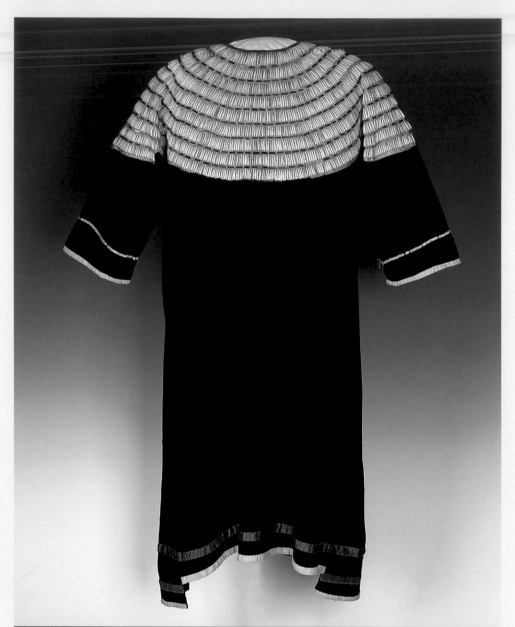

Dress
Lakota (Sioux), ca. 1890
Wool and cotton cloth, satin ribbon, dentalium shells, glass beads, sequins; 55 x 27 inches
Gift of Mrs. Henry H. R. Coe NA.202.368

This type of dress made of trade cloth and decorated with rows of dentalium shells and ribbon was popular among Lakota women in the early reservation period of the 1880s and 1890s. The dentalium shells arrived through trade from the Pacific coast.

lodges, horse raiding, military societies, warfare, and the Sun Dance.

Although women used similar methods to produce goods from raw materials, including fleshing and tanning animal skins for clothing and tipis, preserving the flesh of the hunt, searching for such fruits and vegetables as the ubiquitous "prairie turnip" and medicinal plants and herbs, they did not view this work drudgery. Their arduous labor was recognized as contributions to family and kin group survival. The woman's skill and efficiency in packing and moving the tipi and possessions also added to her status.

Nomadic life was not easy and some groups as the Cheyenne and Lakota had strong religious beliefs about the spacing of children.

The social dimensions of Plains nations might be categorized as families and extended families (*tiospaye* for the Lakota), nested in larger named band-type social organizations, and then nations. Many of these social units were bilateral with a tendency to patrilineal descent, except the Crow, who were matrilineal. Societal constructions were marriages, warrior societies, some sodalities for women, lack of named clans (except the Crow), the Sun Dance as the major religious ritual, and a belief in a latent power. Called *Wakan* among the Lakota, this power could be accessed by the vision quest for men and dreaming for women. It was a source of protection, social control, and action.

As in most human groups, children were highly valued (called *wakan yeja,* or "sacred ones," among the Lakota). These categories were part of their worldview and pursuits, which gave a distinctive and viable lifestyle to the Plains social environment.

But adaptation was strong in these cultures, as the adoption of the horse indicated. Currently called "Indian car," it has allowed the continuation of the Sun Dance, though legally suppressed, and the vital and all-important markers of Indian identity to be manifested in the contemporary Native world. In the sacred realm, the ritual sacred ceremony, the Sun Dance and minor rituals, naming ceremonies, puberty, death, and so forth, articulated the beliefs and values of the various groups.

The activities of males and females were specified by their social roles to foster the harmonious life, which was essential to the smooth functioning of the culture (called *wiconi* in Lakota.) This was accomplished by the correct and efficacious conditioning of the children. Even in play, boys were trained to imitate the hunt and evidence bravery and fortitude.

Female children were similarly conditioned to assume adult roles. Socialization through the rites of passage and by continued exhortations and approved behavior by adult females ensured that a woman would mature to enact the expected ethical and moral codes of her society. Pretty Shield, a Crow woman, observed that

I tried to be like my mother. . . . I carried my doll on my back just as mothers carry their babies; and besides this I had a little tepee (lodge) that I pitched whenever my aunt pitched hers. It was made exactly like my aunt's, had the same number of poles, only of course my tepee was very small.

My horse dragged the poles and packed the lodge skins, so that I often beat my aunt in setting up my lodge, which she pretended made her jealous. And how I used to hurry in setting up my lodge, so that I might have a fire going inside it before my aunt could kindle one in hers! I did not know it then, but now I know I feel sure that she often let me beat her just to encourage me.[1]

In explaining how her aunt became her mother, Pretty Shield said: "About the time when I came to live in this world my aunt, Strikes-with-an-axe, lost two little girls. . . . This aunt, who was my mother's sister, mourned for a long time, growing thinner and weaker, until my mother gave me to her, to heal her heart."[2] This is an example of adoption, which was, and is so, prevalent a social custom among Plains tribes.

In a more recent publication, Agnes Deernose provides a glimpse of sibling respect:

I learned more from my mother's sisters than from my own mother. . . . She taught us girls to be young ladies and cautioned us against shaming our brothers. "Don't make your brothers ashamed of you," she would say. She really made us respect our brothers and told us that we should not play with them after we became young ladies, around eight years of age. We were not to get too close to our brothers that we might touch them.[3]

This also might be interpreted to mean the onset of menstruation, which is seldom described in the ethnographies of women in the Plains, and elsewhere.

Some Lakota maidens were also expected to wear chastity belts for protection against male night-time intruders. The modern term "tipi creepers" might have origins in this phenomenon. Transgression of ideal behavior is described thus:

Big Crow, a man who had dreamt of both the Buffalo and the Elk, gave girls medicine that would stop them from giving birth, but they could never have babies afterwards. Roan Horse's sister and a friend once ate some of his medicine just for fun. But Big Crow whose medicine they stole would not withdraw the power because he was angry. So neither girl ever had children.[4]

Hoebel and Llewellyn in their book on Cheyenne law discuss a case of abortion.[5] Again, this delicate issue is not well documented in the literature. These instances indicate that, as in all societies, women had agency in their actions, despite the consequences.

A very significant event in the lives of women is the menarche. Unfortunately, many ethnographers were males and did not present comprehensive data about women. The exceptions are Frank Linderman and William Powers. Additionally, Plains tribes had strict codes of behavior and women did not readily interact with these intruders (i.e., the ethnographers). But it is possible to search ethnographic accounts to find data.

Among the Lakota, a girl's puberty ceremony was called the Buffalo Sing (*Tatanka Olowanpi*). It was one of the seven sacred rites brought to the Lakota by the White Buffalo Calf Woman, who was the cultural heroine. William Powers wrote,

At the onset of a girl's first menstruation, a puberty rite called *Isnati awicalowan* "They sing over her first menses" was performed . . . and refers both to the act of menstruation and the isolation in which women lived during their menstrual period. The ritual has also been referred to as the Buffalo Ceremony in as much as the buffalo supernaturals guard over woman's chastity and fecundity. It marks the passage from adolescence to womanhood, and during the performance the girl is instructed by a sacred person, before a large congregation, in her responsibilities to her family and people. The ritual also establishes her relationship with the sacred White Buffalo Calf Woman.

Within several days after the girl's menstrual period, her father requests a sacred person to conduct the ritual. The mother and her female relatives erect a new tipi, and the girl is instructed to place her menstrual bundle in a plum tree to safeguard it from the evil influences of *Inktomi*.[6]

In recent times, there have been attempts to revitalize this ceremony, but many contemporary female adolescents refuse to take part in such a public event. A few rituals have been enacted in private homes but this ritual has not achieved universal enactment among the Lakota and is performed in a public sphere only sparsely.

The next major events in a woman's life are courtship, marriage, and childbearing. The Cheyenne Indians are known for the protected chastity of their women and strong social controls regarding marriage. As a Cheyenne woman told Truman Michelson, "My mother would always tell me that the main purpose of her teaching me . . . was to keep me at home, and to keep me from being away to spend my nights with my girl chum. This was done so that there would be no chance for gossip by other people."[7] Furthermore, Grinnell writes,

The women of the Cheyenne are famous among all western tribes for their chastity. In old times it was most unusual for a girl to be seduced, and she who had yielded was disgraced forever. The matter at once became known and she was taunted with it wherever she went. It was never forgotten. No young man would marry her.[8]

The courtship pattern of this Cheyenne followed the general behavior of most of the Northern Plains groups. When a young man was captivated by an attractive and honorable woman, he made his interest known either by subtle ways through the girl's brother, the use of a courting flute, and perhaps by indicating his interest as she went for water for her tipi.

If she did show interest, he came to her tipi, wearing his magnificent courting robe, encased her in it, and then engaged her in talk, always under supervision.

If, however, as among the Lakota, he touched her in inappropriate places, she was violated and could not be chosen for the coveted role as a virgin maiden in the sacred Sun Dance ceremony and was disgraced, as was her kinship unit. Courtship etiquette was specified for each tribe. In general, courtship was supervised and took place during long periods of time during which a woman could reject a suitor if she so wished.

When there was mutual agreement, often through an intermediary, the couple's families began marriage negotiations. Among the Lakota, brothers and male cousins guarded the girl's virginity. They were called *hakatakus* (to "follow after"). According to Hassrick, "If some young man ran off with a girl but didn't marry her and she returned and perhaps ran off again, such a girl was called 'Witkowin' or 'Crazy Woman.' According to one Sioux informant, "Witkowins died young for some reason."[9]

As a part of a marriage agreement, horses were offered to show the success of the suitor at war feats, horse raiding, warfare, and skill as a hunter. In most cases, supplying the tipi and its accoutrements was the future bride's obligation. In some cases, the negotiator often served as a counselor to the newly established family (called in Lakota *tiwahe*), which was nested within the larger kin group, called *tiospaye* among the Lakota.

Crow woman Pretty Shield said of her marriage:

"Ahhh, I was sixteen when my man, Goes-ahead, took me. I have already told you that my father had promised me to Goes-ahead, when I was thirteen. When I became sixteen years old my father kept his promise.

"Did you fall in love with him before he took you?" I asked.

"No, no," she smiled. "I had not often spoken to him until he took me. Then I fell in love with him because he loved me and was always kind. Young women did not then fall in love, and get married to please them-

selves, as they now do. They listened to their fathers, married the men selected for them, and this, I believe, is the best way, There were no deformed children born in those days," she said, thoughtfully. "And men and women were happier, too I feel sure," she added, with a challenge in her words.[10]

When Pretty Shield's son was born, Left Hand, the midwife, wore a buffalo robe with the hair side out, her face painted with mud, her hair tied in a lump on her forehead, and she carried grass. For her services, Pretty Shield's father paid his best horse and several fine robes. The symbolism of the fire, buffalo, grasses, and the number four seem to be metaphors for life on the Plains. Such rich details make possible comparisons with other tribes.

Marriages in any society are not always ideal or long-lasting. Divorce did occur due to incompatibility, abuse, or adultery. Factors which may have contributed to marriage stability were sororal polygyny, and the honor and prestige of successful marriages in which child welfare and responsibility to the larger group loomed large. Additionally, the role of the third gender of "two spirit" males as the *bote* in Crow or the *winkte* in Lakota societies can only be conjectured. Again, this event can only be contextualized for each group of Plains societies.

Women, too, might divorce men, states Hassrick: "Sometimes men leave their families and go around with other women, until their wives finally leave. They always argue as to who should have custody of the children, but if one is nursing an infant, they can't take that one from her. The women usually get the children."[11]

Among the Lakota, it was obligatory for the sister of the father to make and present a cradle for the newborn. A female child is given a name by a respected elder, and the boy is named temporarily by a respected man who had enacted the requirements of a warrior. Usually these childhood names were temporary until a naming ceremony was enacted in a public arena. Temporary names were replaced by earned names in warfare or other exploits.

Moccasins
Apsáalooke (Crow), Montana, ca. 1885
Tanned deer hide, glass beads, brass buttons, rawhide; 10 13/16 x 4 inches
Dr. William and Anna Petzoldt Collection, Gift of Genevieve Petzoldt Fitzgerald NA.202.32

made objects for the Spirit Release ceremony. Some families gave everything away at the time of death; others collected items for the *Wangi Yupahi* (Spirit Keeping) ceremony after a year of bereavement. Then a major "Give Away" was held for other bereaved ones, for the elderly and orphans and for those who had misfortune during the year.[14]

In the life cycle of Plains Indian women, each major rite of passage was observed with ceremony and ritual and obviously was based upon the ethos or world view of each unique nation. Many of these rituals are enacted today.

1. Frank B. Linderman, *Red Mother: The Life Story of Pretty-Shield, Medicine Woman of the Crows* (Rathway New Jersey: The John Day Company, 1932; reprint, *Pretty-Shield; Medicine Woman of the Crows* (Lincoln: University of Nebraska Press, 1974), p. 27.
2. Linderman, p. 20.
3. Fred W. Voget, *They Call Me Agnes: A Crow Narrative Based on the Life of Agnes Yellowtail Deernose* (Norman and London: University of Oklahoma Press), 1995, p. 83.
4. Royal B. Hassrick, *The Sioux: Life and Customs of a Warrior Society* (Norman: University of Oklahoma Press), 1969,) p. 124.
5. Adamson E. Hoebel and Karl N. Llewellyn, *The Cheyenne Way: Conflict and Case Law in Primitive Jurisprudence* (Norman: University of Oklahoma Press), 1941, pp. 117–118.
6. William K. Powers, *Oglala Religion* (Lincoln and London: University of Nebraska Press), 1973, pp, 101. For more detail on the ceremony, see pp. 101–103.
7. E. Adamson Hoebel, *The Cheyennes: Indians of the Great Plains* (New York: Holt, Rinehart and Winston, Inc.), 1960, p. 20.
8. George Bird Grinnell, *The Cheyenne Indians: Their History and Ways of Life* (New Haven: Yale University Press), 1923, 1, p. 156.
9. Hassrick, *The Sioux*, p.123.
10. Linderman, *Pretty Shield*, p. 130.
11. Hassrick, *The Sioux*, p. 131.
12. Marla Powers, *Oglala Women: Myth, Ritual, and Reality* (Chicago: The University of Chicago Press), pp. 91–103.
13. Hassrick, *The Sioux*, p. 337.
14. Hassrick provides many details of Lakota burial ceremonies, See *The Sioux*, pp. 333-338.

Thus, Lakota males may have several names, as they earned them. Lactation periods were long for these groups as a convenience for mothers and to promote a suitable and healthy diet for the baby. Plains women's dresses with yokes that are open to the armpits were so made to facilitate nursing babies and toddlers. Long lactation periods may also have been factors in birth control. Some babies, usually males, were nursed for four or five years.

Feasting is often a way of reinforcing the values and honoring expected behavior of women. As in most rituals, the latent and manifest principles of behavior are highlighted and are seldom seen as social control mechanisms.

After menopause, Lakota women tend to become medicine women (through dreaming) and herbalists, usually by associating and learning from an herbalist. "Respect for the elders" was a tribute to long life. They were seen as "wisdom keepers" and trusted with love and respect. Marla Powers presents a nice treatment of aging and special treatment of Medicine Women and elder women as morticians.[12]

A final rite of passage is death, which was ritualized in Plains societies as it is in most cultures. According to Hassirck, "When a woman died her face . . . was painted with the marks of honor to which she was entitled. Her awl case and sewing kit were placed beside her in the bundle. If she had a favorite horse, it would be killed and its tail placed on a pole."[13]

The body would wear her best dress; frequently a fully beaded quilled pair of moccasins with beaded soles would be placed in the bundle to insure safe journey on the *Canka Wakan* (holy road; Milky Way) to the hereafter. The bundle was then placed on a scaffold. A lock of her hair had been cut and placed in a small bundle for the Memorial Feast, which followed a year of bereavement.

Female mourners wailed and some slashed their legs at the loss of the loved one. Men wore their hair unbraided. Honor songs were sung; during the year, the family (and *tiospaye* extended family) mourned and

Clouds of dust arise, rolling up from the earth,
Spreading onward; herds are there,
Speeding on before,
Going straight where we must journey.

What are those we see moving in the dust?
This way coming from the herd;
Buffalo and calf!
Food they promise for the Children.

—CHATICKS SI CHATICKS (PAWNEE) SONG[1]

Buffalo and the People

When Pawnee bands traveled across the Plains, they sometimes saw great billowing clouds of dust in the distance. Looking closer, they saw that the dust was stirred by running buffalo. At times, a cow and her calf would separate from the herd and come nearer to the people. Pawnee people were taught to be observant when they traveled because such sights signified the promise of abundant buffalo meat that hunters would bring to their families. When this song was recorded at the turn of the nineteenth century, no enormous buffalo herds remained to create great billowing clouds of dust as they ran. The Pawnee no longer sang the song when traveling, but continued to include it in the *Hako*—the Calumet Ceremony—so the people would remember the buffalo and their children would learn about their importance.[2]

From the beginning, the lives of Native people of the Plains and the buffalo have been culturally, economically, and spiritually intertwined. The words of the Pawnee song convey how the presence of the buffalo and her calf represented a promise for the people's survival. Plains Indian people understood that when the buffalo were treated with honor and respect, they allowed themselves to be killed for food and other materials. Buffalo communicated with the people through dreams and visions and were called upon for help during the hunt, war, hunger, illness, and times of need.

When buffalo herds were abundant and within reach and hunters were successful, the people celebrated and gave thanks for this magnificent gift which

Codsiogo (Cadzi Cody) 1866–1912
So-soreh (Eastern Shoshone), Wind River
Reservation, Wyoming
Painted Hide, ca. 1900
Tanned cow hide, pigments; 55 ⅛ x 60 ¾ inches
NA.702.31

From about 1885 to the early 1900s, Shoshone artist Codsiogo, working under the name Cadzi Cody, produced nostalgic pre-reservation scenes of buffalo hunting, warfare, ceremonies, and other traditions. Codsiogo sold numerous hide paintings to tourists who visited the Wind River Reservation. Although he produced the hide paintings for sale, they also served as historical documents of Eastern Shoshone cultural traditions.

provided nourishment and the raw materials from which the necessities of life
were created. The relationship of the buffalo to the Native people of the Plains
has been commemorated and celebrated in traditions, stories, and songs trans-
mitted from one generation to another.

> The old story tellers of the tribe used to . . . tell us buffalo stories. They would say that
> long, long time ago that the buffalo were just like human beings, that they had their own
> chants, their own dances and songs, and they just lived like human beings. They were
> brothers to the human beings of all the tribes. So the animals and the human beings were
> always here together and associated together and considered themselves brothers. . . .

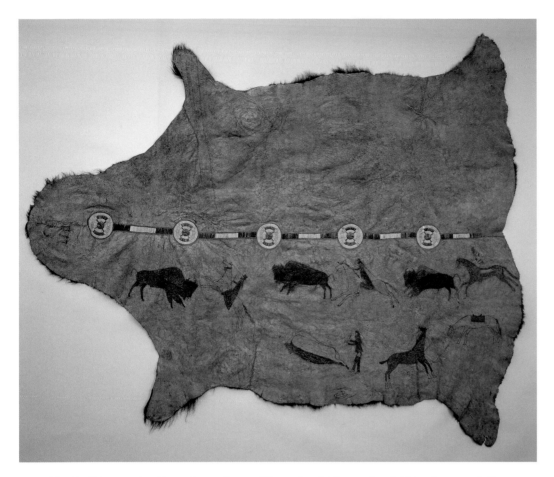

Buffalo Robe
Hidatsa, Northern Plains, ca. 1875
Tanned buffalo hide, dyed porcupine quills, pigments; 88 x 73 inches
Gift of William L. Cone NA.702.30

This robe depicts a successful buffalo hunt. Hunters on horseback, wearing capotes and carrying rifles, chase the buffalo. After the kill, they begin skinning and butchering the buffalo while their horses wait to carry the meat and hides back to camp.

The buffalo, our brother, always here with us, furnishing us food, hides for our clothes, robes for our beds, sinew, bones, everything that they provided for our livelihood. So, we have a special relationship historically and religiously with the *bishée* (we call it *bishée*), bison, or buffalo that is still strong to this very day.[3]

The centrality of the buffalo to Lakota spiritual beliefs is personified in the White Buffalo Calf Woman who, as a messenger from the buffalo nation, brought the ceremonial pipe to the people. This *wakan* (holy) woman appeared to Lakota hunters who were seeking buffalo and other game during a desperate time of starvation. She asked that the people be brought together and then taught them in the ways of the pipe and its ceremonies that were to be used in making peace with other peoples. She also spoke to the women, children, and men, instructing each in their respective roles and responsibilities. She reminded the women of their importance to their families and that they have been given the knowledge to clothe and feed their family members. She talked with the children about their futures and admonished them that they should always lead pure lives. She told the men that the pipe was to be used for nothing but good purposes because the tribe as a whole depended upon it for the necessities derived from elements of the earth and sky. She told them that they should revere these elements and, when in need of buffalo meat, smoke the pipe and pray for what

Crow Women Working on Hides
Crow Reservation, Montana
Photograph by William H. Rau (1855–1920)
Dr. William and Anna Petzoldt Collection, Gift of
Genevieve Petzoldt Fitzgerald PN.95.41

In this camp scene, women are busy scraping hides
which are staked out on the ground with wooden pegs.
Meat is drying on the racks. Women worked long hours
with tools of sharpened bone and horn to clean, soften,
and tan whole skins of buffalo for their families' use.

was needed. "Then, rising, she started, leaving the pipe with the chief who
ordered that the people be quiet until their sister was out of sight. She came out
of the tent [tipi] on the left side, walking very slowly; as soon as she was outside
the entrance she turned into a white buffalo calf."[4] Lakota spiritual leaders have
described the significance of the White Buffalo Calf Woman in their relationship
with the buffalo.

> According to our belief, the Buffalo Woman who brought us the peace pipe, which is at the
> center of our religion, was a beautiful maiden, and after she had taught our tribes how to
> worship with the pipe, she changed herself into a white buffalo calf. So the buffalo is very
> sacred to us. You can't understand about nature, about the feeling we have toward it,
> unless you understand how close we were to the buffalo. That animal was almost like a
> part of ourselves, part of our souls.[5]

Buffalo: Sustenance and Power

From the buffalo—its meat, hide, horns, bones, hooves, hair, and organs—Native
people of the Plains creatively produced the necessities of life. Women worked
long hours with implements of sharpened bone and horn to clean, soften, and
tan hides from which they produced tipi covers, clothing, robes, moccasins, bags,
and bedding. They cut large oblong segments of rawhide and carved them with

designs or painted them with pigments before folding them into parfleches to
hold family belongings. Men made strong shields that deflected arrows from the
rawhide of the necks of buffalo bulls, thickening the pieces by heating them.
Buffalo bones were made into hoes, digging sticks, and painting and hide working tools, and horns were used for cups and spoons. The paunch and bladder
served as containers that could be suspended over cooking fires or filled with
hot stones to boil meat. Sinew served as thread and bowstrings and hair was
braided into ropes. The tail could be used as a fly whisk.

The meat itself was eaten fresh or preserved by cutting it in strips that
were dried in the sun. Stored in hide bags, it could be combined with prairie
turnips, corn, squash, or other vegetables for a nutritious soup. Dried meat
was also pounded and mixed with buffalo fat and chokecherries to make pemmican, which could be kept for several months.

> The buffalo gave us everything we needed. Without it we were nothing. Our tipis were
> made of his skin. His hide was our bed, our blanket, our winter coat. It was our drum,
> throbbing through the night, alive, holy. Out of his skin we made our water bags. His
> flesh strengthened us, became flesh of our flesh. Not the smallest part of it was
> wasted. His stomach, a red-hot stone dropped into it, became our soup kettle. His
> horns were our spoons, the bones our knives, our women's awls and needles. Out of
> his sinews we made our bowstrings and thread. His ribs became rattles. His mighty
> skull, with the pipe learning against it, was our sacred altar.[6]

Storage Bags
Tsistsistas (Cheyenne), Northern Plains,
ca. 1870
Tanned buffalo hide, glass beads, tin cones,
horse hair; 24 x 11 inches
Gift of Mr. Robert Garland NA.106.14A/B

Women made storage bags such as these in
pairs to be carried on either side of a saddle
and for display within tipis.

Images of the buffalo—of the whole figure in profile or representative head and horns, hooves, and tracks—were painted on shields and drums and carved on pipe bowls and stems, representing its significance as an intermediary between humans and the spirit world. Such images were also painted, embroidered in porcupine quillwork, and beaded on moccasins and clothing.

Men recorded buffalo hunts in stories, songs, ledger drawings, and paintings on tanned hides and tipi covers. Members of warrior societies, wearing bonnets made of buffalo hide and horns, performed dances to capture the sacred power of the buffalo. Such power assisted men in attaining success as warriors and providing meat for their families as well as offering physical and spiritual protection in battle. Buffalo horn bonnets were thought to provide protection from arrows and bullets. Buffalo figures carved in stone and wood were used in hunting and other ceremonies.[7] Wooden sticks carved with images of buffalo at one end were carried by members of some Kiowa, Crow, and Hidatsa as emblems of their warrior societies.[8]

For Plains Indian people, the buffalo symbolized sustenance, power, courage, strength, honor, and protection. Men sometimes had dreams concerning buffalo which communicated the protective power of this creature. Brave Buffalo of the Lakota told Frances Densmore about such a dream:

> The buffalo in my dream told me that I would live to be 102 years old. Then they said: "If
> you are to show people the great value of the buffalo one proof which you must give

Bowl
Lakota (Sioux), Northern Plains,
nineteenth century
Buffalo rawhide; 27 ⅝ x 11 inches
Chandler-Pohrt Collection, Gift of Mr. William D.
Weiss NA.106.243

them is a demonstration of your endurance. After properly qualifying yourself you will be able to show that weapons cannot harm you, and you may challenge anyone to shoot you with arrows or with a gun."[9]

Brave Buffalo said that after awakening from his dream, he thought seriously about its meaning. He asked his relatives to put up a large buffalo hide tipi and invited people to come to witness the protective power of the buffalo promised in the dream. Having clothed himself with an entire buffalo hide and head and horns, he challenged anyone to shoot him with arrows. Many people tried, but the arrows did not penetrate his skin. Several years later, he repeated the challenge with guns and, once again, remained unharmed.[10]

Prayers and special rituals and ceremonies were performed under the leadership of individuals who could communicate with the buffalo and had special powers related to the animal that had been given to them through visions or dreams. Such ceremonies helped the people preserve the spiritual connections essential for their physical and cultural survival. Among the Blackfoot, an *iniskin*, or small segment of an ammonite fossil resembling a buffalo, was used in special ceremonies to call buffalo to jumps and places where buffalo could be surrounded and killed.[11]

The Mandan and Hidatsa held a series of buffalo calling ceremonies sponsored by men's and women's societies to increase the herds and draw the buffalo closer to their villages.[12] A major ritual of the Mandan people, the Okipa (O-Kee-Pa) ceremony dramatized tribal origins and the creation of the earth, its plants, animals, and people. The Okipa emphasized the importance of the buffalo to the people and served as an initiation ceremony for young men. The four-day ceremony took place each summer after the corn was planted and before the tribal buffalo hunt. A part of the ceremony was the Buffalo Dance in which men wearing masks of tanned buffalo hide and horns, hide breechcloths, and wrist and ankle decorations of buffalo hair impersonated buffalo bulls. The Okipa ceremony ensured an abundance of buffalo and brought the herds closer to the villages.[13]

Before horses became available in the seventeenth and eighteenth centuries, bands hunted buffalo on foot using buffalo jumps, pounds or corrals, and other resourceful means to gain advantages over the herds. Such hunting methods required knowledge of the migration patterns and habits of the buffalo, skills, cooperation, and careful preparation.

One means of obtaining a large amount of buffalo meat, much of which was preserved for later use, was the buffalo jump—called *pisskan* or *pisská-ni* by the Blackfoot—through which many buffalo could be driven to their deaths over a steep cliff.[14] Buffalo jumps were located throughout the Northern Plains along the foothills of the Rocky Mountains, where large herds of buffalo often win-

Man's Moccasins
Amoskapi Pikuni (Blackfeet), Montana, ca. 1900
Tanned buffalo hide, sinew, dyed porcupine quills, glass beads; 9 ½ x 3 ¾ inches
Simplot Collection, Gift of J.R. Simplot
NA.202.914

These buffalo hide moccasins are decorated in dyed porcupine quillwork and trimmed in beadwork. Although beadwork had largely replaced quillwork by the early reservation period, women continued to use quills on occasion.

Shield

Sahnish (Arikara), Northern Plains, ca. 1875
Rawhide, pigments, bald and golden eagle
feathers, bear claws, glass pony beads, tanned
hide, cloth; 19 inches diameter
Adolf Spohr Collection, Gift of Larry Sheerin
NA.502.66

This shield and its two covers, collected on the
Arikara, Mandan, and Hidatsa reservation at
Fort Berthold, North Dakota, belonged to
Arikara warrior Fighting Bear. Both the shield
with its bear claws and the covers, with images
of standing bears, carry the protective power
of the bear.

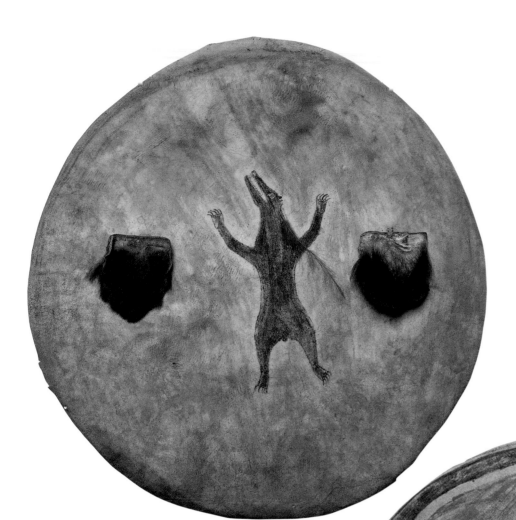

Shield Cover
Sahnish (Arikara), Northern Plains, ca. 1875
Tanned deer hide, pigment, bear fur and hide,
feather; 19 inches diameter
Adolf Spohr Collection, Gift of Larry Sheerin
NA.108.14

Spiritual beings appeared to men in visions and
directed them to make shields and shield covers and to decorate them with images that provide protection in battle. These two shield covers, one of tanned deer hide the other of
muslin, were made to protect the rawhide
shield.

Shield Cover
Sahnish (Arikara), Northern Plains, ca. 1875
Muslin, pigments, feathers; 20 inches diameter
Adolf Spohr Collection, Gift of Larry Sheerin
NA.108.13

tered. Buffalo jumps required cooperation and days
of preparation as many people worked together to
build the V-shaped drive lanes that funneled stam-
peding buffalo over a cliff where they died or
were injured in the fall. Survivors were killed
with arrows and lances. The drive lanes were
constructed of cairns of rocks that extended at
least a mile beyond the edge of the cliff. Piles of
branches and brush were wedged into the cairns
to keep the buffalo running into the ever-narrow-
ing tunnel. According to Joe Medicine Crow, the
concept of the buffalo jump came to the Crow
through Coyote, who challenged a buffalo herd to a
race. Coyote tricked the buffalo by running ahead and
hiding at the end of the jump, where the herd ran over the
edge.[15] According to Blackfoot tradition, the buffalo jump came
to them from their Creator, Napi.[16]

CHIEF
WETS IT
ASSINABOINES
Nº 66

Chief Wets It, Assiniboine
Trans-Mississippi and International Exposition,
Omaha, Nebraska, 1898
Photograph by F.A. Rinehart (1862–1928)
P.72.1.17

OPPOSITE: **Buffalo Horn and Eagle Feather Bonnet**
Tsistsistas (Cheyenne), Northern Plains,
ca. 1860–1865
Eagle feathers, wool and cotton cloth, felt,
glass beads, bison horn, sinew, brass bells, hair;
74 x 16 inches
Trails End Collection, Gift of Dr. and Mrs. Van
Kirke Nelson and Family NA.203.1213

Buffalo jumps were organized in the autumn or early winter. Special preparations, ceremonies, and prayers were made to ensure success, to prevent hunters from being harmed, and to thank the buffalo for their sacrifices. Young men who were good runners—some disguised in wolf or buffalo hides—were selected to lure or force the buffalo into the drive lanes. Other hunters stood along the cairns lighting small fires or waving pieces of buckskin to keep the buffalo running toward and over the jump. Once the buffalo were killed, women removed the hides, butchered, and cut the meat into pieces that could be transported home.

The Head-Smashed-In Buffalo Jump, located in southwestern Alberta overlooking the Oldman River, was used by generations of hunters from approximately 3,000 B.C. until about 150 years ago. The name of the site—"where he got his head smashed in"—comes from a story about a young Piegan man who found himself trapped below the cliff and whose head was crushed by the weight of the falling buffalo.[17] With the arrival of the horse, buffalo jumps fell out of common use by the 1850s, with the last ones used by the Blood in the winter of 1868–69 and the Piegans in about 1874.[18] The Crow woman Pretty Shield remembered coming across a buffalo jump with a visible drive lane which she called "the-dry-cliff" when she was a girl. Although she said that older women told her about the use of buffalo jumps before horses were available, she suggested that the jump had been used by people other than the Crow, saying, "I have heard old women tell of such things being done before the horse came to the plains; and yet this herd of buffalo that went over The-dry-cliff may have been driven to death by another people."[19]

Before the horse arrived on the Plains, Blackfoot and other Plains hunters also procured buffalo by driving them into pounds or corrals built of many upturned dog travois tied together or other enclosures built of branches and brush where they could be killed with arrows or lances. Individual hunters also disguised themselves with the hides of buffalo, coyotes, or wolves so they could approach near enough for the kill. After a big snowstorm, hunters sometimes drove buffalo herds into coulees, where they were killed as they floundered in the deep snow.

Hunting buffalo on foot was a dangerous, arduous, and long process, sometimes lasting several days. The availability of horses on the Plains made the process easier, but by no means easy or less dangerous. For Plains Indian people, however, hunting was essential for survival, not a sport or amusement as it has sometimes been characterized, and men, assisted by women, considered themselves fortunate when they were successful and were thankful for the buffalo and other game.

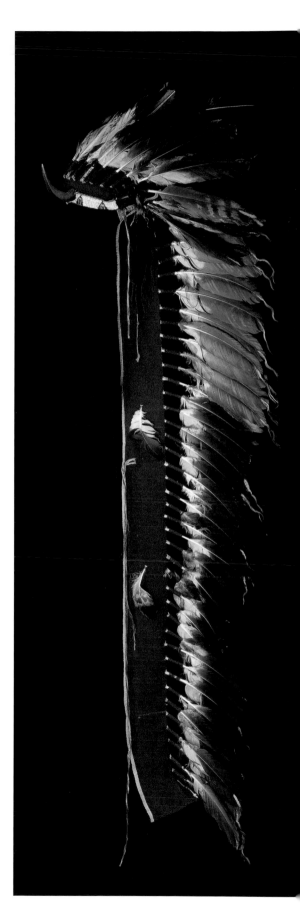

Buffalo Horn Bonnet
Apsáalooke (Crow), Northern Plains, ca. 1860
Split buffalo horns, eagle and hawk feathers,
wool cloth, deer hide, glass beads, brass beads,
string; 55 x 9 inches
Catherine Bradford McClellan Collection, Gift of
The Coe Foundation NA.203.18

OPPOSITE: *Spies on the Enemy, Crow*
Trans-Mississippi and International Exposition,
Omaha, Nebraska, 1898
Photograph by F.A. Rinehart (1862–1928)
P.72.1.15

SPIES ON
THE ENEMY

© F.A RINEHART
OMAHA

Dogs and "The Sacred Dog"

My grandmother told me that when she was young our people did not have any horses. When they needed to go anywhere they put their packs upon dogs in little pole travois drawn by dogs. The people themselves had to walk. In those times they did not travel far nor often. But when they got horses they could move more easily from place to place. Then they could kill more of the buffalo and other animals, and so they got more meat for food and gathered more skins for lodges and clothing.

Iron Teeth[20]

For centuries, Native people traveled the Plains to hunt, to gather plants, and for trade visits, with their dogs dragging lodge poles, and carrying their tipis and other belongings in packs or on travois. For Plains Indian people, dogs served many purposes besides being pack animals. They were camp guardians and companions, but also sources of material wealth that could be used to purchase memberships in societies and in the transfer of sacred medicine bundles. During times of scarcity of game, dogs were sources of foods. For some Plains peoples, dogs were a sacred food eaten during healing and other ceremonies.[21] Images of dogs or, possibly wolves or coyotes, were carved in pipestone and carved and painted in petroglyphs and pictographs.

When interviewed in the early 1900s, Buffalo Bird Woman recalled the role of dogs among the Hidatsa.

In old times we Indian people had no horses, and not as many families of my tribe owned them when I was a girl. But I do not think there ever was a time when we Hidatsas did not own dogs. We trained them to draw our tent poles and our loaded travois. We never used dogs to chase deer as white men do.

Our Hidatsa dogs—the breed we owned when I was a little girl—had broad faces, with gentle, knowing eyes; erect pointed ears; and tails curling, never trailing like a wolf's tail. They had soft silky hair, gray, black or spotted red or white. All had stout heavy legs. I think this sturdiness was because we saved only dogs of stout build to drag our travois.[22]

After the arrival of horses on the Plains, people continued to use the dog-drawn travois for light loads and daily work such as gathering firewood. Dogs were particularly efficient in deeper snows where horses often struggled. Although horses took on much of the significance of dogs in terms of practical value and symbolism, dogs continued to play important roles as companions and guardians of the villages.

Although several historical concepts revolve around when and how Native people of the Plains first obtained horses, it is generally accepted that horses were distributed from the Southwest after the Pueblo Revolt of 1680, when the Spanish were driven out of the region.[23] By the end of the eighteenth century, horses had spread throughout the Plains from Southwestern pueblos along estab-

Buffalo Horn Bonnet
Lakota (Sioux), Northern Plains, ca. 1860
Split buffalo horns, eagle, owl, and other feathers, rawhide, deer hide, hooves, ermine, horse hair, wool cloth, glass beads, pigment;
70 x 12 ¾ inches
Chandler-Pohrt Collection, Gift of Mr. and Mrs. Richard A. Pohrt NA.205.78

Buffalo Horn Bonnet
Amoskapi Pikuni (Blackfeet), Montana ca. 1915
Split buffalo horns, ermine hide and fur, eagle feathers, horse hair, glass beads, ribbons, wool cloth; 24 ½ x 7 inches
The Catherine Bradford Collection, Gift of The Coe Foundation NA.203.10

lished trading networks and through intertribal horse raiding. For Native groups already living on the Plains, horses were a more efficient means of travel, allowing the bands to move more frequently and farther to hunt or trade and to carry larger tipis and more belongings. For Lakota, Cheyenne, Arapaho, and other people with homelands outside of the Plains, horses radically transformed their cultures as they moved into the region and adopted the buffalo-hunting way of life.[24]

Many tribal traditions concern the first time Native people encountered horses and how they became an essential part of their lives. Warring tribes described horses as great advantages in battle. In 1787–1788, Saukamaupee, a Cree who had lived with Piegan people in Canada, told Hudson's Bay fur trader David Thompson about a series of battles between the Piegan and the Shoshone

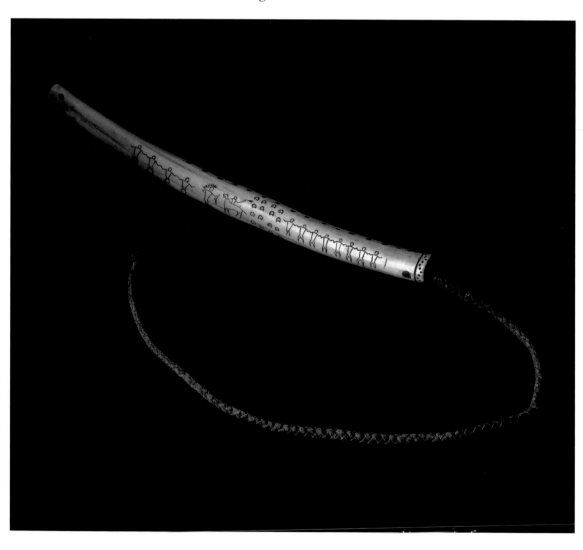

Horse Stealing Charm
Apsáalooke (Crow), Montana, ca. 1890
Rawhide, pigment, clay; 12 ¼ x 9 ⅞ inches
The Crow Indian Collection of Dr. William and Anna Petzoldt, Gift of Genevieve Petzoldt Fitzgerald NA.502.182

Quirt
Osage, Central Plains, ca. 1850
Elk antler, rawhide, 37 ⅜ x 1 inches
Chandler-Pohrt Collection, Gift of Mr. William D. Weiss NA.403.100

This quirt, or riding whip, is made of elk antler engraved in a battle scene, with one warrior on horseback and the other on foot. The engravings in the center suggest many horse tracks flanked by several figures on each side, perhaps representing the owner's coups.

that had taken place in about 1730. Mounted on horses, the Shoshone had the advantage against the Piegan, who were fighting on foot, until the latter were joined by their Assiniboine and Cree allies, who also had no horses, but did have firearms. The Piegan experienced their first close view of a Shoshone horse, which had died from an arrow wound, as described by Saukamaupee: "Numbers of us went to see him and we all admired him; he put us in mind of a stag that had lost his horns; and we did not know what name to give him. But as he was a slave to Man, like the dog, which carried our things, he was named the Big Dog."[25] Later, the Piegans and other Blackfoot people referred to the horse as "elk dog." Among the Lakota, the horse was called "sacred dog." The Crow named the horse *Ichilay,* which means "to search with," perhaps referring to its use in searching for enemies and game.[26] Other names for the horse among Native people that emphasize its spiritual qualities include "mystery dog," "medicine dog," and "sky dog," reflecting the belief of some people that horses descended from the sky.[27]

Saddle Blanket
Upper Missouri region, Montana or North Dakota, ca. 1835
Tanned buffalo hide, wool cloth, glass pony beads; 61 x 27 ¾ inches
Chandler-Pohrt Collection, Gift of Mr. William D. Weiss NA.403.164

This saddle blanket is decorated with trade materials of Euro-American origin: pony beads, red wool stroud cloth, and tin cones. Such embellishment attests to the prestige associated with horse ownership.

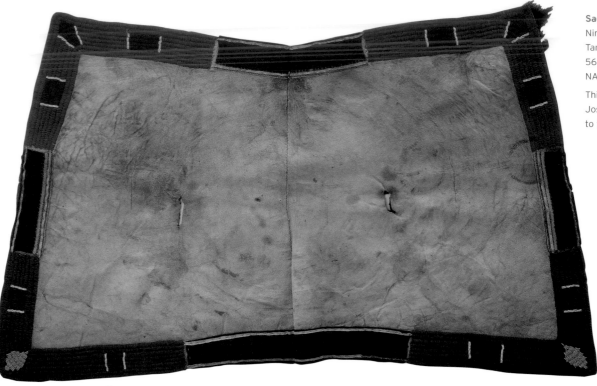

Saddle Blanket
Nimíipu (Nez Perce), Plateau Region, ca. 1870
Tanned buffalo hide and hair, glass beads;
56 x 33 ¼ inches
NA.403.91

This saddle blanket, which belonged to Chief
Joseph, is made with the hair left on one side
to form a cushion for the rider.

Horses represented many positive attributes to Plains Indian people. Besides enhanced mobility, horses also represented power, wealth, and status. Hunters on horseback could pursue buffalo much faster and at greater distances than on foot. Killing the buffalo from horseback was also more efficient than the previous methods of building buffalo jumps and corrals. Families were able to preserve and convey larger reserves of food and more and heavier belongings, as well as larger tipis made of many more buffalo hides. They were able to travel to trading centers such as those established at the Hidatsa, Mandan, and Arikara villages on the Upper Missouri River and Euro-American trading posts. They were also able to more easily transport small children, elders, and relatives who were ill or injured. The Cheyenne Wooden Leg recalled riding in a travois as his family traveled:

> As a little boy I used to ride in a travois basket when the tribe moved camp. Two long lodgepoles were crossed over the shoulders or tied to the sides of a horse. Thus they were dragged over the country. Buffalo skins were used to stretch across between the widely gaping poles behind the horse. Upon or into these bagging skins were placed all of the family property, in rawhide satchels or as separate loose articles. The smaller children also rode there. I have fond recollections of this kind of traveling. Many an hour I have slept in that kind of gentle bed.[28]

The value of horses was universally recognized throughout the Plains and the ownership of many horses, primarily acquired through capture from other tribal groups, symbolized wealth. Losses of horses to enemies—especially horses

Saddle Blanket
Lakota (Sioux), Northern Plains, ca. 1885
Tanned buffalo hide, glass beads;
48 x 30 inches
Gift of Richard W. Leche NA.403.88

Saddlebags
Northern Plains, ca. 1875
Tanned deer hide, glass beads;
44 ½ x 12 ¼ inches
Adolf Spohr Collection, Gift of Larry Sheerin
NA.403.11

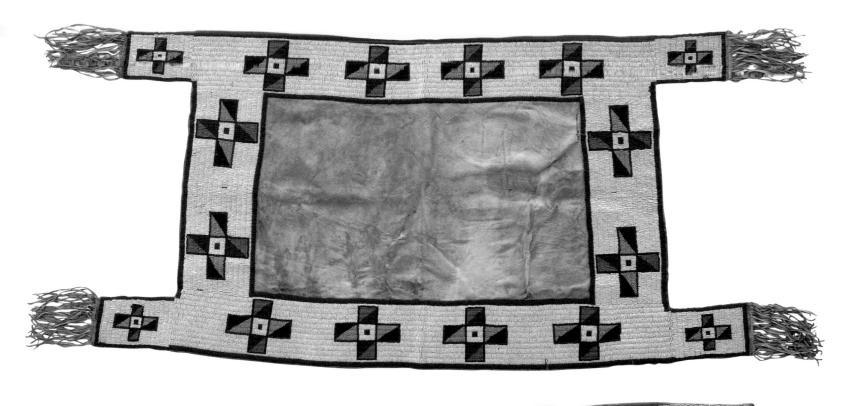

1868

2. Sitting Bull killing a Crow Indian —
One Sioux chased thirty Crows all night caught them
in the morning and killed them all —

Sitting Bull (ca. 1831–1890)
Lakota (Sioux), Fort Randall, South Dakota
Sitting Bull Killing a Crow Indian, 1882
Pencil and crayon on paper;
8 ½ x 10 ¼ inches
40.70.2

This drawing is part of a series completed by Sitting Bull in 1882, during the time he was a prisoner of war at Fort Randall, Dakota Territory. The drawings illustrated important events in Sitting Bull's life and focused on fights with Gros Ventre, Flathead, Chippewa, and Crow warriors and Army scouts. They were made for D.L. Pratt, post trader at Fort Randall.

Upper left: Spotted Horse
Tsistsistas (Cheyenne), Plains
Ledger Drawing, late nineteenth century
Pencil, crayon, watercolor, and ink on paper;
8 ¾ x 5 ⅝ inches
27.78.22

Spotted Horse illustrated encounters with Crow, Ute, Cheyenne, Pawnee, and Kiowa warriors. In this drawing, he shows himself shaking hands with two Osage men, one of whom has a rifle resting on his shoulder.

of high prestige such as those used in running buffalo—were serious matters to be avenged through reciprocal raiding. Men who demonstrated bravery by capturing horses from other people were greatly admired. A Lakota song expresses the message of the horse raider:

> Crow Indian
>
> You must watch your horses
>
> A horse thief
>
> often
>
> am I[29]

Conversely, the Crow warrior Two Leggings described the honor and celebration of a successful horse raid against the Lakota.

> We had captured over a hundred head, the night was still early, and we had a good chance to get away. It would bring me greater honors to lead them back safely without having killed a man, and I did not want to spoil this. I felt that my medicine had kept the Sioux's attention off their horses. . . .
>
> Now there was no danger of being overtaken and we all felt good. As I rode I thought of the celebration waiting for us and of the praise I would receive for being leader. I pictured the older men leading me through camp, singing songs about me, and calling out my name. I was so happy I sang my medicine song: "Anywhere I go, I thank you."
>
> The bunch of horses running before us looked so fine I could not help myself and sang my song again.[30]

Men also increased their prestige by providing horses to less fortunate individuals and families.

Men trained horses that were used in buffalo hunting in maneuvering in and out of buffalo herds, bringing the hunter closer to the animals, and quickly veering away. They also practiced riding on horses trained for warfare. Such war horses were seen as extensions of their owners, with whom they had developed special relationships. "To be alone with our war-horses . . . teaches them to understand us and us to understand them," said the Crow leader Plenty Coups. "My horse fights with me and fasts with me, because if he is to carry me in battle he must know my heart and I must know his or we will never become brothers."[31]

Highly esteemed horses were adorned with painted, beaded, and porcupine quilled horse hoods and masks, bridles, and other equipment and were paraded as men prepared to leave for battle, on return from successful raids, and in other public celebrations. Warriors depended upon their horses to carry them into battle and safely home and were thankful for their assistance. Âiya´āka of the Lakota recounted a dangerous occasion when he was dependent upon the speed and agility of his horse. He dismounted from his horse and spoke to him directly, saying,

We are in danger. Obey me promptly that we may conquer. If you have to run for your life and mine, do your best, and if we reach home I will give you the best eagle feather I can get and the finest *siná lúta*, and you shall be painted with the best paint.[32]

Men celebrated and sang songs in honor of horses who had served them well in battle by carrying them swiftly away from danger.

> Friend
>
> my horse
>
> flies like a bird
>
> as it runs[33]

Children were placed on horses early and generally taught by mothers and fathers to ride by the age of five or six. Cheyenne boys of seven or eight years old usually had the duties related to daily care of horses and drove them to pasture and water. Boys of twelve to thirteen years were often responsible for breaking horses on their own.[34] They practiced riding their horses including the daring maneuvers needed in battle or for chasing buffalo as they assumed their adult roles as hunters and warriors.

> The horse was not just another animal, it caught the imagination of the Lakota "hoksíla" or "boy." It was his first love. He spent as much time as he could on his pony. He learned how to use a rope made out of buffalo hair to capture his pony. He knew how to break a pony for riding. He learned how to stay on his horse while another boy chased him and tried to pull him off when they played war games. He imitated real life. He learned how to use a knife, bow, and arrow. These things he would need to know how to use well in order to survive as a hunter and warrior. Indeed every hoksíla was encouraged to become a "zuyá wichása," a warrior, to protect the helpless, the elderly, the women and children. His reward would be his reputation as a warrior, to have women sing songs for him about how courageous and cunning he was.[35]

Women also owned horses used for riding and pulling travois which they received from relatives or through trade. Among the Blackfoot and other tribes, women were free to give their horses away, trade, or loan them as they wished.[36] Like boys, girls were taught to ride early and Plains Native women like Iron Teeth developed excellent skills as riders.

> The first time I rode alone on horseback occurred when I was about ten years old. My father gave me a yearling colt. When we were traveling, my mother would put packs upon the colt with me. Usually I had two badger skins filled with dried chokecherries behind me, swinging down the colt's sides. Boys teased me by riding up close and lashing my colt to make it jump. At first I was frightened and they laughed at me. But I soon got used to it, and after a little while I became a good rider.
>
> After I grew older I liked to break horses. When I became a woman I never asked

"WHITE HAWK" - CHEYENNE BRAVE - 1879

©L.A. Huffman
109

any man to tame my horses for me. Before trying to ride them, my sister and I used to take the wild animals to a sandy place beside the river. Sometimes we would lead one out into deep water before mounting it. A horse cannot buck hard in deep water. One time a bucking horse threw me into a deep and narrow ditch, where I lit upon my back. My sister had to help me out from the ditch, but I was not hurt.

Lots of wild horses used to be running loose on the plains to the southward. I had a good running horse when I was a young woman, and I always carried with me a lariat rope made of spun and plaited buffalo hair. As a girl I played a romping game we called "wild horses," in which some children would run here and there while others would try to throw lariats about their bodies. In this way I learned to toss the rope. One time, after my marriage, I was riding with my baby strapped to my back when I saw some wild horses. I put the baby in its cradle board down on the prairie and got after the herd. That day I caught two horses.[37]

Plains Indian people developed specialized equipment for riding and handling horses. Women made pad saddles of tanned buffalo, deer or elk hide for her male relatives and saddles with wooden frames covered in rawhide for their own uses. They also made saddles of elk or deer antler covered in rawhide. They made saddle blankets of tanned hide, some of which were undecorated with the hair remaining and others embellished in beadwork. Other specialized horse gear included decorated head ornaments and hoods, bridles and headstalls, martingales, cruppers, and saddlebags.

Like the buffalo, horses also had deep spiritual significance to Plains Indian people that they expressed through ceremonial occasions. Horses appeared to men through dreams and visions and brought them power that ensured their success in capturing and training horses, in hunting, and in warfare. Such visions also brought healing powers to individuals such as the ability to cure illness and those who had been wounded. Joe Medicine Crow described horse medicine as a blessing characterized by the power, stamina, speed, and agility of a horse.[38]

A man with horse medicine had special songs about horses that he would sing in certain ceremonies and dances. Whenever he was asked to name a child, he would invariably use the word horse in the name. By so doing, he expressed a wish and prayer that the child would grow to live up to the meaning of the name. Among the Crows today there are many family names such as Takes a Horse, Rides a Horse, Good Horse, and so on.[39]

Native people expressed their relationship to the horse through images painted and beaded on clothing, carved in stone for pipe bowls, and carved in wood for dance sticks and war clubs. Men recorded successful horse raids in lodge covers, war shirts, hide paintings and, later, ledger drawings. Sometimes such successes and other war deeds were symbolized in paint on the horses themselves. Plains Indian people considered horses to be gifts which made their distinctively mobile way life as buffalo hunters possible and also brought them spiritual blessings. Through prayers, ceremonies, and songs they asked that such gifts and associated powers be bestowed upon them.

> In a sacred manner
> I live
> To the heavens
> I gazed
> In a sacred manner
> I live
> My horses
> are many[40]

Hunters, Warriors, and Their Arts

> At last the day came when my father allowed me to go on a buffalo hunt with him. And what a proud boy I was!
>
> Ever since I could remember my father had been teaching me the things that I should know and preparing me to be a good hunter. I had learned to make arrows and tip them with feathers. I knew how to ride my pony no matter how fast he would go, and I felt that I was brave and did not fear danger. All these things I had learned for just this day when father would allow me to go with him on a buffalo hunt. It was the event for which every Sioux boy eagerly waited. To ride side by side with the best hunters of the tribe, to hear the terrible noise of the great herds as they ran, and then to help bring home the kill was the most thrilling day of an Indian boy's life. The only other event which could equal it would be the day I went for the first time on the warpath to meet the enemy and protect my tribe.
>
> —Luther Standing Bear[41]

Plains Indian men learned their roles and responsibilities, as hunters and warriors—providers and protectors of the people—along with the values, skills, and knowledge needed to fulfill them from an early age. As girls learned from their mothers, aunts, and other adult females, boys found role models in their fathers, uncles, and other male relatives and men of high prestige. They emulated such men, yearning for the day when they would be recognized and celebrated for their prowess as hunters and warriors by their relatives and others within their group. Although they understood that they would be rewarded with great individual prestige for their accomplishments as hunters and warriors, they also were taught that they hunted and fought for the benefit of the people and that the rewards should be shared.

Tomahawk
Lakota (Sioux), Northern Plains, 1881
Wood, metal; 27 ¾ x 6 inches
Dr. Robert A. Anderson Collection NA.205.19A

This tomahawk belonged to Sitting Bull. He surrendered it on September 8, 1881 at Fort Randall, South Dakota, where he was confined with his followers until 1883.

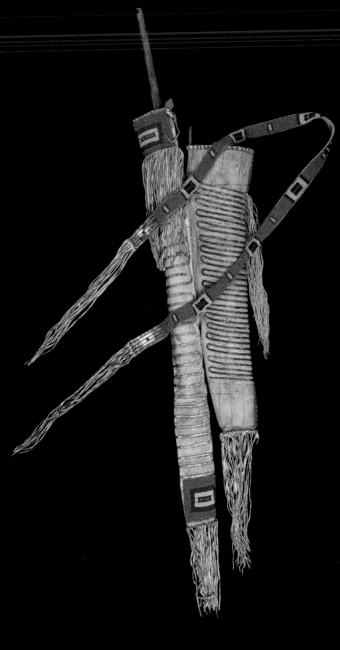

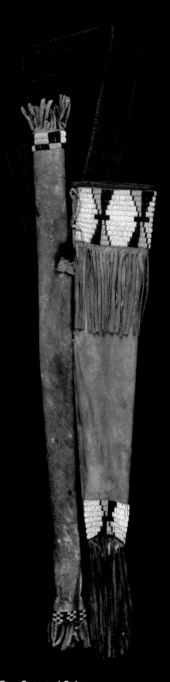

Bow Case and Quiver
Lakota (Sioux), Northern Plains, ca. 1880
Tanned deer hide, glass beads, wool cloth;
46 x 6 inches
Adolf Spohr Collection, Gift of Larry Sheerin
NA.102.40

Bow Case and Quiver
Tsistsistas (Cheyenne), Plains, ca. 1885
Tanned elk hide, felt, glass beads, wool cloth,
wood; 36 ⅜ x 6 ⅛ inches
Adolf Spohr Collection, Gift of Larry Sheerin
NA.102.80

Bow Case and Quiver
Apsáalooke (Crow), Northern Plains, ca. 1875
Otter hide and fur, wool cloth, glass beads,
pigment; 57 x 31½ inches
Adolf Spohr Collection, Gift of Larry Sheerin
NA.102.20

Every Plains Indian man needed a bow case
and quiver to carry his weapons. This example,
made from tanned otter hide, with broad straps
and distinctive beadwork, is typical of those
used by the Crow in the late 1800s.

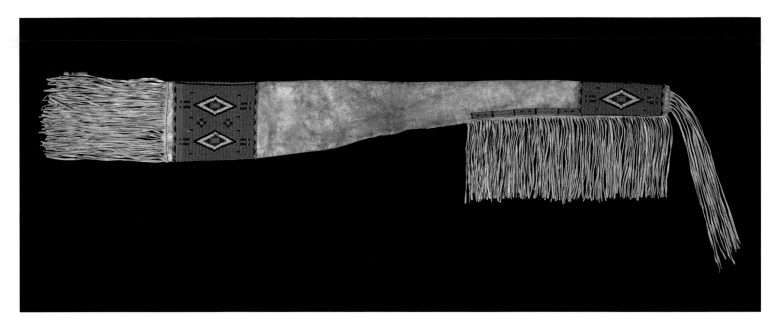

As a boy I spent my evenings listening to the stories of our warriors and medicine men. I wanted to be just as brave and honored, and the following day would train myself that much harder, running and riding and playing war games with my friends.

When we were young we did not speak, we listened to our Wise Ones. Sometimes we were told what to do and sometimes we learned through stories of true things that happened long ago.[42]

Boys were taught directly by their fathers and other male relatives, but they also learned through watching and listening to such men, through playing at adult male activities, and, eventually, by taking on responsibilities related to horse care, hunting, and warfare. Little boys rode their horses bareback, practicing and mastering their riding skills. They had their own small bows and arrows and practiced approaching and killing small game—usually birds or rabbits—as soon as they were capable. They imitated hunting activities including buffalo surrounds, with some boys playing the part of the hunters and some the prey.

Eventually—sometimes by the age of twelve or thirteen—they were able to participate in their first real buffalo hunt, usually going along as assistants by carrying food, going for water, collecting firewood, or tending the horses. The boy's first buffalo kill was publicly recognized, with his father calling out the news to everyone in the camp and often promising to give a horse away in honor of this accomplishment. The boy's mother often put on a feast, inviting several poorer people to share in the family's good fortune. The family gave away blankets and other goods to those who attended. The same public celebration also took place when a boy came home from his first war expedition. Luther Standing Bear of the Lakota recalled the pride of his family at his first buffalo kill. Standing Bear reached this milestone as many changes were taking place within Lakota culture. The buffalo hunting way of life was coming to an end and soon

he would be sent away to boarding school. His first buffalo hunt was also his last, but one he remembered throughout his life.

> Mother now had two hunters in the family and I knew how she was going to make over me. . . . My father was so proud that he gave away a fine horse. He called an old man to our tipi to cry out the news to the rest of the people in camp. The old man stood at the door of our tipi and sang a song of praise to my father. The horse had been led up and I stood holding it by a rope. The old man who was doing the singing called the other old man who was to receive the horse as a present. He accepted the horse by coming up to me, holding out his hands to me, and saying, "Ha-ye," which means "Thank you." The old man went away very grateful for the horse.[43]

The Plains Indian hunting traditions primarily focused on the buffalo, which because of its size was an abundant source of food. Men also hunted elk, deer, antelope, and bighorn sheep, but it was the communal buffalo hunt that

LEFT: **Man's Shirt**
Apsáalooke (Crow), Northern Plains, ca. 1885
Tanned elk hide, pigment, glass beads, wool cloth, horse hair; 36 x 36 inches
Gift of Harriet D. Reed and Betty N. Landercasper, In Memory of W. Guruea Dyer
NA.202.773

ABOVE: *Long-time Dog—Hidatsa*
Fort Berthold Reservation, North Dakota, 1908
Photograph by Edward S. Curtis (1868–1952)

engendered tribal organization, cooperation, restrictions, and spiritual assistance. Although in some instances men did hunt as individuals, when the herds came together in large numbers, the men understood that hunting would be more successful if they cooperated. In preparation for the hunts, leaders would select a few men who were considered reliable to go ahead to scout the location of the buffalo. This selection was considered a great honor which no man would refuse. The hunts were policed by soldier societies—*akí´cita* among the Lakota—and there were restrictions against individual hunters striking out on their own for fear of panicking and scattering the large buffalo herds. The Lakota *Âiya´ka* described the practice in this way:

> Five or more men were selected from the aki´cita to keep order during the hunt. These men went to the council tent and received their final instructions from the chiefs, who told them to be sure to secure beeves for the helpless, the old and the cripples, as well as for women who had no one to provide for them. These aki´cita were men of executive

Man's Shirt
Upper Missouri River Region, ca. 1830-1850
Tanned deer hide, porcupine quills, glass pony beads, pigment, horse hair, sinew, wool cloth; 42 ½ x 56 ¾ inches
Chandler-Pohrt Collection, Gift of Mr. William D. Weiss NA.202.486

The painted line of human figures and horse tracks signify war honors for the wearer and probably symbolize horses captured and enemies defeated. A rosette once sewn on the breast of the shirt is missing.

Man's Shirt
Oglala Teton Lakota (Oglala Teton Sioux), Northern Plains, ca. 1885
Tanned deer hide, glass beads, human hair, wool cloth, dyed porcupine quills; 37 x 44 inches
Gift of Mr. and Mrs. Robert Maxwell James NA.202.208

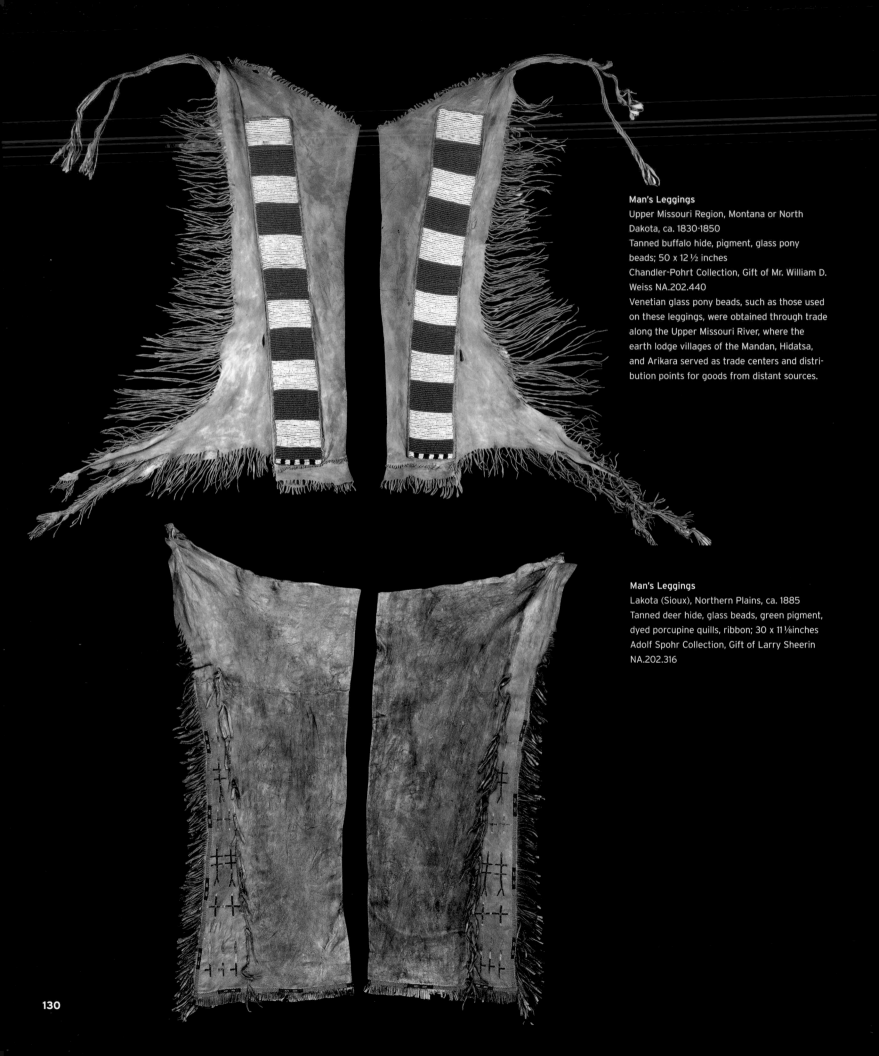

Man's Leggings
Upper Missouri Region, Montana or North Dakota, ca. 1830-1850
Tanned buffalo hide, pigment, glass pony beads; 50 x 12 ½ inches
Chandler-Pohrt Collection, Gift of Mr. William D. Weiss NA.202.440
Venetian glass pony beads, such as those used on these leggings, were obtained through trade along the Upper Missouri River, where the earth lodge villages of the Mandan, Hidatsa, and Arikara served as trade centers and distribution points for goods from distant sources.

Man's Leggings
Lakota (Sioux), Northern Plains, ca. 1885
Tanned deer hide, glass beads, green pigment, dyed porcupine quills, ribbon; 30 x 11 ⅛ inches
Adolf Spohr Collection, Gift of Larry Sheerin NA.202.316

Man's Leggings
Oglala Lakota (Oglala Sioux), Northern Plains,
nineteenth century
Tanned deer hide, yellow ochre, glass beads;
29 ¼ x 10 ½ inches
Adolf Spohr Collection, Gift of Larry Sheerin
NA.202.237

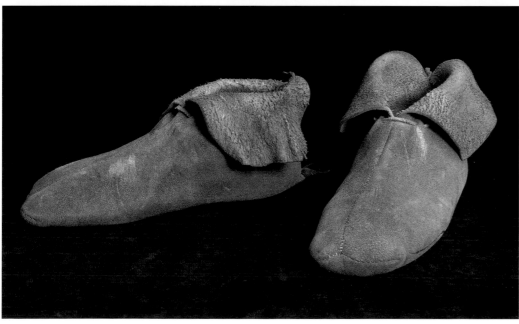

Moccasins
Pawnee (Chaticks si Chaticks), Oklahoma,
ca. 1880
Tanned deer hide; 9 ⅞ x 3 ⅞ inches
Chandler-Pohrt Collection NA.202.459

LEFT: **Man's Breastplate**
Lakota (Sioux), South Dakota, ca. 1890
Commercially tanned leather, bone hair pipes,
brass beads, cowrie shells, silk ribbon;
17 x 11 ¾ inches
Adolf Spohr Collection, Gift of Larry Sheerin
NA.203.236

Plains Indian people acquired tabular beads
known as "hair pipes" from Euro-American
traders. First made of shell, by the late nineteenth century they were manufactured in
large quantities from cow bone.

ABOVE: **Man's Hair Ornament**
Lakota (Sioux), Northern Plains, ca. 1875
Tanned hide, dyed porcupine quills, feathers,
horse hair, silver, glass beads, tin cones,
pigment; 27 ½ x 3 ½ inches
Adolf Spohr Collection, Gift of Larry Sheerin
NA.203.140

ability, and were men to whose authority the people were accustomed. They directed the people on their journey and required them to move quietly so that the buffalo would not become alarmed. . . . In an ordinary hunt the party was divided into two sections, each led by about five aki´cita under whose direction they surrounded the herd, and at whose command they plunged into the chase. Those who were to chase the buffalo took the saddles from their horses. Every man had his arrows ready with the special mark so he could claim the animals he killed. It was like a horse race. As soon as the man shouted "Ready!" they were off, and you could see nothing but dust. The men who had fast horses tried to get the fastest buffalo. Each man tried to get the best possible animals as his trophies of the hunt.[44]

Men did the preliminary butchering of the buffalo, removing the hide whole by cutting along the stomach rather than the back if it was to be used in making a tipi cover. They wrapped the meat in hides and packed it on their horses' backs to take it back to camp for the women to finish cutting and preparing for drying. Women who were good riders sometimes accompanied men on the hunt to help with butchering and tend the horses as they were loaded with the meat.

Turtle Lung Woman said that when the men were successful in a hunt they came home singing the Buffalo Song. She and the other women joined in. They went to butcher the carcasses after they sang. They were the ones who laid claim to their husband's kill. They skinned the buffalo shot by their husband's or son's arrow. They knew from the way the shaft was decorated whose arrow it was. Once they identified it, the carcass belonged to them. They could do with it as they wished. It provided them with material to make new things or to repair old ones.[45]

Curly Bear Wagner of the Blackfeet also has described the butchering and preparation of the buffalo meat.

One of the first things we did when we killed the buffalo, we took a little bit of the buffalo blood in a buffalo horn spoon and we drank that. The reason why we did that is because the buffalo being the strongest critter out on the plains, we wanted his strength; we wanted his spirit within us to make us strong. We honored him that way. . . . The hump of the buffalo was cut and very often cooked right on the spot. It was very tender meat, a very good meat, the best portion of the buffalo. This was given to our elders and our people to be eaten right on the spot.[46]

Spiritual leaders and those with special powers guided the buffalo hunt from beginning to end. They were charged with knowing the locations, assisting the scouts in finding buffalo, or calling the buffalo closer to the camps. They provided prayers and ceremonies to ensure success in the hunt—that the men would return with sufficient meat, plenty for their families and for those in need, and that they would not be injured. Finally, as the feasts of fresh meat took place, the

Man's Hair Ornament
Amoskapi Pikuni (Blackfeet), Northern Plains, ca. 1880
Eagle feathers, ermine skin and fur, brass tacks, wool cloth, glass beads, rawhide; 37 ⅜ x 4 inches
Gift of Mr. and Mrs. Irving H. "Larry" Larom
NA.203.21

people gave thanks for gifts provided by the buffalo. Curly Bear Wagner describes those feasts as celebrations.

> Our people are great story tellers. After the utensils are put away, they may point to the man down there. He may tell of the hunting experience. This story may last three hours and then go on to the next person and tell of a war experience. These stories would last and go on until the early hours of the morning. . . . So, this was a very meaningful and happy event.[47]

Men were also celebrated for their roles as warriors in protecting the land and its people. Tribal cultural values supported military traditions. The role of men as warriors was idealized with specific attributes. Shooter of the Lakota described this idealized male role to Frances Densmore.

> The best part of a man's life is between the ages of 18 and 33. Then he is at his best. He has the strength and ability to accomplish his aims. He is brave to defend himself and others and is free to do much good. He is kind to all, especially to the poor and needy. The tribe looks to him as a defender, and he is expected to shield the women. His physical strength is at its best. He is light on his feet and can reduce long distances to short ones. He is taught true politeness and is very gallant.[48]

It is difficult to estimate the level of warfare that occurred among Plains Indian peoples prior to the eighteenth and nineteenth centuries. The Euro-American presence on the continent began to influence life on the Plains in the seventeenth century, at first indirectly through the introduction of horses and displacement of Native peoples in the east. Throughout the eighteenth century, the new waves of Native emigrants onto the Plains were accelerated by population pressures in the east and by the availability of horses, which made the buffalo hunting way of life more attractive. With the accessibility of firearms acquired at Euro-American trading posts, buffalo hunting became more efficient and competition for hunting territories intensified. As immigrant trails, military forts, and, then railroads and Euro-American homesteads and towns advanced on the Plains during the nineteenth century, intertribal rivalry increased as peoples struggled to protect their homelands and obtain buffalo and other food they had always depended upon. Many tribes also fought against the Euro-American military and colonizers, while others allied with them against traditional tribal enemies. Contributing to the hostilities in the last half of the nineteenth century was the dwindling number of buffalo, which were almost totally annihilated by commercial hide hunters. Native hunters had to travel further from their home territories to find remnants of the scarce herds, bringing them into conflict with other peoples.

During the eighteenth and nineteenth centuries, up until reservations were established, warfare and its attendant preparations, ceremonies, and traditions were elements of the daily life of Plains Indian people. Boys were taught the skills

White Man Runs Him—Apsaroke
Crow Reservation, Montana, 1908
Photograph by Edward S. Curtis (1868–1952)

White Man Runs Him was a Crow warrior, a traditional leader, and a scout attached to the military in the 1870s warfare against the Lakota and Cheyenne. After the Crow were settled on their reservation in Montana, he lived near Lodge Grass and served as a diplomat and delegate for the Crow, making many trips to Washington. One of his grandchildren is Joe Medicine Crow, tribal historian and author.

of warfare just as they were taught the skills of hunting so they would confidently assume their essential future roles as warriors. They also celebrated their first accomplishments in battle. Two Leggings recalled in describing his first killing of an enemy.

> I sang my first victory song. Taking his warbonnet out of its rawhide case I put it on my head and danced around his body. I never thought that a Piegan might surprise me. I was only a boy and now I had my first coup. I sang and thanked the Great Above Person. I danced until the sweat ran down my body. . . .

Buffalo Robe
Lakota (Sioux), Northern Plains, ca. 1870
Tanned buffalo hide and hair, pigments;
78 ½ x 69 ¾ inches
Chandler-Pohrt Collection, Gift of Mr. William D. Weiss NA.203.377

The painting on this robe depicts warriors wearing eagle feather bonnets and mounted on horseback, fighting several men on foot. Some of the warriors are using firearms. Tribal stories describe such battles in which warriors gained advantage because they possessed either horses or guns.

We were singing as we walked into the village, and I held a long willow stick with my scalp tied to the end. For two days and nights the women danced the scalp dance and my name was spoken as the one who had taken revenge on the Piegans.[49]

Much of the warfare occurred through raids for horses—or retaliations for such raids—so individuals and the group could increase their wealth in these essential animals.

I remember when parties of our men used to go afoot from the Black Hills far southward to get horses. Each man took along only his lariat rope, his bows and arrows, his sheath-knife, a little package of dried meat, and two or three extra pairs of moccasins tucked into his belt. Their women were sad in heart as they made these moccasins, for sometimes, the travelers were gone a whole year, or sometimes they were killed.[50]

Men achieved glory in war through counting coup—striking or touching an enemy with their hand or weapons. Almost any heroic deed in battle could count as a coup, but those which occurred within an enemy camp were considered most important. Among the Cheyenne, examples of coups included being the first to locate an enemy, saving a wounded tribesman, having a horse shot out from under a rider, and charging a group of enemies alone. The actual killing and scalping of enemies were also considered coups, although they were not as

Painted Hide
Lakota (Sioux), Northern Plains,
late nineteenth century
Tanned deer hide, pigments, 48 x 41 inches
Gift of Robert G. Charles NA.702.4

This painted hide, showing a battle between
Lakota warriors and Army soldiers, depicts the
Battle of Little Bighorn. Warriors, some on
horseback and others dismounted, are killing
many soldiers, with several depicted as already
wounded or dead. The artist included a tipi village in the lower left and General Custer standing armed with two revolvers. He also painted
several American flags and Army rifles that
have fallen on the ground, and officers, indicated by their shoulder insignia, and non-com-
missioned officers, identified by chevrons on
their sleeves.

highly ranked as touching without harming them. Men were ranked according to their total number of coups and their abilities to successfully lead war parties.[51]

Plenty Coups said that for a Crow warrior to count coup he had "to strike an armed and fighting enemy with his coup-stick, quirt, or bow before otherwise harming him, or take his weapons while he was yet alive, or strike the first enemy falling in battle, no matter who killed him, or strike the enemy's breast-works while under fire, or steal a horse tied to a lodge in an enemy's camp."[52] Plenty Coups said that the first warrior named was the most honorable and that achieving such coups was an indication of bravery A warrior who had counted coup would wear an eagle feather in his hair as a mark of distinction, perhaps one for each coup he counted. If a warrior was wounded while counting coup, he wore an eagle feather painted red to show that he had bled.[53]

Joe Medicine Crow wrote of the Crow tradition of counting coup that "It was the object of every man to win as many coups as possible, for all social priv-ileges and perquisites depended on this achievement."[54] His grandfather Medicine Crow, whose name is more accurately translated "Sacred Raven," had counted many coups and achieved the traditional ranking of chief at the age of twenty-two through the completion of all Crow military requirements. Joe Medicine Crow lists these requirements:

1. To touch or strike the first enemy fallen, whether alive or dead. This was called "counting coup."

2. To wrestle a weapon away from an enemy warrior.

3. To enter an enemy camp at night and steal a horse. Prized war or hunting horses were usually tied to the door of a tepee, or even to the wrist of he owner who was sleeping inside. This feat was called "cutting the halter rope."

4. To command a war party successfully. The warrior was given this command only after completing the other three requirements. If he brought his party back safely and victoriously, he earned a war deed.[55]

Medicine Crow was also a visionary and in later years was an effective reservation leader who traveled frequently to Washington as a diplomat on behalf of the Crow people. Joe Medicine Crow also achieved all the requirements of a chief during his military service in Germany in World War II. By that time, the Crow system of naming chiefs based upon military achievements was no longer practiced.

Men wore clothing that was functional in hunting and war parties and carried shields for their practical and spiritual protective powers. To prepare for hunting and fighting, they made and maintained their weapons and ensured that they were spiritually smudged and blessed. Their horses that were to be used in battle were also blessed by individuals with horse medicine. The men of specific warrior societies had their own prescriptions they followed in preparation and during battle. Eagle Shield described the preparations made by the Lakota Crow-Owners Society:

> When going to war each man carried his crow-skin necklace in a rawhide case and before putting it around his neck he passed it over the smoke of burning sweet grass. Feathers for head decoration were also carried in this case. Eagle Shield said that before a fight the warriors would always put on their finest regalia, so that, if they were killed, they would die in a manner worthy of their position. The sleeves of the war shirts were not sewed, but were tied together under the length of the arm. Before a fight the warrior untied these fastenings and threw back the sleeves to permit free use of his arms.[56]

Men recorded their accomplishments in hunting and warfare through paintings on hides, tipi liners, tipi covers, and their own shirts and leggings. Accompanied with the oral retelling of these accomplishments, such paintings provided biographies of individual men and tribal histories. Paintings on buffalo robes, elk, and deer hides with natural pigments emphasized the action of the story, with figures engaged in battle, chasing and killing buffalo, and other scenes. Individuals and tribes were identified through specific clothing, hair styles, moccasins, shields, and accoutrements. Since the focus was on the narrative action, backgrounds and landscapes were omitted.

TOP: Spotted Horse,
Tsistsistas (Cheyenne), Plains
Ledger Drawing, late nineteenth century
Pencil, crayon, watercolor, and ink on paper;
8 ¾ x 5 ⅝ inches
27.78.3

This self-portrait of Spotted Horse is one of seventy-one drawings depicting episodes in his life. In this drawing, he portrays himself on horseback, wearing his eagle feather bonnet and carrying his distinctive painted and feathered shield, a rifle, and a lance.

Galloping, Littleman, Kiowa, or Sweetwater
Tsistsistas (Cheyenne), Fort Supply, Oklahoma
Ledger Drawing, December 1894–January 1895
Pencil, ink, and crayon on paper;
5 ⅝ x 8 ⅝ inches
Gift of Mr. and Mrs. Joseph M. Katz
48.59.63

Galloping, Littleman, Kiowa, and Sweetwater were four Southern Cheyenne scouts attached to Fort Supply and Fort Reno in Oklahoma. Their drawings are combined in one book with no individual attribution. In this drawing, the artist represented a warrior riding his horse into a volley of shooting rifles. He is hanging onto the side of his horse to avoid being hit and shooting his own rifle. He has a sword by his side and carries a feathered shield. His horse has notched ears and its tail is tied up with red cloth and feather.

The drawings of Galloping, Littleman, Kiowa, and Sweetwater depicted battles, ceremonies, courting, hunting, and camp scenes as well as new invaders to Cheyenne lands—cattle and Euro-Americans.

Wooden Leg Drawing Events from Battle of Little Big Horn, ca. 1927
Northern Cheyenne Reservation, Montana
Photograph by Thomas Marquis (1869–1935)
Thomas Marquis Collection PN.165.1.49

Wooden Leg, a Northern Cheyenne warrior who fought at the Battle of Little Bighorn, told his life story to Thomas B. Marquis, an agency physician for the Northern Cheyenne, in 1922 when he was seventy-three years old. In this photograph, Wooden Leg is shown drawing a scene from the battle in a ledger book.

As buffalo hides became scarce, men turned to new materials to record their biographical experiences. Pencils, ink pens, watercolors, and crayons replaced the natural pigments and stick and bone brushes formerly used in hide painting, and men drew their accomplishments in scenes on canvas, muslin and paper. Painted and decorated canvas and muslins were sometimes used as tipi liners, and, as tribes were settled on reservations in log houses, muslin paintings served as wall liners in much the same manner. From the 1860s until the 1930s, Plains warriors illustrated their battle exploits in biographical drawings in ledger and sketch books acquired from trading and military posts. Many of the muslin and ledger drawings were created for sale to collectors, scholars, and others interested in Plains Indian life.

Some of the ledger books were collected directly by U.S. cavalry soldiers on battlefields and from tipis during raids on Plains Indian villages.[57] Other ledger drawings were produced by prisoners of war and scouts employed by the military. A group of Kiowa, Cheyenne, and Arapaho men confined as prisoners at Fort Marion on St. Augustine, Florida from 1875 to 1878 created a distinctive set of ledger drawings which were sold to tourists and other interested visitors.[58] This work and others from the reservation period dealt with subjects beyond hunting and warfare, such as camp and courting scenes, images of cattle, and Sun Dances and other ceremonial scenes. The Fort Marion ledger art integrated drawings of trains, steamboats, and Florida scenes along with more traditional subjects.

Four Southern Cheyenne ledger book artists—Galloping, Little Man, Kiowa, and Sweetwater—served as army scouts at Fort Supply and Fort Reno in western Oklahoma from 1884 to 1894. As members of Company B at Fort Supply, a company that consisted only of Indian scouts, they were ranked as privates. Like other skilled Cheyenne warriors and horsemen, they had made the transition to military life, perhaps considering it a more attractive life than the farm work promoted by reservation Indian agents and missionaries. As privates, they lived with their families in their own camps at Fort Supply and drew comparable wages to other enlisted men. The images of these Southern Cheyenne ledger drawings consist of battle and hunting scenes, as well as Sun Dance, courting, and other camp subjects.

Plains Indian men also produced other types of art derived from dreams and visions. Such visionary art was often drawn on tipi covers, drums, and rawhide shields and their tanned hide shield covers. Men often sought spiritual guidance from individuals with special medicine and powers in interpreting such dreams and visions and in illustrating them. For tipi covers, they also sought help from

Shield Cover

Apsáalooke (Crow), Northern Plains, ca. 1860
Tanned deer hide, pigments, glass pony beads, rawhide, wool cloth, flicker feather;
21½ inches diameter
Chandler-Pohrt Collection, Gift of Mr. and Mrs. Edson W. Spencer, NA.108.105

The painting on this shield cover shows a bear emerging from a cave into a barrage of bullets. This design has been copied at least three times and is represented in shields in other museum collections. Sometimes Crow men copied shields with especially powerful designs to be given as gifts or traded.

family members who would produce the drawings under their direction.

Men created powerful images on shields and shield covers to provide spiritual as well as physical protection in battle. Grinnell described the shield as the most important part of a Cheyenne warrior's equipment.

> Most shields were believed to possess strong spiritual power. It might exercise in behalf of him who carried it not only the general protective influence due to its sacred character but it might also imbue him with those qualities attributed to the heavenly bodies, birds, mammals, and other living creatures whose images were painted on it, or portions of which were tied to it. It might afford also protection from the elements, for some shields were sacred to the thunder and to the lightning.
>
> A shield adorned with the feathers of the eagle was believed to give its owner the swiftness and courage of that bird. If the feathers of the owl were tied on it, the man perhaps shared the owl's power to see in the dark, and to move silently and unnoticed. The figure of a bear painted on the shield, or its claws attached, gave him the bear's toughness.[59]

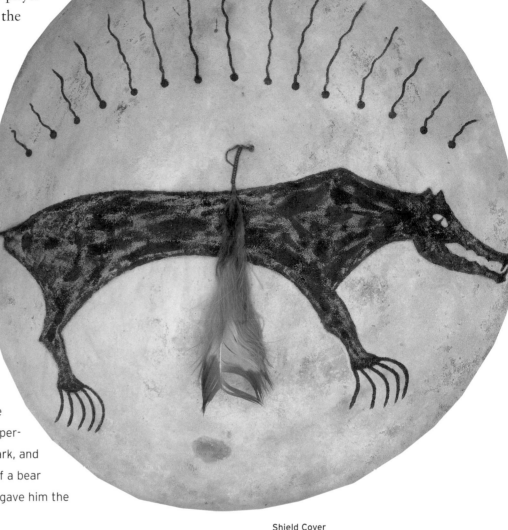

Shield Cover
Apsáalooke (Crow), Northern Plains, ca. 1860
Tanned deer hide, pigments, rawhide, glass pony beads, feathers; 20 inches diameter
Adolf Spohr Collection, Gift of Larry Sheerin
NA.108.15

Men painted their shields with images of powerful beings such as the grizzly bear so they might carry their protection and strength into battle. The image of this bear emphasizes its powerful jaw, teeth, and claws.

Men sought spiritual guidance in the construction of the shield. Every step of the process—heating the circular piece of rawhide from a buffalo bull to shrink and thicken it, creating the tanned deer or antelope hide cover, painting the symbols and other images, and attaching feathers—was guided through smudging with herbs, prayers, and ceremonial singing. Men were also taught the special care that such a powerful shield required. Shields made by nineteenth century warriors that remain in museum and private collections even now carry the inherent powers of their owners and their spiritual protectors.

The near decimation of the buffalo herds of the North American Plains by the 1880s brought the free lives of Native warriors, hunters, and their families—so interwoven with that of the buffalo—to an end and brought the people new challenges. The period of time during which these cultures flourished in the

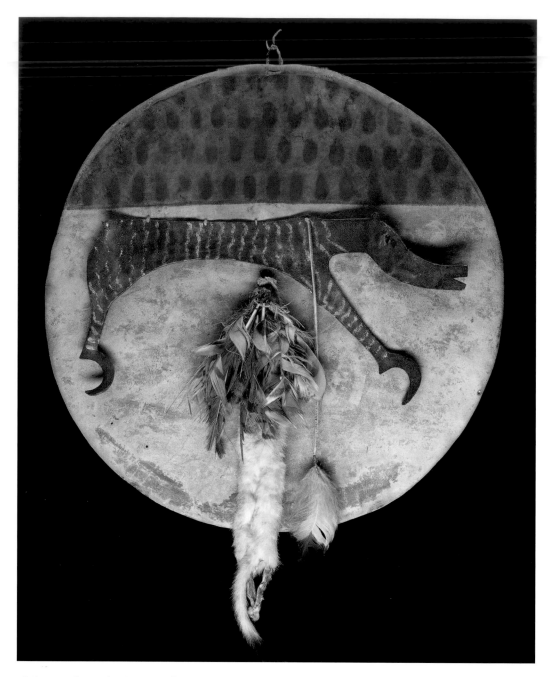

Art was integral to men's lives as warriors and hunters. Visionary experiences prepared men for war and inspired the designs of their shields, shield covers, and other equipment. In addition to the image of a bear, this shield is also embellished with an ermine or winter weasel hide. Weasel hides often decorated men's shirts, feather and horn bonnets, leggings, shields, and war clubs. The animals were admired as fierce fighters and they were known to be good war medicine.

The painted image of the standing grizzly bear on this shield cover symbolizes the bear's inherent strength.

eighteenth and nineteenth centuries was a unique and remarkable era in American history, one still commemorated by descendants of the people who lived through them. As buffalo are restored to reservation lands and tribes and individuals seek to preserve language and cultural traditions, it is heartening to consider and remember Plains Indian people of earlier times and their relatives, the buffalo, and the intrinsic strength, creativity, and courage that characterized their lives. ✪

1. The song is quoted in Alice C. Fletcher, assisted by James R. Murie, *The Hako: Song, Pipe, and Unity in a Pawnee Calumet Ceremony.* Twenty-second Annual Report of the Bureau of American Ethnology (Washington, DC: U.S. Government Printing Office, 1904; reprint, Lincoln and London: University of Nebraska Press, 1996), p. 305. Pawnee scholar James R. Murie provided the translation of this song about the promise of the buffalo. Tahirüssawichi, a Pawnee priest, provided the song and other elements of the Calumet Ceremony recorded by Fletcher during her and Murie's research in 1898–1901.

2. Ibid, p. 81. The Calumet Ceremony, called *Hako* by Murie and Fletcher, was a prayer for children. It was held to ensure that the Pawnee people would increase and be strong and would have long lives and be at peace.

3. Joseph Medicine Crow, interview with author, January 20, 2000.

4. Lone Man in Frances Densmore, *Teton Sioux Music,* Bureau of American Ethnology Bulletin 61 (Washington D.C.: Smithsonian Institution, 1918), p. 66.

5. John Fire Lame Deer and Richard Erdoes, *Lame Deer: Seeker of Visions* (New York: Simon & Schuster, 1972), p. 119.

6. Ibid.

7. John C. Ewers, *Plains Indian Sculpture: A Traditional Art from America's Heartland* (Washington D.C.: Smithsonian Institution Press, 1986), pp. 123–125.

8. Ibid, pp. 149–150.

9. Densmore, *Teton Sioux Music,* p. 175

10. Ibid.

11. Morgan Baillargeon and Leslie Tepper, *Legends of Our Times: Native Cowboy Life* (Vancouver, British Columbia, Canada and Seattle, Washington, U.S.A.: UBC Press and University of Washington Press, 1998), p. 41. Hugh A. Dempsey, "Blackfoot," *Handbook of North American Indians, Plains,* Vol. 13, Part 1 (Washington, D.C.: Smithsonian Institution, U.S. Government Printing Office, 2001), p. 606.

12. Alfred W. Bowers, *Mandan Social and Ceremonial Organization* (Chicago: University of Chicago Press, 1950; reprint, Moscow, Idaho: University of Idaho Press, 1991), pp. 315–328; Alfred W. Bowers, *Hidatsa Social and Ceremonial Organization,* Bureau of American Ethnology Bulletin 194 (Washington D.C.: Smithsonian Institution, 1965; reprint, Lincoln and London: University of Nebraska Press, 1992), pp. 433–466. George Catlin, *Letters and Notes on the Manners, Customs, and Conditions of the North American Indians: Written During Eight Years' Travel (1832–1839) amongst the Wildest Tribes of Indians in North America* (New York: Wiley and Putnam, 1844; reprint, New York: Dover Publications, 1973), p. 127.

13. See George Catlin, *O-kee-pa, A Religious Ceremony, and Other Customs of the Mandans* (London: Trubner and Company, 1867; reprint, New Haven, Connecticut: Yale University Press, 1967, John C. Ewers, ed.), pp. 54–55; Catlin, *Letters and Notes on the Manners, Customs, and Conditions of the North American Indians,* pp. 155–177; Bowers, Mandan Social and Ceremonial Organization, pp. 111–163.

14. Dempsey, "Blackfoot," p. 606.

15. Joseph Medicine Crow, *From the Heart of the Crow Country: The Crow Indians' Own Stories* (New York: Orion Books, 1992), pp. 86–87.

16. Gordon Reid, *Head-Smashed-In Buffalo Jump* (Calgary, Alberta: Fifth House Press, 2002), p. 10.

17. Reid, *Head-Smashed-In Buffalo Jump,* pp. 16–17.

18. Dempsey, "Blackfoot," p. 607.

19. Frank B. Linderman, *Red Mother: The Life Story of Pretty-Shield, Medicine Woman of the Crows* (Rathway, New Jersey: The John Day Company, 1932; reprinted as *Pretty-Shield; Medicine Woman of the Crows,* Lincoln: University of Nebraska Press, 1974), p. 49.

20. Thomas B. Marquis, "Iron Teeth, A Cheyenne Old Woman," *Cheyenne and Sioux: The Reminiscences of Four Indians and a White Soldier* (Stockton, California: University of the Pacific, 1973), p. 53.

21. Baillargeon and Tepper, *Legends of Our Times: Native Cowboy Life,* p. 48.

22. Gilbert L. Wilson, *Waheenee: An Indian Girl's Story: Told by Herself to Gilbert L. Wilson* (St. Paul Minnesota: Webb Publishing Company, 1927; reprint, Lincoln and London; University of Nebraska Press, 1981), p. 73.

23. John C. Ewers. *The Horse in Blackfoot Indian Culture: With Comparative Material from Other Western Tribes,* Bureau of American Ethnology Bulletin 159 (Washington, DC: Smithsonian Institution, 1955), p. 3; Herman J. Viola, *After Columbus: The Smithsonian Chronicle of the North American Indian* (Washington, DC: Smithsonian Institution, 1990), pp. 60–61. Ewers provides detailed information based upon historical documentation concerning the diffusion of the horse among the Blackfoot and other Plains peoples (pp. 3–19).

24. Preston Holder, *Hoe and the Horse on the Plains: A Study of Cultural Development Among North American Indians* (Lincoln and London: University of Nebraska Press, 1970), pp. 90–107.

25. Quoted in Ewers, *The Horse in Blackfoot Indian Culture,* p. 16.

26. Medicine Crow, *From the Heart of the Crow Country,* p. 101.

27. Baillargeon and Tepper, *Legends of Our Times: Native Cowboy Life,* p. 25.

28. Thomas B. Marquis, *A Warrior Who Fought Custer* (Minneapolis: Midwest Company, 1931; reprinted as *Wooden Leg: A Warrior Who Fought Custer,* Lincoln: University of Nebraska Press, 1957), p. 5.

29. Densmore, *Teton Sioux Music,* p. 337

30. Peter Nabokov, *Two Leggings: The Making of a Crow Warrior* (New York: Thomas I. Crowell, Publishers, 1967), pp. 191–192.

31. Frank B. Linderman, *American: The Life Story of a Great Indian, Plenty-coups, Chief of he Crows* (Rathway, New Jersey: The John Day Company, 1930; reprinted as *Plenty-coups, Chief of the Crows,* Lincoln: University of Nebraska Press 1962), p. 100.

32. In Frances Densmore, *Teton Sioux Music,* p. 298. *Siná lúta* is described by Densmore as a strip of red cloth that would be fastened around the horse's neck.

33. Lakota Horse Society song in Frances Densmore, *Teton Sioux Music,* p. 299.

34. E. Adamson Hoebel, *The Cheyennes: Indians of the Great Plains* (New York: Holt, Rinehart and Winston, 1960), p. 92.

35. Delphine Red Shirt, *Turtle Lung Woman's Granddaughter* (Lincoln and London: University of Nebraska Press, 2002), pp. 129–130.

36. Ewers, *The Horse in Blackfoot Indian Culture,* p. 29.

37. Marquis, "Iron Teeth, A Cheyenne Old Woman," p. 58,

38. Medicine Crow, *From the Heart of the Crow Country,* p. 103.

39. Ibid.

40. Densmore, *Teton Sioux Music.* p. 237

41. Luther Standing Bear, *My Indian Boyhood* (Boston: Houghton Mifflin, 1931; reprint, Lincoln and London: University of Nebraska Press, 1988), pp. 176–177.

42. Nabokov, *Two Leggings: The Making of a Crow Warrior,* pp. 6–7.

43. Ibid, pp.189–190.

44. Densmore, *Teton Sioux Music,* p. 442.

45. Red Shirt, *Turtle Lung Woman's Granddaughter,* p. 17.

46. Curly Bear Wagner, interview with the author, January 20, 2000.

47. Ibid.

48. Densmore, *Teton Sioux Music,* p. 178.

49. Nabokov, *Two Leggings: The Making of a Crow Warrior,* p. 36.

50. Marquis, "Iron Teeth, A Cheyenne Old Woman," p. 53

51. Hoebel, *The Cheyennes: Indians of the Great Plains,* p. 70.

52. Linderman, *American,* p. 55.

53. Ibid, pp. 55–56.

54. Medicine Crow, *From the Heart Of The Crow Country,* p. 42.

55. Ibid, p. 45.

56. Densmore, *Teton Sioux Music,* pp. 319–320.

57. See Jean Afton, David Fridtjof Halaas, and Andrew E. Masich, *Cheyenne Dog Soldiers: A Ledgerbook History of Coups and Combat* (Denver: Colorado Historical Society, 1996) for the history and interpretation of Southern Cheyenne drawings collected at the Summit Springs fight in 1869.

58. Karen Daniels Peterson, *Plains Indian Art from Fort Marion* (Norman: University of Oklahoma Press, 1971), pp. 63–73. *Plains Indian Drawings 1865–1935: Pages from a Visual History,* Janet Catherine Berlo, ed. (New York: Harry N. Abrams, Inc., 1996), p. 14.

59. George Bird Grinnell, *The Cheyenne Indians: Their History and Ways of Life,* Vol. 1 (New Haven: Yale University Press, 1923), pp. 187–188.

The Buffalo as Part of the Mandan-Hidatsa Way of Life

GERARD BAKER

My father, the late Paige Baker, Sr., whose Mandan name is "Sacred Horse," and my mother Cora, whose Indian name is "Sweet Grass," told many stories of the importance of buffalo in our culture. My father was fluent in the Mandan, Hidatsa, and English languages, and my mother is fluent in Hidatsa and English. I am a member of my mother's Clan, Apukawika. One of the first stories I remember hearing about the buffalo was a story of a man that went on a fast on top of Singer Butte, now known as the Killdeer Mountains. This is in western North Dakota, approximately ten miles from the Fort Berthold Indian Reservation, where I grew up on our cattle ranch. A fast takes place when an individual goes to a sacred area, many times on a high hill, and prays for four days and nights. The entire four days is devoted to prayer, day and night, with no sleep, water or food. Sometime within the four days, the individual could either get visited by a spirit that will give him or her direction, or the person may hear or experience something beneficial. This man had gone up for the required days and saw in his vision that the buffalo were coming out of the hole, as they have always done since time began. My father said that he was told that this could indicate two primary events—that the buffalo were still populating the earth, which indicated the people's survival as well.

In this vision, this man saw very few buffalo coming out of this area and the ones that were coming out were very, very poor and thin. After he had come back from his vision, he prayed, as he believed this was a bad omen that they should pray to forestall. After this man was leaving this area with his companions, they saw one lone buffalo, and as a people that are always looking for the opportunity to get food for the people, they hunted and killed it. What they found surprised them—they said the buffalo was very thin and poor and when they opened it up to prepare the meat, they found nothing in the stomach but a ball of clay earth. The man told the others that his vision was indeed real and this only proves it, as this buffalo must have come out of the hole on top of the mountain. It also had extremely soft hoofs, indicating that this was a "new" buffalo, so soft one could press finger marks into its flesh. To some, this indicated the demise not only of the buffalo, but also of a way of life for the Village Indians known as the Mandan and Hidatsa.

The buffalo played a major role in all facets of life from the time of creation for these tribes that lived in earth lodge villages along the Knife and Missouri Rivers. The Mandan and Hidatsa were at one time very strong independent nations made up of many earth lodge villages. In the late 1700s and early 1800s, these villages numbered five and were located in two types of villages, winter and summer. Winter villages are located along and in the river bottoms for protection of the cold, and the summer villages are on higher terraces. The residents of these villages were a well organized group, with many people living in one fortified village complex that could have more than 100 earth lodges and several hundred people within the high cottonwood palisades. These agricultural people, like other nations on the Northern Plains, had various organizations such as Clans and Societies to help govern them. The Clans were matrilineal—children were born into their mothers' clans and remained in that clan their entire lives, whereas the Societies were age-grade organizations and an individual advanced into Societies as he or she aged and fulfilled the obligations of each. Admittance was gained into a Society by two primary means, through purchase or inheritance. A person did not have to belong to the same Society, although most did, but also had the opportunity to join other Societies.

The tribes had many ceremonies centered on the Creation Beings of the earth, the Creator, the Cultural Heroes, and others, who had saved mankind countless times. The ceremonies were done throughout the year for various needs. The buffalo played a major role in many of the stories and ceremonies. Even in some of the creation stories the buffalo and the "buffalo name" are very important in not only identifying locations, but also for successful buffalo hunts. Some ceremonies were also meant to assure that the buffalo would always be on earth to help their human relatives. In the Earth Naming Ceremony, for example, there were four buttes that were said to be known as the "Buffalo Spirit Places." These four are "Buffalo Comes Out Butte," "Singer Butte," "Buffalo Home Butte" and "Rosebud Butte." These buttes were located mostly in the western part of the tribe's territory and were identified by the Creators when they made this land. The buttes are very well defined, but due to many circumstances, they are no longer utilized as they once were. While on summer hunts, the men would take offerings to the buttes—sometimes a buffalo skull with eagle feathers as offerings for a successful hunt and to ask the buffalo to keep returning. As I understand it, they would also leave some additional medicine at the various buttes and collect them after the hunt.

The buffalo played a role in the older men's Buffalo Bull society which had many responsibilities, including teaching young boys to be adults through learning the prayers, hunting skills, and the making of implements used in the hunt and for warfare. The famous Mandan Ceremony, the O-Kee-Pa, had the buffalo as a major element in one part of the ceremony called the "Buffalo Calling Ceremony." This ceremony is very difficult to explain, as there have been many changes to our Societies since the arrival of "modern" religions. At this time, all life in these villages had been learned from the Creator and his helpers, the buffalo and others. The various ceremonies that the non-

Indian saw and reported on were extremely different from the European way of life and religion. What the foreign visitor thought to be risqué and improper was very important to the tribes for their future existence. Lewis and Clark, George Catlin, and others described one part of the Buffalo Calling Ceremony as immoral because at one point during this ceremony, a wife is given to an older man to assure success in warfare, plentiful buffalo, and successful hunts in coming years and assuring that the tribe will live on. The entire O-Kee-Pa ceremony is a four day event, with the Buffalo Calling Ceremony taking place in one evening. Dressed up as buffalo, the men would imitate the buffalo in mock fights and in their breeding season.

As all tribes, we believed that the buffalo had a spirit and at one time in our early creation, we learned that like all of the animals that the Creator made, the buffalo could talk. The stories that are still passed down to younger generations were meant as teaching stories and there was always a lesson in each story, even the humorous ones. Stories about the Bison and the Coyote's adventures, as an example, would tell many a lesson about greed. This is a brief version of the story that tells of the hunger of the Trickster, Coyote and the Buffalo Bull. The Coyote through his greed tricked the buffalo into going over the cliff and getting killed, just so the Trickster could prepare and eat all the buffalo. The Trickster then chases away the other animals so they wouldn't eat his food. In the end, the Trickster is so tired from butchering that he starts to fall asleep on a rock. This was caused by buffalo and the rock. To stay awake Coyote puts sticks in his eyelids, but he sticks to the rock anyway. All the other animals come and once they discover that he is stuck to the rock, they eat up the buffalo. The message is, of course, that if you get greedy, in the end you will lose. In the end of most of the stories, the buffalo come back to life and goes to on to live another day.

If a person were to fast and have a buffalo give him or her medicine, that was highly respected. The buffalo represented strength, wisdom, fierceness, and bravery,

and the people believed that the buffalo taught them a lot. All buffalo parts were used in many ways, from tipi covers, to bed covers in the Earth lodge, robes, war shields, food, clothing, tools, and games. The list goes on and on. Many of the older men would also make hats to wear for dancing. At one time in our history, an individual had to have the right to wear and use these materials. Today, with many mixed feelings and beliefs, people young and old wear parts of the buffalo in their dance outfits.

The buffalo is making a comeback. The elders in my family have told me, "The buffalo is like us Indians. The white man put us on reservation, like the buffalo in a zoo, they also killed our game and degraded our ceremonies and our way of life." But they add that we will never go away, and neither will the buffalo. We still need them and we still need to recognize the spirits through ceremony.

Many of our ceremonies regarding the buffalo are gone because of the introduction of smallpox that came to our villages on two occasions, the first in 1782 and the last one in 1837. Along with the arrival of the European trade, that further introduced elements that contributed to the decline of our nation. The last two factors that helped decimate the tribes were the introduction of organized religion and the U.S. government. Representatives of organized religions believed that the Indian people were worshipping false gods and that the animals did not have spirits. Many times, they forcibly took our medicine bundles, even some of our buffalo bundles, and either burned them or sold them to museums across America. The U.S. government's role included but was not limited to forced education and relocation of entire tribes to Indian reservations. These actions resulted in the loss of many aspects of our culture.

Many tribes, including the Mandan, Hidatsa and Arikara of the Fort Berthold Reservation, now have a very healthy herd of buffalo that once again roam parts of our homeland and reservation. We utlize and sell the meat and bi-products, and also use the

Buffalo Mask
Nueta (Mandan), Northern Plains, ca. 1860
Buffalo hide, horns, rawhide, wood; 19 ¼ x 11 inches
Chandler-Pohrt Collection, Gift of Mr. William D. Weiss
NA.203.359

This type of mask was worn during the Mandan Okipa ceremony. During the four-day summer ceremony, men danced the Buffalo Dance during which they wore buffalo masks and impersonated buffalo bulls. The Okipa Ceremony brought the buffalo herds closer to the village and ensured the success of the hunt.

buffalo for tourism activities. The buffalo and the spirit of the buffalo are still very important to the tribe. We believe and hope that in this day, we all once again will look to the buffalo as a survival tool for our generations to come, not only as a food source, but more importantly as a spiritual source that once again will strengthen us and the generations to come.

The white man's government promised that if we, the Shoshones, would be content with the little patch allowed us, it would keep us well supplied with everything necessary to comfortable living, and we would see that no white man should cross our borders for our game, or for anything that is ours. But it has not kept its word! The white man kills our game, captures our furs, and sometimes feeds his herds upon our meadows. And your great and mighty government. . . . It does not protect us in our rights. It leaves us without the promised seed, without tools for cultivating the land, without implements for harvesting our crops, without breeding animals better than ours, without the food we still lack, after all we can do, without the many comforts we cannot produce, without the schools we so much need for our children.

—WASHAKIE[1]

Honor and Celebration

4

Washakie, the long-lived leader of the Eastern Shoshone people, thus protested to John W. Hoyt, governor of Wyoming Territory, in July, 1878. At the time, the Eastern Shoshone were struggling to retain reservation lands assigned to them in the Wind River Valley through the Fort Bridger Treaty of 1868—a treaty of peace between the Shoshone, Bannock, and the United States—and to compel the government to fulfill other requirements of the treaty.

The land itself, a variable terrain populated with diverse plants and animals, had economic and spiritual significance to the Shoshone people. They had long camped along the Big and Little Wind Rivers and the Popo Agie and hunted elk, mule deer, and big horn sheep in the mountainous areas and antelope on the plains and plateaus. The people traveled seasonally north and east of the reservation to the Big Horn and Powder River Basins to hunt buffalo and gather needed plant foods and to Fort Bridger to trade. Under the Fort Bridger Treaty, the Shoshone retained the right to hunt off reservation lands and were promised an agency, schools for their children, annuities, and allotment of lands, seeds, and farm implements to heads of households. Under the Brunot Treaty of 1872, the Shoshone had lost additional lands. Beginning in March, 1878, they were required to share their Wind River Reservation and its scarce rations with the Northern Arapaho.[2]

Throughout his life, Washakie had demonstrated and reinforced his credentials as a Shoshone leader through his accomplishments as a hunter and as a war-

Shirt
Lakota (Sioux), Northern Plains, 1870s
Tanned deer hide, pigment, human and
horse hair, glass beads, porcupine quills;
42½ x 58 inches
Adolf Spohr Collection, Gift of Larry Sheerin
NA.202.598

This shirt belonged to the Oglala Lakota leader
Red Cloud, who had achieved the ranks of
"shirt wearer" in the 1860s and chief in the
1870s. Red Cloud's position and responsibilities
among the Lakota are symbolized by the elaborate embellishment of the shirt, with two hundred and thirty-eight locks of human hair and
sixty-eight locks of horse hair, all wrapped in
porcupine quills and attached with thongs decorated with large faceted beads. Little Wound
appears to be wearing this shirt in the photograph of the 1880 Lakota delegation to
Washington, D.C.

rior in battles against the Crow, Ute, Arapaho, and Blackfeet. He had also served as a scout for the U.S. Army in campaigns against the Lakota in the 1870s. Washakie's life, which spanned most of the nineteenth century, corresponded with many changes and turbulence for Shoshone people. When he was born in approximately 1804–1810, the Shoshone then were living as free buffalo hunters on the Plains.[3] By the time he died in 1900, he had experienced the final disappearance of the buffalo in the 1880s, concomitant losses and adjustments in tribal culture and traditions, and the escalating reduction of available territory and resources as increasing waves of gold miners and settlers trespassed into Shoshone lands and treaties were signed to alleviate resultant conflicts.

When he was recognized by the federal government as principal chief of the Eastern Shoshone, Washakie assumed the role of reservation leader and diplo-

Sioux Delegation in Washington, Red Dog, Little Wound, Red Cloud, American Horse, Red Shirt, John Bridgeman, interpreter (standing)
Washington, D.C., June 1880
Vincent Mercaldo Collection P.71.831.1

Native political leaders who were delegates to Washington, D.C. were often attired in Euro-American clothing for meetings with the President and government representatives. This photograph shows leading men of the Lakota wearing a mixture of Euro-American and Native clothing. Little Wound is wearing the shirt identified as belonging to Red Cloud, while Red Cloud wears a cotton shirt, vest, and pants.

mat. Out of the necessity of dealing with the U.S. government, he and other late nineteenth-century Plains chiefs created a new style of political leadership. Many of these leaders, sometimes called "reservation chiefs," became convinced that their old ways of life were disappearing and they accepted the necessity of negotiating with government representatives to preserve their lands, support their people, and enforce the treaties. They also learned that their new style of political leadership required seemingly inconsistent qualities of perseverance and outspokenness, diplomacy and tact, and, often, accommodation and conciliation.

When the Northern Arapaho were settled with the Shoshone on the Wind River Reservation in March, 1878, the United States government failed to provide additional rations or other accommodations that had been promised for their support. Black Coal of the Northern Arapaho, who also met with Governor Hoyt in July, 1878, echoed Washakie's concerns.

> This was the country of my fathers, now dead and dying. When, last fall, we saw the Great Father, we asked for either this place, the country along the Sweetwater, or that about Fort Laramie. It was agreed we should come here. . . . We promised the Great Father several things and we have kept our word. We have come to the place given us and have behaved like good Indians. We have made friends with the Snakes and the Utes, and we shall see the Crows and make peace with them. But the government has been slow in fulfilling its promises to us. The government promised us a separate agency: but we are still under the Shoshone agent. . . . When we came from Washington, General Crook told us he would come out in the spring and see that everything was made right. But he has not come, and many things, you see, are not right. We have many children. We love our children. We very much want a good school house, and a good man to teach our children to read your language, that they may grow up to be intelligent men and women, like the children of the white man.[4]

Like Washakie, Black Coal had distinguished himself as a warrior and leader of war parties. The Northern Arapaho had allied with the Lakota and Northern Cheyenne in war against Euro-American incursions into their territories in 1865–1868. Later, Black Coal encouraged Northern Arapaho warriors to serve as Army scouts in campaigns against the Lakota and Northern Cheyenne in 1876–1877. He acted as a spokesman for the Northern Arapaho to the federal government when they resisted settlement with their Southern Arapaho relatives in Indian Territory (Oklahoma) and requested a separate reservation in Wyoming. In 1877, Black Coal traveled with a delegation of Northern Arapaho leaders to meet with President Rutherford B. Hayes and other government officials to remind them of the Northern Arapaho's service as scouts and to express the tribe's unwillingness to move south. Although the Northern Arapaho did not receive their own separate reservation or agency, they remained in Wyoming, where they were settled on the Wind River Reservation.

Chief Washakie
Wind River Reservation Wyoming, 1883–1885
Baker & Johnston Studio
Vincent Mercaldo Collection P.71.761.1

Washakie holds a pipe with a stem decorated with hair and wears an eagle feather bonnet with a trailer. He also holds a rifle across his lap. When this photograph was made, Washakie was an established leader and a representative of the Eastern Shoshone in negotiations with the United States government.

Black Coal was a significant band leader of the Northern Arapaho, as were Sharp Nose and Friday. In the eyes of government officials, however, he became the principal chief of the Northern Arapaho, a position he held until his death in 1893, when Sharp Nose assumed that office. Late nineteenth-century chiefs and leaders such as Washakie, Black Coal, and Sharp Nose served as intermediaries between the United States government and its representatives and their own people and consequently sometimes found themselves in contradictory positions as they tried to satisfy the needs of both parties.

In their separate presentations to Governor Hoyt, both Washakie and Black Coal strenuously insisted that the needs of their people be met and the requirements of treaties and agreements be fulfilled. At the same time, they reassured the governor that they were "good Indians" who wanted to settle down to live as farmers and send their children to school where they would learn to speak and read English. As skillful negotiators, they had learned how to communicate with government authorities to receive the concessions they required. However, as traditional chiefs they demonstrated to their own tribal members that they supported their interests and, additionally, embodied in their personal lives the prerequisites of Plains leadership—success as warriors and hunters, fortitude, bravery, moderation, and generosity, demonstrated through the redistribution of material goods. Related to these qualities were personal power and supernatural blessings acquired through the intercession of spiritual beings, which made it possible for men to excel and accrue their many successes.

Men's Paths to Honor

> How I wished to count coup, to wear an eagle's feather in my hair, to sit in the council with my chiefs holding an eagle wing in my hand.
>
> —Plenty Coups[5]

As a respected man of many accomplishments, Plenty Coups fulfilled his desire to be a prominent leader and a man of great influence, to wear an eagle feathered bonnet, and to carry an eagle wing fan at tribal ceremonies as insignias of honor and distinction. Plains Indian men like Plenty Coups achieved prestige through their exploits in war by counting coups and through the hunt by providing food for their families and for those in need. As they accumulated more honors and accomplishments, they might be given the authority of leading hunting and war expeditions, which made them responsible not only for the success of the undertaking but also for the safety of all the participants. Such leadership tended to be fluid and was neither permanent nor absolute, and leaders were continually required to demonstrate their influence and abilities as warriors and hunters. With age and experience, men could rise to the level of band headmen or chiefs, which brought additional responsibility for looking out for the well-being of their followers.

The role of chief among Plains Indian people has often been misconstrued by Euro-American representatives and government officials, who wanted to deal with one leader who had absolute authority to negotiate and sign treaties on behalf of entire tribes. In practice, however, such leaders made major decisions by consulting with other senior advisors to arrive at a consensus and, consequently, to ensure the support of their followers.

The path to political leadership for Plains Indian men required participation in warrior societies—associations that trained and encouraged warriors, organized war expeditions, and celebrated victorious outcomes. Among the Cheyenne, there were six military associations open to any boy old enough to go to war, each with their own distinctive organization and symbols: Fox (or Kit Fox), Elk (or Elk-horn Scrapers), Shield, Dog, Bowstring, and Crazy Dog.[6] The societies were responsible for policing and carrying out the decisions of the chiefs, although they also advised leaders on matters related to peace and war, movement of camps, and details of the buffalo hunts. They maintained order on buffalo hunts and when bands traveled, they built the medicine lodge for the annual Sun Dance, and sponsored their own dances.[7] Wooden Leg described the warrior societies as "the foundation of tribal government among the Cheyennes."[8]

Cheyenne Chief Two Moon, at Fort Keogh
Fort Keogh, Montana, ca. 1879
Photograph by L.A. Huffman (1854–1931)
P.100.1950

The Northern Cheyenne war leader Two Moon fought in the Battle of Little Bighorn in 1876, but surrendered with his band at Fort Keogh in April, 1877, where they remained until the Tongue River Reservation was established in 1884. He later served as an Army scout and a reservation leader who traveled to Washington, D.C. in 1888 and in 1914, three years before he died. In this photograph, he wears an eagle feather bonnet with a magnificent trailer.

> I joined the Elk warriors when I was fourteen years old. We were camped then at Antelope creek near the Black Hills. Their herald chiefs were going about the camp circle calling, "All Elk warriors come for a dance and a feast." They were gathering at a large tepee made of two family lodges combined into one. Left Handed Shooter, at that time leading chief of the Elks, came to my father's lodge and said to me: "We want you to join the Elk warriors."
>
> Oh how important I felt at receiving this invitation! I had been longing for it, waiting to be asked, wishing I might grow older more rapidly in order to get this honorable standing already held by my father and my two older brothers. Seventy or more Elks were dancing. Occasionally one fired a gunshot into the air. As they danced they were scraping their "rattlesnake sticks," the special emblem of Elk membership. Each of these sticks was made of hard wood, in the form of a stubby rattlesnake seven or eight inches long. On each stick was cut forty notches. Another stick was used for scraping back and forth along the notches. The combined operation of many instruments made a noise resembling the rattlesnake's warning hum. Each member owned his personal wooden stick, but there was one made from an elk horn that was kept always by someone as a trustee for the society.[9]

Among the Lakota, besides other warrior societies there was a specialized soldier society, the *akicita*, that enforced laws and maintained order, especially during the summer buffalo hunt, the Sun Dance, and other large tribal gatherings. This association was open to any young man who had experienced at least one hunting or war expedition. Altogether there were six *akicita* societies—each

Shirt
Lakota (Sioux), Northern Plains, ca. 1880
Tanned deer hide, pigment, glass beads, human hair, wool cloth, thread; 33 x 22 inches
NA.202.205

with its own distinctive organization and ceremonies—a different one was chosen each year to police a band.[10] Black Elk described the role of the *akicita* in a buffalo hunt of his youth:

> Then we are started for where the bison were. The soldier band went first, riding twenty abreast, and anybody who dared go ahead of them would get knocked off his horse. They kept order, and everybody had to obey. After them came the hunters riding five abreast. The people came up in the rear. Then the headmen of the advisors went around picking out the best hunters with the fastest horses, and to these he said, "Good young warriors, my relatives. Your work I know is good. What you do is good always; so today you should feed the helpless. Perhaps there are some old and feeble people without sons, or some who have little children and no man. You shall help these, and whatever you kill shall be theirs." This was a great honor for young men.[11]

Black Elk was describing how able young men were encouraged to be generous by giving buffalo meat to people in need. Besides being good hunters and warriors, Plains Indian men who hoped to become leaders had to demonstrate their generosity by sharing food and other resources, lending horses to those who needed them, and by assisting the elderly. Among the Lakota, such leaders belonged to the Chief Society, made up of men aged forty or over who served as a governing council and in turn selected seven chiefs known as *wicaŝitancan,* "leaders of men." These seven chiefs delegated authority to four younger men who were known as *wicaŝayatanpi,* or "praiseworthy men." These men were also called "Shirt Wearers" because of their distinctive symbol of office, a shirt fringed with human, and sometimes horse, hair.[12] According to Hassrick, such embellishments of hair on a shirt symbolically represented the people for whom the wearer had responsibility.[13] Older leaders presented the shirts, which were decorated with representations of the warriors' individual war exploits, to the Shirt Wearers in a formal ceremony. They were expected to lead in battle and to act for the well-being of all the people.[14]

Together the Chiefs Society, the seven chiefs, and the Shirt Wearers appointed four men, *wakicunze,* who, working through the *akicita,* were responsible for organizing and controlling the camps. All such leaders governed through consensus and influenced policy and decisions made through councils.

For the Cheyenne, leadership was vested in the Council of Forty-four, a tribal council of peace chiefs representing all of the bands. All the peace chiefs were proven warriors, but upon being named a peace chief, a man was required to resign his membership in a military society. Such peace chiefs were characterized by the attributes of wisdom, courage, generosity, and a concern for the well-being of the people. Most importantly, although they previously may have been aggressive warriors, as peace chiefs they were expected to be even-tempered and good-natured in their deliberations.[15]

Among some Plains peoples such as the Hidatsa, Mandan, and Arapaho, males and females followed separate paths through hierarchical stages or societies from childhood to old age. Through this progression, individuals accumulated knowledge and skills as well as prestige and authority in both sacred and secular matters and accompanying expectations of appropriate behavior for each stage of life. Age-graded systems for males of these tribes consisted of a series of military societies, each with its own name, symbols of membership, ceremonies, songs, dances, rights, and responsibilities. The societies reflected the fact that warfare was interwoven with ceremonial and spiritual life.

Hidatsa boys entered this system at about thirteen to sixteen years of age, when a group of age peers collectively purchased their membership in the Stone Hammer Society, an association characterized by the distinctive ceremonial war clubs decorated with hawk and eagle feathers that its members carried.[16] When

Sitting Bull (Tatanka Iyotake) and Family
Fort Randall, Dakota Territory, ca. 1883
Cabinet photograph by John Pitcher Spooner, ca. 1887, most likely reprinted from a photograph
P.69.1844

The famed Hunkpapa Lakota political, military, and spiritual leader Sitting Bull consistently defended tribal lands against Euro-American encroachment and after 1868 led a united resistance against the United States military. Inspired by a Sun Dance vision, he led his followers to victories against the United States military at the Battles of the Rosebud and Little Bighorn in July, 1876. In this photograph, Sitting Bull's mother, Her Holy Door, is seated to his right and his daughter, Many Horses is seated with her son to his left. Standing are his two wives, Seen by the Nation (left) and Four Robes (right).

Dance Shield

Brule Lakota (Brule Sioux), South Dakota, ca. 1890

Tanned deer hide, yellow ochre, wood, hawk and other feathers, wool cloth, horsehair; 20 inches diameter

Gift of Dr. Harold McCracken NA.502.14

OPPOSITE: **Dance Shield Cover**

Lakota (Sioux), South Dakota, ca. 1890

Tanned deer hide, pigments, eagle feathers, wool cloth, dyed horse hair; 19¼ inches diameter

Gift of Corliss C. and Audrienne H. Moseley NA.502.3

Nineteenth-century warriors recorded their achievements in paintings on buffalo robes, tipi covers, shields, and shield covers. The painting on this dance shield depicts a warrior on horseback wearing an eagle feather bonnet with long trailer counting coup on another man armed with firearms. Carrying such a shield in a dance proclaimed the owner's accomplishments.

Wolf Chief joined the Stone Hammer Society at the age of sixteen, an older member told him, "The Stone Hammers are the first society; and they are the first in war, for you are now young and vigorous. Sometimes young men who want to see a vision, have a vision of a stone hammer; such a man always gets to strike an enemy with a stone hammer. For this Stone Hammer society is a very sacred organization."[17] As a part of the several-day-long transfer ceremony through which aspirants acquired membership in the organization, the older boys taught the younger society dances and songs.

The Black Mouth Society, characterized by a distinctive painting of the members of the organization, was an intermediate association between youth and old age which maintained order at ceremonies and carried out the decisions of the tribal council about movement of the camp and tribal buffalo hunts.[18] Wolf Chief recalled that Black Mouth Society members were the police of the village.

I remember quite well when I was about eight years old, seeing these Black Mouths come around ordering a clean-up. They all came together in a little crowd and went around calling:

Ankle Trailers

Apsáalooke (Crow), Northern Plains, ca. 1870
Skunk hide, canvas, wool cloth, glass beads, tanned deer hide, yarn; 46 x 12 inches
Katherine Bradford McClellan Collection, Gift of The Coe Foundation NA.203.356

Men wore specialized regalia in their society dances such as this set of ankle trailers made of decorated skunk hide.

Roach Headdress and Spreader
Osage, Oklahoma, ca 1890
Dyed deer hair, turkey beard,
cloth; 13½ x 2¼ inches
Dr. Robert L. Anderson Collection
NA.203.12A/B

Men in warrior societies wore
roaches made of deer, horse,
badger, turkey neck, and porcupine guard hair, on their heads as
symbols of war honors and as a
part of Grass Dance regalia. The
roach was spread and secured by
a hide thong passing through a
roach spreader of bone, elk antler,
or wood. An attached eagle
feather waved above the roach
with each of the dancer's movements.

"You women, go and clean up outside of your lodges!" These Black Mouths had all the lower part of their faces painted black and very often, although it was not necessary, the upper part of the face was painted red. . . . As the Black Mouths passed, every woman came out with a basket and native-made broom and swept up the debris about her lodge into the basket. This she carried down to the bank of the Missouri and emptied it over the bank.[19]

The ultimate association for Hidatsa men was the Bull Society, limited to men with sacred bundles and rights related to the buffalo. The Bull Society conducted the buffalo dances that took place four times a year and during the Okipa Ceremony.[20]

As Hidatsa men progressed through each society and recorded achievements as warriors and war leaders, they received increasing public praise, rights, and honors. Some became village or band chiefs or members of tribal councils—positions held by men who had shown they could govern through consensus, participate in tribal ceremonies, and act with generosity, good judgment, and kindness to the elderly. In retrospect, Wolf Chief described his early training as "equivalent to a wagon drawn along a deeply-rutted road; there was no way to get out of the road except by going forward in the same path as others had done before—one could make no progress backing up, and the depth of the ruts prevented one from taking a different course."[21]

The Mandan age-graded societies closely resembled that of the Hidatsa, with whom they had lived in close proximity on the Missouri River and within the same village, Like-a-Fishhook, since 1845.[22] The smallpox epidemics of 1782 and 1837 which nearly annihilated Mandan and Hidatsa populations disrupted their cultures and affected the composition of the societies.[23]

The Arapaho considered an individual's life a journey through four significant stages or hills of life: childhood, youth, mature adult, and old age. They believed old age to be a supernatural blessing and accomplishment; thus, it was

Dance Stick
Oto, Central Plains, ca. 1875
Wood, mirror; 25 x 3¾ inches
Chandler-Pohrt Collection, Gift of Mr. William D. Weiss NA.203.373

Men carried dance sticks and mirror boards as accessories imbued with spiritual powers during the Grass or Omaha Dance. This dance stick with a mirror is carved with the profiles of two facing horses, emphasizing the significance of the horse and horse raiding to Plains warriors.

Horse Dance Stick
Lakota (Sioux), South Dakota, ca. 1890
Wood, pigment; 33½ x 5¼ inches
Adolf Spohr Collection, Gift of Larry Sheerin NA.502.4

Men sometimes carved horse dance sticks in honor of favorite horses that had been wounded or killed or had performed heroically in battle. This horse dance stick is composed of a horse head carved at one end and the horse's leg and hoof for the handle. In the middle of the stick are three triangular marks signifying the wounds suffered by the horse in battle.

OPPOSITE: **Mirror Bag**
Apsáalooke (Crow), Montana, ca. 1900
Tanned deer hide, glass beads, wool cloth; 9⅛ x 5 inches
Adolf Spohr Collection, Gift of Larry Sheerin NA.109.55

Face paints and other supplies for dances and special occasions were stored in mirror bags. Men carried these finely beaded bags as part of a formal ensemble or dance accessories.

important to seek and cultivate the good will of elders throughout one's lifetime. Parents asked elders to choose their children's names and to participate in ceremonies and prayers at various stages to ensure that they would have successful lives. Youth deferred to elders, gave them gifts, and sought their advice in spiritual matters and other spheres of life, while older people were expected to assist, instruct, and indulge young people. Elders monitored the behavior of younger Arapaho and encouraged them in the cultural values of bravery, generosity, and level-headedness by publicly recognizing those who demonstrated those characteristics. In ceremonial and social celebrations, older women often sang songs that praised individuals for achievements and bravery in warfare and expressed approval for accomplished leaders.[24] According to Kroeber, old age was characterized by the red pigment made from red earth and tallow that elders applied to their faces for ceremonies. "Old people confine themselves to red exclusively, so that red paint is often symbolic of old age."[25] The very physical appearance of these elders reminded those around them of their central role in the security and welfare of the people.

Beginning in adolescence, Arapaho males organized into age sets of peer groups and progressively passed through a series of seven ceremonial lodges, including two for youth, four for adult men, and one for elders. These lodges in the order in which they were entered were the Kit Foxes, Stars, Tomahawks, Spears, Crazies, Dogs, and Old Men. As men progressed through each of the lodges, they accumulated increasing sacred knowledge and were responsible for teaching younger men at the levels below their own. Membership in the lodges, each with its own regalia, dances, and songs, also had secular connotations. Men who had achieved war honors and led war expeditions also were leaders within their lodges. Membership in a lodge was required for participation in war parties.[26]

Elders who entered the Old Men's lodge, the seventh grade comprised of men who no longer went to war, were considered the definitive authorities in ceremonial and spiritual matters They were instructed by a group known as "Water-Pouring Old Men" which held a status above all other Arapaho, based upon their experience and knowledge of sacred matters. This group of seven elderly spiritual leaders, who had earned honors through personal ordeals and sacrifices and were keepers of the seven tribally owned men's medicine bags, were ultimately responsible for directing all tribal ceremonies.[27] Such elders also had other influence because Arapaho chiefs consulted with them and relied upon them for public support.[28]

Through military societies and lodges, Plains men prepared for and celebrated their victories in battle with special ceremonies, dances, and songs. When the tribes were confined to reservations and the buffalo had been nearly exterminated, men no longer had opportunities to hunt and go to war, and the functions of the societies and lodges became less relevant in those arenas. The age-grade

societies of the Arapaho and Hidatsa had broken down by the early twentieth century. Men, however, continued to celebrate their past victories and achievements as warriors through the Grass Dance.

The Grass Dance originated in an Omaha dance that had spread across the Plains before 1860 and developed into a society that celebrated and honored the role of men as warriors among several tribes in many variations. By 1880, the Grass Dance had been adopted by tribes from the Southern to far Northern Plains.[29] Each of the societies had its own songs, dances and dance practices, specialized clothing, regalia, and accessories. Men carried dance shields painted with images imparting spiritual power and protection, and dance sticks decorated and carved with images of vanquished enemies or horses taken in raids. Men often carved dance sticks in the images of favorite horses that had carried them into battle and had, perhaps, suffered wounds. They also carried dance mirrors, reminiscent of the mirrors they had used as warriors to signal to other members of a war party, as a way to reflect light as they danced.

Spiritual Guidance Through Visions

The path to leadership also required supernatural protection and blessings that men received through visions or dreams. As a young man, Plenty Coups undertook a vision quest in an isolated high place of the Crazy Mountains. The vision he had, earned through fasting and personal sacrifice, significantly influenced his life and, because of his prominence, also affected the lives of many other Crow people. This vision first came to him through a spiritual intermediary in the form of a buffalo bull which transformed into a man and images of many buffalo.

> Out of the hole in the ground came the buffalo, bulls and cows and calves without number. They spread wide and blackened the plains. Everywhere I looked great herds of buffalo were going in every direction, and still others without number were pouring out of the hole in the ground to travel on the wide plains. When at last they ceased coming out of the hole in the ground, all were gone, all! There was not one in sight, anywhere, even out on the plains. I saw a few antelope on a hillside, but no buffalo—not a bull, not one calf, was anywhere on the plains.
>
> I turned to look at the Man-person beside me. He shook his red rattle again. "Look!" he pointed.
>
> Out of the hole in the ground came bulls and cows and calves past counting. These, like the others, scattered and spread on the plains. But they stopped in small bands and began to eat the grass. Many lay down, not as a buffalo does but differently and many were spotted. Hardly any two were alike in color and size. And the bulls bellowed differently too, not deep and far-sounding like the bulls of the buffalo but sharper and yet weaker in my ears. Their tails were different, longer, and nearly brushed the ground. They were not buffalo. These were strange animals from another world.

Chief Plenty Coos and Daughter

Plenty Coups with Adopted Daughter
Crow Reservation, Montana, ca. 1915-1920
P.42.27.3

Plenty Coups understood through his vision that he would never have sons or daughters of his own, although as a leader he considered himself responsible for the well-being of all Crow people. He adopted Crow children and encouraged Crow youth to go to school to get an education, and to return to the reservation to protect Crow lands and interests in negotiations with the federal government. In this photograph, Plenty Coups wears a traditional Crow leader's insignia of an eagle feather bonnet and hide shirt decorated with beadwork and ermine and carries a blanket with beaded blanket strip. Mary Man with a Beard (1910–1921), his adopted daughter, wears a traditional Crow-style elk tooth dress and beaded leather belt.

I was frightened and turned to the Man-person, who only shook his red rattle but did not sing. He did not even tell me to look, but I did look and saw all the spotted-buffalo go back into the hole in the ground, until there was nothing except a few antelope anywhere in sight.[30]

During this vision quest, other revelations came to Plenty Coups. He saw the image of an old man sitting in the shade of a grove of trees near a spring. He experienced a strong wind storm that destroyed many trees, leaving only one standing. In this tree was a nest of a chickadee, a bird Plenty Coups described as wise rather than physically strong, and which learned by observing the successes and failures of others. A voice told him, "Develop your body, but do not neglect your mind, Plenty-coups. It is the mind that leads a man to power, not strength of body."[31]

After his vision experience, Plenty Coups was guided by elders to understand that the spotted buffalo represented cattle of the white men who would inevitably dominate the Crow homelands. The chickadee became Plenty Coups' personal medicine. To him it represented the Crow people, a small nation surrounded by many enemies. He believed that in order for the Crow to survive, they were required to seek peace with the whites, develop their minds, listen, and learn like the chickadee. He understood that the old man of his vision was Plenty Coups himself, who eventually built his home near the spring of his revelation and lead the Crow through the transitions of the late nineteenth and early twentieth centuries until his death in 1932.

Joe Medicine Crow, who as a young man knew Plenty Coups—an associate of his grandfather Medicine Crow—described the Crow concept of a vision quest as a way to achieve supernatural power through "animal emissaries of the First

Eagle Headdress
Apsáalooke (Crow), Northern Plains, ca. 1870
Golden eagle head and body, buffalo hide and hair, brass bells and buttons; 11 x 26 inches
The Irving H. "Larry" Larom Collection
NA.203.168

The man who wore this distinctive headdress carried with him the power and supernatural protection of both the buffalo and the eagle—significant creatures of the earth and sky with great spiritual significance to Plains Indian people.

Eagle Feather Bonnet
Amoskapi Pikuni (Blackfeet), Northern Plains, ca. 1860
Golden eagle feathers, wool cloth, ermine, brass tacks and bells, horse hair, rawhide, wood, porcupine quills; 31 x 8¼ inches
Chandler-Pohrt Collection, Gift of Mr. and Mrs. Richard A. Pohrt NA.203.357

This style of bonnet, distinctive to the Blackfeet, was made of a crown of eagle feathers standing straight up in a rawhide headband that was covered with red cloth and decorated with pieces of ermine skin. Other pieces of ermine hang down on each side. Only a few respected leaders wore such bonnets, which were imbued with supernatural protection, during battles, ceremonies, or in dress parades. The design for the bonnet was said to have originated in a vision experienced by Many Tail Feathers at the time of the last Blackfeet buffalo jump.

Maker (or Great Spirit)" that would assist a man in becoming a better warrior and, eventually, becoming a chief.[37]

> The Crow called this spiritual experience "Going Without Water." It was basically a fasting supplication. Through suffering from exposure to the elements, from the pangs of thirst and hunger, and from the pain of blood sacrifice (cutting off a finger and bleeding into unconsciousness), the faster hoped to gain the pity of the animal spirits (the Ones Without Fires). Thus to receive an early "visit" by them and to be given instructional dreams and visions were the sure signs of "receiving the Baxbe, the Sacred Power."[33]

Among the Lakota, the vision quest is called *hanbleceya*, meaning, "crying for a vision." A vision quest was undertaken under the supervision and guidance of a man who had already achieved the sacred capability to gain power or understand dreams, or to predict the results of hunting or war expeditions. A male's first vision quest normally was undertaken during adolescence, although he could pursue such spiritual revelations as often as he felt necessary throughout his life.[34]

Not all Plains tribes practiced the vision quest, although dreams and revelations came to men, and women, under other special circumstances. Sometimes such visions brought curative powers from spiritual emissaries such as eagles, hawks, elk, deer, and buffalo, which taught the individual how to heal people. Such healers were also greatly respected among Plains Indian people.

According to Joe Medicine Crow, the vision quest was voluntary for Crow men who wished to become successful warriors. Others went directly to a veteran warrior or chief with medicine or special power and obtained his blessings by paying a certain fee.[35]

One can still identify rows of stones marking vision quest sites of the nineteenth century in remote and mountainous locations of the Crow reservation. Seven of these "fasting beds" are located on Dryhead Overlook in the Pryor Mountains and are thought to have been used by Plenty Coups, Medicine Crow, Two Leggings, and four other Crow men in the 1860s.[36] In his remembrance, Plenty Coups said that three of his closest friends accompanied him on his early vision quest, each separating to go to his own fasting bed once they reached the mountains. In addition to the nineteenth-century vision quest sites, other such places constructed by young Crow men in more recent years can be identified in the Pryor and Crazy Mountains.[37]

Medicine Crow is reported have undertaken at least three vision quests to gain the spiritual power to become an accomplished warrior and eventually a chief. Like Plenty Coups, his visions were prophetic and included images of the railroad that would much later come to the region, large numbers of white men who told him they would in time dominate Crow territory, and white men's houses and cattle.[38] Like other Crow young men, he trained to become a warrior by going on expeditions where he gained valuable experience and achieved honor

Eagle Feather Bonnet
Apsáalooke (Crow), Montana, early twentieth century
Eagle feathers, glass beads, ermine hide and fur, horsehair, dyed porcupine quills; 24 x 17 inches
The Crow Indian Collection of Dr. William and Anna Petzoldt, Gift of the Genevieve Fitzgerald Estate NA.203.934
This eagle feather bonnet was given to the Baptist missionary Reverend William A. Petzoldt by White Man Runs Him in 1928, one year before he died. A former Army scout in campaigns against the Lakota and Cheyenne, in his later years he traveled far beyond the Crow Reservation to appear at celebrations, parades, fairs, and dedications, where he was often photographed.

and recognition as a leader in warfare. Like Washakie, Black Coal, and Plenty Coups, these accomplishments served to reinforce Medicine Crow's authority in the late nineteenth century as a reservation chief and leader.

Specialized clothing, regalia, insignia, and other symbols of office signified the honors, abilities, and status of the men who wore them. An eagle feather was a mark of distinction, the highest honor that a Plains Indian man could attain, although the feather's specific symbolism—whether painted, cut, or worn in a particular manner—varied among tribes. As Plenty Coups described when he was preparing for his first vision quest, eagle wing fans were carried by prominent distinguished men in tribal councils. When such older men of the Arapaho carried eagle wing fans, which have an origin deeply rooted in tribal traditions, they were "for the good of all the tribe."[39]

Eagles were considered the most powerful birds that flew highest in the sky and warriors were encouraged to emulate them by demonstrating their strength, abilities, and valor in battle. The Northern Cheyenne elder John Stands In Timber recalled, "They say an eagle can take in nearly the whole world with his eyes, and see it as clearly as a man looks at the ground by his feet."[40] The eagle itself was symbolic of the thunderbird, the creature of the sky that controlled the storms. Because of eagles' inherent physical and spiritual powers, only certain men undertook their capture, an endeavor that required not only stealth and strength, but also dedication, fasting, prayers, and spiritual assistance.

An eagle feather bonnet created from the bird's tail feathers and often elaborated by a magnificent flowing trailer of many feathers is among the most recognizable of Plains Indian icons and, in the popular imagination, considered representative of all Native Americans. Distinguished warriors and leaders wore such feathered bonnets as symbols of their own personal acts of bravery or of the combined war honors of many men in their tribe. Men wore eagle feather bonnets in battle to inspire bravery, remind other men of past war honors, and summon supernatural power to defeat the enemy. The feathers of the bonnet were considered by the Lakota to hold the protective power of the eagle, which prevented men from being hit by bullets or arrows.[41]

Wooden Leg recalled that eagle feather bonnets were not worn by all warriors, but only a few distinguished men in each Cheyenne warrior society. Such men were experienced and skilled fighters, some of whom had been told by distinguished senior warriors and leaders that they had earned the rights to wear eagle feather bonnets.

The act meant a profession of fully acquired ability in warfare, a claim of special accomplishment in using cunning and common sense and cool calculation coupled with the bravery attributed to all warriors. The wearer was supposed never to ask mercy in battle. If some immature young man pretended to such high standing before it seemed to his com-

panions that he ought to do so, he was twitted and shamed into awaiting his proper time. I
first put on my warbonnet when I was thirty-three years old, fourteen years after I had
quit the roaming life. After a man had been accepted as a warbonnet man he remained so
throughout his lifetime.[42]

According to Wooden Leg, the eagle feather bonnet was not a symbol of
office but represented a man's fighting ability. Although war chiefs and tribal
chiefs often wore such feathered bonnets, some particularly modest but very
capable and bravest men did not. As a protective device connected to warfare, a
man made his own feather bonnet, although his wife, mother, or sister made the
beaded brow-band.[43]

After tribes were settled on reservations, distinguished men continued to
wear eagle feather bonnets as symbols of their achievements and to remind people of their tribal histories. As Lakota and Cheyenne men wearing eagle feather

Shirt

Lakota (Sioux), Northern Plains, ca. 1885
Tanned deer hide, glass beads, dyed porcupine
quills, human hair, yellow and green pigments;
34½ x 22½ inches
Gift of Corliss C. and Audrienne H. Moseley
NA.202.267

bonnets performed in Buffalo Bill's and other Wild West shows in the United States and Europe in the late nineteenth and early twentieth centuries, their dramatic appearances became the public personifications of all Native people. This stereotypical image of Indian people has been reproduced in countless books and films. In more recent years, Indian leaders from outside of the Plains region have adopted eagle feather bonnets to represent their own accomplishments and to identify themselves as Native Americans. Plains Indian people also continue to honor their leaders in this way and to bestow eagle feather bonnets upon returning soldiers—most recently from wars in Afghanistan and Iraq—and other tribal members who have completed achievements.

Nineteenth-century Plains Indian men of honor wore shirts made of deer, elk, or antelope hides embellished with human and horsehair and decorated with strips of dyed porcupine quillwork or beadwork sewn on the shoulders and sleeves. Such shirts were symbolic of the wearers' accomplishments and positions within Plains societies. Some of the shirts exhibited paintings illustrating the war deeds of their owner—the coups counted, the horses captured, or the enemies defeated. As with the Shirt Wearers of the Lakota, the shirts themselves represented the fortitude, valor, and leadership of the men who wore them.

During the early reservation period as men were no longer actively involved in warfare, the decorated hide shirts were made by women for their male relatives to wear at ceremonial and social events. Chiefs and other leaders of tribal delegations sometimes wore the shirts when they conferred with government representatives in Washington, D.C., and other locations to indicate to all that they were men of honor and importance.

Among the Pawnee, Otoe, Omaha, Ponca, and Meskwaki, men wore bear claw necklaces as symbols of honor. Such necklaces were made from the long broad claws of grizzly bears that once roamed the Southern and Eastern Plains. The creation of such necklaces was specialized among the Pawnee and required attaching many claws to a circle of otter skin and sometimes elaborated with beadwork decorations. The otter also had spiritual significance—only honored men were allowed to wear the circle of hide that formed the base for the necklace. Plains Indian men held grizzly bears in high esteem because of their strength, power, and fighting abilities—qualities universally admired by Native warriors.

Other symbols of leadership came to Plains Indian men from sources outside of their cultures. When Plains nations came together to confer or trade, reciprocal gift exchanges served to establish relationships and to sanction agreements that occurred during the meetings. Early visitations between European representatives and traders followed this pattern, with gifts being presented to Plains Indian leaders in recognition of their positions and to establish and strengthen future relations. Representatives of the United States government also provided presentation objects of diplomacy—notably presidential peace medals and pipe

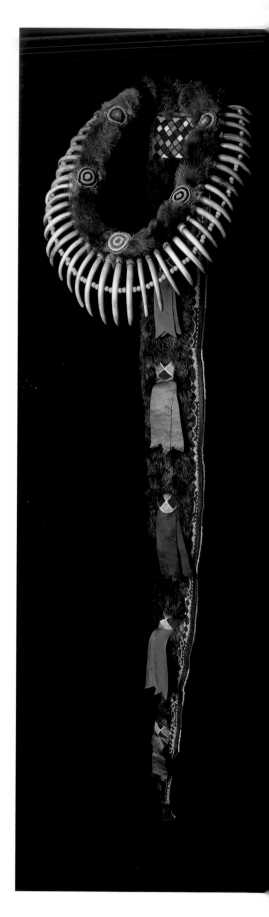

Pipe Tomahawk
Apsáalooke (Crow), Northern Plains, ca. 1865
Wood, iron, tanned deer hide, glass beads, wool cloth, ermine hide and hair, dyed horse hair, 43½ x 10 inches
Adolf Spohr Collection, Gift of Larry Sheerin
NA.504.1

European and American traders and government representatives presented pipe tomahawks to Plains chiefs and band leaders during visits and treaty negotiations and during meetings to establish trade. By the middle of the nineteenth century, firearms had become available to Native people and pipe tomahawks transitioned from weapons to ceremonial use. To Plains Indian leaders, pipe tomahawks were symbols of prestige often displayed in nineteenth century photographs of tribal delegations.

tomahawks—which were highly desired by Plains Indian men.

As a ceremonial weapon, the pipe tomahawk combined the significance of the pipe in Native spiritual practices with the symbolic importance of warfare. Pipe tomahawks were first manufactured by the English for Native American trade in the seventeenth century, followed by the French and Americans. The pipe tomahawks were introduced to Native peoples of the Plains by the earliest Euro-American expeditions to the region. Manufactured of steel, brass, or pewter, they had handles of ash, walnut, hickory, or maple. The pipe tomahawks sometimes were decorated by their Native owners with brass-headed tacks on the handles and attachments of cloth, beadwork, and other materials.

Women's Honors: Sacred Arts

The fact that women are the primary socializers of children underlies their duties as teachers of values, language, culture, world view, rituals, and practices, and underlies the beliefs and behaviors of the Lakotas. As Lakota women and men, we must constantly keep in mind the meaning of our word for children, the "sacred ones." By valuing the Lakota way and teaching it to our children, we will ensure that this lifestyle that we cherish will continue.

—Beatrice Medicine[44]

OPPOSITE: John Young Bear (1883–1960)
Bear Claw Necklace
Meskwaki, Tama, Iowa, ca. 1920
Bear claws, glass beads, otter hide, ribbon; 14 x 60 inches
Adolf Spohr Collection, Gift of Larry Sheerin
NA.203.213

A bear claw necklace is a symbol of power worn by a respected leader. The claws represent the bear's strength and courage, while the otter hide signifies power over both land and water. The animals' qualities guided the wearer during warfare, treaty negotiations, and other important events during his lifetime. This necklace, made by accomplished Meskwaki artist John Young Bear, is composed of otter hide and prairie grizzly claws and features a long hide trailer decorated with beautiful beadwork.

As men were respected for their achievements in hunting and warfare and as
leaders, Plains Indian women also were honored for caring for and instilling values in children, their work in the arts, and their roles in ceremonial life.[45] To a
great extent, the examples of material culture—primarily physical remnants of
nineteenth- and early twentieth-century Plains Indian life—now residing in museums and private collections were created by women. The artists who created
them were admired within their own tribes for their exquisite artistry in making
hide clothing and objects of daily or ceremonial use, which were embellished
with beautiful designs in porcupine quillwork and beadwork. More recently,
non-Indian scholars, artists, and art collectors have also developed an apprecia-

tion of the arts produced by Plains Indian women. Paradoxically, these women artists remain largely anonymous, since most of those who collected their works did not record their names.[46] Critical information about the role of art in the lives of nineteenth-century Plains Indian women as well as the details of their daily lives and their influence and positions in ceremonial and political areas also is still missing. Early ethnographers rarely recorded it, though whether because of a lack of interest or inability to communicate directly with women cannot be determined.

Women's societies or guilds devoted to the decorative arts fostered and encouraged excellence in tanning and working with hides, creating tipis and their furnishings, and in porcupine quillwork. Such societies operated in much the same way as men's societies, with their own ceremonies, initiations, feasts, and sponsored events. Also like the men's societies, these associations provided venues for recognizing and celebrating those women who had attained the highest level of achievement in their artistic production. For example, Cheyenne women who had tanned thirty buffalo robes and decorated them with porcupine quillwork or made a complete tipi by tanning and softening buffalo hides, fitting them together and sewing them, and preparing the lodge poles, were considered to be at the highest level of arts producers and, thus, worthy of special recognition.[47]

Membership in the societies was limited to experienced, knowledgeable, and skilled women who had reached significant artistic milestones. One of the most important societies, the women's quilling society, was dedicated to the production of the sacred arts—the ceremonial decoration in quillwork of buffalo robes

Child's Moccasins
Tsistsistas (Cheyenne), ca. 1890
Tanned deer hide, glass beads, rawhide;
6½ x 2½ inches
Adolf Spohr Collection, Gift of Larry Sheerin
NA.202.179

and other objects made of hides. Members of this association were expected to be highly moral and virtuous in their personal lives. Among the Northern Cheyenne, women were ranked within the society according to the degree of difficulty associated with the items they had produced, ranging from lowest degree to highest: moccasins, baby cradles, tipi decorations, buffalo robes, and tipi linings, back rests, and storage bags.[48] According to Grinnell, women considered quillwork "of high importance, and when properly performed, quite as creditable as were bravery and success in war among the men. The guild of quillers included the best women in the camp. Its ceremony and ritual have been handed down from mythic times."[49]

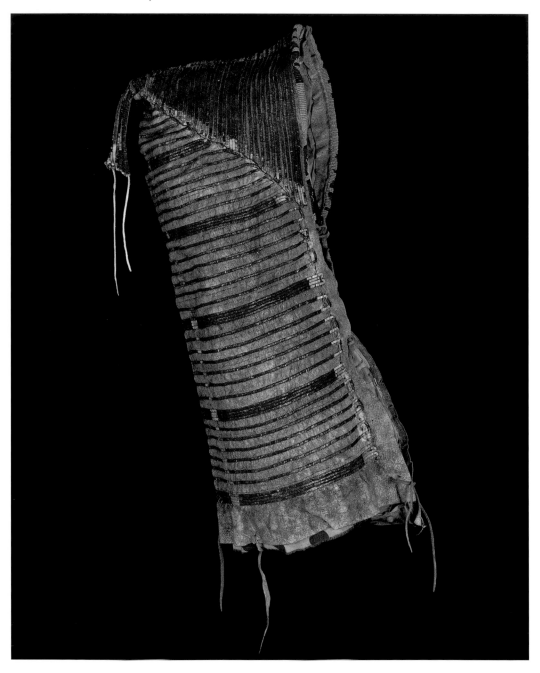

Cradle
Lakota (Sioux), Northern Plains, ca. 1880
Tanned deer hide, dyed porcupine quills, wool cloth, glass beads, feather; 25 x 11 inches
Irving H. "Larry" Larom Collection NA.111.27

The art of quillwork was considered by Lakota women to be a gift from Double Woman and a highly honored form of decoration for baby cradles, clothing, buffalo robes, bags, and other items. This cradle combines porcupine quillwork and glass beadwork.

One means of gaining membership in this society was for a young woman
to pledge to complete an object such as a buffalo robe decorated with quillwork
to achieve good fortune for a family member, such as a husband or brother going
to war or an ill child or other relative. The young woman would approach a
member of the women's quilling society, most often a family member, and ask for
instruction in completing the work properly. The process of initiating work on
the robe and fulfilling the woman's vow involved considerable ritual, a ceremonial feast, and giveaways as women of the society came together to support the
young woman in her first endeavor. The actual quilling of the robe was a sacred
undertaking that required that the artist follow specific procedures and restrictions.[50] With the completion of the robe, the young woman was admitted to the

Cradle
Hinono'ei (Northern Arapaho), Wyoming, ca.
1880
Sackcloth, tanned hide, dew claws, dyed and
natural porcupine quills, 32 x 13 inches
Chandler-Pohrt Collection, Gift of Mr. William D.
Weiss NA.111.47

Arapaho women who were members of quillwork societies or guilds created baby cradles
with designs rooted in tribal traditions. Such a
cradle ensured the spiritual as well as physical
well-being of the child within.

society and could attend its feasts and other ceremonies and give instruction to
other potential candidates. Grinnell noted that during the ceremonies, the women
of the society described the quillwork they had completed in much the same way
as men publicly recounted their coups. Later, women of the society would provide detailed instruction and patterns for the design of the quillwork.[51]

Members of such societies had special designs with accompanying rituals
that they precisely reproduced on robes, cradles, tipi decorations, moccasins, and

other items. Like men, women also had dreams or visions in which they received new designs considered to be the individual's personal property, which were not to be copied.

Northern Arapaho women learned the skills and accompanying rituals of quillwork through apprenticeship with an older woman who was a holder of one of seven sacred medicine bags. The bags, which contained the tools needed for quillwork and for tipi painting, signified the high ritual authority of the women who held them.[52] Like the Cheyenne, a woman could vow to create a cradle or a buffalo robe decorated with a quillwork design to win supernatural assistance for a family member in need. After the completion of this undertaking and additional work that demonstrated her skill and artistry, she could eventually inherit the bag along with the rights to instruct other women in quillwork and its accompanying ceremonies. Such a woman named Firewood inherited a sacred medicine bag from her mother in about 1885 and earned honors through the completion of sixty baby cradles, fourteen buffalo robes, five decorated tipis, ten calf robes, and one buffalo backrest cover.[53]

Northern Arapaho cradles have distinctive quillwork designs variously interpreted as representing the baby who would use the cradle or the tipi in which the child would someday live. In the first interpretation, the quillwork circular design on the top of the cradle is symbolic of the child's head, the strips of quillwork along each side represent the child's hair, and the long quill-wrapped thongs that wrap around the cradle symbolize his ribs. In the second interpretation, the overall construction and shape of the cradle with its interior framework of sticks represents the tipi entrance. The circular decoration and pendants in quillwork at the top of the cradle represent Arapaho tipi ornaments, which are similar in design. The looped quillwork pendants along the opening of the cradle stand for the peg holes at the bottom of a tipi.[54]

Lakota and Blackfeet quill workers also considered that their art had sacred connotations. Lakota women who excelled in quillwork and in hide work were said to have received their abilities through a vision of Double Woman. Associations of such women were sometimes called together under the leadership of older women for feasts and to exhibit their works to one another. Proficient hide tanners and tipi makers also came together for the cooperative making of tipis.[55] Blackfoot women began working in quillwork only after initiation and ceremonies which protected them from going blind or experiencing swelling in their finger joints.[56]

In much the same way that men wore insignia to signify their military honors, Hidatsa women wore rings and bracelets which indicated the number of buffalo robes they had tanned or tipis they had made. Metal bracelets were precious and expensive adornments that were made from wire acquired from traders. According to Buffalo Bird Woman, a woman who had quilled a tipi cover was

Moccasins
Lakota (Sioux), South Dakota, ca. 1890
Tanned deer hide, dyed porcupine quills, cotton cloth, horse hair, tin cones, glass beads; 9 ⅞ x 4 inches
NA.202.7

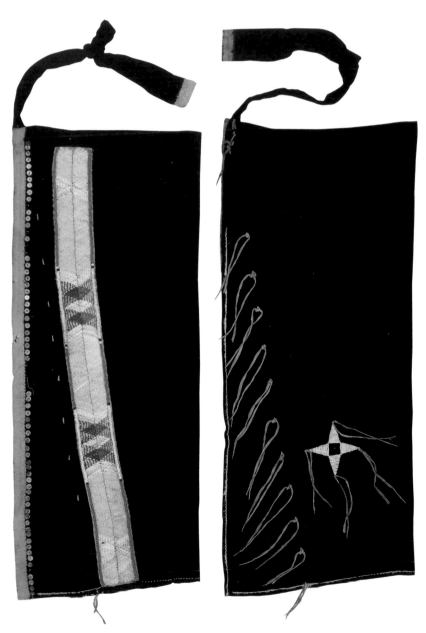

Man's Leggings
Hidatsa, North Dakota, ca. 1885
Wool cloth, dyed porcupine quills, glass beads, metal tacks; 32 x 9 inches
The Catherine Bradford Collection, Gift of The Coe Foundation NA.202.47

Moccasins
Lakota (Sioux), South Dakota, ca. 1885
Tanned deer hide, glass beads, sinew;
9⅞ x 3½ inches
Chandler-Pohrt Collection, Gift of Mr. and Mrs.
Barron G. Collier, II NA.202.859

entitled to wear two bracelets, while a man who had led a war expedition might wear one in recognition of this achievement. A woman could wear a ring to indicate that she had completed the quillwork of a buffalo robe.[57] Women also received gifts in recognition of their completion of such work. Buffalo Bird Woman was honored in this manner by her Aunt Sage for the tipis and buffalo robes she had completed. "If a girl was a worker and tanned hundreds of hides her aunt might give her an honor mark. My aunt Sage gave me such, a *maípsukaśa* or woman's belt. These were broad as a man's suspender and worked in beads. . . . One could not purchase or make such a belt; it had to be given."[58]

After groups of the Cheyenne and Arapaho people were moved to reservations in Indian Territory, porcupine quillwork gave way to paint and beadwork as decorative devices. By the middle of the nineteenth century, glass beads had became readily available through Euro-American trade, so Northern Plains women also began to predominately use beadwork over quillwork. Women's fine beadwork on their families' clothing and household items was greatly admired as artists elaborated on old designs or created new ones. After the transition to reservation living in the late 1800s, women concentrated on creating beautiful clothing with beadwork designs for formal wear such as ceremonies and other times when people came together to share their cultural identities. In a less formal structure than the quilling societies, older women continued to instruct their younger relations in the art of beadwork and to come together to display their creations.

The role of Plains Indian women within the larger nineteenth-century ceremonial organizations has not been well documented, although there is evidence that it was significant in bringing about success in hunting buffalo, warfare, and the cultivation of gardens. Arapaho women performed a buffalo dance that corresponded with the dances of the men's societies. In this dance, which occurred as a result of an individual woman's vow, the women participants of many ages

represented the buffalo. They wore specialized paint and regalia and carried accouterments related to the roles they played in the ceremony—cows, bulls, or calves—consisting of a buffalo headdress, decorated belt, and eagle bone whistles. The women's headdresses were composed of caps of buffalo hide with two horns and painted and quilled brow-bands.[59]

The ceremonies of Mandan, Hidatsa, and Arikara women's societies were directed toward ensuring success in warfare without loss of life and celebrating victories, growing abundant gardens with good harvests and giving thanks for them, and calling buffalo closer to the villages.[60]

The series of age-graded societies of the Hidatsa began with the Skunk Society, which included young women from about fifteen to twenty years of age. They were associated with the men's Stone Hammer Society and each group

Buffalo Society Woman's Headdress
Hinono'ei (Northern Arapaho), Wyoming,
ca. 1880
Buffalo hide, fur and horns, sinew, dyed
porcupine quills, feathers; 17 x 11 inches
Chandler-Pohrt Collection, Gift of Mr. William D.
Weiss NA.203.358

Arapaho women who were members of the
Buffalo Woman Society wore headdresses such
as this in dances performed to bring about an
abundance of buffalo.

assisted the other on occasions when they celebrated victories in warfare. The Enemy Society, composed of young married women, also celebrated warfare and the victories of battle.[61]

The ceremonies of the Goose Society, considered to be of Mandan origin and comprised of women of about thirty to forty years of age, ensured bountiful gardens through a series of rituals and prayers throughout the growing and harvesting season. Many members of the Goose Society had received visions associated with the growing of corn and they were called upon in times of drought and insect infestations.[62]

During the winter, the White Buffalo Cow Society, made up of older women who were past menopause, performed ceremonies to call the buffalo closer to the villages. A highly respected association roughly equivalent to the men's Bull Society, the women wore distinctive headdresses created from tanned white buffalo hide decorated with eagle, hawk and other feathers.[63]

Mandan and Arikara women's societies were similar in organization and purpose as those of the Hidatsa. Women achieved prestige and respect for participating in their societies as well as the support of their peers as they undertook their daily work and ceremonial obligations. They often received gifts and payments for their efforts.[64] As women, they were also able to contribute to their families and to their tribe as they performed the valuable daily work of rearing children and providing food, clothing, and other necessities, and carried out the prayers, ceremonies, and rituals that brought spiritual assistance and protection to the people.

Ceremony and Celebration

We call ourselves Pté Oyáte, or Female Buffalo People. We depended on the buffalo for our way of life. In April when the young buffalo calf was born, the cycle of life on the plains began. In October when the great hunts began, the young calves were mature and we began to accumulate what we needed for the winter. We as a people were aware of these things and lived our lives according to these natural cycles.

—Delphine Red Shirt[65]

Plains Indian ceremonial life followed and supported the yearly seasonal cycle of economic endeavors such as hunting buffalo, gathering plants, preserving and storing of foods, traveling to new camps and trade gatherings, and, for farming peoples, planting, tending, harvesting, and preserving their crops. Each tribe followed its own ceremonies, which were deeply rooted in cultural traditions that provided spiritual meaning and reinforcement for their values, traditions, and ways of life. One of the yearly ceremonies, the Sun Dance, was a significant component of the ceremonial cycle for many Plains tribes. Held during the summer when abundant grass supported large herds of buffalo, the Sun Dance provided

an opportunity for many bands and small family groups to come together to celebrate as a people.

Sun Dance Lodge (Medicine Lodge)
Northern Cheyenne Reservation, Montana,
1920s
Photograph by Thomas Marquis (1869–1935)
Thomas Marquis Collection P.165.1.184

> The Sun Dance was a complex, beautiful, and powerful ceremony that during the nineteenth century was the highlight of the annual summer encampments of almost all the Plains buffalo hunters. While it may not have been the most important religious ritual of a particular tribe, it was among the most public and dramatic. It was a communal ceremony that for many tribes required the participation of the entire group, or, in the case of larger groups such as the Teton Sioux, at least as many bands as could camp together.[66]

For peoples such as the Lakota and Cheyenne, which were composed of several bands that lived apart throughout much of the year, the Sun Dance was a time when leaders met in tribal councils, men's societies came together to discuss common interests, trading took place, young men and women courted and families made marriage arrangements, and relatives renewed kinship ties. During this encampment, military societies organized large buffalo hunts and sometimes war parties and raids on enemy camps. The spiritual focus of this gathering was the performance of the Sun Dance ceremony itself.

Although the term "Sun Dance" has come to be the most popular contemporary name for this ceremony, each of the tribes have their own specific terms

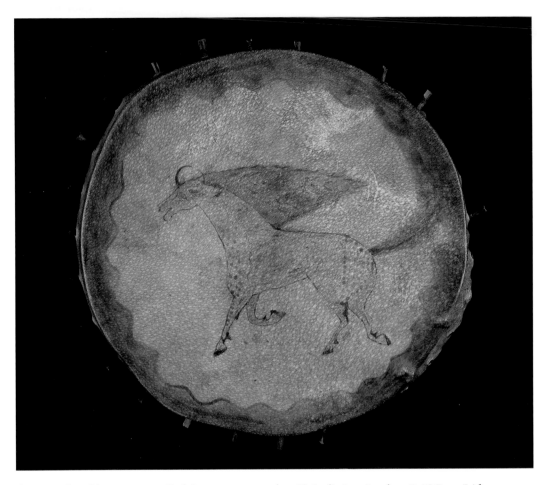

for it. The Cheyenne call this ceremony the "Medicine Lodge," "New Life
Lodge," or "Medicine Tipi Ceremony," and the Arapaho used the terms
"Sacrifice Lodge" or "Offerings Lodge." The Lakota called it the "Sun Gazing
Dance."[67] There are many tribal variations of the Sun Dance as well, all of which
involved fasting, prayer, and suffering. Among the Lakota, Cheyenne, Arapaho,
and Blackfoot, the ceremony also required additional sacrifices made to fullfil
vows by dancers. Chased By Bears of the Lakota described this ritual:

> My first Sun dance vow was made when I was 24 years of age. I was alone and far from
> the camp, when I saw an Arikaree approaching on horseback, leading a horse. I knew that
> my life was in danger, so I said, "Wakan'tanka," if you will let me kill this man and capture
> his horse with this lariat, I will give you my flesh at the next Sun dance."[68]

Through the Sun Dance, participants prayed and suffered for the well-being
of the entire tribe so the buffalo would be abundant and the people would
increase and live good lives. Arthur Amiotte has explained the place of the Sun
Dance within world views and traditions of Plains peoples.

> At the heart of the Sun Dance prayer is a cyclical view of time and process, this great cir-
> cle of life that various tribes call "That Which Moves," "The Great Holy," "The Great
> Spirit," or "The Great Mystery."

It is this concept, or its perceived parts, that the tribe in their sacred lodges have demarcated and manifested as symbol in their visual arts, music, oratory, poetry, dance, drama, and vernacular architecture. Through the use of these forms in ritual, tribal people interact, they express, celebrate and reaffirm their relationship to the originating powers of their very being and their particular roles in the great cyclical potency that governs all dimensions of the environment that sustains them—as long as they behave as stewards and respect it and reciprocate in a benevolent manner.[69]

Tribal cultures of the Plains were diverse and not all peoples followed the ritual of the Sun Dance. The Pawnee, who did not celebrate the Sun Dance, observed a rich and complex ceremonial cycle that was intertwined with preparation for and celebration of the hunt, planting, growing, and harvesting of corn and other crops, and a recognition of the place of the people within the great universe and all elements of the earth and sky. The significance of corn or Mother Corn was the overriding element of many of the ceremonies, reflecting its importance in the survival of Pawnee people.

Crow Tipi Village, Riverside
Crow Agency, Montana, ca. 1906
Photograph by Joseph Henry Sharp
(1859–1953)
P.61.1.5

During the annual Crow Fair which began in 1904, Crow tribal members camped north of Crow Agency on the banks of the Little Bighorn River. The daily parade, during which participants dressed in traditional hide clothing embellished with beading or quillwork and horses were decorated with beautiful saddles, bridles, and other equipment, was a central element of the Fair. During this long parade, the procession forded the river and proceeded to Crow Agency before returning to the other side en route to the fair grounds.

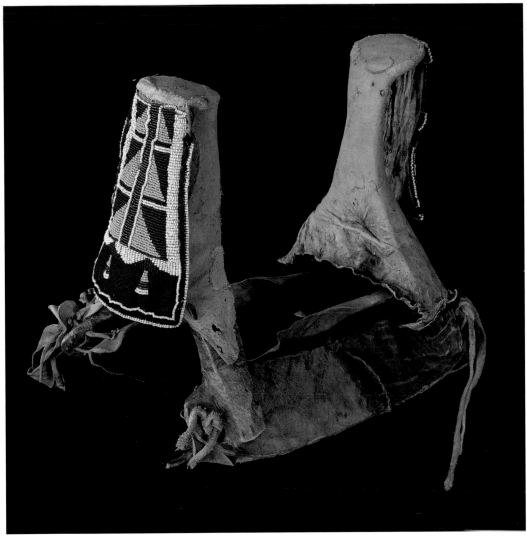

Girl's Saddle

Apsáalooke (Crow), Montana, ca. 1890
Wood, rawhide, tanned hide, glass beads, wool
cloth; 15½ x 8⅜ x 12⅝ inches
Gift of the Irving H. "Larry" Larom Estate
NA.403.102

Horses were introduced by the Spanish, and
Plains tribes borrowed the Spaniards' basic
forms of riding equipment—saddles, bridles,
and stirrups. Plains artisans embellished these
basic forms with beading, quillwork, and other
decorations.

During the 1880s, the federal government restricted performances of all
Native religious ceremonies as they attempted to break tribal cohesiveness and
cultural identities and compel people to set aside their traditions and belief systems and emulate the lives of the farmers and ranchers whose settlements
increasingly encircled the reservations. Christian missionaries assisted by
demanding that adherents of tribal traditions discard their sacred bundles
together with the spiritual beliefs that supported them. Children were removed
from families and sent to boarding schools at a distance where they could be separated from tribal life and trained as farmers and homemakers in keeping with
Euro-American ideals.

Despite these restrictions, Native people strove to hold onto their traditions
and ceremonies by performing them away from reservation headquarters in
remote locations where they were less likely to be noticed by government agents.
By the early 1900s, they also learned that they could continue to practice certain
Native traditions if they could convince the agents that their tribal gatherings

In Traditional Dress (on horse, left to right), Bright Wings and Beth Iron Horse, (standing left to right), Annie Talking Pipe and Nellie Scratches Face

Crow Reservation, Montana

Photograph by Rev. W. A. Petzoldt, D.D. (1872–1960)

Dr. William and Anna Petzoldt Collection, Gift of Genevieve Petzoldt Fitzgerald PN.95.158

Reminiscent of the excitement of moving camp in the buffalo hunting days, Crow women of the reservation period dressed up themselves and their horses for parades and celebrations. They created beautifully dec-orated saddles, martingales, bridles, and cruppers for such occasions.

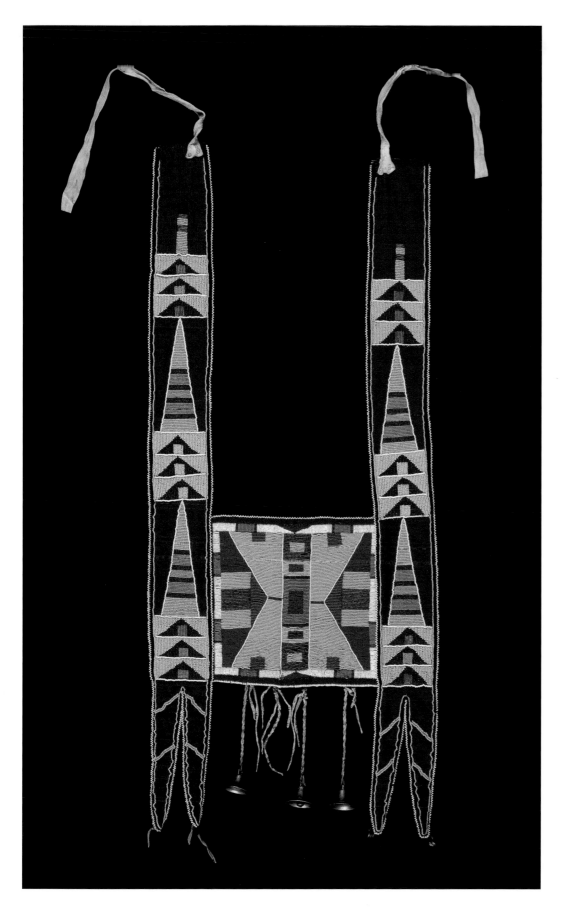

Crupper
Apsáalooke (Crow), Montana, ca. 1885
Commercially tanned leather, glass beads, wool
cloth, tanned hide; 31 x 20½ inches
NA.403.18

were social and secular rather than ceremonial, and if they scheduled such activities to correspond with significant holidays of the Euro-American calendar.

Federal authorities on the Crow Reservation strictly prohibited the Sun Dance, vision quests, and other visibly religious ceremonies as well as those that brought the people together in traditional gatherings that lasted several days. During the early reservation period, however, on the Fourth of July each year, Crow tribal members were allowed to assemble for a day of dances in full traditional attire, battle reenactments, and parades. These activities apparently also provided entertainment for agents, missionaries, and others near the reservation. Christmas and New Year's Day also provided a justification for traditional dancing and feasts, as did George Washington's Birthday, Easter, and Decoration Day. Occasionally, Crow leaders such as Plenty Coups and Pretty Eagle were granted permission to sponsor dances and other gatherings, although individual agents were often inconsistent in their attitudes and decisions about these celebrations.[70]

Social dances such as the Owl Dance and Hot Dance predominated at these gatherings. The Hot Dance was the Crow rendition of the Grass Dance or Omaha Dance, which was organized under the direction of men's societies and

Lance Case
Apsáalooke (Crow), Montana, ca. 1890
Rawhide, glass beads, wool cloth;
51½ x 12¾ inches
NA.108.95

During reservation-era parades, lance cases representative of men's weapons used to defend the people were tied to a woman's saddle. This tradition continues today during the annual Crow Fair when women display beautiful clothing, cradles, horse equipment, and the painted and beaded lance cases in the daily parades through camp.

Martingale
Apsáalooke (Crow), Montana, ca. 1905
Canvas, glass beads, wool cloth, tanned hide,
brass hawk bells; 36 5/8 x 15 inches
Gift of Mrs. Henry H.R. Coe NA.403.86

Pad Saddle
Cree, Northern Plains, ca. 1880
Tanned deer hide, metal rings, wool cloth, canvas, glass beads, yarn; 21¼ x 29 inches
Gift of Mrs. F.W. Walrous, The Colonel John F. Guilfoyle, U.S. Cavalry West Point 1877, Collection of American Indian Material NA.403.97

celebrated the achievements of men much as the pre-reservation associations once did. Much to the disapproval of government agents, Crow participants in these celebrations demonstrated the cultural value of generosity by giving away food and other goods to those in need and by sponsoring feasts.[71]

Parades in which Crow men and women dressed in their finest regalia rode horses decorated in beautifully made saddles, bridles, cruppers, horse collars, and other accouterments took place at many celebrations. This demonstration of artistry combined with horsemanship had its roots in earlier periods when the bands moved in organized processions to new locations or on seasonal buffalo hunts. There were antecedents also in the rides of victorious returning warriors back into their villages after successful raids and battles, with their horses painted and decorated with feathers. The parade tradition can be still observed at the annual Crow Fair at Crow Agency, Montana, the North American Indian Days near the Blackfeet Reservation at Browning, Montana, and other Native celebrations throughout the Plains and Plateau regions.

During the first decades of the twentieth century, the Crow Tobacco Ceremony apparently increased in significance as well as in the number of chap-

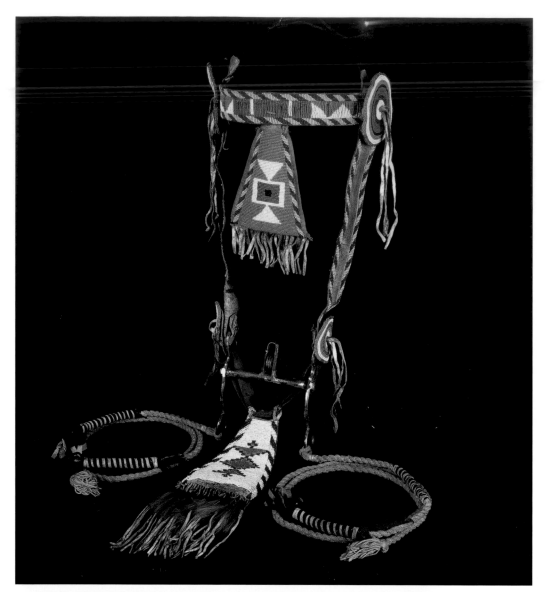

Bridle
Amoskapi Pikuni (Blackfeet), Montana, ca. 1895
Rawhide from a parfleche, metal bit, tanned
hide, wool cloth, glass beads, cotton rope, dyed
horsehair, tin cones, pigment; 33 x 9 inches;
reins 66¼ inches
Gift of Mr. William Magee NA.403.112

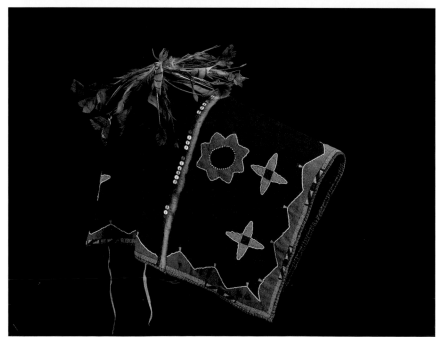

Horse Mask
Nimíipu (Nez Perce), Plateau, ca. 1895
Wool cloth, brass, leather ties, owl feathers,
glass pony beads; 37 x 31¾ inches
NA.403.170

Horses arrived among the Nez Perce around
1730, and quickly spread to the neighboring
Cayuse, Walla Walla, Umatilla, and other
Plateau tribes. Like their neighbors on the
Plains, Plateau people valued horses highly,
outfitting them with lavishly beaded equipment. Horse masks such as this one are still
used in parades in the Plateau region.

194

ters and adherents.[72] The ritual adoption of new members, which in pre-reservation days had taken place in winter months, was moved to the Fourth of July celebration, to suggest to government agents that it was another harmless secular
activity. The Crow Arrow Throw also continued through the early reservation
period. This competition, in which men attempt to land arrows nearest a target
arrow, emphasizes strength and accuracy, both important skills for warriors.

Although there were many losses of tribal ceremonies during the devastating
early reservation period, the Crow and other Plains Indian peoples strove to survive as cohesive communities and to preserve tribal values and traditions. Their
leaders—brought up as free hunters and warriors of the Plains but cognizant of
the necessity of dealing with the United States government—were part of those
efforts. Through it all, Plains Indian people managed to carry basic tribal values
into the twentieth century. These values included respect for the women and men
who excelled in their undertakings, honoring the elders who embodied ancient
traditions, the spirit of generosity, and their connections to the lands that fostered their cultures. ✵

1. Chief Washakie of the Eastern Shoshone in July 1878 to John W. Hoyt, governor of Wyoming Territory, quoted in Grace Raymond Hebard, *Washakie: Chief of the Shoshones* (Cleveland: A.H. Clark Co., 1930; rpt., Lincoln and London: University of Nebraska Press, 1995), p. 213.

2. Henry E. Stamm, IV, *People of the Wind River: The Eastern Shoshones 1825–1900* (Norman: University of Oklahoma Press, 1999), pp. 47–53.

3. Washakie's birth date has been variously recorded as 1798 and 1804. Stamm argues that the year of birth was approximately 1808–1810. Stamm, *People of the Wind River*, pp. 25–26.

4. Quoted in Loretta Fowler, *Arapahoe Politics, 1851–1978: Symbols in Crises of Authority* (Lincoln and London: University of Nebraska Press, 1982), p. 71.

5. In Frank B. Linderman, *American: The Life Story of a Great Indian, Plenty-coups, Chief of the Crows* (Rathway, New Jersey: The John Day Company, 1930; reprinted as *Plenty-coups, Chief of the Crows*, Lincoln: University of Nebraska Press 1962), p. 57.

6. E. Adamson Hoebel, *The Cheyennes: Indians of the Great Plains* (New York: Holt, Rinehart and Winston, 1960), pp. 33–34. George Bird Grinnell, *The Cheyenne Indians: Their History and Ways of Life*, Vol. 2 (New Haven: Yale University Press, 1923), p. 48.

7. Grinnell, *The Cheyenne Indians*, pp. 49–53.

8. Thomas B. Marquis, *A Warrior Who Fought Custer* (Minneapolis: Midwest Company, 1931; reprinted as *Wooden Leg: A Warrior Who Fought Custer*, Lincoln: University of Nebraska Press, 1957), p. 56.

9. Ibid., pp. 58–59.

10. Royal B. Hassrick, *The Sioux: Life and Customs of a Warrior Society* (Norman: University of Oklahoma, 1969), pp 16–17. James R. Walker, *Lakota Society*, Raymond J. Demallie, ed. (Lincoln and London: University of Nebraska Press, 1992), pp. 28–29. William K. Powers, *Oglala Religion* (Lincoln and London: University of Nebraska Press, 1982), p. 41. Marla N. Powers, *Oglala Women: Myth, Ritual, and Power* (Chicago and London: The University of Chicago Press, 1986), pp. 26–27.

11. John G. Neihardt, *Black Elk Speaks: Being the Life Story of a Holy Man of the Oglala Sioux* (Lincoln and London: University of Nebraska Press, 1932; rpt. 1979), p. 56.

12. William K. Powers, *Oglala Religion*, pp. 40–41. Marla N. Powers, *Oglala Women*, 26–27. Hassrick, *The Sioux*, pp. 8, 27–28.

13. Hassrick, *The Sioux*, p. 90. An alternative interpretation for the significance of the fringes of hair on shirts is that they represent the enemies vanquished by the owners.

14. Barbara A. Hail, *Hau, Kóla! The Plains Collection of the Haffenreffer Museum of Anthropology* (Bristol, Rhode Island: Haffenreffer Museum of Anthropology, Brown University, 1980), p. 68.

15. Grinnell, *The Cheyenne Indians*, Vol. 1, pp. 336–340. Hoebel, *The Cheyennes*, pp. 37–39.

16. Alfred W. Bowers, *Hidatsa Social and Ceremonial Organization, Bureau of American Ethnology Bulletin 194* (Washington: Smithsonian Institution; U.S. Government Printing Office, 1965; rpt., Lincoln: University of Nebraska Press, 1992), pp. 180–181. Carolyn Gilman and Mary Jane Schneider, *The Way to Independence: Memories of a Hidatsa Indian Family, 1840–1920* (St. Paul: Minnesota Historical Society, 1987), pp. 88–89.

17. Quoted in Gilman and Schneider, *The Way to Independence*, pp. 90–91.

18. Bowers, *Hidatsa Social and Ceremonial Organization*, pp. 184–185.

19. Quoted in Gilman and Schneider, *The Way to Independence*, p. 38.

20. Bowers, *Hidatsa Social and Ceremonial Organization*. pp. 198–199.

21. Ibid., p. 220.

22. Ibid., p. 175.

23. Ibid., pp. 175–177.

24. See Loretta Fowler, *Arapahoe Politics, 1851–1978: Symbols in Crises of Authority* (Lincoln and London: University of Nebraska Press, 1982), p. 8.

25. Alfred L. Kroeber, *The Arapaho, Bulletin of the American Museum of Natural History 18*, 1902, 1904, 1907 (rpt., Lincoln: University of Nebraska Press, 1983), p. 28.

26. Kroeber, *The Arapaho*, pp. 153–159. Fowler, *Arapahoe Politics*, p. 9. Loretta Fowler, "Arapaho," *Handbook of North American Indians*, Vol. 2 (Washington: Smithsonian Institution, 2001), pp. 844–846.

27. Kroeber, *The Arapaho*, 207–208. Fowler "Arapaho," p. 846.

28. Fowler, *Arapahoe Politics*, p. 77.

29. Gloria A. Young, "Intertribal Religious Movement," *Handbook of North American Indians*, Vol. 2. (Washington: Smithsonian Institution, 2001), p. 996.

30. Linderman, *American*, pp. 63–64.

31. Ibid., p. 67.

32. Joseph Medicine Crow, *From the Heart of the Crow Country: The Crow Indians' Own Stories* (New York: Orion Books, 1992), p. 80.

33. Ibid.

34. William E. Powers. *Oglala Religion*, p. 91.

35. Medicine Crow, *From the Heart of Crow Country*, p. 80.

36. Ibid., p.82.

37. Ibid.

38. Ibid., p. 44.

39. Kroeber, *The Arapaho,* p. 22.

40. John Stands In Timber and Margot Liberty with the assistance of Robert M. Utley, *Cheyenne Memories* (New Haven: Yale University, 1967; rpt., Lincoln and London: University of Nebraska Press, 1972), p. 52.

41. Hassrick, *The Sioux,* p. 86.

42. Marquis, *A Warrior Who Fought Custer,* p. 85.

43. Ibid.

44. Beatrice Medicine, "Indian Women and Traditional Religion," in *Sioux Indian Religion,* Raymond J. DeMallie and Douglas R. Parks, eds. (Norman and London: University of Oklahoma Press, 1987), p. 170.

45. Some Plains women also were honored for brave exploits in warfare. Beatrice Medicine explored the role of such women in "Warrior Women—Sex Role Alternatives for Plains Indian Women," in *The Hidden Half: Studies of Plains Indian Women,* Patricia Albers and Beatrice Medicine, eds. (Washington, D.C.: University Press of America, 1983), pp. 267–280. For specific examples of women's war exploits, see John C. Ewers, "Women's Roles in Plains Indian Warfare," *Plains Indian History and Cultures: Essays on Continuity and Change* (Norman and London: University of Oklahoma Press, 1997), pp. 191–204; and Grinnell, *The Cheyenne Indians,* Vol. 2, p. 47.

46. In her publication on Kiowa and Comanche cradles, Barbara Hail was able to connect cradles in museum collections with known cradle makers through consultations with the descendants of the artists. It may still be possible to identify additional artists for limited collections in this way. See Barbara A. Hail, *Gifts of Pride and Love: Kiowa and Comanche Cradles* (Bristol, R.I.: Haffenreffer Museum of Anthropology, Brown University, 2000), 18–19.

47. Grinnell, *The Cheyenne Indians,* Vol. 1, p. 159.

48. Ibid., p. 161.

49. Ibid., pp. 159–160.

50. Ibid., pp. 160–164. Hoebel, *The Cheyennes,* pp. 63–64.

51. Ibid., pp. 160–163. Grinnell attributed the description of the quilling society ceremony in this publication to a woman he identified as Picking Bones Woman who had achieved the highest honors of a quiller, the completion of thirty buffalo robes.

52. Kroeber, *The Arapaho,* p. 30.

53. Fowler, *Arapahoe Politics,* p. 112.

54. Kroeber, *The Arapaho,* pp. 67–68.

55. Hassrick, *The Sioux,* p. 223. William K. Powers, *Oglala Religion,* pp. 58–59. Marla N. Powers, *Oglala Women,* pp. 73–74.

56. John C. Ewers, *The Blackfeet: Raiders on the Northwestern Plains* (Norman: University of Oklahoma Press, 1958), pp. 119–120.

57. Gilman and Schneider, *The Way to Independence,* pp. 56.

58. Ibid., p. 53.

59. Kroeber, *The Arapaho,* pp. 210–226. Fowler, "Arapaho," *Handbook of North American Indians,* Vol. 2, p. 846.

60. Virginia Bergman Peters, *Women of the Earth Lodges: Tribal Life on the Plains* (New Haven, Conn.: Archon Books, 1995), p. 56.

61. Bowers, *Hidatsa Social and Ceremonial Organization,* p. 200.

62. Ibid., pp. 200–204.

63. Gilman and Schneider, *The Way to Independence,* pp. 82–83.

64. Peters, *Women of the Earth Lodges,* p. 60.

65. Delphine Red Shirt, *Turtle Lung Woman's Granddaughter* (Lincoln and London: University of Nebraska Press, 2002), p. 17.

66. JoAllyn Archambault, "Sun Dance," *Handbook of North American Indians,* Vol. 2. (Washington: Smithsonian Institution, 2001), p. 983.

67. Grinnell, *The Cheyenne Indians,* Vol. 2, p. 152, 211. John H. Moore, *The Cheyenne Nation: A Social and Demographic History* (Lincoln and London: University of Nebraska Press, 1988), p. 38. William K. Powers, *Oglala Religion,* p. 95. Archambault, "Sun Dance," p. 983. Moore suggests that the Medicine Tipi in the Cheyenne terminology referred not just to the lodge where the ceremony took place, but the entire tribal circle.

68. Quoted in Frances Densmore, *Teton Sioux Music, Bureau of American Ethnology Bulletin 61* (Washington D.C.: Smithsonian Institution, 1918), p. 96.

69. Arthur Amiotte, "The Sun Dance" in Charlotte Heth, *Native American Dance: Ceremonies and Social Traditions* (Washington D.C.: National Museum of the American Indian, Smithsonian Institution, 1992), pp. 135–136.

70. Frederick E. Hoxie, *Parading Through History: The Making of the Crow Nation in America, 1805–1933* (Cambridge: Cambridge University Press, 1995), pp. 209–210.

71. Ibid., pp. 211–212.

72. Ibid., p. 214. Robert H. Lowie, *The Crow Indians* (New York: Farrar and Rinehart, 1935, rpt., Lincoln and London: University of Nebraska Press, 1983), p. 174.

Crow Tribal Leaders

JOSEPH MEDICINE CROW

I welcome the opportunity to tell about the lives of certain important Crow Indian leaders who helped found a small band into a large, powerful, and rich tribe known as Crow Indians of the State of Montana. A leader emerges because of the conjuncture of an event or a situation, a person possessing innate capabilities, and this person's definition of the situation. Since 1600 A.D., when a man called No Insides, or No Vitals, seceded from the Earthen Lodges, now called Hidatsa, and migrated westward, there have been many great leaders, or chiefs, ruling a fledgling new tribe eventually called "Crow Indians" by white men. These people called themselves Apsàalooke, meaning "children of a large beaked bird."

A few years before the turn of the seventeenth century, about 1590, the ancestral tribe of the Hidatsa and the Crows was migrating west from the Lake Winnipeg area. Enroute No Vitals, the leader, fasted at present-day Devil's Lake of North Dakota. Here the First Maker appeared to him and gave him sacred seeds (*Ichi-chay*) and told him to take them to the high mountains in the west and plant the seeds. There the First Maker would come and instruct No Vitals' people in the sacred ways of planting and harvesting the seeds. So long as the Crow people do this, the First Maker would give them a good place to live and in time they would become rich and powerful.

No Vitals and about 400 people left their village on the Missouri River, in what is now North Dakota, about 1600 A.D., looking for the Promised Land. No Vitals died and his protégé Running Coyote carried the sacred bundle of *Ichi-chay* and continued the search.

The migrants traveled on and on throughout the west covering thousands of miles and taking about 100 years! Stories tell of a large salty lake (Utah), a large river flowing east from the mountains which the migrants called Arrow Head River (the Canadian River of north Texas and Oklahoma), a hot and humid land in the south (Oklahoma), and finally back west to northern Wyoming and southern Montana. After exploring the region for some time, they concluded that they had finally reached the Promised Land. Indeed, it was a wonderful land; the landscape was not only beautiful but full of game animals and a vast variety of wild fruits.

No Vitals was the first of a succession of great leaders of the Apsàalooke, the progenitor of a new tribe which may be regarded as the forerunner of creating the so-called Northern Plains Indian Culture Area.

Prior to the coming of Lewis and Clark, new and unusual events occurred that quickly and drastically changed the nomadic pedestrian way of life. The coming of the white man's horse about 1730 gave the people mobility, thus expanding their territory. The acquisition of metal tools made domestic life much easier and the white man's gun made hunting more efficient and fostered conflict with other tribes. Finally, the appearance of the white man himself about 1775 dramatically affected the culture of a growing new tribe. These new things challenged Apsàalooke men to find solutions to new situations.

As surrounding tribes had also acquired the horse and the gun and started to come into the Crow territory, intertribal warfare started in the Northern Plains. Before long, these tribes, including the Apsàalooke, had become militaristic. Men became leaders by performing four dangerous battlefield acts of bravery. Leaders, heretofore called "good men," were now called "war chiefs." Two of them, Young White Buffalo and Plays with His Face, were very important.

Young White Buffalo was instrumental in transforming the pedestrian Apsàalooke into superb horsemen about 1732. This was a great event in tribal history. Plays With His Face was regarded as a chief at the turn of the nineteenth century. He belonged to the fool-hardy class of warriors. He was a strong defender of the Crow Country for many years and terrorized tribes then coming into the Crow territory. Enemy arrows and bullets could not harm him; he was invincible. But smallpox brought him down. As he was taking his last breath, he killed himself.

Between the arrival of Lewis and Clark and the establishment of the Crow Indian Reservation in 1870, several other leaders helped direct tribal activities. Red Feather at His Temple, called Chief Long Hair by white men, was born in the late 1700s. He was a great chief by 1825. He was indeed a super man—a great warrior, a successful war chief, a powerful spiritual man, and a wise leader. This man exemplified the "orphan-to-riches" type success story. As a boy he was homeless, begging food and a place to sleep. A widow took pity on him and adopted him "as a husband." She sent him to the Medicine Lodge Site (now called Medicine Wheel on the Big Horn Mountains) to fast and seek vision power. He was given sacred powers by the Sun and the Little People who live there. Yet a boy, he would join war parties and quickly earned enough war deeds to be recognized as a war chief.

In the meantime it was noticed that his hair was growing rapidly. He told the people that this was the sign of his sacred powers and when the braids reached over one hundred hands' measurement, the Apsàalooke will have reached their peak of greatness.

Since 1843, the whole Apsàalooke tribe had camped on the Yellowstone at a sacred place they called "Where the Mountain Lion Sits," called "Pompey's Pillar" by William Clark. Chief Long Hair called a council and many chiefs came and all sat in a large tipi. Here he unwrapped his hair and had the men measure it by hand. It was over one hundred hands long (about twenty-nine feet). He dispatched several men to take census by going from lodge to lodge. There were 1,140 lodges containing about 9,000 people. The new Apsàalooke tribe had grown large, rich, and

Pillar, the sacred shrine of the Crow people. The next day, several young men were dispatched to Heart Mountain, more than one hundred miles away. When they got there, they saw a huge land slide on the west side of the peak and there clearly visible was the profile image of Long Hair. To this day, this natural statue is evident.

Chief Long Hair signed a treaty of friendship and cooperation with the United States of America in 1825. It still stands today. This legalized the early chief's philosophy of being friends and allies of the white men who will some day take over the Indian and his land. He would advise sub- and future chiefs to get along and work with the white men. I consider Long Hair as one of the greatest, if not the greatest, Crow leader of all Crow history.

The contribution that Twines His (Horse's) Tail, called Rotten Tail by white men, made to the development of the Apsàalooke was his exploratory expedition far beyond the borders of the Crow Country. The party was gone about two and half years and came back with valuable information about the surrounding regions and the people living there. They visited some Indians living in lodges made of square blocks of dried mud. The cactus there was as large and tall as trees.

Arapooish, called Rotten Belly by white men, was a good and able chief. He described the Crow Country to Robert Campbell of the American Fur Company in 1843 as, "a good country; there is no other country like it. The First Maker made it just right, put it in exactly the right place, and gave it to his red children, the Apsàalooke." Such was the description of No Vitals' Promised Land.

Sits In The Middle Of The Land, called Black Foot by white men, carried on the legacy of Chief Long Hair by legalizing the Crow Country. He made a treaty with the

powerful. Yes, this is the fulfillment of the First Maker's promise to No Vitals as he set forth looking for the Promised Land.

As the pipe was going around for the last time, the Chief also said that when his hair grew over one hundred hands that his spiri-

tual protectors would come after him and at that moment a part of Heart Mountain Peak (near Cody, Wyoming) would also die.

He leaned against his back-rest, closed his eyes, and died with a triumphant smile on his face. He was buried in a ledge on Pompey's

Shirt
Apsáalooke (Crow), Montana, ca. 1890
Tanned deer hide, glass beads, yarn, ermine, human and horsehair, wool cloth; 21 x 24½ inches
Adolf Spohr Collection, Gift of Larry Sheerin NA.202.351

After they were confined to their Montana reservation in the late nineteenth century, Crow men who had achieved leadership positions in the traditional manner continued to represent their people in negotiations with federal officials. As leaders, they wore beautifully crafted hide shirts with decorations of strips of glass beadwork, ermine, and human and horsehair. Dances, society gatherings, and parades provided opportunities to wear such clothing as symbols of tribal unity and identity during difficult times.

United States in 1868. He was assisted and given good advice by a Frenchman named Pierre Chien, who had married into the tribe. He was reputed to speak the Crow language perfectly. This treaty not only enabled the Crow people to deal with the government's harsh assimilation process rather easily, but also gave the Crow Nation a strong sovereignty position with the United States government. The Crow leaders can go directly to the Executive Branch concerning the administration of the Crow Indian Reservation. This so-called Treaty of Fort Laramie of 1868 is still in effect and serves the Crow Tribe well to this day. Chief Sits In The Middle lived seven years after the reservation was established. He enforced the terms of the treaty with good results.

In 1877, the Chief and a party were hunting in Northern Wyoming when he suddenly died of pneumonia. He was buried up a river named after him with the poor spelling of Meeteetse River, about thirty miles southeast of Cody. In 1978, some Crow people retrieved his remains and brought them back for reburial with proper ceremony at Crow Agency, Montana. The grave is now a shrine.

In the early part of the period immediately after the reservation was established, the Crow leaders were young war chiefs who had to contend with a different antagonist on a vastly different field of battle—the government's complicated assimilation policy. The Secretary's Orders of 1887 outlined a harsh unilateral program to quickly subdue and abolish Indian cultures; the Indian was to be transformed into a white man. These leaders, now called Reservation Chiefs, also had to vigorously oppose and prevent Montana senators and congressmen from opening the Crow Reservation to white settlers.

A misguided young man named Wraps Up His (Horse's) Tail nearly nullified the good works and accomplishments of the leaders and brought tragedy to the Crow people. One day he proclaimed that with his magic sword he could swing at the soldiers at Fort Custer, located inside the Crow Reservation, and kill them all as if by lightning. Tribal leaders were alarmed and tried to dissuade him, but he would not listen. Local newspapers proclaimed with bold headlines that the Crows are planning war and that Sitting Bull himself was making his "second coming" to help the Crows! On November 17, 1887, Wraps Up His Tail struck, but the magic sword didn't work. The Indian Agent's Indian Police caught him and summarily executed him.

The Reservation Chiefs like Pretty Eagle, Medicine Crow, and Plenty Coups went to Washington, D.C., to protect the Crow people and their reservation. They would take an educated young man as their interpreter. The foremost of these was Robert Yellowtail, a graduate of Sherman Institute of California who had studied law. In 1917, a Senate hearing of Montana Senator Walsh's bill to open the Crow Reservation to white settlers was held. The night before the hearing, Chief Medicine Crow and Plenty Coups, the top tribal leaders of the time, opened their war medicine bundles. They prayed and claimed victory. Their prayers were answered through the powerful oratory of their interpreter. Robert Yellowtail was given five minutes to present the Crow case. He spoke over an hour, holding the committee spellbound. Several Senators said that if the bill went to the Senate floor, they would filibuster it. Senator Walsh withdrew his bill.

In 1934, John Collier was appointed Commissioner of Indian Affairs under the new Roosevelt Administration. When the Indian Reorganization Act was passed, Collier immediately launched his program to restructure the Indian Service, giving the tribes wise and generous latitude in managing their own reservation affairs. The commissioner appointed Robert Yellowtail, then forty-three years old, as the new superin-tendent of his own Crow Indian Reservation. He immediately launched an ambitious program of long-range economic rehabilitation plans for his Crow people. His main goals were to restock the reservation with horses, as well as buffalo and elk. The buffalo program was quickly accomplished, as several hundred head of bison were donated by Yellowstone Park, the National Bison Range of western Montana, and by some private individuals. Before long, the horses too were back. Lost concepts and values in Crow culture were revived.

5

Adversity and Renewal

*A long time ago my father told me what his father told him,
that there was once a Lakota holy man, called Drinks Water,
who dreamed what was to be; and this was long before the
coming of the Wasichus. He dreamed that the four-leggeds
were going back into the earth and that a strange race had
woven a spider's web all around the Lakotas. And he said:
"When this happens, you shall live in square gray houses, in
a barren land, and beside those square gray houses you shall
starve." They say he went back to Mother Earth soon after
he saw this vision, and it was sorrow that killed him. You can
look around you now and see that he meant those dirt-roofed
houses we are living in, and that all the rest was true.
Sometimes dreams are wiser than waking.*

—BLACK ELK[1]

When Oglala Lakota spiritual leader Black Elk narrated his life story and
described his vision to John G. Neihardt in 1930, he was almost seventy years
old and had experienced firsthand the transitions in his tribe as the people sought
to recover from the loss of the buffalo and their freedom and independence and,
ultimately, the deaths of so many relatives. In his youth, Black Elk had traveled
on the great tribal buffalo hunts; in 1876, at the age of thirteen, he had participated in the Rosebud and Little Bighorn Battles; and, in 1890, he survived a
wound he suffered at the massacre at Wounded Knee. Facing the illness, poverty,
and despair of the Lakota on the Pine Ridge Reservation, in 1886, Black Elk
joined Buffalo Bill's Wild West Show and traveled through American and
European cities until 1889, when he returned to the reservation. He hoped to
gain insights from his travels into the Euro-American world that had brought
about so many changes to the Lakota, so he could help to repair the nation's
"sacred hoop," which had been broken and scattered, and the disrupted and
destroyed lives of the people.[2]

Other elders whose stories were recorded in the early twentieth century
found it difficult to address the dire circumstances of the previous decades. With
the near extinction of the buffalo and devastation of the traditional economic
pursuits of hunting, gathering, and cultivation of their customary crops, people
could not provide for themselves and their families. Government agents and missionaries prohibited traditional cultural and spiritual expressions and, above all,

Ghost Dance Dress
Hinono'ei (Arapaho), Oklahoma, ca. 1890
Tanned elk hide, eagle feathers, pigments;
54 x 54 inches
Chandler-Pohrt Collection, Gift of Mary J. and
James R. Jundt NA.204.4

Arapaho adherents of the Ghost Dance created
shirts and dresses painted with images of the
earth and sky with traditional spiritual signifi-
cances and often drawn from personal visions.
Full and crescent moons represent the heavens
and painted mountains signify the earth. The
sacred cedar tree, characterized by its ever-
green foliage, fragrance, durability, and red
heart wood, and the crow, an important Ghost
Dance symbol revered for its inherent omnis-
cience and as a messenger from the spirit
world, are both represented on the dress.

strove to separate children from their parents to hasten the process of forcing Indians to abandon their Native practices and assume the lives of Christian farmers, ranchers, and homemakers.

Two Leggings, who had devoted his life to seeking honor and respect as a Crow hunter and warrior, expressed his frustration at the inactivity of reservation life when he said: "Nothing happened after that. We just lived. There were no more war parties, no capturing of horses from the Piegans and the Sioux, no buffalo to hunt. There is nothing more to tell."[3] When he said this in 1919, he had lived almost forty years beyond the disappearance of the buffalo from the Plains and the final Crow participation in warfare against the Lakota, Cheyenne, and Arapaho. In Two Leggings' estimation, nothing worth recounting happened during those long decades.

It was no doubt difficult for Native elders to reminisce about the occurrences of the late nineteenth century because there was so much sadness to recount. The Native American population in North America had been decimated by smallpox, cholera, measles, and other diseases for which they had little resistance, increasing warfare with the United States and each other, and, finally, starvation.

Consequently, it was probably less traumatic for some Plains Indian people to concentrate on the pre-reservation days when the people were strong and vibrant and leading lives independent of government interference. Because of Native people's dependence upon the federal government and the decisions of its representatives, it was also no doubt difficult to speak candidly to Euro-American researchers of the disastrous policies and events that created the arduous reservation conditions for fear of reprisals.

Early researchers who visited Plains Indian reservations in the late nineteenth and early twentieth centuries also had limited interest in learning about the current lives of the people living there. Many mistakenly believed that Native people of the Plains would inevitably disappear like the buffalo—they would finally pass on from the numerous afflictions of reservation life or melt into the general population once the old had died and the young had been assimilated.

The anthropologists, historians, museum representatives, and others who attempted to record the ways of life that they believed would soon vanish most often concentrated on collecting representative remnants of those "dying" and "disappearing" cultures—clothing, implements, personal belongings, and sacred materials central to tribal traditions, as well as the physical remains of the people themselves. These objects and the human remains became the foundations of European and American natural history museum repositories. Despite the radical changes occurring in the reservation lives of Plains Indian people, museums commonly exhibited such collections as manifestations of seemingly static and unchanging nineteenth-century buffalo cultures. Researchers documented such pre-reservation cultures by seeking out elders to record tribal knowledge, ceremonies, songs, traditions, histories, and practices, and by photographing them in traditional nineteenth century dress so future generations would learn about the Native North American peoples of the bygone past.

Those researchers who did inquire about personal lives and conditions on reservations reportedly were answered in much the same way as Plenty Coups to Frank Linderman: "You know that part of my life as well as I do. You saw what happened to us when the buffalo went away."[4] Pretty Shield reluctantly elaborated on the nineteenth-century losses experienced by Crow after the demise of the buffalo: "Our old men used to be different; even our children were different when the buffalo were here."[5]

> We believed for a long time that the buffalo would again come to us: but they did not. We grew hungry and sick and afraid, all in one. Not believing their own eyes our hunters rode very far looking for buffalo, so far away that even if they had found a herd we could not have reached it in half a moon. 'Nothing; we found nothing' they told us; and then, hungry, they stared at the empty plains, as though dreaming. After this their hearts were no good any more. If the Great White Chief in Washington had not given us food we should have been wiped out without even a chance to fight for ourselves.[6]

With the loss of freedom to practice their most important spiritual traditions and the passing of elders—the spiritual leaders with ritual knowledge—some became adherents of the Ghost Dance, which promised a return to the old and better way of life. The Ghost Dance came to Plains Indian people in 1889–1890 under the leadership of the Paiute visionary Wovoka, whose father had participated in a version of this Native revitalization movement in the 1870s. Originating near the Walker River Reservation in Nevada, this movement spread rapidly throughout the Plains as tribal delegations came to experience Wovoka's doctrines.

Wovoka taught that people could return to their old ways of life by doing the Ghost Dance in a four-day ceremony, living peacefully, and working hard. The earth would be regenerated and the buffalo and other game would return and once again be plentiful. Relatives and friends who had passed on would return, white men would disappear, and the people would live free of disease, death, and misery.[7] Both men and women participated in the dance, which was adapted by each tribe with diverse manifestations consistent with its own cultural traditions.

Sacred clothing created for the Ghost Dance was rich with symbolism and often derived from the visionary experiences of adherents. Dresses, shirts, and leggings were painted with powerful representations of the earth and sky—mountains, plants, the sun, moon, and stars—and creatures with importance in the spirit world—the turtle, which supported the earth, and eagles, crows, and magpies, which served as messengers to heaven. The materials and designs used in Ghost Dance clothing varied among individuals and tribes. People of the Southern Plains made their clothing of tanned deer or elk hide painted with natural pigments and sometimes decorated with eagle feathers, often omitting the glass beads and metal decorations that had come through Euro-American trade. The Lakota made fringed shirts and dresses of cotton muslin which they believed were impenetrable to bullets.[8] Sweat ceremonies, ceremonial smoking and smudging, and ritual painting of faces with images derived from visions were also incorporated into the ritual.

Ghost Dance Shirt
Hinono'ei (Arapaho), Oklahoma, ca. 1890
Tanned elk hide, eagle feather, pigments;
40 x 29 inches
Chandler-Pohrt Collection, Gift of The Searle
Family Trust and The Paul Stock Foundation
NA.204.5

The shirt is painted with images significant in
Arapaho traditions and Ghost Dance symbolism. Eagles, magpies, and crows serve as spiritual messengers to the heavens. The turtle is
the supporter of the earth, which causes the
earth to tremble as it moves. The human figure
carries a pipe and has the design of the crescent on his chest.

Ghost Dance Dress
Hinono'ei (Arapaho), Oklahoma, ca. 1890
Tanned deer hide, mescal seeds, brass beads,
ermine tails, feathers, satin ribbon, hawk bells,
mirror; 56 x 33 inches
Gift of J.C. Nichols NA.204.1

Performance of the Ghost Dance rekindled traditional forms of ritual and prayer and celebrated the individual and direct nature of
Plains Indian religious experience. The creator
of this dress depicted elements of the universe
as a whole—the mountains of the earth and
the heavens above represented by the evening
sky and its stars. Trade materials including ribbons, brass hawk bells, and a mirror have been
added together with the more traditional feathers and strips of ermine.

Ghost Dance Shirt
Lakota (Sioux), South Dakota, ca. 1890
Muslin, pigment, eagle and owl feathers;
35 ½ x 27 ½ inches
Gift of The New Hampshire Historical Society
NA.204.2

Lakota Ghost Dancers believed that their Ghost
Dance shirts would protect them from bullets
and other weapons. Wovoka supplied red ochre
to Ghost Dancers through traveling emissaries
for use on faces and clothing. Lakota dancers
used the sacred red paint on fringe, trim, and
sacred designs of their cloth shirts.

Followers of the Ghost Dance created songs that addressed the misery of the reservations and their visionary hope for a new world as well as the movement's ritual symbolism. A particularly plaintive song of the Arapaho told of the hunger and dependence of reservation life.

> Father, have pity on me,
> Father, have pity on me:
> I am crying for thirst,
> I am crying for thirst;
> All is gone—I have nothing to eat,
> All is gone—I have nothing to eat.[9]

Another Arapaho song told of the promise of Wovoka of the spiritual new earth that would begin with a tremor.

> My children, my children,
> Look! The earth is about to move,
> Look! The earth is about to move,
> My father tells me so,
> My father tells me so.[10]

The crow as a messenger to the spirit world is omniscient and sees and hears everything both on earth and in the sky. This Northern Arapaho song related the power of the crow.

> I hear everything,
> I hear everything,
> I am the crow,
> I am the crow.[11]

The Ghost Dance movement came to an abrupt conclusion for Lakota followers after the Wounded Knee Massacre of 1890. For other peoples, including the Wichita, Pawnee, and Shoshone, the ceremony continued for many years. The Ghost Dance and accompanying songs are sometimes performed today on special occasions. The continuing power of Ghost Dance symbolism also is reflected in contemporary artistic expressions that refer to this spiritual movement and incorporate images of the significant elements of the universe characteristic of earlier manifestations.

The Native American Church also brought spiritual succor to Plains Indian people during the difficult and disruptive early reservation period. This movement combined elements of traditional Native religious beliefs with the teachings of Christianity and is based upon the ritual consumption of peyote—a medicinal cactus used among Indian people for thousands of years—as a sacrament. The Native American Church originated around 1880 among the Southern Plains tribes living on reservations in southwestern Oklahoma under the early leadership of men such as Quanah Parker of the Comanche and John Wilson of the Caddo. The movement quickly disseminated to other Native people in Oklahoma and the surrounding region, assisted by the establishment of intertribal educational institutions such as Carlisle Indian School in Pennsylvania and the Haskell Institute in Lawrence, Kansas. In 1928, the Native American Church was established formally as a legally incorporated entity at a time when the federal government was attempting to prohibit the use of peyote.

Members of the Native American Church in the early reservation period created specialized art for ritual use, including gourd rattles, carved and beaded staffs, fans, water drums, carrying boxes, and other ceremonial materials. Most of these objects were made by practitioners of the religion for their own use or for other participants rather than for sale. The Native American Church also inspired the creation of distinctive beadwork and jewelry and other items produced of German (or nickel) silver in styles that have proliferated among Indian people through the United States in much the same manner as the religious movement itself has spread. Twentieth-century artists also created paintings and drawings depicting ceremonial scenes and elements of Native American Church symbolism, following a spiritual inspiration that continues to the present day.

Fan
Omaha, ca. 1910
Dyed eagle feathers, glass beads, tanned hide; 26 ¼ x 11 inches
Chandler-Pohrt Collection, Gift of Mr. and Mrs. Richard A. Pohrt NA.502.183

Native American Church members created loose feather fans with beaded handles, carved and beaded staffs, and gourd rattles for their all-night ceremonies. The handle is beaded in a distinctive style known as gourd stitch, also sometimes referred to as peyote stitch because of its predominant use on ceremonial objects of the Native American Church.

Our Hearts Were Like Stone

I entered into the Staked Plains and turned north. At some point in my journey it became clear to me that I was moving against the grain of time.

I came to a great canyon in the plain and descended into it. It was a very beautiful place. There was clear water and high green grass. A great herd of buffalo was grazing there. I moved slowly among those innumerable animals, coming so close to some that I could touch them, and I did touch them, and the long, dusty hair of their hides was crinkled and coarse in my fingers. In among them they were so many that I could not see the ground beneath them; they seemed a great thick meadow of dark grain, and their breathing was like the sound of a huge, close swarm of bees. Guadal-tseyu and I, we picked our way, going very slowly, and the buffalo parted before us—it was like the careful tearing of a seam, stitch by stitch – and otherwise they paid us no mind. We were a long time in their midst, it seemed a long time passing through. And farther on there were tipis, some of them partly dismantled, and little fires gone and going out, embers smoldering, and many things were strewn about, as if a people were breaking camp. But there were no people; the people had gone away. And for a long time after that I followed their tracks.

—N. Scott Momaday[12]

By the middle of the nineteenth century, the herds of buffalo that once covered the Great Plains were visibly declining in numbers. Environmental historians and biologists have proposed various factors for this decline, including droughts or depredation from wolves, over-hunting by Native and Euro-American commercial hide hunters, and premeditated mass killings sanctioned and encouraged by the United States Army.

For nineteenth-century Native people, the diminishment of the herds became increasingly noticeable as hunters were forced to travel far beyond their traditional territories to locate the scarce and scattered herds. In retrospect, they associated the disappearance of the buffalo with the destruction of their traditions and communities. Plenty Coups described the unspeakable sadness this brought to the people: " . . . when the buffalo went away the hearts of my people fell to the ground, and they could not lift them up again. After this nothing happened. There was little singing anywhere."[13]

The periodic occurrence of drought on the Plains, which limited the amount of grass and forage available, set the stage for the decline of the buffalo. On the Northern Plains, a fifteen-year drought occurred between 1836 and 1851, with other dry spells occurring during the latter eighteenth and early nineteenth centuries. The Central Plains experienced droughts from 1761 to 1773, from 1798 to 1803, and from 1822 to 1832.[14] Until the nineteenth century, the resilient and nutritious short grasses preferred by the buffalo tended to recover along with the animals themselves. By the middle of the nineteenth century, however, recovery from droughts became much more problematic because of competition from increasing numbers of cattle, horses, and sheep and restrictions on bison migrations as Euro-Americans moved into the region.

Beginning in the 1840s, emigrants traveling to California through the Central Plains brought with them livestock, which trampled or consumed grasses for miles on either side of the trail along the Platte River, effectively destroying the buffalo's forage. In 1853, emigrants herded over one hundred thousand cattle and forty-eight thousand sheep along the Platte. It is estimated that by 1860, emigrants had driven over half a million cattle and an equal number of sheep along the Oregon and California trails. Similar destruction of forage occurred in the Southern Plains along the Santa Fe Trail. Adding to this stress was the emigrants' sport of shooting any buffalo that approached their wagon trains as they traveled west.[15] The establishment of Euro-American homesteads and ranches as well as the construction of transcontinental railroads also limited the migration of the buffalo.

As the buffalo herds were destabilized, the introduction of commercial hide hunting—a profitable business on the Plains by the middle of the nineteenth century—brought about their final devastation. Eastern and European manufacturing interests instigated the market for the thick and durable buffalo hides, which were used to make belts to drive the machinery in increasing numbers of factories. Heavy buffalo robes also were much in demand for lap robes and warm winter coats.

The commercial hunters killed as many buffalo as possible using powerful long-range rifles. Since they only wanted the hides, the hunters skinned the buffalo, leaving the meat behind. Sometimes, they also took the tongues, which were salted or smoked and sold as delicacies. There are numerous anecdotes of hunters killing thousands of buffalo over brief periods of time and leaving acres and acres of dead and skinned buffalo unused on the plains. Although the commercial hide hunters likely exaggerated their individual exploits and early chroniclers overstated the immensity of some of the kills, railroad shipping records attest to the large number of hides that were transported east, and period photographs document scenes of many dead and skinned bison lying on the ground, immense mounds of buffalo hides piled at train depots awaiting transportation, and enormous piles of buffalo bones that were later collected to be manufactured into fertilizer. Pretty Shield described the desolation of the Crow after seeing the mass slaughter of buffalo.

> Ahh, my heart fell down when I began to see dead buffalo scattered all over our beautiful country, killed and skinned, and left to rot by white men, many, many hundreds of buffalo. The first I saw of this was in the Judith basin. The whole country there smelled of rotting meat. Even the flowers could not drown the bad smell. Our hearts were like stone.[16]

Nineteenth-century trade in buffalo hides intensified with the development of new means of transportation that brought both settlers and buffalo hunters to

In the track of the skin hunters 1878 Timber creek North Montana
© by L.A Huffman.

In the track of the skin hunters, 1878
Timber Creek, North Montana
Photograph by L.A. Huffman (1854–1931)
P.100.3104

Commercial hide hunters who proliferated on the Plains from the 1870s to early 1880s destroyed the once vast herds of buffalo. Interested only in the hides or tongues which could be shipped for commercial uses in Eastern and European cities, the hunters killed enormous numbers of buffalo. The hides and sometimes the tongues were taken, and the rest of the animal was left behind.

the heart of buffalo country and made possible large shipments of robes to eastern markets. Steamboats began ascending the Missouri River in the 1820s, and in 1832, an American Fur Company steamboat reached the mouth of the Yellowstone River at Fort Union.[17] During the 1830s and 1840s, there was a significant increase in the buffalo hide trade in the Missouri River region, with the American Fur Company shipping approximately 110,000 robes a year to St. Louis by the late 1840s.[18] As buffalo became scarcer in that region in the 1850s, the Upper Missouri River hide trade began to decline.

The establishment of railroad lines throughout the Plains exponentially increased the number of buffalo killed and hides shipped to market in the 1870s and early 1880s, until there were essentially no remaining herds. By 1869, the Union Pacific Railroad joined the Central Pacific in Utah and traveled across the plains through Nebraska and Wyoming Territory. In 1870, the Kansas Pacific Railroad reached Denver, Colorado, and in 1872, the Atchison, Topeka, and Santa Fe reached Dodge City, Kansas, which almost immediately became the center of the hide trade. In 1880, the Northern Pacific Railroad was extended to Glendive, Montana Territory.[19]

By 1875, market hunting had obliterated the herds of the Southern Plains and by 1883, wild buffalo herds were nearly eradicated everywhere. The last

commercial shipment of hides took place in 1889, and by 1894, the only free buffalo remaining in the United States could be found in Yellowstone National Park. By 1902, poachers had reduced the Yellowstone herd to only twenty-eight animals.[20]

Obviously, commercial hide hunting had a devastating effect upon the lives of Plains Indian people. In the short run, it also provided new opportunities for those Native and Métis hunters who participated in this economy by exchanging hides for new and desirable Euro-American goods at Fort Union, Bent's Fort, Fort Pierre, and other trading posts. The United States military also encouraged this slaughter by providing ammunition, supplies, and safe passage along the railways into the Plains territories to Euro-American hunters. In the end, the destruction of the buffalo herds—the "Indian's commissary" in the words of General Philip Sheridan—was successful in helping subjugate the Native people of the Plains and making their lands available for Euro-American settlement.[21]

Prominent in oral histories and winter counts of many Plains Indian peoples are the remembrances of the final disappearance of buffalo from their regions and the last bison hunts. For the Kiowa of the Southern Plains, this occurred in 1882. The Kiowa believed that the buffalo had once lived underground and the actions of the whites who came into their lands to establish forts, railroads, settlements, the buffalo soldiers—African American troops of the Ninth and Tenth Cavalry—and hide hunters had driven them back down. The ancient ceremonies of the Kiowa had failed to bring the buffalo back to the people.

The buffalo saw that their day was over. They could protect their people no longer. Sadly, the last remnant of the great herd gathered in council, and decided what they would do.

The Kiowas were camped on the north side of Mount Scott, those of them who were still free to camp. One woman got up very early in the morning. The dawn mist was still rising from Medicine Creek, and as she looked across the river, peering through the haze, she saw the last buffalo herd appear like a spirit dream.

Straight to Mount Scott the leader of the herd walked. Behind him came the cows and their calves, and the few young males who had survived. As the woman watched, the face of the mountain opened.

Inside Mount Scott the world was green and fresh, as it had been when she was a small girl. The rivers ran clear, not red. The wild plums were in blossom, chasing the red buds up the inside slopes. Into this world of beauty the buffalo walked, never to be seen again.[22]

The loss of the buffalo influenced all spheres of Plains Indian life that had centered on both the practical endeavors of the hunt and the spiritual aspects of respect and gratitude the people held for this magnificent creature. Although government agents attempted to introduce cattle ranching and farming to tribes once they were settled on reservations, many of the essential prerequisites for such occupations were not provided and individuals were slow to adopt this new way of life. The meat of the cattle issued by the federal government provided much needed nourishment and a rare opportunity of excitement for men, who sometimes hunted and killed the cattle as a poor substitute for buffalo hunting. However, cattle failed to fulfill the peoples' spiritual needs. Those ceremonies, dances, and songs related to the buffalo became less frequently performed, creating a spiritual void in the lives of the people.

"The Nation's Hoop is Broken"

I am an old woman now. The buffaloes and black-tail deer are gone, and our Indian ways are almost gone. Sometimes I find it hard to believe that I ever lived them.

My little son grew up in the white man's school. He can read books, and he owns cattle and has a farm. He is a leader among our Hidatsa people, helping teach them to follow the white man's road.

He is kind to me. We no longer live in an earth lodge, but in a house with chimneys; and my son's wife cooks by a stove.

But for me, I cannot forget our old ways.

Often in summer, I rise at daybreak and steal out to the cornfields; and as I hoe the corn I sing to it, as we did when I was young. No one cares for our corn songs now.

Sometimes at evening I sit, looking out on the big Missouri. The sun sets, and dusk steals over the water. In the shadows I seem again to see our Indian village, with smoke curling upward from the earth lodges; and in the river's roar I hear the yells of the warriors, the laughter of little children as of old. It is but an old woman's dream. Again I see but shadows and hear only the roar of the river; and tears come into my eyes. Our Indian life, I know, is gone forever.[23]

The American public is somewhat familiar with the Trail of Tears, a dramatic event during which approximately seventeen thousand Cherokee people were forcibly removed from their homelands in the southeastern United States to Indian Territory in 1838, a trip that resulted in an estimated four thousand deaths. As a Plains Indian elder once remarked, each tribe also experienced its own Trail of Tears during which they were brought to the nadir of their existence. Many tribes such as the Ponca, Otoe and Missouria, and Pawnee of the Central Plains experienced actual physical relocations from their traditional homelands to reservations in Indian Territory. In other cases for tribal peoples who retained a remnant of their lands in the Northern and Southern Plains, their Trail of Tears consisted of a spiritual dislocation, brought about by the loss of the buffalo and concomitant challenges to their life ways and essential beliefs.

In 1877, the Ponca were forcibly removed from their Nebraska reservation and eventually relocated on the Salt Fork River in Indian Territory. During the long trip south, more than a third of their people died of starvation and disease, and those remaining were in extremely poor condition. On January 1, 1879, Standing Bear, carrying the remains of his son who had died in Indian Territory for burial in their Nebraska homelands, left the reservation with thirty followers to return north to the Niobrara. Once the group arrived and settled with allies on the Omaha Reservation, Standing Bear was arrested by federal troops under General George Crook and informed that he would have to return to Indian Territory. With the help of individuals interested in Indian policy reform, the story of Standing Bear's plight reached sympathetic audiences first in Omaha and then in Eastern cities where he toured from 1879 to 1883.[24]

> We told them that we would rather die than leave our lands; but we could not help ourselves. They took us down. Many died on the road. Two of my children died. After we reached the new land, all of my horses died. The water was very bad. All our cattle died; not one was left. I stayed till one hundred and fifty-eight of my people had died. Then I ran away with thirty of my people, men and women and children. Some of the children were orphans. We were three months on the road. We were weak and sick and starved. When we reached the Omaha Reserve the Omahas gave us a piece of land, and we were in a hurry to plough it and put in wheat. While we were working, the soldiers came and arrested us. Half of us were sick. We would rather have died than have been carried back; but we could not help ourselves.[25]

The Pawnee also experienced physical relocation, first to a reservation at Genoa, Nebraska, in 1859, and then to Black Bear Creek in Indian Territory in 1874–1875. Their subsequent losses are reflected in declining population numbers that demonstrate the combined effects of epidemics, starvation, and warfare with other Plains people. In 1800, Pawnee population estimates range from 10,000 to 12,500 people.[26] By 1840, they were counted at 6,244 individuals, and

Two Crow Children

Crow Reservation, Montana, early 1900s
Photograph by Rev. W. A. Petzoldt, D.D.
(1872–1960)
Dr. William and Anna Petzoldt Collection, Gift of
Genevieve Petzoldt Fitzgerald PN.95.185

The dress of the two Crow children shows the contrasting styles of the early reservation period. The girl wears her traditional dress decorated in elk teeth, necklace, earrings, and moccasins. The boy wears the clothing of a cowboy—cotton shirt and silk scarf, leather gloves, a hat, and chaps.

in 1872, they were reported to number 2,447.[27] In 1890, fifteen years after being removed to Indian Territory, Pawnee people numbered 804 individuals. By 1900, Pawnee population numbers reached the low point of 650.[28]

The destructive effects of Old World diseases on tribal populations were overwhelming, particularly for horticultural people who lived large parts of the year in densely populated earth lodge villages. Such diseases had already taken their toll on Plains populations during the eighteenth century, and beginning with the 1801–1802 smallpox pandemic, recorded in Lone Dog's winter count, became even more widespread and destructive. Researchers have documented thirteen smallpox epidemics affecting North American Indians during the nineteenth century, as well as five of measles, three of cholera, and two of influenza.[29]

A major smallpox pandemic swept throughout the Plains, Northwest, Canada, and Alaska between 1836 and 1840, resulting in thousands of American Indian deaths. The epidemic was recorded in a Kiowa winter count as Smallpox Winter in 1839–1840 and documented in tribal oral traditions and accounts of outside observers throughout the Plains. Plenty Coups described the arrival of the smallpox to a group of Crow who were camped north of present Billings, Montana.[30] Not knowing the origin of the disease and frightened by the number of deaths, Plenty Coups said that two young warriors rode their horses over a bluff to their deaths as sacrifices to save their loved ones from the disease.[31]

The epidemic was brought to the Northern Plains in the summer of 1837 by travelers on the American Fur Company steamboat St. Peter to Fort Union and, in only a few short weeks, caused the deaths of approximately 10,000 Native people.[32] In July, the disease reached the Mandan who lived in two earth lodge villages on either side of the Missouri, reducing their population from an estimated sixteen hundred to two thousand individuals to only one hundred and thirty-eight by October of that year.[33] Four Bears, a leader who had welcomed many Euro-Americans travelers, including the artists George Catlin in 1832 and Karl Bodmer in the winter of 1833–1834, died on July 30, 1837 denouncing the men who had brought the disease to the Mandan people.

> Listen well what I have to say, as it will be the last time you will hear Me. Think of your Wives, Children, Brothers, Sisters, Friends, and in fact all that you hold dear, are all Dead, or Dying, with their faces all rotten, caused by those dogs the whites, think of that My friends, and rise all together and Not leave one of them alive. The 4 Bears will act his part.[34]

Buffalo Bird Woman also recalled the impact of the 1837 smallpox epidemic on the Mandan and Hidatsa people: "We had corn aplenty and buffalo meat to eat in the Five Villages, and there were old people and little children in every lodge. Then smallpox came. More than half of my tribe died in the smallpox winter. Of the Mandans only a few families were left alive. All the old people and little children died."[35]

An estimated 6,000 to 8,000 Blackfoot, Piegan, and Blood individuals died from this epidemic. Mike Bruised Head of the Kainai described the effects of the smallpox, which he characterized as a "price the Blackfoot paid for the fur trade," as "vast and enormous."

> Smallpox affected every core of our being. As a result of the smallpox, we lost a large body of knowledge from our people, the old people. You can consequently say that the disease had a profound impact on the Blackfoot physically, culturally and spiritually. Their whole being was affected. The smallpox outbreak reduced the number of society members for years. It affected society transfers of bundles and sacred items. Sacred items could not be transferred because they became infected. Pipes and bundles were buried with the people, if the people were buried at all. There was a fear that touching these sacred articles would transmit the disease and affect more people.[36]

Smallpox continued to devastate Plains populations throughout the nineteenth century. Vaccinations were available by the early 1800s and were sometimes provided for in treaties, but they were only intermittently available until the late nineteenth century.[37] Cholera, malaria, measles, tuberculosis, scarlet fever, whooping cough, mumps, and influenza also incapacitated Plains peoples during the nineteenth and early twentieth centuries. Reservations were rampant with disease, most likely resulting from the generally unhealthy environments, poor medical treatment, malnutrition, and the overall weakened condition of the people.

As railroads, forts, trails, and settlements increasingly encroached on tribal homelands during the last half of the nineteenth century, warfare between Plains Indian people and the U.S. military intensified. Many conflicts were severe and dramatic, sometimes resulting in such glorious victories for Plains Indian people as the Little Bighorn Battle or in crushing defeats at massacres at Sand Creek, the Marias River, the Washita, and Wounded Knee. The Blackfeet and Gros Ventre writer James Welch described such conflicts as a "clash of cultures."

> The Indians would say they were defending their territory, or exercising their right to be free upon it, to follow the buffalo as they had for centuries; the white authorities would say that they were punishing the Indians for depredations against the white settlers, traders, rivermen, wood gatherers, and miners, or for leaving the reservations without permission. In any case, contrary to some opinions, these actions resulted from a clash of cultures. What caused this clash is evident. The Indians lived on territories that the whites wanted. Most such collisions occur when one culture wants something from the other. It is always astonishing when the invading culture feels it has the divine right (call it Manifest Destiny or whatever) to take that something, in this case, land—from the other.[38]

In writing about Little Bighorn, Welch observed that, in retrospect, people tend to dwell upon their defeats rather than their victories. This is exemplified by the commemoration and glorification of General George Custer's and the Seventh Cavalry's defeat at Little Bighorn, which began immediately after the event on June 25–26, 1876, and continues today. For almost one hundred and fifty years, Plains Native people also have memorialized fatal conflicts with the United States military through oral and recorded histories of their own tribes. In recent years, they have brought such events to public recognition through art, literature, and dedications of memorials—sometimes in cooperation with government agencies—to Black Kettle, Big Foot, and others who died on the Washita and Sand Creek and at Wounded Knee and sites of other nineteenth-century conflicts.

> Defeat touches people deeply because of the sheer weight of loss. Victory is generally fleeting, a good, often exhilarating feeling, a celebration, but loss lingers long after the event. Loss in battle means the death of loved ones, hardship, and suffering. It often means the death of an ideal, or in the Indian case, of a way of life too. And so loss stays with a people, often at the fringe of the desperation of getting on with life, but always there. Loss is a hard legacy to pass on to their children and to their children's children.[39]

The Cheyenne, Lakota, and Arapaho participants in the victory at Little Bighorn also suffered losses of leaders, warriors, and family members. The Cheyenne warrior Wooden Leg characterized the scene in camp immediately after the battle as a time of mourning rather than boisterous celebration.

> There was no dancing nor celebrating of any kind in any of the camps that night. Too many people were in mourning, among all of the Sioux as well as the Cheyennes. Too many Cheyenne and Sioux women had gashed their arms and legs in token of their grief. The people generally were praying not cheering."[40]

Plains Indian people continue to carry the memories of such losses as the massacres at the Marias River, during which one hundred and seventy-three Blackfeet under the peaceful leader Heavy Runner were killed on June 23, 1870, and Sand Creek, during which the Third Colorado Cavalry under the command of Colonel John M. Chivington massacred over one hundred and fifty Cheyenne and Arapaho, mostly women and children, who were part of Black Kettle's and White Antelope's peaceful camp on November 29, 1864. At Sand Creek, the old warrior White Antelope, seventy-five years of age, was killed by soldiers as he sang his death song:

> Nothing lives long
> Except the earth and the mountains.[41]

Black Kettle survived Sand Creek but died four years later on the banks of the Washita River as the Seventh Cavalry under Lieutenant Colonel George A. Custer attacked his village, killing Cheyenne men, women, and children and destroying lodges, winter food supplies, and horse herds on November 27, 1868.

Girls Dormitory, Crow Boarding School
Pryor, Montana, ca. 1899
Photograph by Fred E. Miller (1868–1936)
P.32.94

Day schools and boarding schools were built to educate children on reservations and other regions away from home. The girls here, lined up in order from the oldest to the youngest, are shown in their cotton dresses with their teachers and other school workers standing behind.

Woman using a sewing machine (treadle)
Photograph by Rev. W. A. Petzoldt, D.D.
(1872–1960)
Crow Reservation, Montana, early 1900s
Dr. William and Anna Petzoldt Collection,
Gift of Genevieve Petzoldt Fitzgerald PN.95.270

When treadle sewing machines became available on Plains reservations, women used them to make canvas tipis, wall, tents, canvas and muslin liners for log houses, quilts, and clothing.

The infamous Wounded Knee Massacre has come to symbolize the tragedy and brutality of nineteenth-century conflicts between Plains Indian peoples and the United States military, as well as the end of the old way of life. Wounded Knee occurred as a reaction of the federal government—specifically the War Department—to the Ghost Dance as it spread among the Lakota, beginning in March, 1890 after a visit of Short Bull, Kicking Bear, and other delegates to the Paiute visionary Wovoka. Increasingly fearful that the Ghost Dance would inspire Lakota resistance and armed conflict, government officials prohibited such gatherings and sent troops to arrest the Lakota leader Sitting Bull at Standing Rock and to quell this spiritual movement. The tragic results were the death of Sitting Bull on December 15, 1890, and the massacre of more than three hundred men, women, and children at Big Foot's Ghost Dance encampment by members of the Seventh Cavalry armed with Hotchkiss guns on December 29. In the following year, American Horse, a Lakota delegate to Washington D.C., testified about the killing of women and children at Wounded Knee.

There was a woman with an infant in her arms who was killed as she almost touched the flag of truce, and the women and children of course were strewn all along the circular village until they were dispatched. Right near the flag of truce a mother was shot down with

her infant; the child not knowing that its mother was dead was still nursing, and that especially was a very sad sight. The women as they were fleeing with their babies were killed together, shot right through, and the women who were very heavy with child were also killed.[42]

Black Elk described the impact of the Wounded Knee Massacre on the Lakota people:

And so it was all over.

I did not know then how much was ended. When I look back now from this high hill of my old age, I can still see the butchered women and children lying heaped and scattered all along the crooked gulch as plain as when I saw them with eyes still young. And I can see that something else died there in the bloody muck, and was buried in the blizzard. A people's dream died there. It was a beautiful dream.

And I, to whom so great a vision was given in my youth—you see me now a pitiful old man who has done nothing, for the nation's hoop is broken and scattered. There is no center any longer, and the sacred tree is dead.[43]

Other struggles with Euro-American authorities took place away from the battlefield, in meetings, conferences, and treaty negotiations. Some of these conferences were held in tribal homelands and on reservations, although many occurred during formal visits of tribal delegations to Washington, D.C., where they met with the President and other government officials to express the con-

Half Leggings
Dakota (Eastern Sioux), South Dakota, ca. 1860
Tanned deer hide, canvas, cotton cloth, glass beads; 17 ½ x 25 inches
Chandler-Pohrt Collection, Gift of Mr. William D. Weiss NA.202.468

Métis men sometimes wore half leggings such as this pair decorated with Eastern Sioux beadwork in floral designs, over buckskin trousers. Native women made such leggings for husbands and other family members or for trade.

Shirt
Hidatsa or Mandan, Fort Berthold Reservation, ca. 1880–1900
Muslin cloth, dyed porcupine quills, tanned hide; 27 x 44 inches
The Catherine Bradford Collection, Gift of The Coe Foundation NA.202.197

Once tribal people settled on reservations, traditional materials such as hides were sometimes scarce, so they relied upon materials from trading posts and stores. This shirt is made of muslin but decorated in porcupine quillwork and fringed as in pre-reservation times.

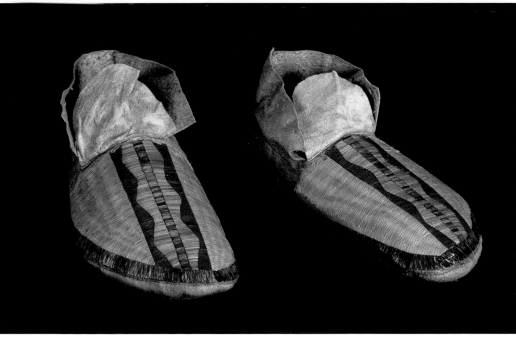

Moccasins
Hidatsa, ca. 1900
Tanned deer hide, dyed porcupine quills, glass beads, brass buttons; 10 ⅛ x 4 ⅛ inches
Dr. William and Anna Petzoldt Collection, Gift of their daughter Genevieve Fitzgerald NA.202.31

cerns and needs of their people. For government representatives, the purpose of such visits to Washington was to impress upon Indian people the wealth and power of the United States by showing them firearms, railroads, steamboats, battleships, telegraphs, tall buildings, and the immense cities and seemingly inexhaustible populations that inhabited them.[44] The feeling was that once Indian leaders became aware of such technological and population advantages, they would no longer resist the government's efforts at territorial and cultural domination.

Plains Indian delegations to Washington expressed dismay at the sheer number of white people they encountered in Chicago, Philadelphia, Washington, and

New York. Sometimes, they were disappointed and frustrated at their failure to impress upon the government officials the needs of their people, discussions of which were often met with empty promises. In 1891, Young Man Afraid of His Horses, an Oglala Lakota leader, reported of his Washington meeting that "We had some promises, but they are like all other promises of the Great Father. We are not fooled and we go home with heavy hearts."[45] Despite the setbacks, tribal leaders such as Red Cloud and Medicine Crow became more adept at dealing with government officials and made several trips to Washington to protect their diminishing lands and their peoples' interests.

Life and Art of the Reservation

We had everything to learn about the white man's road. We had come to a country that was new to us, where wind and rain and rivers and heat and cold and even some of the plants and animals were different from what we had always known. We had to learn to live by farming instead of by hunting and trading; we had to learn from people who did not speak our language or try to learn it, except for a few words, though they expected us to learn theirs. We had to learn to cut our hair short, and to wear close-fitting clothes made of dull-colored cloth, and to live in houses, though we knew that our long braids of hair and embroidered robes and moccasins and tall, round lodges were more beautiful.

—Carl Sweezy[46]

The Southern Arapaho artist Carl Sweezy (ca. 1880–1953) described the dilemmas faced by tribal members as they adapted to the radical and rapid changes of life on the Cheyenne and Arapaho Reservation in Oklahoma and attempted to meet the expectations of Euro-American officials and missionaries by learning farming and ranching skills. He also recalled the excitement that occurred when cattle were issued to reservation families and men brought their weapons and fastest horses to the agency headquarters for a hunt reminiscent of the days of hunting buffalo on the Plains. After the hunt, women butchered the cattle, saving the hides for future use, prepared feasts, and preserved remaining meat by drying. In 1896, reservation officials decided to change this method of beef issue "to shorten the time required for the issue, and to do away with the celebrating that went with it."[47] The cattle were slaughtered and only the meat was distributed, much to the disappointment of the Cheyenne and Arapaho people, whose leaders protested this decision to no avail.

A principal foundation of the federal government's program of assimilation involved the physical removal of children from the influences of their elders and their cultural traditions—essentially breaking family bonds. The children were sent to government vocational boarding schools many miles away from home. After experimenting with educating Indian students at Hampton Normal and Agricultural Institute in Hampton, Virginia, a school for African Americans, in

1879 Captain Richard Henry Pratt established the first off-reservation boarding school in an abandoned army barracks in Carlisle, Pennsylvania. Luther Standing Bear was in the first class at Carlisle Indian School, which he later said he left the Lakota reservation to attend as an act of bravery.[48]

> One day some white people came among us and called a meeting of the parents. We children did not know what it was all about, but I sensed something serious, for my father was very thoughtful for a time. Then he asked me one day if I would like to go away with the white people. They had come after some boys and girls and wanted to take them a long way off to a place about which we knew nothing. I consented at once, though I could think of nothing else but that these white people wanted to take us away and kill us.[49]

Young Indian students like Standing Bear embarked upon a radically new experience when they attended schools where they shed their Indian names, languages, their long hair, hide clothing, and individual and tribal identities to be immersed in Euro-American philosophies and practices. Standing Bear described the boarding school practice of renaming children, in which—in contrast to

Dress
Apsáalooke (Crow), Montana, ca. 1900
Wool cloth, imitation elk teeth (bone),
glass beads; 43 x 26 inches
Irving H. "Larry" Larom Collection NA.202.65

Crow, Cheyenne and Lakota women used elk teeth to decorate distinctive dresses, as symbols of prestige, wealth, and the hunting abilities of husbands and fathers. Because only the rare upper canine teeth—symbols of endurance and longevity—were used on the dresses, substitutes were sometimes carved of bone or elk antler and stained to look like real ones. During the late 1800s, Crow women and girls wore dresses of blue or red wool such as this one in a tribally distinctive style which has carried through to today.

tribal naming ceremonies—they were told to choose names from a list on the blackboard which was never read or explained.

> The teacher had a long pointed stick in her hand, and the interpreter told the boy in the front seat to come up. The teacher handed the stick to him, and the interpreter told him to pick out any name he wanted. The boy had gone up with his blanket on. When the long stick was handed to him, he turned to us as much to say, "Shall I—or will you help me—to take one of these names?" He did not know what to do for a time . . . .
>
> Finally, he pointed out one of the names written on the blackboard. Then the teacher took a piece of white tape and wrote the name on it. Then she cut off a length of the tape and sewed it on the back of the boy's shirt. Then that name was erased from the board . . . . Soon we all had names of white men sewed on our backs.[50]

After the opening of Carlisle, other government boarding schools were established, with twenty-four in operation by 1899, including Chilocco Indian Agricultural School in Indian Territory, and Haskell Institute, both of which

Jacket (front and back)
Apsáalooke (Crow), Montana, ca. 1885
Tanned deer hide, pigment, cloth, otter fur and hide, ribbon, glass beads, dyed horse hair; 38 ⅝ x 22 inches
Irving H. "Larry" Larom Collection NA.202.592

This jacket is painted in yellow pigment and features floral designs sometimes used in Crow beadwork. It is trimmed with otter hide, ribbons, and bundles of dyed horse hair on the back of each sleeve.

Dress

Amoskapi Pikuni (Blackfeet),
Montana, ca. 1890
Wool and cotton cloth, buttons,
glass beads, brass beads, bells,
thimbles, ribbon;
51¼ x 39⅝ inches
Chandler-Pohrt Collection, Gift of
Mr. and Mrs. Charles W. Duncan, Jr.
NA.202.466

The embellishment of this dress
reflects the centuries' old custom of
adopting new materials. Beads of
glass and metal cover the bodice
with a shimmering design of simple
stripes and ribbons decorate the
lower part. Beads, bells, and thimbles were added for color and
sound.

Girl's Dress
Lakota/Tsistsistas (Sioux/Cheyenne),
South Dakota or Montana, ca. 1890
Tanned deer hide, glass beads, tin cones,
cotton cloth; 33 ½ x 31 inches
Gift of Harriet D. Reed and Betty N.
Landercasper, In Memory of W. Guruea Dyer
NA.202.386

Lakota Girls
South Dakota, late 1800s
Vincent Mercaldo Collection P.71.1142

The four girls in this studio photograph are
dressed in their finest dresses, with fully
beaded yokes made in a style characteristic of
Lakota and Cheyenne beadwork of the early
reservation period, beaded moccasins, and
leggings.

opened in 1884 and throughout their long histories served students from the
Plains as well as other regions.[51] Although some children like Luther Standing
Bear voluntarily traveled far from their homes to attend schools, others were compelled to attend, when pressure was applied to their families to let them go. There
were many runaways and tragic stories of children who were physically and emo-
tionally abused or who died of foreign diseases, far from home and their families.

Despite the vocational emphasis of the boarding schools, there were also
programs in the arts that focused on studies of Euro-American cultural traditions. In music classes, students were organized into choirs and bands and were

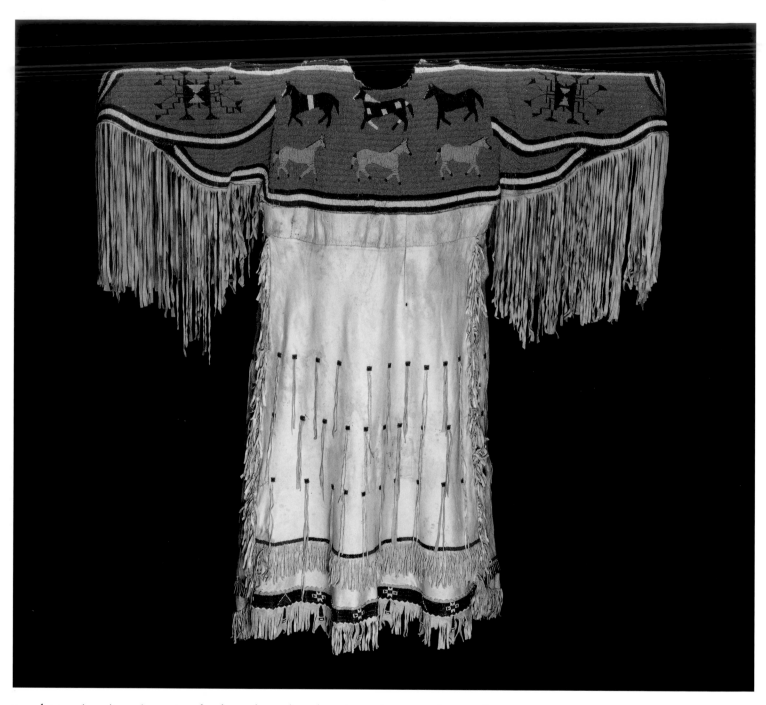

taught to sing American standards and to play the piano, brass, string, and woodwind instruments. In art classes, they learned easel painting following the forms of the European masters. In the early 1900s, Native cultural studies were introduced into the curriculum at Carlisle and other boarding schools under the political influence of Indian policy reformers.[52] These programs flourished intermittently until later educational reforms during the 1930s formalized this approach. Boarding schools also became the venues where cultural and artistic exchanges occurred as students from many tribal traditions and regions came together.

Dress

Lakota (Sioux), Northern Plains, ca. 1920
Tanned deer hide, glass beads, tin cones;
45 x 21¾ inches
Gift of Hon. and Mrs. William Henry Harrison
NA.202.70

This beautifully beaded dress features the pictorial designs of the reservation era with several horses—paints, black, brown, and white—on both the front and back.

LEFT: **Dress**
Lakota (Sioux), South Dakota, ca. 1880
Tanned deer hide, glass beads;
43 x 24 inches
Chandler-Pohrt Collection, Gift of Mr. William
D. Weiss NA.202.355

RIGHT: **Dress**
Lakota (Sioux),South Dakota, ca. 1890
Brain tanned deer hide, glass beads;
63 x 58 inches
Gift of Harriet D. Reed and Betty N.
Landercasper, In Memory of W. Guruea Dyer
NA.202.869

Lakota beadworkers favored blue beads as the
background for reservation-era dresses such
as this one featuring a fully-beaded bodice
with geometric and abstract tipi designs with
the typical U-shaped form at the center, said
to represent a turtle rising from the water.
Such dresses, beautiful yet too heavy for daily
wear, were made for formal dress.

233

Boy's Vest

Lakota (Sioux), South Dakota, ca. 1880
Tanned deer hide, glass beads, cloth;
15 x 16 inches
In memory of Frank O. Horton and Henriette S.
Horton NA.202.970

Beginning in the 1870s, women made vests for
men and boys of their family following the
Euro-American basic design but decorated with
elaborate, tribally specific beadwork. This vest
made for a favored young boy exhibits the
complexity of reservation-era Lakota design,
incorporating decorative lines, diamonds, and
forked forms with triangular bases.

Boy's Pants

Lakota (Sioux), South Dakota, ca. 1880
Tanned deer hide, glass beads, cloth,
14 ⅛ x 20 inches
In memory of Frank O. Horton and Henriette S.
Horton NA.202.971

During the transitions of the early reservation,
Lakota women excelled in making clothing
and other items fully covered in beadwork in
exquisite designs. Mothers, and especially
grandmothers, made distinctively decorated
moccasins, shirts, vests, dresses, and pants
for children to wear for ceremonies and other
special occasions.

Jacket (front and back)
Oglala Lakota South Dakota (Sioux), ca. 1890
Tanned deer hide, glass beads;
29 ½ x 19 ¾ inches
NA.202.378

This jacket was purchased from the Oglala
Lakota warrior and leader Iron Tail, who fought
in the Plains wars of the 1860s and 1870s. He
later performed in Buffalo Bill's Wild West
Show.

Boarding school experiences together with other changes and cultural encounters of the late nineteenth and early twentieth centuries profoundly influenced Plains Indian arts. Women and girls learned to use sewing machines through missionary classes and domestic arts programs in the schools. The machines were widely used for making canvas tents and tipis, clothing, quilts, bedding, curtains, and other household items adapted to the log houses that proliferated in reservation settings.

During the early reservation period encompassing the years 1880–1920, an unexpected and remarkable flowering of tribal arts transpired, with the creation of beautiful works in hide, beadwork, and porcupine quillwork combined with newly introduced materials and designs. Just at the point when Plains Indian peoples confined to the discouraging conditions of the reservations seemed to have reached the nadir of their existence, they did not die off or disappear into the larger American society. Instead, they experienced a renewed sense of creativity.

Women used porcupine quillwork with glass beads, fabrics, tin cones and other metals, and other materials available through trading posts and stores. During the 1880s, Lakota and Cheyenne women began to illustrate men's war exploits in representational images in quillwork and beading, an innovation from

earlier, predominately geometric designs. They created battle scenes with beaded images of men dressed in traditional clothing, riding on horseback, carrying weapons, and wearing eagle feather bonnets with long trailers. They also beaded figures of horses, buffalo, deer, elk, and birds as well as the cows and cowboys that eventually became part of their lives.

In keeping with the characterization that "Sioux women beaded everything that didn't move," Lakota beadworkers introduced a new style of decoration in which entire objects, including moccasins and even glass bottles, were covered in beadwork.[53] Using their skills in producing soft, white, tanned hides and beading, they created beautiful dresses with fully beaded yokes for ceremonies, dances, parades, and other formal occasions. They beaded men's vests of Euro-American style in geometric and representational designs. They also made cradles with tribal designs, beautiful clothing for their children and grandchildren as smaller versions of adult styles, and unique fully beaded pants and vests for little boys. The creation of such clothing signified to others the women's artistry and devotion to their beloved family members.

During this period, women began using the American flag as a decorative motif, most likely selected at first for its strong colors. Perhaps later, as Plains men joined the United States military in the early 1900s and went to fight in wars in European soil, the flag design took on deeper significance as representative of their homelands and the battles fought to protect them.

Jacket (front and back)
Lakota (Sioux), South Dakota, ca. 1920
Tanned deer hide, glass beads;
30 x 19 ¼ inches
Gift of Mrs. Howell Howard NA.202.193

This jacket of Euro-American cut is decorated front and back with beaded images of men wearing eagle feather bonnets and horses of many colors and trimmed with strips of geometric beadwork. Such a coat could have been made for a family member or for sale.

On the Southern Plains, as tribes from the Northeast and Great Lakes regions were relocated to reservations in Indian Territory, they brought with them floral designs that influenced Kiowa, Otoe, and other Plains beadworkers. The Crow and Blackfoot had earlier adopted floral designs from eastern peoples who had accompanied nineteenth-century fur traders. Fabrics with floral patterns also may have been inspirations for innovative beadwork designs.

Scholars have suggested that Plains Indian women produced beautifully embellished examples of material culture once they were settled on reservations, simply because they had more time without their traditional time-consuming duties associated with the buffalo hunting way of life. They had easier access to commercial materials, including silk ribbons, glass beads, cotton thread, fabrics, and brass bells and other metal decorations.

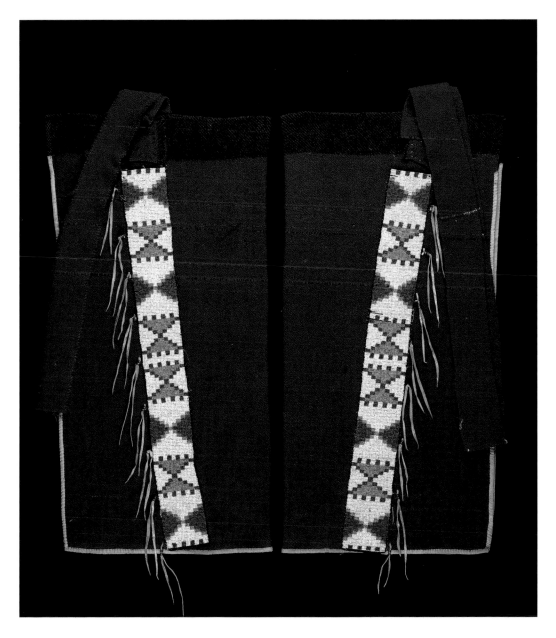

Man's Leggings
Blackfeet, Montana, ca. 1900
Wool cloth, glass and brass beads, tanned hide;
30 ¼ x 14 ¾ inches
NA.202.235

Shirt
Amoskapi Pikuni (Blackfeet), Montana ca. 1905
Tanned deer hide, ermine, glass beads;
32 x 21 inches
Adolf Spohr Collection, Gift of Larry Sheerin
NA.202.48

Once settled on reservations, men of distinction continued to wear decorated hide shirts for ceremonies, special occasions, and meetings with government representatives.

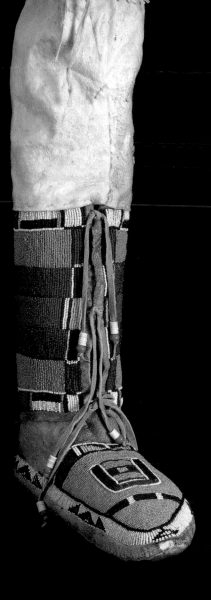

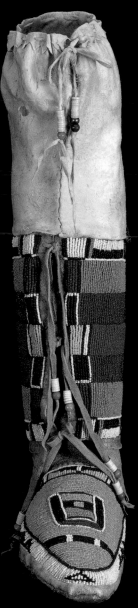

Top left: **Moccasins**
Tsistsistas (Cheyenne),Oklahoma, ca. 1910
Tanned deer hide, glass beads, rawhide;
10 ¼ x 3 ½ inches
Gift of Irving H. "Larry" Larom Estate
NA.202.10

Top right: **Moccasins**
Gaigwa (Kiowa), Oklahoma, ca. 1910
Tanned deer hide, glass beads, pigment;
10 ⅞ x 3 ¾ inches
Gift of Mr. Richard W. Leche NA.202.20

These moccasins show the use of pigment,
long fringes, and sparsely applied beadwork
characteristic of Southern Plains decoration.
The fringes embellish the seam and the back
of the heel.

Right: **Woman's Moccasins with Leggings**
Apsáalooke (Crow), Montana, ca. 1920
Tanned deer hide, glass and brass beads,
shell, rawhide; 9 ⅜ x 3 ¼ inches
Gift of Mr. and Mrs. William Henry Harrison
NA.202.62

Dress

Gaigwa (Kiowa), Oklahoma, ca.1920
Tanned deer hide, elk teeth, glass beads,
mescal beans, pigment; 45¾ x 31¾ inches
Chandler-Pohrt Collection, Gift of Mr. William D.
Weiss NA.202.442

Kiowa and other Southern Plains women created dresses of softly tanned deer hide featuring long fringes and beadwork trim and
abstract floral designs rather than fully beaded
bodices. This dress also has traditional materials of elk teeth and pigment.

Blanket
Otoe, Oklahoma, ca. 1905
Wool cloth, glass beads, ribbon;
53½ x 58 inches
Adolf Spohr Collection, Gift of Larry Sheerin
NA.203.672

John Young Bear (1883–1960)
Meskwaki, Tama, Iowa
Turban, ca. 1920
Otter hide, German silver, glass beads, horse
and deer hair, eagle feather, wool and cotton
cloth, feathers; 5 x 11⅝
Adolf Spohr Collection, Gift of Larry Sheerin
NA.205.16

This turban combines the powers of the bear—
represented by the bear paw rendered in
German silver—eagle, and otter with beautiful
Prairie beadwork design. John Young Bear was
a notable Meskwaki wood carver and maker of
traditional regalia.

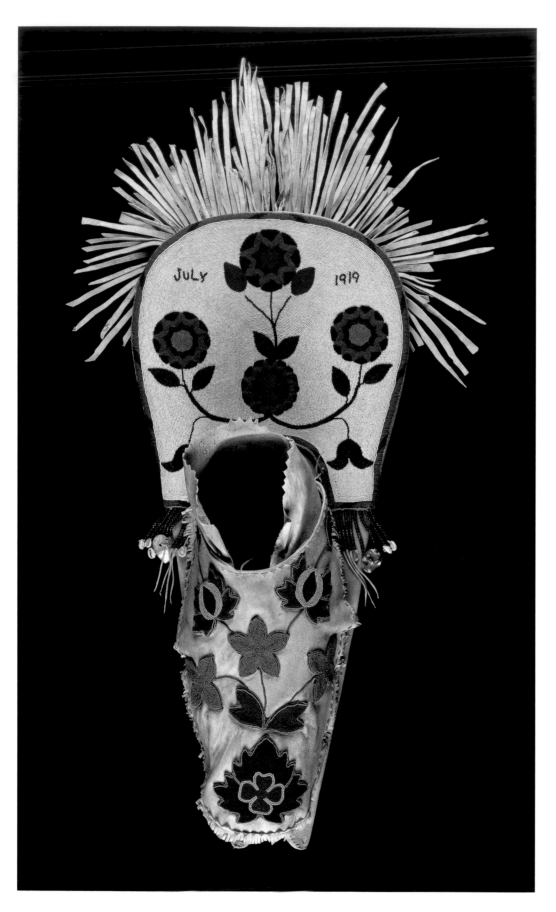

Cradle
Squeliy'u (Salish), ca. 1919
Tanned deer hide, wood, glass beads, wool and cotton cloth, cowrie and abalone shells, mother of pearl; 35 x 15 inches
Simplot Collection, Gift of J.R. Simplot NA.111.57

This cradle, with its distinctive floral design and date of July 1919, was probably made for a parade or other special occasion. During the reservation era of the late 1800s and early 1900s, women created special clothing, horse equipment, and accouterments for Fourth of July parades and tribal celebrations. Salish and other Plateau peoples often participated in such events on the Crow and other Northern Plains reservations, much as Plains tribal members frequently traveled to the Plateau.

Storage Bag
Lakota (Sioux), 1890
Tanned deer hide, dyed porcupine quills, tin cones, dyed horse hair; 14 ⅜ x 24 ½ inches
Chandler-Pohrt Collection, Gift of Mr. William D. Weiss NA.106.245

This storage bag exemplifies the representational art in beading and porcupine quillwork by Lakota women during the early reservation years. In this depiction, a warrior on horseback counts coup on an enemy.

However, it is likely that the motivations for early reservation artistry in the Plains, which has come to symbolize excellence in Native American arts, can be found in the sometimes difficult experiences that shaped their lives. On the reservations, Plains tribal members struggled with physical survival as they also attempted to maintain their cultural identities while government agents, missionaries, and schools pressed them to set aside their languages, beliefs, ceremonies, and communal lives. Reservation arts, manifested in beautifully embellished creations in tribal designs, became a means of establishing and maintaining cultural identities. Through perseverance, Plains Indian people survived the adversities of the late nineteenth and early twentieth centuries and through artistry and creative innovation they renewed and expressed their cultural identities and heritages.

1. John G. Neihardt, *Black Elk Speaks: Being the Life Story of a Holy Man of the Oglala Sioux* (New York: William Morrow & Company, 1932; reprint, Lincoln and London: University of Nebraska Press, 1979), pp. 9–10.

2. Neihardt, *Black Elk Speaks*, p. 214.

3. Peter Nabokov, *Two Leggings: The Making of a Crow Warrior* (New York: Thomas I. Crowell, Publishers, 1967), p. 197.

4. Quoted in Frank B. Linderman, *American: The Life Story of a Great Indian, Plenty-coups, Chief of the Crows* (Rathway, New Jersey: The John Day Company, 1930; reprinted as *Plenty-coups, Chief of the Crows*, Lincoln: University of Nebraska Press 1962), p. 311.

5. Frank B. Linderman, *Red Mother: The Life Story of Pretty-Shield, Medicine Woman of the Crows* (Rathway, New Jersey: The John Day Company, 1932; reprinted as *Pretty-Shield; Medicine Woman of the Crows*, Lincoln: University of Nebraska Press, 1972), p. 251.

6. Linderman, *Red Mother*, pp. 250–251.

7. James Mooney, *The Ghost-Dance Religion and the Sioux Outbreak of 1890, Fourteenth Annual Report of the Bureau of Ethnology, 1892–93*, Part 2 (Washington, D.C.: U.S. Government Printing Office, 1896; reprint, Lincoln and London: University of Nebraska Press, 1991), p. 777.

8. Mooney, *The Ghost-Dance Religion*, p. 790.

9. Mooney, *The Ghost-Dance Religion*, p. 977.

10. Mooney, *The Ghost-Dance Religion*, p. 973.

11. Mooney, *The Ghost-Dance Religion*, p. 994.

12. N. Scott Momaday, *The Names: A Memoir* (Tucson and London: University of Arizona Press, 1976; reprint, 1987), pp. 163, 166.

13. Quoted in Linderman, *American: The Life Story of a Great Indian*, p. 311.

14. Andrew C. Isenberg, *The Destruction of the Bison: An Environmental History, 1750–1920* (Cambridge: Cambridge University Press, 2000), p. 27.

15. Isenberg, *The Destruction of the Bison*, p. 109.

16. Linderman, *Red Mother*, p. 250.

17. Isenburg, *The Destruction of the Buffalo*, p. 93.

18. Isenburg, *The Destruction of the Buffalo*, p. 106.

19. Isenburg, *The Destruction of the Buffalo*, p. 131–132.

20. Valerius Geist, *Buffalo Nation: History and Legend of the North American Bison.* (Stillwater, Minnesota: Voyageur Press, 1996), p. 91.

21. In 1875, General Philip Sheridan addressed a joint session of the Texas House and Senate as they considered legislation to protect the region's few remaining buffalo. He stated that the hide hunters should be considered national heroes deserving of medals because of their role in destroying the "Indian's commissary" and making way for "speckled cattle and the festive cowboy, who follows the hunter as a second forerunner of an advanced civilization." The legislation subsequently failed to pass. See Francis Paul Prucha, *The Great Father: The United States Government and the American Indians* (Lincoln: University of Nebraska Press, 1986), p. 561.

22. From a story told by Old Lady Horse (Spear Woman) and published in Alice Lee Marriott and Carol K. Rachlin. *American Indian Mythology* (New York: New American Library, 1968), p. 170.

23. Gilbert L. Wilson, *Waheenee: An Indian Girl's Story: Told by Herself to Gilbert L. Wilson* (St. Paul Minnesota: Webb Publishing Company, 1927; reprint, Lincoln and London: University of Nebraska Press, 1981), p. 176.

24. David J. Wishart, *An Unspeakable Sadness: The Dispossession of the Nebraska Indians* (Lincoln and London: University of Nebraska Press, 1994), pp. 208–212. The dilemma of Standing Bear and his followers led to the significant legal case of *Standing Bear v. Crook*, which resulted in a ruling that an Indian is a "person" entitled to petition for his rights.

25. From Helen Hunt Jackson, *A Century of Dishonor* (Boston: Roberts Brothers, 1893), quoted in Peter Nabokov, ed., *Native American Testimony: A Chronicle of Indian-White Relations from Prophecy to the Present, 1492–1992* (New York: Penguin Books, 1978; reprint, 1992), p. 169.

26. Wishart, *An Unspeakable Sadness*, p. 160.

27. Ibid., p. 82, 190.

28. George E. Hyde, *The Pawnee Indians* (Denver: University of Denver Press, 1951; reprint, Norman: University of Oklahoma Press, 1974), p. 365.

29. Russell Thornton, *American Indian Holocaust and Survival: A Population History Since 1492* (Norman and London: University of Oklahoma Press, 1987; reprint, 1990), p. 91.

30. Smallpox came to the Crow in 1840 and resulted in the deaths of approximately one-third of their total population of 3,000 individuals. Thornton, *American Indian Holocaust*, p. 95.

31. Linderman, *American: The Life Story of a Great Indian*, pp. 111–112.

32. Linderman, *American*, pp. 94–95.

33. Linderman, *American*, p. 98.

34. This speech was recorded by a fur trader Francis A. Chardon, who witnessed the effects of the epidemic, and published an account of it in Francis A. Chardon, *Journal at Fort Clark, 1834–39* (Pierre, South Dakota: State of South Dakota, 1932), quoted in Thornton, *American Indian Holocaust and Survival*, p. 99.

35. Linderman, *Red Mother*, p. 9.

36. Mike Bruised Head, "The Impact and Effects of the Lewis and Clark Expedition from the Eyes of the Blackfoot." Paper presented at the Plains Indian Museum Seminar, Native Perspectives on the Lewis and Clark Expedition, Buffalo Bill Historical Center. October 4, 2003.

37. Thornton, *American Indian Holocaust and Survival,* pp. 100–102.

38. James Welch with Paul Stekler, *Killing Custer: The Battle of the Little Bighorn and the Fate of the Plains Indian.* (New York and London: W.W. Norton & Company, 1994), p. 285.

39. Welch with Stekler, *Killing Custer,* p. 45

40. Thomas B. Marquis, *A Warrior Who Fought Custer* (Minneapolis: Midwest Company, 1931; reprinted as *Wooden Leg: A Warrior Who Fought Custer,* Lincoln: University of Nebraska Press, 1957), p. 256.

41. Quoted in Donald J. Berthong. *The Southern Cheyennes* (Norman: University of Oklahoma Press), 1963), p. 219.

42. American Horse at Council of Lakota delegation in Washington D.C., February 11, 1891 in *Report of the Commissioner of Indian Affairs for 1891,* volume 1, p. 181. Excerpted in Mooney, *The Ghost-Dance Religion and the Sioux Outbreak of 1890,* p. 885.

43. Neihardt, *Black Elk Speaks,* p. 276.

44. Herman J. Viola, *Diplomats in Buckskins: A History of Indian Delegations in Washington City* (Bluffton, South Carolina: Rivilo Books, 1995), pp. 9–10.

45. Viola, *Diplomats in Buckskins,* p 92.

46. Quoted in Althea Bass, *The Arapaho Way: A Memoir of an Indian Boyhood* (New York: Clarkson N. Potter, 1966), p. 45.

47. Bass, *The Arapaho Way,* p. 55.

48. Luther Standing Bear, *My People the Sioux,* E.A. Brininstool, ed. (New York: Houghton-Mifflin, 1928; reprint, Lincoln and London: University of Nebraska Press, 1975), p.135.

49. Luther Standing Bear, *My Indian Boyhood* (Boston: Houghton Mifflin, 1931; reprint, Lincoln and London: University of Nebraska Press, 1988), p. 156.

50. Luther Standing Bear, *My People the Sioux,* pp. 136–137.

51. Margaret L. Archuleta, Brenda J. Child, and K. Tsianina Lomawaima, eds., *Away From Home: American Indian Boarding School Experiences, 1878–2000* (Phoenix: Heard Museum, 2000), pp. 17–18; K. Tsianina Lomawaima, *They Called It Prairie Light: The Story of Chilocco Indian School* (Lincoln and London: University of Nebraska Press, 1994), pp. 8–9.

52. Archuleta, Child, and Lomawaima, *Away From Home,* pp. 85–97.

53. Marla N. Powers, *Oglala Women: Myth, Ritual, and Reality* (Chicago: The University of Chicago Press, 1986), pp. 137–138.

A New and Different Life on a Small Part of a Very Old Place

Traditional Arts in the Early Reservation Period in the Dakotas, 1870–1920

ARTHUR AMIOTTE

The treaty-making period that began around 1851 marked rapid and sometimes violent change from the autonomy the Plains Indian tribes had known to confinement and profound adversity. By the later 1860s and early 1870s, reservations were slowly being occupied by some tribal people willing to live the new life, though some notable leaders like Crazy Horse of the Oglala Lakota, Sitting Bull of the Hunkpapa Lakota, and Chief Joseph of the Nez Perce continued to resist relocation. But the destruction of animal and plant species on which the tribes relied prior to and after resettlement dealt them a critical blow, depriving them not only of food, but also of materials for clothing, shelter, and their traditional arts. The physical accoutrements and patterns of life would change, and in the process, give rise to new traditions and art forms.

Plains Indian peoples had been trading since about 1700 for non-Indian-made items—metal, cloth, dyes, paints, needles, thread, and glass beads—which they incorporated into their material culture. The artist-artisan was free to use newer foreign media according to his or her aesthetic choice. Consequently, many hybrid art forms flourished—the use, for instance, of glass seed beads along with embroidered or wrapped porcupine quills. Initially rare and precious, vibrantly colored trade cloths were combined with glass seed beads and porcupine quills. Favored fabrics were stroud and Hudson's-Bay wool-trade blankets, made specifically for the North American Indian trade.

Surrender and relocation ended many warrior traditions once integral to rites of passage, attained status, and certain men's societies at the heart of tribal leadership and governance. Traditional objects signifying society membership not only protected the bearer in battle, but also made up important parts of society bundles, rites, music, and dance. Being elected to these societies augmented, and in some cases reaffirmed, one's identity as an accomplished man of the people and hence, an ideal tribe member. Objects such as distinctive headdresses and tanned mountain sheepskin shirts, sometimes with matching leggings, decorated with distinctive designs related to a particular warrior or civil society, affirmed that the wearer had attained tribal ideals, and served as visual texts of metaphysical and social significance. Other elaborately adorned shirts and headdresses were reserved for venerated civil leaders recognized for their prudence, bravery, and generosity. These garments were worn almost like robes of office or vestments of honor on public occasions.

Photographs of Plains tribal people, including those present at the deliberations of the famous Laramie Treaty of 1868, show that 80 percent were dressed in cloth garments and robes, dispelling the notion that anything made after 1870 or 1890 is not genuinely "Indian." But on the reservations, the style of everyday wear did change for both men and women. Those who entered white educational institutions were compelled to adopt non-Indian fashions. Beef and cowhides now came as monthly rations distributed at agency headquarters. People resided in small enclaves in canvas tipis and military style house-shaped "wall tents," the canvas of which or the wall tent itself was issued as treaty payments or annuities. The 1887 Dawes Act mandated that individual land allotments be made, and families, or extended families, were moved onto their homesteads. With a handful of exceptions, tribal gatherings where one would don tribal ceremonial garb were forbidden or discouraged.

But pre-reservation social and governance traditions endured. The adult population had declined because of disease, malnutrition, and inadequate living and environmental conditions, but those individuals were still governed by pre-reservation tribal institutions and leaders. Such notables as Red Cloud, Sitting Bull, Spotted Tail, and their faithful followers continued to command and receive proper due as official spokesmen in dealings with the federal agency and Washington forces of change. Traditional garments and symbols of authority, usually made by women artists, were central to this ongoing tradition. Relying on skills learned from female relatives and artisans, the makers interjected into the reservation setting ancient techniques and designing dynamics which would be perpetuated by the next generations. In this sense, the early reservation period did not spell the loss and disjuncture of artistic traditions to the extent that some believe.

The U.S. government envisioned that on individually allotted parcels of land, Indians would become self-sustaining farmers and ranchers. The fruits of such labors would support a nuclear or small extended family, replacing the collective tribal consciousness that had guaranteed an equitable distribution of food and indigenously manufactured goods. The old system had offered reasonable hope of survival to all tribal members, including elders without family, widows, and orphans, and it cemented bonds within the entire band. Indeed, it underpinned many social and sacred institutions, including marriages. After thousands of years, it became institutionalized by those aspiring to leadership, and became a formal part of all major rituals and ceremonies.

The "giveaway" has various levels of meaning, from sheer selfless charity to reciprocity, including rewarding others for exceptional service to the people. Memory played a key role in these occasions, because the group witnessed the giveaways, and the recipients always remembered the occasion and character of the givers. On another level, the young saw examples of good character and behavior, sanctioned by tribal ethos and elders.

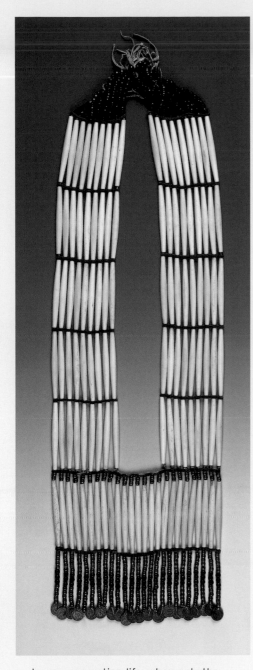

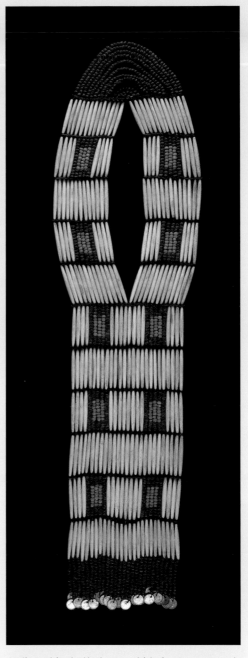

In pre-reservation life, when only the industriousness of the hunter and the manufacturer of goods limited one's potential for personal wealth, givers could completely divest themselves of all their possessions in an act of public passion and compassion, because through industry and gregariousness they could ultimately recoup everything they had given away. This dimension of tribal spirituality and valuing is one of the most potent motives for making cultural material objects. As they grew up, young women were consistently encouraged to make things, moccasins and household goods in particular, so extras would be available should the need to give some away arose.

The U.S. government, on the other hand, favored more concern for one's own, in a sense urging Native Americans to adopt a more capitalistic attitude. The missionary efforts of various Christian denominations worked hand-in-hand with government efforts. Indeed, Christian groups in the East lobbied for passage of the Dawes Act, to save Indians from avaricious white settlers near or on Indian reservations. If Indians accepted the white work ethic, the theory went, all would eventually blend in, or possibly even disappear, as civilization spread across the West. Rules were established that outlawed many traditional practices, and these rules were strenuously enforced.

Such dictums might have diminished or ended altogether the production of tribal arts, but between 1870 and 1890, many Indian objects that now abide in museum collections were collected. This may have been because Indian people continued to produce tribal arts for ceremonies held in isolated places, away from the scrutiny of federal authorities.

At this time, stores and trading posts were established near the reservations to supply not only food and household goods, but also larger quantities of materials for manufacturing traditional goods. Many pre-reservation-made articles now in collections

were obtained in trade, gathered from battle-fields and gravesites, and given to non-Indians. Similar objects became media of exchange as storekeepers accepted both fine newly made and older items for groceries, dry goods, and other materials. Traders and storekeepers became middlemen, making tribal arts available to individual and institutional collectors.

Once a Native American gave an object away, the new owner was free to do whatever he liked with it. In the new economy of barter and currency exchange, many a recipient cashed in his gift at a store or trading post for immediate essentials or cash, thus blurring or losing altogether the true provenance of the object. This also explains why many items in collections appear brand new. Certain artisans also became well known for the fine quality of their work. As the network of trading, purchase, and exchange became more elaborate, some collectors commissioned pieces from particular artists and artisans, which is another reason some items in collections are in near-mint condition.

The Western show performances that began in the 1880s and continued into the first three decades of the twentieth century also affected traditional tribal arts. The best known of these was Buffalo Bill Cody's Wild West. In 1883, he enlisted his first Indian participants, who were Pawnee. By 1885, he had recruited Sitting Bull and others for his performances before U.S. and international audiences. The performances were held in arenas much like modern rodeo settings, and Cody was the star. The Indians, dressed in tribal regalia, played buffalo hunters chasing on horseback a small herd of bison around the arena, warriors attacking a covered wagon and stage coach, and later, warriors re-enacting the battle at the Little Bighorn, with Cody riding in to save the day.

Cody himself actively recruited Indians on the Pine Ridge reservation, where they demonstrated their riding and shooting skills before they were hired. If those chosen to make the tours East and abroad did not own the needed outfits, families hurriedly gathered dance bustles, headdresses, and other items once worn by members of warrior societies, many of which had been disbanded. The man's traditional war dance outfit we now know was emerging at this time, as

Indians were increasingly allowed to gather at social events. Some families made new garments especially for Cody's performances and a proliferation of shows and exhibitions, including the Chicago Columbian Exposition in 1893.

"Show" Indians were well paid, receiving their savings at the end of the tour. Women also performed in these shows as keepers of simulated tipi camps and as dancers. Their wages enabled them to purchase more goods for further production.

By 1889, Christian denominations, principally Roman Catholic and Episcopalian, were establishing small churches, major missions, and boarding schools on the Sioux reservations, often close to tribal administration headquarters, usually called "the agency." The U.S. government also entrusted Christian missionaries with creating educational institutions intended to remove young people from tribal society and immerse them in non-Indian culture, so that eventually they would not return to their people or even want to be tribal people. Though some of these schools were near the reservations, others were deliberately built great distances away.

In time, some parochial schools were replaced by government-run day and boarding schools. Being a good Christian and practicing Christian commandments and values—some diametrically opposed to tribal values—were precepts overtly and subtly imbedded in every discipline taught in these schools, even to the point of portraying Indian people as evil savages, something of the past, superstitious, or worshippers of the devil and witchcraft, when they were mentioned at all.

Formal classroom education held Indian youth hostage, in some cases, literally. One early practice in the Dakotas was to withhold annuities from families who kept their children from school. But those who believed the

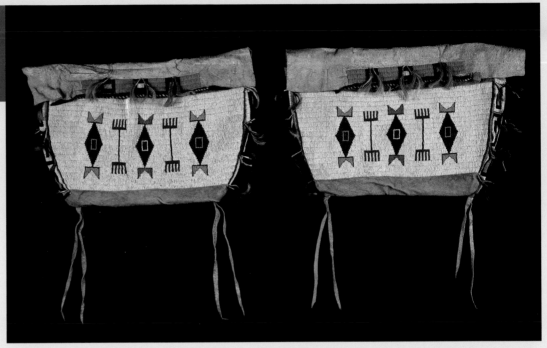

formal classroom could forever change Indian people overlooked the teaching of profound tribal values within Indian communities. Still, young people from five to eighteen years of age were delivered over to the new establishments. While great numbers of pre-reservation-born residents resisted conversion, many accommodated or embraced these overtures, in some cases to make the social atmosphere more amenable for their children.

Photographs of the first generation of Indian children attending these schools show them adorned with their tribal best. These treasured outfits were promptly replaced by uniforms and stiff leather shoes, and children underwent close-cropped haircuts as a part of a disinfecting bathing regime. Many of these Indian objects were added to school collections, as were gifts sent to children and to kind teachers and administrators. On some reservations, parents presented finely made and elaborately decorated traditional objects to institutions when their children graduated or, in some cases, upon the death of a beloved child in residence. Such items were also given to the clergy, associates, or their wives for their help at funerals, weddings, and baptisms. And inevitably, some objects were sold for cash.

The clergy objected to bodies being bared in celebratory dances during the early reservation period, so men adopted long underwear beneath their dance accoutrements. Métis woven sashes and beaded and metal concho belts with pendants and beaded drops were also worn to conceal bare legs and thighs not covered by leggings.

By 1893, in the wake of the Wounded Knee Massacre of 1890, a changing reservation economy, and the influence of formal education on the now-returning first generation, those in charge sought new approaches for mollifying the growing population. The

churches began allowing the people to congregate at the local missions for testimony to the graces of conversion and belief in the new-found faith. These gatherings eventually became huge gatherings of representatives from different reservations who traveled by wagon train, horseback, and railroad, some from great distances, with camping gear in tow. Services, preaching, and testimony occurred in large bowers, reminiscent of the historical Sun Dance lodges. There were also feasts and social activities during these conclaves. Certain denominations, particularly the Episcopalians, were more relaxed about the wearing of tribal dress on these occasions. From a Lakota perspective, it was an opportunity to practice the ancient customs, called the *saiciya*, and to adorn oneself in finery indicative of one's tribe, band, extended family and/or personal accomplishment, as much to say, "I am a Lakota and we are the Lakota and this great display of beauty reflects our finest values." Such liturgical gatherings were usually held every two or three years.

With some expendable resources and less intense demands on their time, women had more leisure to devote to art production. By this time, many women had mastered use of the foot-pedal sewing machine at school.

This innovation increased both the production and complexity of fabric arts. The machine also made production of canvas wall tents and tipis for summer use and camping more efficient.

Elaborately beaded dresses, leggings, and women's accoutrements emerged, as did beaded covers for hymnals and prayer books, stoles, and vestments, altar cloths and coverlets for statue pedestals with beaded liturgical symbols, and beaded or quilled picture frames. Such objects were sometimes donated to the hosting congregation, which sold them to defray the cost of feeding and housing such a great gathering. In good tradition, many were also given to friends and distant relatives not seen for a long time.

The sanction of reservation-based annual gatherings also occurred at this time. Initially held on the Fourth of July, the occasion was aimed at encouraging patriotism and the notion that though conquered and colonized, Indian people were nevertheless part of a great nation, and that if they endured, they would be saved from their primal ways and would share in the great bounty of America. The descendents of the original reservation leaders were expected to provide the bulk of the largesse on these occasions, as was the custom in pre-reservation times. Those who had gained through travels in Western shows and benefited from the new educational experience but had embraced the traditional beliefs of their forebears assumed and were granted new status.

Another important group was composed of white men married to Indian women, half-breeds, and mixed bloods. These first benefited financially from the new reservation system because they were bicultural and bilingual, gaining wealth as salaried interpreters in Indian-government transactions, as employees at the newly established reservation agencies, and as storekeepers or state employees. They had a finer understanding of potentially lucrative land allotment policies, cattle and livestock programs designed for Indian people, and business, trade, and the cash economy. Their children also had advantages in the Euro-American ethnocentrically oriented schools and thus would become some of the earliest successes. Depending on the persistence of the Indian ethos in these families, many became instrumental in the traditional ways of the people and some were central to the success of the early gatherings.

Many of these mixed blood families were prolific producers of elaborate traditional objects simply because they had more money to spend and more leisure to create, and were not compelled to sell their creations, but could continue to embellish them. Many family collections became remarkable because the members could also purchase and commission works of other artists and artisans. Since fortunes do rise and fall, however, even these exceptional pieces sometimes ended up in collections far from their origins.

By the early decades of the twentieth century, adaptation of farming and ranching brought more stability to reservation dwellers. Programs in animal husbandry, gardening, farming, ranching techniques, and domestic skills, sometimes using the latest technologies, brought further changes in the economy and material culture, most notably in the synthesis of artistic media or forms. Home economists in reservation communi-

ties taught women not only sewing machine skills, but also needlework, tailoring, homemaking, and food preservation techniques. Corn, squash, and beans were preserved using ancient tribal techniques, and new crops of potatoes, cabbages, and a host of other vegetables were grown. Wild foods, the prairie turnip, berries, mushrooms, teas, and herbs, augmented the new food varieties.

Heirloom tools and implements, some handed down from pre-reservation times, continued to be used. Berries, parched corn, and dried prairie turnips were mashed into meal with pounding tools. Wooden and rawhide bowls and horn spoons, now made from cow horn, continued to be manufactured.

Tin and tin enameled cups and spoons and purchased wooden bowls were sometimes embellished with beads and quillwork for certain ceremonies. Heirloom and newly manufactured parfleche containers held dried meat, pemmican, personal possessions, and heirloom tools. Principal among these were hide-tanning tools of bone and elk antler, some incised with dots and circular bands as a record of how many hides had been tanned.

Young women were increasingly returning from boarding schools with homemaking skills commensurate with those taught in Indian communities, but they learned them in institutional settings with more precision and with machines and materials more in line with non-Indian homemaking conventions and fashions. And the literate Indian homemaker could also order materials from businesses such as Montgomery Ward and Sears and Roebuck.

Out of these developments, the patchwork quilt emerged as an alternative to purchased blankets. Early quilts were made from recycled garments, muslin, flour, and salt sacks, and were filled with burlap feed and potato sacks. Used clothing from Eastern benefactors many times went into colorful quilts. Particularly functional were quilts made of fine broadcloth, serge, and flannel wool. The female tradition of designing in straight edged geometrics seems to have

made a natural transition, as early quilts were predominantly geometric blocks reminiscent of parfleche designs. The radiating star design did not gain its popularity, ascribed tribal meaning, and significance until the 1950s. Fine quilts in cottons, silks, satins, and velvets were further embellished with dainty embroidery and stitchery learned in the classroom. Women subscribed to fashion and needlework magazines that featured patterns, including those for infant wear. Combined with traditional techniques, such patterns were rendered with unusual but charming ingenuity.

By the first decade of the twentieth century, some reservation dwellers had prospered to the point that individual communities were sponsoring local celebrations with public feasting and giveaways. Sometimes these coincided with the Fourth of July or other dates significant to Indian people, such as June 25th, the day of the Battle of the Little Bighorn. Extended families and communities provided the resources as expressions of community pride and status.

There arose at this time the custom of selection, by a distinguished body of elderly leaders, a surrogate leader or leaders of the people, which by custom included those people's families. The appointed person or persons were accorded the status and respect once accorded headmen or chiefs. At the installation of their reign, which would last one or two years, the chief's honoring song was sung as they lead the procession in a solemn round dance of the entire community. Blessed with a ritual sacred pipe ceremony, the leaders were presented with a circular pouch containing an oversized copper penny, probably obtained as a souvenir or commemorative coin. They were advised to be strong and industrious, and to care for the people.

Until the next celebration, those selected were expected to create, gather, and garner great wealth. Individuals within the group also made themselves new outfits and other accoutrements so that at future events they would be well adorned.

At the next public celebration, the surrogate leaders on their elaborately adorned

mounts, wearing their new garments, led the procession around the entire encampment, followed by their adorned family, carrying and displaying the wealth they would give away after the entire camp feasted. Following traditional games, horse racing, dancing, adaptations of historic ceremonies, including phases of the Sun Dance without the piercing of flesh, the ceremony of selecting the next surrogate leaders would take place and the people would then pack up and return home.

The annual tribal fair, which emerged as community gathering in this period, was usually held at or near agency headquarters, frequently the largest community and business centers on reservations. These towns grew up around the only hospital, the main boarding school, and numerous Bureau of Indian Affairs offices, commissaries, and privately owned butcher shops, grocery, dry goods, and mercantile stores.

A unique feature of these tribal fairs was the displaying of traditionally made quilled and beaded items. By this time, the non-Indian authorities, government and religious, while espousing dislike for dancing and traditional sacred ceremonies, were also aware of the positive and lucrative practice of Indian people making and selling traditional tribal arts to augment their incomes. Indeed, the businesses at the agency purchased and traded in Indian-made objects, often displaying them prominently alongside manufactured goods.

Besides the exhibition of produce, livestock, and traditionally made items, the tribal fair was also a place for newly learned and some older "arts and crafts." Large displays of the latest quilt forms were popular as women continued to experiment using new

fabrics. Some of these were quilted, others tied with rows of knots. Generally speaking, those quilts made for giving away were only the newly made quilt tops. Recipients then took these home and recovered existing quilts as fillers.

The fairgoers camped on a great plain not at, but near, the agency, in a great circle with community members camping in a historically designated place reminiscent of their historical place in pre reservation gatherings. As a matter of community pride, the first quill- and bead-decorated tipis of community members were pitched prominently in front of the camp, declaring to other community camps, forming a great circle of smaller circles, that "we of [such and such] community, declare our presence by showing you the finest that we have made and own."

The emergence of the Indian rodeo took place at this time as well. Once again on a grand reservation-wide scale, horse races and games of competition took place. Afternoon and evening traditional dances were held in the central circular constructed bower, which was also the focus of some ceremonies and public oratories praising and admonishing the people to further embrace their traditions and beliefs. Of course, this

was an occasion for the people to adorn themselves in traditional beauty and dance regalia, affirming their identities and pride.

A rarely recognized aspect of these gatherings was their growing intertribal quality, wherein visitors from other non-Sioux reservations also participated. These visitors and guests were from neighboring reservations or from great distances. Some of these alliances were from pre-reservation times; others were established through marriages and friendships made by young people attending intertribal boarding schools in the East or regional schools serving tribes from several states. Non-Sioux tribes dressed in their distinctive styles, exchanged gifts and received Lakota-made gifts as a matter of hospitality.

Plagued by drought, poverty, malnutrition, epidemics and chronic diseases, and the unrelenting efforts of government and churches, the early reservation period could have devastated a lesser people, but the Lakota rose to the occasion. With their anciently bred strengths of character, intellect, and aesthetic sensibilities driven by spirituality, they strode confidently into twentieth-century modernity, and persist into the twenty-first.

Far from the fires of the camps, out on the rain-dark prairies,
in the swales and washes, on the rolling hills, the rivers of
great animals moved. Their backs were dark with rain and
the rain gathered and trickled down their shaggy heads. Some
grazed, some slept. Some had begun to molt. Their dark
horns glistened in the rain as they stood guard over the sleep-
ing calves. The blackhorns had returned and, all around it
was as it should be.

—JAMES WELCH[1]

6 Our People Today
ENDURING LEGACIES

The history of Plains Indian people has been one of endurance and survival despite seemingly overwhelming adversities. At the beginning of the twentieth century, few would have suggested that Native people would continue to exist as sovereign Indian nations more than a hundred years later. Indeed, few would have predicted that Indian people would continue to exist at all. There must have been an inner strength in our ancestors—one that is not always apparent today— that supported them through the difficult times when their economies, their cultures, and their very lives were threatened. Those ancestors created significant and unique cultures and patterns of life and expressed them through languages, oral traditions, ceremonies, songs, spiritual beliefs, and the arts that they attempted to preserve for their children and grandchildren. Many Plains tribal members today remember, research, and renew elements of that ancient way of life—the continuous threads that have been passed down through generations— for the education, cultural and spiritual grounding, and welfare of their own children and grandchildren.

This does not mean that Native people are frozen in the nostalgic past, but rather that they revere and honor the accomplishments of their elders and those who came before them while living as vital members of their own communities. They respect and celebrate the tribal heritages, histories, and traditions that have provided a sense of cohesion and identities for their people, but they also actively innovate and create their own futures on reservations and in small towns and cities throughout North America.

Coyote Legend, 1976
Alabaster; 26 ½ x 20 x 18 inches
William E. Weiss Contemporary Art Fund 9.76

Doug Hyde studied sculpture under Allan Houser at the Institute of American Indian Arts in 1963–66 and attended the San Francisco Art Institute in 1967. Of Nez Perce, Assiniboine, and Chippewa heritage, Hyde interprets Native American traditions told to him by his grandfather and other elders, historical events, and contemporary Indian life in stone and bronze. This sculpture is based on a story about Coyote and His Daughter. In carving this work, Doug Hyde allowed ". . . the individual characteristics of the material—the shape, the color, the grains and the texture—to suggest the flow of the design."

Allan C. Houser (Haozous) (1914-1994)
Warm Springs Chiricahua Apache
Drama on the Plains, 1977
Alabaster; 21¾ x 27 x 8¾ inches
William E. Weiss Contemporary Art Fund 16.77

Born in 1914, Allan Houser was the first child born out of captivity of the Warm Springs Chiricahua people in Oklahoma. As followers of Geronimo, the Chiricahua had been held as prisoners of war for twenty-seven years. Houser lived near Apache, Oklahoma among the Kiowa, Plains Apache, and Comanche before studying watercolor art at the Santa Fe Indian School in 1934–1939. He then began a long and productive career as one of the twentieth century's most significant American sculptors. As a teacher at the Institute of American Indian Arts from 1962 to 1975, he also greatly influenced younger Native American artists. In this work, Houser shows the close relationship of a Plains warrior with his horse.

Once Plains Native people regained control of their lands, governing structures, religious rights, and education, they turned to restoring significant cultural elements that had been lost or nearly lost. Tribal language programs for preschool through college have proliferated in recent years to preserve those languages still in common use among tribal peoples and reintroduce others which are threatened with extinction. On the Wind River Reservation of Wyoming, for example, both the Arapaho and Shoshone languages are taught at the Wyoming Indian School—itself established by elders who had experienced the cultural deprivations of the boarding school system—and the newly established Wind River Tribal College. For several years both the Northern Arapaho and Eastern Shoshone tribes have sponsored language and culture classes through which young people learn and practice their languages, arts, songs, histories, and oral traditions under the instruction of elders and others with cultural knowledge.

Plains Indian scholars, writers, and museum professionals have taken more active roles in the public interpretations of their own histories, cultures, and arts, once the domain of Euro-American "experts," and have introduced new insights based upon their knowledge and experiences as Native people. Under the Native American Graves Protection and Repatriation Act of 1990, Plains Indian communities have reclaimed for reburial the physical remains of ancestors long in storage in museum collections, as well as sacred bundles and ritual objects central to traditional spiritual beliefs and practices. They also continue to seek the protection of their sacred sites and landscapes so future generations can experience the powerful spiritual connections to the lands that created and nurtured their beliefs and cultural traditions.

The powerful relationships of Plains Indian peoples to the buffalo, once lost, have again been rekindled. While millions of buffalo lived within the Great Plains, a good portion of the yearly seasonal cycle was devoted to hunting the magnificent creature that provided nourishment and other material benefits to the people. The buffalo dances and calling ceremonies, the spiritual preparations for the hunt, and the ritual prayers and songs of thanksgiving were interwoven with this cycle. When the herds disappeared, Native people lost the strength to resist confinement to reservations as well as their abilities to lead lives independent of the federal government. Also lost or put aside were many ceremonies that had brought an abundance of buffalo close to villages and ensured success in hunting.

Although buffalo were no longer a focus of the economic lives of the people, they remained a subject of oral traditions and artistic representations. Reservation beadwork artists continued to depict buffalo in their work. Men painted images of buffalo and buffalo hunts on hides, paper, and cloth and

Wind River High School Students
Butchering Buffalo
Wyoming, 1999
Photograph by Sara Wiles

Phyllis Trosper and Gloria Goggles lead students Brian Trosper and Derek Sandall in butchering a buffalo. Through this experience, students learn about the economic and spiritual significance of the buffalo within Plains cultures. The Wind River Reservation community uses meat from the buffalo for traditional feasts, including dinners for veterans and elders.

carved them in pipestone and wood. Artists such as Codsiogo of the Eastern
Shoshone produced hide paintings of buffalo hunts and ceremonial scenes that
interested collectors and others who traveled through the Wind River
Reservation in the early 1900s. However, the continuing respect for the buffalo
manifested in oral traditions and the arts was deeper than a simple response to
market forces, but related to the spiritual well-being of the people.

After being absent from the lives of Plains Indian people for fifty to more
than one hundred years, the buffalo returned. A new chapter of the relationship
of the people with the buffalo began on the Crow Reservation in Montana. In
1934, Indian Commissioner John Collier appointed Robert Yellowtail as superintendent of the Crow Reservation, the first tribal member to hold that position.
Yellowtail began to work on economic development on the reservation, including
establishing a buffalo herd there.[2]

The Crow built their herd from buffalo from Yellowstone National Park
and the National Bison Range. Because of conflicts with neighboring ranchers
when the buffalo roamed into private lands and the presence of brucellosis
among some animals, the herd was eliminated in 1962–1964 under the direction
of the U.S. Bureau of Sport Fisheries and Wildlife. The Crow Tribe reintroduced
buffalo in 1971 with approximately four hundred animals and today has the
largest herd under tribal management, over 1,500 head.

Frances G. Yellow (b. 1954)
Cheyenne River Lakota (Sioux)
Tatanka Wan, A Buffalo Bull, 1993
Bronze; 9 ½ x 17 x 4 ⅛ inches
Gift of Dr. Patricia L. Hutinger 20.98

A poet as well as an artist, Francis Yellow is
inspired by traditional hide paintings and
ledger drawings and adapted this pictorial style
to his own paintings, drawings, and sculptures.
Sometimes satirical, his work addresses Lakota
culture, historical experiences, contemporary
political issues, and personal identity.
According to Yellow, elders teach that the
Lakota are descendants of the *Pte Oyate*—
"Buffalo People." He sees his identify as evolving from the Pte Oyate and the *Ikce Wicasa*—
"Common Man"—and Lakota *Oyate* or
"Friendly People."

The buffalo graze on a pasture of approximately twenty-two thousand acres in the Big Horn Mountains region. The tribe manages the buffalo with roundups and brucellosis testing—an ongoing concern of the area's private cattle ranchers—and has fenced part of their pasture to keep the herd on reservation lands. The buffalo meat is available for tribal elders, Sun Dances and other ceremonies, powwows and celebrations, and other cultural events. The Crow have also assisted other Montana tribes in establishing their own herds. In this way, the preservation of the buffalo—*bi'shee* in the Crow language—has become a meaningful element of the economic, cultural, and spiritual lives of Crow people today.

An organization of Native American tribal representatives, the Inter Tribal Bison Cooperative, provides technical assistance and grant funding to nations interested in establishing buffalo herds on reservation lands. Founded in 1990, the cooperative first met in 1991 in the Black Hills of South Dakota with representatives of nineteen tribes in attendance and a common mission: "To restore bison to Indian lands in a manner which is compatible with our spiritual and cultural beliefs and practices."[3] The cooperative has grown to forty-two tribes in sixteen states, with twenty-five of their constituents located within the Northern Plains.

The restoration of the buffalo to tribal lands symbolizes a spiritual and cultural rebirth for Plains people, reminding them of their ties to the land and their heritage as free hunters the Plains.

> Man is dependent on nature. When the health of the environment is threatened, so is the health of mankind. This is evident in history. When the white man upset the balance of nature by nearly destroying the buffalo, the health of the Native American declined. By bringing back the buffalo, we will improve the health of the Native people as well as the health of the environment.
>
> —Mike Fox[4]

Many Native Americans, historically and in the present, associate the disappearance of the buffalo with the declining health of Indian people on reservations. The poor and meager food that replaced buffalo, other game, and wild and cultivated plant foods definitely led to malnutrition in early years. More recently, Native people have experienced drastic increases in the incidence of diabetes, which now also is affecting children and teenagers, and heart disease, both of which have been attributed to poor nutrition.

Tribal officials are motivated by health concerns and potential economic benefits to re-establish herds of buffalo on reservation lands. In 2001, buffalo were returned to the Fort Peck Reservation of Montana. The Assiniboine and Sioux tribes at Fort Peck had ten years earlier set aside the pastureland for the beginnings of their herd—one hundred animals purchased from the Gros Ventre

Crow Riders at Indian Memorial Dedication
Little Bighorn Battlefield National Monument, Montana, June 25, 2003
Photograph by Emma I. Hansen

On the anniversary of the Little Bighorn Battle in 2003, the National Park Service dedicated the Indian Memorial in recognition of the Lakota, Cheyenne, Arapaho, Crow, and Arikara who fought there. The memorial with the theme "Peace Through Unity" was authorized under legislation in 1991 that also renamed the formerly Custer Battlefield National Monument. At the day-long dedication, tribal representatives—some on horseback like these Crow men and boys dressed in tribal regalia—participated in ceremonies honoring the warriors who fought there. They also presented programs on their respective cultures, histories, and perspectives on the battle.

and Assiniboine at Fort Belknap—and hoped that restoring the buffalo would bring about economic and environmental benefits, improved diets, employment, educational opportunities, and a spiritual rebirth for their people. As the animals were released into the pasture, the people celebrated with a powwow and ceremonies.

Assiniboine and Sioux spiritual leaders and tribal officials held a pipe ceremony. Several female elders served a traditional meal of corn soup, berry pudding, and fry bread in a nearby barn on the ranch. Busloads of tribal leaders and schoolchildren watched as the buffalo charged from livestock trailers and into a huge corral, where fresh hay and water awaited them.

"I'm glad they're back," said Brockton elementary student Trent Spotted Bird as the buffalo rushed off a livestock truck. "They make us stronger."[5]

Restoring the Rhythm of Life

When my people moved to the reservation, the old rhythm of life was broken. The old reasons for separating and then getting together ended. But the Crow people were used to doing things together, and by my day they had developed a new rhythm that combined some of our own celebrations with White ones. The ceremonies might be changed to fit in with our own, but the Crow kept a seasonal circle in their living.

—Agnes Yellowtail Deernose[6]

Federal policy of the early reservation period was based upon assimilation or "Americanization" of Indian people. With the assistance of Christian missionaries, some of whom were appointed reservation agents and superintendents, the federal government sought to suppress the practice of Native religions and in 1883 prohibited the Sun Dance and other ceremonies. Violators of this prohibition against "Indian Offenses" were subject to loss of rations, fines, or imprisonment.[7] Federal officials and missionaries objected to specific elements of the Sun Dance that involved physical self-sacrifice, but they also disapproved of any ceremony that brought Native people together. They hoped to break down the cultural cohesion supported by such gatherings and substitute the value of individualism as they strove to make Indians self-sustaining farmers and ranchers. Suppression of Native religious practices, the education of children in off-reservation boarding schools, and the Dawes General Allotment Act of 1887, which authorized subdividing reservation lands into individual plots, all were designed to further this process.

Despite the prohibition of the Sun Dance, many traditionalists continued to travel to remote locations or to hold their ceremonies in secret. But for other tribal peoples, the Sun Dance was performed only sporadically in the late nineteenth and early twentieth centuries.

> The government stopped the Sun Dance in many tribes in 1881. The last Cheyenne ceremony was later than that, though around 1887 or '88. I was old enough to see the lodge in the middle of a big flat, and hear the singing. It did not begin again until after I returned from school in 1905. I think the Cheyennes may have had it in secret now and then during those years. Since then there have been many attempts to get it stopped again, but it has gone on steadily, sometimes twice a year, almost every year now for half a century.
>
> –John Stands In Timber[8]

Under John Collier's tenure as Commissioner of Indian Affairs, the ban on the Sun Dance and other religious practices was lifted in 1934. The ceremony was reintroduced among some cultures in which it had ceased. The Crow held their last traditional Sun Dance in about 1875, but in 1941 they adopted a different version from the Eastern Shoshone.[9] This ceremony was brought by Shoshone Sun Dance leader John Trehero at the invitation of William Big Day, who had been inspired by his experiences at a ceremony he attended in 1938 in Fort Washakie.[10] Once introduced to the Crow, this sacred ceremony continues and remains a focus of spiritual life today. According to Crow belief, it benefits the entire world.

> In the Sun Dance way, the individual benefits from his prayers, but this is not all. The entire tribe benefits from the Sun Dance because, one part of our prayers is especially for

Memorial at Old Scouts Cemetery
Fort Berthold Reservation, North Dakota,
August 22, 2001
Photograph by Emma I. Hansen

The Arikara people honor tribal members' military service at the Indian Scout Post No. 1 cemetery built by the U.S. Volunteer Indian Scouts, consisting of Arikara warriors who had served as Army Scouts between 1867 and 1883 and their relatives. Originally established at Like-A-Fishhook village, the cemetery was moved to its present location near White Shield in 1953—when reservation lands were flooded under the Garrison Dam Project—and rededicated in 1994 as a memorial to the old scouts and all Arikara veterans. Arikara people gather on Memorial Day each year to recognize this service and sing honor songs in memory of the scouts.

the tribe and for all creation. Without these prayers from all of the different Indian tribes, the world might not be able to continue. You can see how important the Sun Dance is. In our morning Sunrise Ceremony, when we sing the four sacred songs after we have greeted the rising sun, we bring forward all of the Medicine Fathers and all of the sacred beings in the universe hear our prayers. When I say the morning prayer after we finish the songs, I ask that the tribe and the entire creation be blessed for another year until the next Sun Dance. All of the other dancers share in this prayer. This is a very important time, and anyone who is present can sense that we are all at the heart of creation during these prayers.

–Thomas Yellowtail[11]

In recent years, the Sun Dance among the Lakota has experienced growth and revitalization, although it had never actually been suspended despite the federal regulations.

Contrary to what many people say, or what we may read in the literature, even though the Sun Dance was officially prohibited during the 1880s, it never became extinct. From oral tradition we have evidence of people on numerous Sioux reservations having sneaked off to the badlands or to hidden places in the hills where these formal ceremonies took place in as close to their original form as they could be. Beginning as early as 1924 and developing especially during the 1960s and seventies, we had the revival of the ceremony proper, gradually moving out of its transitional phase where it was part powwow and part Sun Dance and part annual fair. We have seen a renaissance take place recently in which the Sun Dance was returned somewhat to its formal, intensely sacred character, with many of the same restrictions and dimensions that it had in its historical setting.

–Arthur Amiotte[12]

Arthur Amiotte has noted that elements of the Lakota Sun Dance have often been misunderstood as "self-torture," and this misunderstanding historically provided federal authorities and missionaries a justification for prohibiting it. The ceremony, however, provides participants who understand it with a spiritual awakening and recognition of the unity and power of the universe that has not diminished through time nor the innovations of the present.

But for the one who understands it, there is a profound realization in the dance, a sacred ecstasy, a transformation whereby he realizes the wholeness and unity of all things. The spiritual, the temporal, the gross, the profane, the common all come together at one time. Through this the individual transcends all what we know of this life and finally arrives at the real world, the real place.

Today, we may hear criticisms of the use of tin buckets, kettles, loudspeakers at the Sun Dance. I think we should realize, however, that Lakota culture has never been static; it never has been monolithic. It always has been undergoing a process of change. In fact, the process of life itself is one of transformation. As cultural beings what is important to us is, that despite our having taken on many aspects of modern technology, the sacred intent continues to remain the same. That is the very core of the meaning of sacred Lakota tradition.[13]

Beatrice Medicine has stated that since about 1963 the Lakota Sun Dance "has assumed an almost intertribal character as a nativisitic movement"—partly because of its association with the American Indian Movement that arose during that period—and diffused to other Native peoples, some of whom were not fully integrated within the norms and values of Lakota culture.[14] But the Sun Dance continues to have a central and significant relevance for Lakota people.

> There is something intrinsically valuable about the Lakota life-style. That view persists, no matter what kinds of culturally repressive measures–intellectual, social, or religious–we have had to endure. This is what is so important to us when we hear Lakota songs, such as the Sun Dance songs–Lakota hymns, really, because they are about cultural values and attitudes. The words of the ceremonial songs and the dances convey these values and attitudes. Surely this is what Lakota rituals and belief are all about.[15]

The Native American Church, with origins in the Southern Plains religious movements of the 1870s and 1880s, remains an important and expanding force

Emil Her Many Horses (b. 1954)
Oglala Lakota (Sioux)
Native American Church Set, 1999
Wood, glass beads, horse hair, feathers, metal, deer hide, pigments, string, gourd, silk hat; staff 38 ¼ x 2 ⅜ inches; fan 29 ½ x 3 ½ inches; rattle 22 ¼ x 2 ½ inches; hat 6 x 10 inches, diameter 12 ¼ inches
Gift of the Pilot Foundation NA.502.215.1, .3-.5

The loose fan, gourd rattle, and beaded staff—instruments of prayer central to the ceremonies of the Native American Church—are typically encased in colorful beadwork using the gourd or peyote stitch which diffused along with the spiritual movement. Included in this set is a black silk top hat decorated with feathers and a beaded hatband featuring the church's symbols of waterbirds. A tipi is depicted on the rosette. A German silver waterbird is pinned on the front. This motif is repeated in beadwork on the fan, rattle, and staff.

in contemporary spiritual expression. Like the Sun Dance, Ghost Dance, and other Native religious practices, the Native American Church was subject to the prohibitions enacted at the time of its origin as well as persistent legal prosecution for over one hundred years. In 1888, the Indian agent for the Kiowa, Apache, Comanche, Wichita, Caddo, and Delaware issued an order prohibiting the use of peyote—mistakenly referring to it as "mescal beans"—and threatened those who violated this rule with losing annuity goods and rations.[16] In 1899, the Oklahoma legislature passed a statute criminalizing the religious use of peyote, repeating the mistake of using the term "mescal beans."[17] As peyote use spread to other reservations, practitioners faced similar prohibitions and legislation. The formal establishment of the Native American Church in Oklahoma in 1918 and subsequent chapters in other states were responses to the attempts to suppress this religious practice.[18] Since its beginnings, the Native American Church has diffused throughout the United States and into Canada and Mexico and is considered the largest intertribal Indian religious practice in North America today.[19]

Members of the Native American Church created a body of art replete with symbols for use during meetings, the basic styles of which are still being followed. Men produce rectangular boxes of cedar or leather, known as feather or peyote boxes, beautifully carved or painted with scenes of peyote ritual and motifs rich in symbolism. Sometimes the boxes are painted or lined with felt in the red and blue colors of the Native American Church, representing day and night. The boxes hold the necessary ritual paraphernalia—the fan, gourd rattle, staff, and sweet grass, and other items of personal spiritual significance. During the meetings, each participant opens his peyote box and unfolds the scarf containing the ritual objects within before the ceremony begins.

The feather fans, made of eagle, hawk, scissortail flycatcher, magpie, waterbird (anhinga), pheasant, flicker, and brightly colored macaw feathers, are made in flat or loose forms, the latter providing movement during the meeting rituals. The gourd rattles are used to accompany participants as they sing their personal vision songs and the long staffs are held or set upright as symbols of leadership during the ceremonies. The staff is usually made in two or three sections which when separated can be carried in the peyote box. Each of these items is usually decorated with colorful beadwork in the gourd or peyote stitch design often representing feathers, tipis, crosses, and waterbirds together with characteristic zigzag patterns. Unlike most Plains Indian beadwork, men do the majority of the decorative work on Native American Church ritual objects. Although the artistry and technique lavished on these ritual objects—often the most treasured of personal possessions—personifies excellence in Plains Indian art, their deeper significance lies in the spiritual beliefs and extreme devotion that inspired their creations.

Other Plains artistic traditions also have helped to bring about recognition of this religious movement. German silver jewelry with designs related to the spiritual use of peyote and symbols of the Native American Church is a unique and innovative art form that developed in concert with the church's growth.[20] German silver, an alloy of nickel, copper, and zinc, became available through trade on the Southern Plains in the mid-1800s and was widely used throughout the reservation period. The formation and expansion of the Native American Church converged with the recognition of such master artists in German silver as Julius Caesar of the Pawnee, and later his son, Bruce Caesar.

In the Northern Plains, Mitchell Zephier (Pretty Voice Hawk) from the Lower Brule Reservation in South Dakota, who began working in the 1970s, has been the most productive and recognized artist in German silver and other metals. Zephier's work is based upon Lakota cultural symbolism and values with designs inspired by the Native American Church and his own experiences. His work is characterized by "the marriage of metals technique" in which German silver is combined with metals such as copper and brass.[21] In the 1980s, Zephier decided to teach metalwork to other Lakota artists because he believes that, "If you create something of beauty, it increases your self esteem."[22] He also considers it important to assist tribal members in making a living through creating art, as well as passing on the artistry and skills that have helped him to preserve and express Lakota cultural traditions.

Although Zephier learned the basics of metalworking through classwork and informal instruction in Vermont and Chicago, his artistry flourished on the Rosebud Sioux Reservation where he found inspiration through his participation in the Sun Dance and the Native American Church—both potent sources of artistic and literary expression for Native people. Monroe Tsatoke, a renowned Kiowa painter of Native American Church rituals and symbolism, addressed the "devout spiritual feeling" that Indian people convey through tribal rituals and ceremonies and often express through their arts.

> The Indian in his art expressed this emotion. This unsatisfied desire for the things of the spirit. By his art he strives to express his own concept of the divine creator. Wrong it may be, but according to the light he has it is the best thing he can do.
>
> He has the ceremonies invoking the blessings of the only god he knows, all of which are expressed in his art.[23]

Contemporary Cultural Celebrations: Powwows and Homecomings

> We've been going to powwows ever since I can remember. We have a big family here. . . . We've all danced. We've all traveled to powwows extensively, not only to become champion dancers or to be well known but to keep our culture alive. One of the things I get out of it for myself, personally, is that I feel like I'm contributing to our people that have left us, our ancestors. In that aspect I think and we believe they are still here today watching us.
>
> —Cassie Soldier Wolf[24]

Mitchell Zephier (Pretty Voice Hawk) (b. 1952)
Lakota (Sioux)
Native American Church Cross, 1979
German silver, brass; 9 x 4½ inches
NA.502.48

The cross shows Mitchell Zephier's distinctive "marriage of metals" technique, in which German silver is layered with brass or other metals. The designs of the cross, which are inspired by Lakota culture and the symbolism of the Native American Church, include the central motif of the pipe and star, crescent and waterbird, and the gourd rattle, fan, staff, and water drum with drumstick. Four tipis, where the ceremonies take place, are on either side of the center.

Dance Bustle
Dakota (Sioux), Manitoba, Canada, 1987
Pheasant feathers, deer hide, wool cloth,
glass beads; 40 ½ x 25 inches
NA.203.795

During many summer weekends, Northern Arapaho tribal member Cassie Soldier Wolf and her family members pack their dance clothing, regalia, and camping equipment and travel to powwows across the Plains. Among Plains Indian people, the dynamic and evolving tradition known as powwow has become not only the most visible expression of tribal arts and cultures, but also one of the strongest.

The roots of the contemporary powwow lie in the eighteenth and nineteenth century warrior societies through which men sought special protection for warfare and celebrated their individual war deeds and tribal victories. Each of these societies carried their own name, insignia, dances, songs, and symbols. As participation in these specific warrior organizations subsided, a new men's dance society movement known as the Omaha Dance or Grass Dance—named for the braided sweet grass tied to dancers' belts and bustles—diffused throughout the Plains from the 1860s to 1880s.

The Omaha Dance may have originated from the Pawnee *Iruska*, meaning "the fire is in me," a powerful medicine society whose members were immune from burns and had the ability to treat burns others suffered.[25] This society dance, characterized by regalia consisting of a porcupine hair roach and specialized Crow belt or bustle, spread to the Omaha, who called it the *Hethuska* and taught it to the Lakota and to tribes throughout the Northern Plains. As the dance spread, it lost many of its ceremonial elements and incorporated new conventions, including the use of a large drum and, on the Northern Plains, the wearing of the hair roach with a different style of bustle, otter hide breastplates, and long strings of bells. On the Southern Plains, the dance became known as the *O-ho-mah* among the Kiowa, the *Hethuska* or *Heluska* among the Ponca, and the *I'n-lon-schka* among the Osage with each tribe incorporating culturally specific elements. The transfer of the dance from one people to another occurred during tribal visitations of the late nineteenth century during which members taught the dances and songs and reciprocally received gifts of horses and goods.[26]

Women Traditional Dancers
Plains Indian Museum Powwow, Cody,
Wyoming, June 18, 2005
Photograph by Sean Campbell

Traditional dancers Renee Tossitsie (Eastern
Shoshone), Shelley Charging (Three Affiliated
Tribes/Eastern Shoshone), and Fay Ann Soldier
Wolf (Northern Arapaho) enter the dance circle
during the Powwow Grand Entry.

Other precursors of the contemporary powwow can be found in summer gatherings when the bands came together for the Sun Dance and other ceremonies. The powwow has also been influenced by early reservation-era intertribal visitations and celebrations, trade fairs, meetings, councils, and other venues where dancing occurred. Such exchanges became commonplace in Indian Territory in the late nineteenth century as more than thirty tribes were settled there in relatively close proximity.

When Indian soldiers came home after World War I and II, the warrior society dances of the past century acquired new meaning. Those returning warriors were honored at "Homecoming Dances," as they were sometimes called in Oklahoma. In these celebrations, important social ties and cultural traditions were also renewed, including the honoring of elders, naming and adoption ceremonies, welcoming of families back into public life following a period of mourning, and general bonding between families and friends. These early powwows also resembled the summer dance celebrations of the past century and included gathering families in encampments at celebration grounds, the use of camp criers or announcers, and social interaction among participants.

The word "powwow," derived from a Southern New England Algonquian term for a "medicine man" or "curing ceremony," was not generally used by Native people to identify such gatherings until the 1920s in western Oklahoma.[27] Powwows gained further prominence in the 1950s and 1960s throughout the Plains region when Lakota, Crow, and Blackfeet peoples began to sponsor large intertribal events. Now powwows take place on reservations, in small tribal communities, or in more diverse settings such as universities, tribal colleges and other educational institutions, urban convention centers, casinos, and museums. The phenomenon of the contest powwow with cash awards that emphasize the individual dancer's ability and achievement has also flourished. In the late twentieth century, powwows became a venue for reinforcing community ties and the culturally significant value of generosity, demonstrated through giveaways.

Powwows are not commercial events, nor purely entertainment, but important spiritual and social gatherings to celebrate the arts, dance, music, and cultural traditions, and to reinforce familial and social relationships. As Crow tribal member Richard Singer says,

> Powwows are really welcoming places. . . . I go to enjoy it, listen to good songs, see good dancing, and visit with friends and family that I haven't seen in awhile. It's kind of a place where everybody meets and catches up on things. It reinforces a lot of the friendships that have occurred and it's a good place to learn new songs or see things that you haven't seen before.[28]

Although the warrior societies and early Plains Homecoming powwows were primarily the domain of male dancers, in the last fifty years women have

OPPOSITE: Alice New Holy Blue Legs (1925–2003) Oglala Lakota (Sioux)
Man's Hair Ornament, ca. 1970
Eagle feathers, dyed porcupine quills, tanned hide, cotton and wool cloth, rawhide, metal cones, mirror, shell beads; 35 x 9¼ inches
Gift of Arthur Amiotte in Memory of Lloyd Kiva New NA.203.1314

Alice New Holy Blue Legs said that when she was young, every Lakota girl was expected to learn how to tan hides and do beadwork and porcupine quillwork. Her mother had died, so her father instructed her in quillwork and other skills. She became a premier quillwork artist who was awarded a National Endowment for the Humanities National Heritage Fellowship Award in 1985. She also taught her art to her husband, daughters, and grandchildren.

taken more active roles and children are encouraged to attend, dance, and learn their cultural traditions.

It's a way for us to express our songs. It's a way for us to strengthen our family and, you know, a celebration of life. . . . We go to competition powwows, but we also go to traditional powwows because it honors who we are. You have naming ceremonies at powwows; you have memorial contests, memorial dances. It's a way for us to remember who we are as a people. . . . For us, it's just a way of life.

—Sandra Iron Cloud[29]

Throughout the histories of Plains Indian people, those who have served in the military have been honored for defending their homelands and protecting their people. Ceremonies for veterans often take place at powwows and other cultural celebrations.

We always honored our veterans. This is one of the most important things in our society because they put their lives on the lines for us. We always honored them, just as a long time ago when they'd come home we always did an honor dance for our veterans, or, for our warriors. . . . Today, it's the same thing. The first thing they start talking about is the importance of the veterans, putting their lives on the lines for their loved ones, for their families, for their nations, for all Indian people. So, therefore, we always look at it in a good way, that these guys come home and we'll honor them.

—Curly Bear Wagner[30]

A color guard of military veterans who served in World War II, the Korean, Vietnam, the Gulf War, and recent Middle Eastern conflicts, carrying eagle feather staffs, the American flag, and tribal nation flags, lead the dancers into the circle during the Grand Entry or Parade In that begins each powwow. They stand at attention during the singing of the flag song and post the colors before the Victory Dance. Families often honor men and women entering or returning from military service and those scheduled to be posted to overseas duties with honor songs and giveaways. When eagle feathers fall from dancers' regalia during the powwow program, the veterans lead rituals to retrieve the feathers. These ceremonies are culturally specific and in some cases involve dancing, "counting coups" upon the feathers by veterans, and the recitation of war experiences.

The association of warrior traditions and respect for military service is demonstrated in annual tribal celebrations such as the Pawnee Homecoming, which formally began in 1946 to honor the Pawnee soldiers returning from World War II, although its roots run much deeper in tribal tradition. It originated in the Lance Society Dances and Victory Dances from the days when the Pawnee lived along the Platte River and its tributaries, and was reinforced in the first service of Pawnee warriors in the United States military as Army scouts between 1864 and 1877. Traditional warrior societies, leaders, and individual

Grand Entry Ceremonies
Plains Indian Museum Powwow, Cody,
Wyoming, June 17, 2005
Photograph by Chris Gimmeson

Members of V.F.W. Apsáalooke Post 5503 of
Crow Agency carrying the eagle staff and
American and Crow Nation flags lead dancers
during the Grand Entry and opening ceremonies at the Plains Indian Museum Powwow.

tribal members respected this military service and ritually prepared the scouts for
warfare and honored them through ceremonies, songs, and prayers.

Later, Pawnee soldiers enlisted in the Spanish American War, during which
one tribal member, William Pollock, served in the Rough Riders. When Pawnee
men came home from World War I in 1919, a two-day celebration took place on
June 6 and 7 and the people honored their young men and offered thanks that
among forty men who served—many in extremely hazardous duties—only one
life was lost.

When the soldiers returned by train to Pawnee, Oklahoma, families went down to the station to welcome them and followed as they marched down the street. Some of the soldiers sought out the old warriors who had served as scouts and asked for their blessings. The celebratory dance was held in the Skidi ceremonial roundhouse located north of Pawnee. Hundreds of Pawnee and other tribal members as well as non-Indian onlookers from the surrounding area attended. The soldiers—some in uniform and others in traditional Pawnee regalia—danced with their families and friends in a Victory Dance during which one mother carried a pole topped with a German helmet and knife that her son had captured. A male elder spoke: "While the boys were away we prayed for their safe return. We did this at every public gathering and it looks as though our prayers had been answered."[31]

Both men and women had prominent roles, giving speeches, recounting war experiences, conducting giveaways, dancing, and singing individual honor songs of the Lance Society, and old war songs with new verses referring to the German Kaiser, planes, and submarines. An elder sang a song that had come to him in a dream, in which he heard a voice saying it would not be long before he would see the Pawnee boys again, as well as thousands of white people dancing, singing, and waving flags. A few days later, he heard of the signing of the Armistice. He later gave the song to Pawnee people to be sung at celebrations honoring returning soldiers.[32] Amid the celebration, the people mourned and prayed with the family of the young man who had been lost to illness in France.

A similar celebration took place after World War II during which many Pawnee served, including three who had been prisoners of war. World War I veterans organized the feast and dances to honor returning veterans in the first Pawnee Homecoming which took place in July 1946. In 1947, World War II veterans organized the Homecoming, which has continued since under the leadership of the Pawnee Indian Veterans Association as an annual celebration each July in honor of all veterans and current military members and to welcome all Pawnee people home. Assisting in hand games and other activities throughout the celebration is the Pawnee Chapter of the American War Mothers, organized in 1940 and composed of the mothers of sons and daughters who served in the military during wartime.

The Homecoming also includes a parade, an art show, a softball tournament, and a five-mile Hawk Chief Run, named in honor of the Pawnee scout and runner, who in 1876 was said to be the first man to run a mile in under four minutes. The powwow, however, is the focus of this four-day celebration. In recognition of Pawnee traditions, after the Parade In, the chiefs of the four bands—Skidi, Pitahawirata, Kitkehahki, and Chaui—enter the circle to dance, dressed in the traditional straight dance regalia.

Crow Fair: "Where They Make The Noise"

As in the old days, Crows begin the New Year with lots of good fun, good-luck wishes, and plenty to eat. We do this with our fair and rodeo held in August at Crow Agency. Sometimes, there are over eight hundred tipis. We take bedsprings and rollaway beds to sleep on in tents pitched in back of our tipis. This is a good time for women to sew, cook, and visit. We all dress up in our best parade outfits, and the best ones are given first, second, and third prizes. We parade with our clan, and there are prizes for Indian dancing. Lots of Indians come—Nez Perce, Blackfeet, Bannock, Shoshoni, Cheyenne, and Sioux. We make a big camp of tipis for our guests. They eat well on buffalo meat from our tribal herd, and the most important fair officers are sure to hold giveaways; the fair officers always give presents to the visiting Indians to give them a good feeling when they leave.

—Agnes Yellowtail Deernose[33]

The tribal name for Crow Fair is *Uhba'asaxpiluua*, a term for any celebration, dance or social gathering meaning "where they make the noise."[34] Held each August, Crow Fair is an opportunity to experience tribal artistry in action. Dancers from throughout the Great Plains come to the powwow to compete for recognition and prize money, wearing their finest traditional clothing and regalia. Crow tribal members from the very young to the elderly reenact the parades that have characterized their cultural histories, with contemporary flourishes. Led by veterans carrying the American and Crow Nation flags, Crow men and boys wearing beaded hide clothing and eagle feather bonnets and women and girls wearing the traditional red, blue, and green elk tooth dresses ride horses outfitted with beaded gear and carry painted lance cases, beaded rifle scabbards, cradles,

Riders in Crow Fair Parade
Crow Agency, Montana, August 23, 2003
Photograph by Emma I. Hansen

Crow tribal members celebrate their heritage and arts through the daily parade at Crow Fair. Women wearing their elk teeth dresses, men in beaded hide clothing and eagle feather bonnets, and children in tribal clothing ride through the camps in remembrance of earlier processions across the Plains.

Kevin Red Star (b. 1943)
Apsáalooke (Crow)
Crow Indian Parade Rider, 1982
Oil on canvas; 42 x 31⅞ inches
Gift of Mr. and Mrs. W.D. Weiss 7.94

Kevin Red Star researches the culture, clothing, and history of the Crow, who provide the subject matter for his paintings. He states that he gets involved in the image by photographing and sketching contemporary scenes such as Crow parades and dancing. His brilliant personal interpretations of Crow life are characterized by exaggerated color and simplified form.

and other accouterments. The cars, trucks, and floats—each covered with Pendleton blankets, elk tooth dresses, shawls, and cradles and carrying dignitaries and dancers—follow the horse procession.

This celebration was first organized in 1904 by the government agent for the Crow, Samuel C. Reynolds, using tribal funds to encourage men in agricultural pursuits and women in Euro-American-style domestic work. At the fair, families were encouraged to exhibit their farm produce and animals, women's handicrafts, canned goods, and other domestic products for ribbons and cash prizes. To promote Crow participation in the fair, Reynolds relaxed the federal prohibition against traditional and social gatherings and allowed ceremonies, parades, horse racing, singing, and dancing.

The cultural and celebratory activities of the fair were powerful inducements for the Crow to gather in encampments at the fairgrounds. In time—much to the disappointment and disdain of government agents and superintendents— the parades, dancing, traditional arts, horse racing, battle reenactments, and ceremonies eclipsed the agricultural and domestic exhibits.[35]

> The old chiefs and elders, true pre-reservation Crows, took advantage of the agent's relaxation of the strict rules and heightened the festive mood of the gathering with sham battles, reenactments of events from the former days of intertribal warfare, victory dances, public recitals of war deeds by veteran warriors, and gift distributions to clan relatives, thus reviving rituals heretofore prohibited by the government.[36]

The fair was suspended in 1919 because of drought and was held only intermittently during the next ten years. During that time, the Crow organized and joined cultural celebrations and fairs in Lodge Grass, Pryor, and in the non-reservation towns of Sheridan and Billings, outside of the supervision of federal authorities.[37] In the 1930s, Robert Yellowtail revived the fair, although it was discontinued again during World War II. By the time Crow Fair was resurrected after the war, the agricultural and domestic features were forgotten and the social and cultural aspects expanded and intensified. Visiting and cultural exchanges with other tribal representatives of the Plateau and Northern Plains, integral to this celebration from its early years, also extended to include people from throughout the world.

> The modern Crow Fair and Celebration is much more than dancing, horse racing, and rodeoing. It is a big family reunion; Crow Indians living in the various parts of the large reservation camp together to visit, feast, and recount old stories and history. It is a time when members of other tribes come to visit their Crow friends. Many non-Indians come to look, take pictures, and move on; others come purposely to participate in the various activities. Europeans, mainly members of "Indian clubs" in Germany, France, and England, come to live like real Indians for a week. There is joy, friendliness, and even frivolity throughout the camp!
>
> —Joseph Medicine Crow[38]

The final day of Crow Fair is reserved for the tribe to conduct the "Dancing Through the Camp" ceremony, through which all pray for a good year until the people gather again.

> Four leaders are selected to lead the participants in a long procession around the main sector of the encampment. At each of four designated stops, a leader tells a good-luck or good-deed story and prays that the people will have similar good experiences during the

coming year. Here four songs are sung by the drummers, and the procession moves to the next stop. The fourth and final stop is made inside the dancing arbor.

Joseph Medicine Crow[39]

After the procession, fair officials present gifts to tribal elders, visitors and special clan relatives to show appreciation for having been selected to manage the event. They provide a feast and the officials for next year's fair are elected.[40]

Through this ceremony, fair leaders articulate the cultural histories, traditions and values of the Crow—the ancient migrations that brought them to the Northern Plains, the processions they followed as they moved their villages seasonally as they hunted buffalo, the ideals of generosity and respect for elders, and the spiritual foundation that guides all aspects of life.

Contemporary Artistic Expressions

The American Indian has tenaciously held on to his arts, not in the sense of the object alone, but rather as a fabric that binds and holds together many dimensions of his very existence. The arts are to him an expression of the integrated forces that tie together and unify all aspects of life. . . . [The Indian artist] is therefore, the eyes, ears and voice of his own age. More than that, he has his personal record which, to a culture without a written language is the partial repository or encyclopedia of its oral tradition.

–Arthur Amiotte[41]

Innately connected to cultural values, mores, and life experiences, the art of Plains Indian peoples reflects traditions, transitions, adaptations, and innovations as they have moved from their ancient past into the present. Artists have always had integral roles and responsibilities within historic Plains cultures as providers of both secular and sacred materials, recorders and interpreters of cultures and events, and visionaries of the future. They have long adapted materials and technologies to produce multi-layered works that were functional and relevant to cultural and spiritual lives.

Although Indians of the past probably never considered themselves to be practicing artists in pursuit of art for its own sake, art was nonetheless integral to the growth of Indian culture. For them, art and culture are inseparable–art is essential to the shaping of culture and simultaneously shaped by it.

–Lloyd New[42]

Contemporary artists preserve cultural identities while meeting new challenges and experimenting with new media. Among contemporary traditionalists—those who work in the "traditional" media of hide work, porcupine quillwork and beadwork—the art forms of an earlier era are carried into the present in recognition of cultural identity and appreciation for the technical ability and

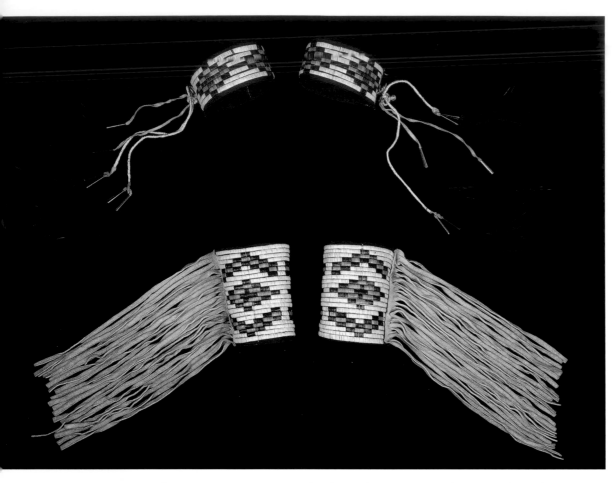

Sophie New Holy (1916–1984)
Oglala Lakota (Sioux)
Man's Cuffs and Arm Bands, 1971
Tanned hide, dyed porcupine quills, cotton
cloth, rawhide, feathers, tin cones; cuffs 5¼ x
9½ inches, arm bands 2¼ x 12 inches
Plains Indian Museum Acquisitions Fund
Purchase NA.203.1311, NA.203.1310

Although beadwork largely replaced porcupine
quillwork during the late nineteenth century,
Lakota women continued to decorate clothing,
bags, accessories, and dance regalia with
quilled designs into the contemporary period.
The New Holy family has been prominent in the
preservation of the skills of porcupine quillwork
among the Lakota, including Sophie New Holy,
who was the stepmother of Alice New Holy
Blue Legs.

ingenuity of past generations. Rarely do such artists simply reproduce those ancient designs, however, but rather introduce their own ideas and new meanings. Although many of these artists have academic art instruction, they may have also learned from older generations in an age-old transfer of traditional knowledge. Other artists are working in new media, perhaps addressing new issues and concerns or applying new techniques and materials to the interpretations of eighteenth- and nineteenth-century cultural and historical experiences and ancient traditions.

Contemporary beadwork artists create for family and personal use for powwows and other celebrations as well as for income. Although most beadwork artists are women, men are also working in this medium more frequently. Traditionally, beadwork skills and designs have been learned within the family, although this art form is also now taught through tribal and cultural programs on reservations and in urban areas and in art programs in high schools and tribal colleges.

Three beadwork artists from one family, Wilma Jean McAdams-Swallow, Vivian Swallow and Sandra Swallow-Hunter, Eastern Shoshone tribal members from the Wind River Reservation, excel in creating Shoshone dresses, moccasins, beaded belts and bags, and other contemporary powwow clothing. Swallow and

Wilma Jean Swallow (b. 1934), Sandra Swallow Hunter (b. 1961) and Vivian Swallow (b. 1962)
So-soreh (Eastern Shoshone)
Dress, 2000
Native tanned elk hide, glass beads, imitation hairpipes; 54 x 35 inches
Gift of Mr. and Mrs. Harold R. Tate NA.202.1139

Wilma Jean Swallow (b. 1934), Sandra Swallow Hunter (b. 1961) and Vivian Swallow (b. 1962)
So-soreh (Eastern Shoshone)
Woman's Moccasins, 2000
Native tanned elk hide, glass beads;
54 x 35 inches
Gift of Mr. and Mrs. Harold R. Tate NA.202.1138

Wilma Jean Swallow, Sandra Swallow Hunter, and Vivian Swallow make dresses, moccasins, belts, and bags featuring the distinctive Shoshone rose design for family members and other Shoshone powwow dancers. In this design, the beading of the rose on the dress and moccasins follow the lines of the petals, stems, and leaves. The three women work as a team and hope to inspire other talented Eastern Shoshone artists in hide and bead-work.

Swallow-Hunter learned beading from their mother, McAdams-Swallow, who has beaded for over thirty years. Swallow began learning as a small child by stringing together beads of mixed colors left over from her mother's work. By her late teens, she was working on her own projects.[43] The three women first began designing and creating dresses, most featuring the distinctive Shoshone rose design, for their own family members and have continued to work as a team.

The Shoshone rose design has become one of the dominant and most recognizable patterns used since World War II and often differentiates Shoshone pow-wow dancers from individuals of other tribes. Swallow describes the Shoshone preference for the rose and other natural designs in the following way:

> The Shoshone, like other Native Americans, use elements that surround us, like the mountains seen as geometric designs on our moccasins. Roses are something beautiful in nature, which surrounds us. Originally, we used the wild rose, but after the Shoshone were exposed to embroidery through the boarding schools we began making more elaborate designs.[44]

Debra Lee Stone Jay lives at Fort Hall, Idaho, on the Shoshone-Bannock Reservation. A Shoshone-Bannock tribal member who is also of Paiute descent, she creates beaded dresses, vests, moccasins, cradles, purses, and other accessories featuring distinctive floral, geometric, and animal designs as well as portraits of Shoshone-Bannock people.

Debra Lee (Stone) Jay (b.1957)
Shoshone–Bannock
Vest, 2002
Smoke tanned hide, glass beads, cotton cloth;
23 ½ x 22 ½ inches
Plains Indian Museum Acquisitions Fund
Purchase NA.202.1008

This vest shows a different approach to the use of the Shoshone rose design. The vest is made of smoked tanned hide, which provides a soft brown color as background. The beadwork features a combination of Shoshone geometric designs and the rose pattern.

276

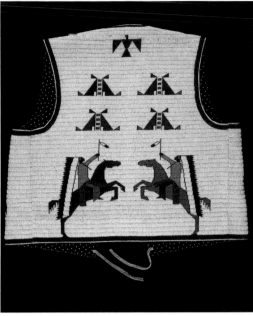

Marcus Dewey (b. 1956)
Hinono'ei (Northern Arapaho)
Beaded Vest, 1997
Hinono'ei (Northern Arapaho), 2003
Tanned deer hide, glass beads, cotton cloth;
24 x 25 inches
Plains Indian Museum Acquisitions Fund
Purchase NA.202.1276

The vest made by Northern Arapaho beadwork artist Marcus Dewey is reminiscent of the fully beaded Northern Plains men's vests of the early reservation period, when women began illustrating men's war deeds through pictographic beadwork designs on clothing, pipe bags, and other objects. This vest features tipi and thunderbird designs with two facing warriors on horseback on the front and back. The warriors wear eagle feather bonnets with long trailers and hold shields, coup sticks, a tomahawk, and lance.

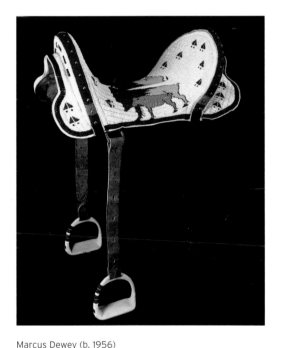

Our family was raised in the traditional manner with all the language, customs, and traditions of the tribe. Our grandmother was known as a master in the art of hide tanning and beadwork specializing in intricate floral and geometric designs of the Intermountain tribes. Our grandfather also helped us by telling us about the colors of the sky and the animals, explaining to us about the markings and the movements of certain wildlife.[45]

Northern Arapaho beadwork artist Marcus Dewey is known by Native American art specialists and collectors for his distinctive beaded saddles. McClellan military saddles—standard issue from the Indian Wars until World War I—are the foundations of his beadwork designs, which feature representations of buffalo beaded in traditional Arapaho colors of white, blue, red, and yellow. He also beads men's vests reminiscent of the fully beaded Northern Plains men's vests of the early reservation period, with warriors on horseback wearing eagle feather bonnets with long trailers and holding weapons of war—shields, coup sticks, a tomahawk, and lance—and fully-beaded cradles featuring Arapaho geometric and representational designs. Dewey conducts historical research on early and reservation-era beadwork and consults with older family members as he develops his designs, although he states that many of his designs come to him through dreams.[46]

Vanessa Jennings (Paukeigope) is the rare beadwork artist who has achieved public recognition, receiving a National Heritage Fellowship from the National Endowment for the Arts for her mastery of Kiowa traditional arts in 1989, the Honored One award from the Red Earth Arts Festival in Oklahoma City in 2004, first place awards at the Santa Fe Indian Market and Red Earth, and numerous museum commissions. Ironically, like many other beadwork artists, Paukeigope has supported her dedication to traditional Kiowa culture and arts throughout her life by working outside of the art field.

Marcus Dewey (b. 1956)
Hinono'ei (Northern Arapaho)
Beaded Saddle, 1997
McClellan saddle, glass beads, metal, wool cloth, brass tacks; 31 x 19 ½ inches
Museum purchase with funds provided by the Pilot Foundation NA.403.203

Marcus Dewey reinterprets Plains representational painting in this fully beaded saddle. Buffalo and their tracks are depicted against a ground of blue and white—traditional Arapaho colors. Immaculate rows of beadwork, colorful bands of trade cloth, and brass tacks embellish a buckskin surface. Through his artistry, Dewey transforms the appropriated McClellan saddle into a decidedly Arapaho work of art.

Vanessa Paukeigope Jennings (b. 1952)
Gaigwa (Kiowa)
Cradle, 1996
Wood, glass beads, tanned deer hide, metal
tacks, cotton cloth; 49 x 9 inches
Museum purchase with funds provided by the
Pilot Foundation and Arthur Amiotte NA.111.59

Vanessa Jennings based the design for this
cradle on a photograph of her grandfather
Stephen Mopope as a baby in a cradle on the
back of his mother Etta Mopope. The cradle,
long gone from the family's possession but
recently discovered in a museum collection,
had been made by Etta Mopope and her
mother Keintaddle. Jennings hopes that her
version of the cradle would have made
Keintaddle and her grandmother Jeanette
Mopope proud. The pink-colored beads came
from acquaintances in France and remind the
artist of the subtle pink and purple hues of the
prairie grasses in Oklahoma moving in the
wind.

Jennings comes from a long and distinguished artistic tradition as the oldest grandchild of renowned Kiowa Five painter Stephen Mopope and Plains Apache traditional artist Jeanette Berry Mopope. She credits her grandparents, who brought her from Arizona where her parents were working to live with them on their Oklahoma allotment when she was a year old, for teaching her traditional Kiowa and Apache philosophies, manners, and arts that have guided her throughout her life.

> I had two really wonderful people in my life and those were my grandparents. My grandfather, up until the end, was a very traditional man. He painted, he was a singer, he played the flute, he did wonderful things with his life. My grandmother was an accomplished singer, she was a beadworker, she was an extraordinary person. And, they were willing to share what they had. I am the product of that compassion and that kindness.[47]

Jennings was named for her maternal great-grandmother Paukeigope (Etta Mopope) who with her mother Keintaddle were beadwork artists known among the Kiowa for the excellence of their work. Another great-grandmother (the mother of Jeanette Berry Mopope) was Anna E. Jones Berry, who was also a beadworker and cradle maker. Jennings describes her life as a part of an ancient continuum built upon the accumulated knowledge and experiences of her familial ancestors that carries on in her children and grandchildren's generations.[48]

Eva B. McAdams (b. 1927)
So-soreh (Eastern Shoshone)
Belt and Bag, 1993
Tanned hide, glass beads; belt 44 x 3⅛ inches;
bag 27¼ x 5¼ inches
Plains Indian Museum Acquisitions Fund
Purchase NA.203.1331

Eva B. McAdams learned to bead from her mother Eloise St. Clair and her grandmother, Mary Washakie. Through the years she has created Eastern Shoshone powwow dresses, leggings, moccasins, belts, and bags, and accessories for family members, art shows, and museum collections. In 1990, she received the Wyoming Governor's Award for the Arts and in 1996 she was awarded a National Heritage Fellowship Award from the National Endowment for the Arts. Although much of McAdams' beadwork uses the Shoshone rose pattern, this belt and bag features morning glories and petunias.

Jennings' grandmother taught her beadwork and passed on her very strict beliefs about colors and designs. She taught her to respect other families' designs and to use only designs that belonged to their family. To copy another family's would be disrespectful and dishonest because each design has a life and history of its own. The only time she should use another family's design is if they were given to her by a family member such as an elderly beadworker with no daughters or granddaughters who wanted to ensure that a design would be preserved.[49]

Jennings' traditional artwork includes dresses, leggings, cradles, lances, horse equipment, shirts and jackets, and dolls. Recently, she has concentrated on distinctive and highly decorated cradles created because

> The color, design, and artistry of cradleboards impress me as a celebration of life. These cradleboards are symbols of humanity, honoring our unnamed sisters and grandmothers who rose up against overwhelming odds of war, cultural genocide, death, and other monumental events to celebrate a newborn's life as only women can: to represent the promise of hope for the future.[50]

Southern Ute artist Austin Box began working in the traditional art forms of hidework, beadwork, and quillwork after his retirement from the United States Army as a means of reconnecting with his cultural traditions after an absence of twenty-one years from his home in Colorado.[51] A self-taught artist, Box has focused on reviving traditional Ute work and has based his designs for men's shirts, leggings, shields, bandolier bags, and knife sheaths on older examples in museum collections. He introduces into these traditional objects designs and symbols derived from his military experiences—particularly his service in the Vietnam War—thus using these older traditional means of recording accomplishments in war to tell the story of his own life.

During the difficult early reservation period, Plains Native women adopted new vehicles of artistic expression as they began creating clothing and household items using cloth, thread, needles, and sewing machines to fill practical and ceremonial needs of their new lives. Women on the Northern Plains began making patchwork quilts in the late nineteenth century as substitutes for buffalo robes to provide warmth in early reservation houses. The skill of quiltmaking was introduced to Native women by women missionaries and wives of government agents on the reservations as well as through classes at religious and federal boarding schools aimed at teaching Euro-American domestic arts. Initially, women made patchwork quilts with square or geometric patterns for everyday use utilizing scraps from used clothing or flour sacks. To teach quilting and exchange patterns, women often cut and sewed their quilts together and Lakota women, in particular, formed quilting groups similar in function to the earlier porcupine quillwork societies through which their skills and contributions to their families and tribal communities were recognized. In time, the women created many dif-

Austin Box (b. 1930)
Nuche (Southern Ute)
Shirt, 1989
Tanned deer hide, glass beads, commercial dyes, paint, ermine hide and hair, dyed porcupine quills, sinew; 30 x 22 ⅞ inches
Gift of Mr. and Mrs. William D. Weiss
NA.202.1007

Austin Box began making hide shirts and regalia to wear to powwows and tribal ceremonies after he retired from the military and returned to Colorado. He bases his creations on examples from museum collections, but incorporates traditional Ute designs with his own personal innovations and symbols drawn from his experiences in the military in Southeast Asia.

ferent geometric patterns for quilting, with the most prevalent contemporary design integral to cultural and ceremonial life being the star quilt known as *wichapi shina*, meaning "star robes."[52]

Seldom is a star quilt used as an ordinary bed covering in reservation homes; rather star quilts are used in ways that distinguish their meaning and role within Lakota Sioux life. They are employed as door coverings for dwellings or shelters at ceremonial events and are worn by healers in the yuwipi (curing) ceremonies. More importantly, star quilts have long been a critical element in giveaways and from birth to death, the life-cycle events of Sioux peoples.[53]

Freda Goodsell (b. 1929)
Oglala Lakota (Sioux)
Star Quilt, 2000
Cotton cloth, thread, batting; 132 x 84 inches
Museum purchase with funds provided by the
Pilot Foundation NA.302.144

With dynamic bursts of pattern and color, star quilts recall the feathered circles of eagle feather headdresses, the rays of the sun, and the morning star. Like similarly patterned hide robes of the buffalo days, star quilts may be worn for momentous occasions or given to mark significant events in a person's life. Characterized by craftsmanship and beauty, they are presented to honored individuals/persons at powwows funerals and ceremonies. Oglala Lakota quilt maker Freda Goodsell estimates that she has made thousands of quilts for family members and friends, for ceremonies, and as donations for fundraisers.

Small star quilts are made by family members for newborn babies. They are given to young people at naming ceremonies, graduations, weddings, and as gifts of honor and prestige during giveaways at memorial feasts and powwows. They are also draped over coffins at funeral rites as buffalo robes were once used to wrap the bodies of the deceased. The star pattern of the quilts represents the morning star, a significant symbol in Lakota beliefs and ceremonial life and, although it may have derived from introduced Euro-American designs, it also has antecedents in earlier symbolic hide-painting traditions.[54]

Oglala Lakota quilt maker Freda Mesteth Goodsell has made numerous quilts for ceremonies, giveaways for family members and friends, and for donations for raffles to raise funds for schools or other community fundraisers. Although Goodsell grew up in a home surrounded by the quilts her mother, Christina Standing Bear Mesteth, had made, she is self-taught and did not begin making quilts until she was in her thirties. Her quilts combine prints and solid colors of fabric in complimentary shades and tones in a starburst pattern that radiates from the center.

Goodsell grew up in a log house on White Horse Creek south of Manderson, South Dakota, a home built by her grandfather Standing Bear, an

OPPOSITE: Arthur Amiotte (b. 1942)
Oglala, Lakota (Sioux)
The Visit, 1995
Acrylic and collage; 19 ⅜ x 23 ⅜ inches.
Gift of Mrs. Cornelius Vanderbilt Whitney 17.95

Through his collages, Amiotte addresses continuity, adaptation, and innovation among Lakota people during the early reservation period of 1880 to 1930. Here, a man and woman on horseback and wearing traditional dress arrive at the home of Standing Bear's family and inspect the fine car parked out front. Above are Ghost Dancers looking at the crescent moon and heavenly constellations. The handwritten text evocative of early ledger drawings, says: "I dreamed my long ago ancestors over for a visit to see my grandchildren and our new house. They said my grandchildren were good. Some of them sat in that automobile. They liked it."

artist of the early reservation period who produced painted scenes on cloth of warfare and Lakota camp and ceremonial life, drawings, and illustrations for the book *Black Elk Speaks*. Many of his works are in private and museum collections. Goodsell's nephew Arthur Amiotte finds his inspiration in the experiences of his great grandfather Standing Bear, his family, and other Lakota during the early reservation period approximately between 1880 and 1930, "a period when culture change and adaptation were drastically taking place in the areas of technology; printed media and language; fashion; social and sacred traditions; education; and, for Sioux people, an entirely different world view."[55] He also describes the effects such cultural changes had on later generations.

> My early experiences of "real culture" began with my grandparents. My art makes a statement about native existence—not of a mythical, romantic Indian riding across the Plains, but rather the story of the Indian today who was born into a reservation home. For example, we lived in a log house on the reservation, drank water from the creek, and made wastunkala (dried corn) and dried berries for wojapi (pudding). We were allowed to experience life through all the senses, growing into the age of reason, where one is able to understand as an adult the true meaning of things.[56]

A student of the Yanktonai Dakota artist Oscar Howe, Amiotte worked in paintings, drawings, and textile and fiber arts until 1988, when he began his

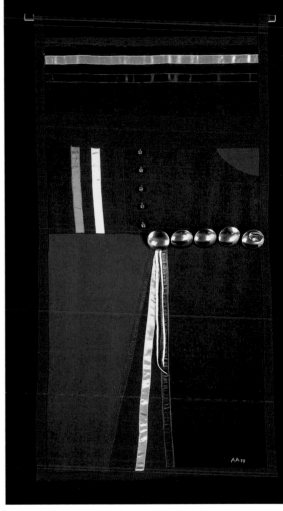

ABOVE: Arthur Amiotte (b. 1942) and Rose Gibbons (1916–1988)
Oglala Lakota (Sioux)
Banner, 1972
Wool, satin, ribbons, brass bells, nickel silver, deer hide, felt; 52 x 27 inches
NA.302.102

This banner represents a ribbon dress of the type worn by Lakota women on reservations from the 1880s until about 1930. Half of the blue wool dress trimmed with satin ribbons is shown together with the belt of silver conchos. The dress was created by Arthur Amiotte and his aunt Rose Gibbons, as a part of a series of works cooperatively produced by members of one Lakota family. This creative process is reminiscent of the traditional collaboration of Plains family members in daily activities as well as in artistic production.

Kevin Red Star (b. 1943)
Apsáalooke (Crow)
Crow Winter Camp in Teepees, 1999
Oil on paper; 22 ⅝ x 30 ¼ inches
William E. Weiss Fund Purchase 15.99.4

The cool, clear silence at the end of a perfect winter day is evoked in this painting. "I wanted it to be a tranquil, serene setting," Red Star said. "I was thinking about dusk—seeing the light reflecting from the setting sun."

series of collages composed of family photographs, Standing Bear's drawings, old magazine advertisements, ledger book pages, and his own photographs and paintings. The handwritten texts of the collages—reminiscent of those used in nineteenth-century ledger drawings—are statements of Lakota people about their lives and cultural adaptations during the transitional early reservation period.

The paintings of Kevin Red Star also address early reservation life, when his Crow ancestors traveled with wagons rather than travois and dressed in a mixture of Euro-American and tribal clothing, but put on their finest moccasins, elk teeth dresses beaded hide clothing, and eagle feather bonnets to parade with their horses, which were decked out in beautifully beaded gear. He also depicts Crow of an earlier time—warriors and war parties, portraits of medicine men and other great leaders, tipis with pictographic images, and groups of tipis arranged in camps. His images of contemporary Crow life focus on powwow dancers, the continuing tradition of parading, and the mountain landscapes of Crow country. Much of Red Star's work is based upon his research of historical photographs and pre-reservation arts, including parfleches, hide paintings, and ledger drawings, and on recording the contemporary celebrations of Crow Fair and powwows.[57]

Red Star was immersed in Crow traditional art from an early age because of his mother, Amy Bright Wings who created beaded hide clothing, shawls, and powwow regalia for dancers from the Northern and Southern Plains. He attended the Institute of American Indian Arts (IAIA) in Santa Fe as a member of its first class in 1962, where he was introduced to new ideas and methods in

Earl Biss (1947–1998)
Apsáalooke (Crow)
General Custer in Blue and Green, 1996
Oil on canvas; 39 ⅞ x 30 inches
Gift of Mr. and Mrs. Charles D. Israel of Arpon, Colorado 18.00

Earl Biss studied painting and jewelry making at the Institute of American Indian Arts in 1963–1965 under Allan Houser, Charles Loloma, and Fritz Scholder. His subsequent study at the San Francisco Art Institute and travels in Europe in 1974 where he studied the European master artists also helped him to develop his own creative approach. A leader in Native American contemporary art, Biss was noted for his oil paintings of Crow warriors on horseback, buffalo hunting scenes, portraits, and mountain landscapes, rich with color and emotion. Biss based this portrait of George Custer on a photograph taken by Matthew Brady on May 23, 1865. His great-grandfather White Man Runs Him served as an Army scout under Custer in 1876 in the campaign against the Lakota and Cheyenne.

classes in art history and techniques of art in media ranging from jewelry and printmaking to drawing and painting. At IAIA, Red Star studied under Allan Houser and worked with other young Native artists who later achieved prominence, including T.C. Cannon, a Kiowa-Caddo painter from Oklahoma, Doug Hyde, a Nez Perce sculptor from Oregon, and Earl Biss, a jeweler and painter also from the Crow Reservation. Red Star, Hyde, and Biss later received scholarships to attend the San Francisco Art Institute.

T.C. Cannon (1946–1978)
Gaigwa-Hasinai (Kiowa-Caddo)
Buffalo Medicine Keeper, ca. 1974
Oil and acrylic on canvas; 39¼ x 39¼ inches
William E. Weiss Fund Purchase 8.02

T.C. Cannon is considered one of the most eloquent and innovative of Native American artists of the 1970s. He and other early students at the Institute of American Indian Arts who were influenced by modernist artistic movements played significant roles in changing the direction of contemporary Indian art. Within his paintings, he integrated diverse interpretations of Native beliefs and traditions, historical and contemporary cultural conflicts, and his own experiences. The strength and intensity of the Sun Dance is shown in the strong colors of *Buffalo Medicine Keeper*. The man with a buffalo horn bonnet wears a combination of traditional and contemporary clothing. The buffalo skull has been painted for use as a Sun Dance altar.

Under the leadership of Cherokee textile artist and educator Lloyd New, students at the school were encouraged to experiment with innovative techniques and styles while understanding their tribal traditions and maintaining their own cultural identities. The founding and development of IAIA in the early 1960s also coincided with a growing political awareness of the issues that continue to affect Indian people—land, governance, and cultural and spiritual practices which were addressed in the art of several of the students.

T.C. (Tommy Wayne) Cannon, an innovator among Native American artists, was influential in creating a new direction in paintings depicting the contemporary daily lives and histories of Indian people. He sometimes painted portraits of Native individuals as solitary figures and, using bold reds, yellows, and blacks, integrated elements of the historic and contemporary Plains as well as world cultures. After his return from serving in the Army in Vietnam, many of his works focused on conflict and his emotional responses to Native American experiences. Although Cannon's successful art career was tragically cut short by a car accident in 1978, his artistic body of work remains significant and memorable.

Oreland C. Joe (b. 1958)
Nuche-Diné (Ute-Navajo)
Star Blanket, 1996
Alabaster; 26 ⅝ x 11 x 8 inches
William E. Weiss Purchase Award—1996 Buffalo
Bill Art Show 9.96

Oreland C. Joe draws his cultural inspiration
from his mother's musical talent, his father's
work as a silversmith and painter, and his
grandfather's knowledge of traditional songs
and dances in his sculptural work. He also was
influenced by his travel to France and Italy,
where he studied art, and later research into
Japanese and Egyptian art. He integrates these
studies with research on Native culture, songs,
and dances of the period 1800 to the 1920s.
Star Blanket shows the artist's masterful carving in stone with intricate details, powerful use
of texture, and expressive color.

T.C.'s contribution to the flow of American Indian cultural annals is impressive in that he broke through the barriers of confusion and unnecessary prevailing constraints that had become an impediment to progressive creativity in Indian art. He managed this through an unusually deep—and sometimes anguished—searching philosophic commitment and devotion to his own personal accomplishments—not only in the realm of painting, but in personally expressive music and art.

—Lloyd New[58]

Bently Spang pursues innovation in sculptural interpretation using a combination of natural materials—stone, wood, bone, hide, and animal sinew that represents the traditions and symbolism of his Northern Cheyenne heritage—and man-made materials—cast aluminum, glass, and steel that symbolize the modern world. Much of his work addresses his search for cultural identity as a tribal member who spent most of his formative years living in small towns and cities away from the Northern Cheyenne Reservation. His creations attempt to bridge the gaps between the two worlds. Spang considers his work autobiographical

Neil Parsons (b. 1938)
Amoskapi Pikuni (Blackfeet)
A Grandmother's Lodge, 1987
Fabric, crayon, tempera on paper; 17 x 17 inches
William E. Weiss Purchase Fund, 1987 Plains Indian Invitational Art Exhibit 4.87

In this abstract collage, Parsons recalls the warmth and security of his grandmother's home. The dark patterned cloth reminds him of his grandmother, who wore dresses of such floral fabrics. The brown heart represents his grandmother and the green heart symbolizes the artist. According to Parsons, "There is an abstract visual language which has few barriers as to time and place. . . . Native American artists have understood it well. An abstract beaded bag or painted parfleche created in the nineteenth century speaks the same language and solves the same visual problems as an abstract painting does today."

Jaune Quick-to-See Smith (b. 1940)
Salish-Cree-Shoshone
Painted Pony Series: Games People Play, 1985
Mixed media on paper; 46 x 34 inches
Gift of Miriam and Joe Sample 5.00.1

Jaune Quick-to-See Smith addresses through her art concerns about the environment, perceptions of the land, and contemporary political issues. She says that her work has always been concerned with an inhabited landscape of plants and animals. In *Games People Play,* her pictographic forms describe past and present-day games of Native American people, while her earth tones and layered textures poetically convey the feeling of the rugged Western landscape.

and interpretive of his personal experiences which, although informed by the past, take place within a vital contemporary, Cheyenne society that respects its traditions while innovating and adapting to contemporary conditions.

There is a prevailing stereotype about Native Americans that we long to return to a nineteenth century way of life and that we are, in fact, resistant to change. This notion fails to take into account that Plains Indian and other Native societies were in a constant state of transition both before the arrival of Euro-Americans and afterward as environmental changes occurred, new peoples were encountered, and ideas were exchanged. Plains Native people regret and mourn the drastic and sudden losses of the late nineteen and early twentieth centuries—the lands, the buffalo, the ceremonies, and the lives of our ancestors. We value the traditions that survived and our cultural heritages, but understand that within living cultures, change is inevitable. Artistic interpretation, innovation, and creativity provide the foundations for understanding, interpreting, and adapting to changing environments and situations.

> Art is a way to express a people's struggle for cultural survival. Each generation's thinking about the world in which they find themselves is evidenced in the art of that culture. As new materials and new ideas came along, Indian artists reacted to the new stimuli. Ideas about art, culture, beauty and truth have always been evolving.
>
> —Rick Hill[59]

Although Plains Indian arts can be admired for their inherent beauty and the technical skills of the makers, an understanding of cultural and historical contexts provides a far deeper appreciation and awareness of its functional and spiritual significance. It is also enlightening to explore such cultural histories

Kim Knife Chief (b. 1957)
Chaticks si Chaticks (Pawnee)
Cradleboard Pendant, 2000
Copper, brass, sterling silver;
3 ¾ x 1 ⅜ inches
Gift of the Pilot Foundation NA.203.1209

A graduate of the Institute of American Indian Arts, Kim Knife Chief creates jewelry using metals, clay, jewelry, and beads in modern designs representing traditional themes. This pendant is made of copper, brass, and sterling silver to represent the traditional style of a Pawnee cradleboard, which traditionally would have been made of wood and carved and painted with the morning star design. Stars—powerful symbols in Pawnee traditions—are carved on the cradle's straps and the cradle's ties are rendered in copper.

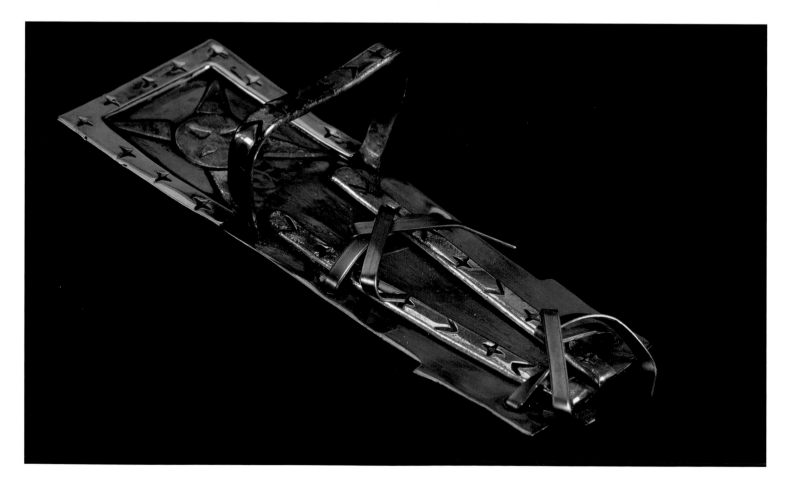

through the eyes of the participants—the oral accounts and writings of past and present Plains Indian men and women who experienced firsthand the many transitions and adaptations that occurred or who have striven to acquire the cultural and ritual knowledge. As in past generations, contemporary Plains tribal members will continue to reaffirm and preserve their cultural identities, arts, traditions, and heritages as they create innovative means to convey their knowledge and beliefs to their descencants. Such efforts demonstrate the vitality of the cultures and communities of Native people of the Great Plains. ✦

1. James Welch, *Fools Crow* (New York: Penguin Books, 1986), pp. 390–391.

2. Frederick E. Hoxie, *Parading Through History: The Making of the Crow Nation in America, 1805–1935* (Cambridge: Cambridge University Press, 1995), pp. 329–336, 306–307. Joseph Medicine Crow, *From the Heart of the Crow Country: The Crow Indians' Own Stories* (New York: Orion Books, 1992), pp. 108.

3. Inter Tribal Bison Cooperative, *Annual Report* (Rapid City, South Dakota, 1998), p. 1.

4. Statement by Mike Fox, Gros Ventre, President of the Inter Tribal Bison Cooperative, 1997–1999, Inter Tribal Bison Cooperative *Annual Report* (Rapid City, South Dakota, 1998), p. 2.

5. From Richard Peterson (Assiniboine/Sioux), *American Indian Magazine* (Summer, 2001), p. 16.

6. Fred W. Voget, assisted by Mary K. Mee, *They Call Me Agnes: A Crow Narrative Based on the Life of Agnes Yellowtail Deernose* (Norman and London: University of Oklahoma Press, 1995), p. 169.

7. Francis Paul Prucha, *The Great Father: The United States Government and the American Indians,* Volume II (Lincoln and London: University of Nebraska Press, 1986), pp. 646–648. Mario Gonzalez and Elizabeth Cook-Lynn, *The Politics of Hallowed Ground: Wounded Knee and the Struggle for Indian Sovereignty* (Urbana and Chicago: University of Illinois Press, 1999), p. 379. On April 10, 1883 the Commissioner of Indian Affairs issued regulations defining "Indian offenses" including participation in the Sun Dance and similar dances and the practice of medicine men and authorizing each reservation agent to establish a Court of Indian Offenses which would have jurisdiction over these offenses. Individual Indian agents varied widely in the establishment of the court and enforcement of the regulations.

8. John Stands In Timber and Margo Liberty with the assistance of Robert M. Utley, *Cheyenne Memories* (New Haven, Conn.: Yale University Press, 1967; reprint edition, Lincoln and London: University of Nebraska Press, 1972), p. 94. Liberty notes that the Cheyenne Sun Dance had three main periods of disruption: two or three years following their surrender in 1877, in 1890 and in 1904 because of suppression by the Indian Bureau, and in 1919 under pressure from local missionaries. The other dates of Stands In Timber's narrative are speculative, although his point was that the Sun Dance continued among the Cheyenne despite the official prohibition which caused its disappearance among other tribes.

9. Fred W. Voget, *The Shoshoni-Crow Sun Dance* (Norman: University of Oklahoma Press, 1984), pp. 78–79.

10. Voget, *The Shoshoni-Crow Sun Dance*, p. 129.

11. Thomas Yellowtail in *Yellowtail: Crow Medicine Man and Sun Dance Chief, An Autobiography as told to Michael Oren Fitzgerald* (Norman and London: University of Oklahoma Press, 1991), p. 103.

12. Arthur Amiotte, "The Lakota Sun Dance," *Sioux Indian Religion*, Raymond J. DeMallie and Douglas R. Parks, eds. (Norman and London: University of Oklahoma Press), 1987, pp. 75–76.

13. Ibid., p. 89.

14. Beatrice Medicine, "Indian Women and Traditional Religion," in *Sioux Indian Religion*, Raymond J. DeMallie and Douglas R. Parks, eds. (Norman and London: University of Oklahoma Press, 1987), p. 163.

15. Medicine, "Indian Women and Traditional Religion," pp. 159–160.

16. Omer Stewart, *Peyote Religion: A History* (Norman: University of Oklahoma Press, 1987), pp. 128–129.

17. James Botsford and Walter B. Echo-Hawk, "The Legal Tango: The Native American Church and the United States of America," in *One Nation Under God: The Triumph of the Native American Church*, Huston Smith and Reuben Snake, eds. (Santa Fe, N.M.: Clear Light Publishers, 1996), p. 126.

18. For a summary of other legal challenges to the use of peyote in Native American religious practice leading to the Native American Cultural Protection and Free Exercise of Religion Act of 1994, see Botsford and Echo-Hawk, "The Legal Tango," pp. 128–141.

19. Dennis Weidman and Candace Greene, "Early Kiowa Peyote Ritual and Symbolism: The 1891 Drawing Books of Silverhorn (Haungooah)," in *American Indian Art Magazine* (Autumn, 1988), p. 34.

20. Rosemary Ellison, *Contemporary Southern Plains Indian Metalwork* (Anadarko, Oklahoma.: Southern Plains Indian Museum and Crafts Center, 1976), p. 16.

21. Mitchell Zephier. "Taking the Best of the White Man's Road: New Traditions in Northern Plains Metalwork," *Plains Indian Museum Seminar,* Buffalo Bill Historical Center, Cody, Wyoming, September 30, 1995.

22. Ibid.

23. Monroe Tsatoke, *The Peyote Ritual: Visions and Descriptions* (San Francisco: The Grabhorn Press, 1957), pp. xv–xvi.

24. Cassie Soldier Wolf, interview with Lawrence Johnson for Plains Indian Museum, June 14, 2006.

25. James R. Murie, "Pawnee Indian Societies," *American Museum of Natural History Anthropological Papers,* Vol. 11, Part 7, 1914, p. 608. Clyde Ellis, *A Dancing People: Powwow Culture on the Southern Plains* (Lawrence: University Press of Kansas, 2003), pp. 40–50.

26. Gloria A. Young and Erik D. Gooding, "Celebrations and Giveaways," *Handbook of North American Indians,* Vol. 2 (Washington, D.C.: Smithsonian Institution, 2001), p. 1012. Ellis, *A Dancing People,* pp. 48–52.

27. Young and Gooding, "Celebrations and Giveaways," pp. 1012–1013.

28. Richard Singer, interview recorded by Lawrence Johnson Productions for Plains Indian Museum, June 13, 2006.

29. Sandra Iron Cloud, interview recorded by Lawrence Johnson Productions for Plains Indian Museum, June 13, 2006.

30. Curly Bear Wagner, interview recorded by Lawrence Johnson Productions for Plains Indian Museum, June 16, 2006.

31. Frances Densmore, "Pawnee Music," *Smithsonian Institution Bureau of American Ethnology Bulletin* 93 (Washington D.C.: U.S. Government Printing Office, 1929), pp. 64–69.

32. Ibid.

33. Voget, *They Call Me Agnes,* p. 169–170.

34. Medicine Crow, *From the Heart of the Crow Country,* pp. 120.

35. Hoxie, *Parading Through History,* p. 307.

36. Medicine Crow, pp. 120–121.

37. Hoxie, *Parading Through History,* p. 307.

38. Medicine Crow, *From the Heart of the Crow Country,* p. 123.

39. Medicine Crow, *From the Heart of the Crow Country,* p. 122.

40. Ibid.

41. Arthur Amiotte, quoted in Rick Hill, *Creativity Is our Tradition: Three Decades of Contemporary Indian Art at the Institute of American Indian Arts* (Santa Fe: Institute of American Indian and Alaska Native Culture and Arts Development, 1992), p. 10.

42. Lloyd New in *Creativity Is Our Tradition,* p. 168.

43. Vivian Swallow, interview with the author, March 3, 2003.

44. Ibid.

45. Information provided to author by Debra Lee Stone Jay.

46. Marcus Dewey, interview with the author.

47. Vanessa Paukeigope Jennings in a presentation at the Plains Indian Museum Seminar, Buffalo Bill Historical Center, September 1996.

48. Ibid.

49. Vanessa Paukeigope Jennings, interview with the author, March 11, 2004.

50. Vanessa Paukeigope Jennings, "Why I Make Cradleboards," *Gifts of Pride and Love: Kiowa and Comanche Cradles,* Barbara A. Hail, ed. (Providence, R.I.: Haffenrefer Museum of Anthropology, Brown University, 2000), p. 96.

51. Cathy L. Wright, "Contemporary Ute Crafts: Revival and Innovation" in *Ute Indian Arts & Culture From Prehistory to the New Millennium,* William Wroth, ed. (Colorado Springs: Taylor Museum of the Colorado Springs Fine Arts Center, 2000), p. 219.

52. Beatrice Medicine, "Lakota Star Quuilts: Commodity, Ceremony and Economic Development," *To Honor and Comfort: Native Quilting Traditions,* Marsha L. MacDowell and C. Kurt Dewhurts, eds. (Santa Fe: Museum of New Mexico Press and Michigan State University, 1997), p. 113.

53. Ibid.

54. Ibid., and Patricia Albers and Beatrice Medicine, "The Role of Sioux Women in the Production of Ceremonial Objects: The Case of the Star Quilt," *The Hidden Half: Studies of Plains Indian Women,* Patricia Albers and Beatrice Medicine, eds. (Washington D.C.: University Press of America, Inc.), p. 129.

55. Arthur Amiotte, "Artist's Statement," *Arthur Amiotte Retrospective Exhibition: Continuity and Diversity,* John A. Day, ed. (Pine Ridge, S.D.: The Heritage Center, Inc., Red Cloud Indian School), p. 5.

56. In Arthur Amiotte, *This Path We Travel: Celebrations of Contemporary Native American Creativity* (Golden, Colorado: Fulcrum Publishing and the Smithsonian Institution, 1994), p. 26.

57. Kevin Red Star, *A History of the Contemporary Artist.*" Plains Indian Museum Seminar, Buffalo Bill Historical Center. September 28, 1995.

58. Lloyd New. Letter to the National Hall of Fame for American Indians in support of T.C. Cannon's induction, February 23, 1983 quoted in *Creativity Is Our Tradition,* p. 92.

59. Rick Hill, *Creativity Is Our Tradition,* pp. 46–47.

A Cheyenne in Cyber Space

BENTLY SPANG

Yesterday, my obsession got the best of me again. Resistance faded into futility and, just like a thousand times before, I did *another* internet search on the word "Cheyenne." I've tried to cut back, even tried to quit cold turkey, but it never lasts. This time I sat myself down and had a good talk with myself. "Who cares what people think?" I told myself reassuringly. "You're a fully formed Northern Cheyenne man-child, artist-person who is secure in your Cheyenne-ness. You go back to the rez all the time, you camp at the Fourth of July powwow every year, you love dried meat, and you know what *Tsistsistas* and *bunist* mean. And that's just the tip of the iceberg." I put my arm around my shoulder and squeezed hard. "Let it go, bro, who cares what the world thinks of Cheyennes?" If it were only that simple.

Then the little anthropologist on my shoulder started running his mouth and it was all over. Most Indians have one of these little fellas; they just don't admit it. Anyway, he went on and on about his "Cheyenne research" and his "findings" (for the umpteenth time) and then, get this, he tried to use the Great-White-Father-in-Washington line. That never works, it just gets me riled up. He's actually kind of cute, though, all dressed up in his little khaki shirt and shorts, black socks and a tiny pith helmet, like the action figure no kid wants that ends up in the thrift store bin. "Do it," he said, grinning and picking his teeth with one finger like Dr. Evil, "Do your little internet search, my Indian friend, doooo it. And then you shall see the true magnitude of my power. Oh, and when you're done, don't forget to e-mail me any new characteristics and physical anomalies. I'll need that to continue my world domination thing." He's a little creepy.

So, after all the anthropological wrangling and gnashing of teeth, I gave in and began my typical cycle of preparation for an internet search. I like to start all my Cheyenne internet searches with a little pep talk, gets the blood flowing. "Okay, man," I told myself in my best shaky Crispin Glover voice, "this time things will for sure be different, gosh darn it. It is 2007, and we're all grown up, and I just know the dominant society has made gigantic, cultural strides since last week's search. I'm pretty sure that racism has almost been eradicated and then infomercials will be next, you'll see. Then maybe, just maybe, we can finally put a Cheyenne on the moon. Oh yeah, I forgot, we've already been there." I did a lip point and punched the air with a hard "Yes!" fist.

Falsely fortified, I pushed forward with what was fast becoming an Odyssean-like internet search. As I settled in to begin typing, my attention strayed and I stared off into the air absently. Everything started to get real wavy and blurry and (FADE IN—DREAM SEQUENCE—PAN THROUGH THICK WHITE FOG TO REVEAL A PATIENT ON A TABLE, ATTENDED BY A DOCTOR) just for a moment I imagined I was a young, fresh-out-of-medical-school doctor working his first gig in an emergency room. Cheerful and still annoyingly ideological, I was trying desperately to get a cultural pulse on a fading society. "I've got something!" I shout, fingers on the neck of an Anglo mannequin-ish figure, "Get me three ccs of Vine Deloria stat! Ahhh yes, there it is, thank god, we've got a pulse. It's pretty stereotypical and faint but, frankly, it is within normal parameters for a society like this one. Hmmm, that's odd, the patient seems to be surviving primarily on a diet of sports mascots and Turner Indian movies. Oh, I see what the problem is now, they've got their cultures crossed and it's caused a short circuit. They're defining the word 'culture' statically as only art and music, with no regard for living cultures. Fascinating. Uh-oh, the pulse is getting weaker, we're losing him. Nurse, hand me the paddles quick! Stand back everyone. All clear!" (FADE OUT TO WHITE—EXIT DREAM SEQUENCE—FADE IN TO A YOUNG, BLINDINGLY CHARASMATIC AND HUMOROUS CHEYENNE MAN, SITTING AT A COMPUTER WRITING THIS ESSAY.) The wavy lines vanished and everything snapped back into focus. Back in search mode, my cursor easily found the little search box with the big "G" on it in the corner of my browser. I typed "C-h-e-y-e-n-n-e" in the box, misspelling it at least three times.

Believe me, I know it's the most popular children's name of the moment, but listen up, folks, Cheyenne also happens to be the *given* name of my nation of origin—*Northern Cheyenne*, to be more specific. I say "given" because in our language we actually call ourselves something completely different (do some research on it, it's out there). It's a situation faced by many Native American-American Indian-Indigenous-Aboriginal-First Nations-nations in this country (take your pick folks, lump-sum descriptors are a dime a dozen in Indian country). Just like the Lakota (*still* incorrectly referred to as "the Sioux") and the Dine' (also wrongly called "the Navajo"), we Cheyenne (both northern and southern groups, yeah, I know it's complicated) have endured this misnomer courageously. In fact, the name "Cheyenne," according to one of several stories I've heard, is really some white settler's "pronunciational" twist on what the Lakotas used to call us (look that up too, while you're at it). Either that, or it's like this Lakota guy once said, "We called you Cheyenne because we couldn't say 'Chinese.'" Whatever the case, for better or for worse, for richer or for poorer, and at any rate, the name "Cheyenne" has stuck.

So, as my pinky finger raised ever so slightly, frozen dramatically in midair and poised to push the "enter" button, I said to myself, "Self, your obsessive cyber-searches are so much more than a mere and simple internet search, why, they're actually like an Indian Gallup poll (sorry, not *that* Gallup, my Dine' friends). Granted, my version is a bit more unscientific, but it is no less significant.

Bently Spang, Montana (b. 1960)
Tsistsistas (Northern Cheyenne)
Pevah, 1991
Cast aluminum, marble, cedar, redwood;
29 inches x 24 ¾ inches x 5 ¾ inches
Stanley N. Landgren Bequest Purchase Fund 4.97

The land and the people of the Northern Cheyenne provide powerful connections to the past for Bently Spang. "My pieces are personal icons," he says. "The aluminum is a metaphor for the contemporary world in which I live, the non-Indian part of me. The stone, cedar, buckskin all represent the Northern Cheyenne part of me. The metal binds the stone, the wood binds them both. I am bound by my culture; we are still here after all. . . . *Pevah* means 'good' in Cheyenne."

human in their eyes? My fondest secret hope is that, with my poll, I will one day discover a brave new public. This new and improved public will know that Cheyennes are not a former and used-to-be culture who didn't survive the unprovoked attacks and extermination policies of the U.S. government. This extra-absorbent public, with the new advanced formula, will understand that we didn't vanish as predicted by the anthropologists of the day and end up in the "happy hunting grounds," which, I just discovered, is really a media-created space just above the bill of your average baseball cap.

Less filling and better tasting, this new public will know instinctively that Native peoples are in no way connected to those ill-conceived and patently destructive, mass reproduced, and mockingly cartoonish stereotypes that are Chief Wahoo of the Cleveland Indians, Chief Illiniwak of the University of Illinois, and the Washington Redskins of the National Football League (to name only a few). My new public will, in fact, have already banned these hurtful stereotypes, knowing that these seemingly innocent sports mascots, made wrong-headedly to honor us (and stubbornly defended as such, though no one thought to ask us how we wanted to be honored), are really the cartoonish manifestation of a lingering pustule of racist hate in a country that knows better (not all y'all, you know who you are). In so banning, the public of my wildest dreams will have helped free

As a matter of fact, I'm not one bit ashamed to admit that my poll is highly subjective and self-serving with a margin of error plus or minus more than 50 percent. I took two semesters of statistics in college (or *sadistics,* as we called it), so I know almost everything that's wrong with my poll, believe me. But what's so right about my poll is that it's designed, executed, and compiled by a Native person (me) and it is about Native life. In fact, to my knowledge, it is the first poll of its kind in modern history. It's societies' worst nightmare folks, an Indian with a poll. And it's not just any poll, this is a poll with some power. For it is a poll of the Indian, by an Indian, for Indians, and it shall not be ignored."

Feeling much more cutting-edge and less like an obsessive kook, I sprang into action. In achingly slow, slow motion (for dramatic effect) my now-gigantic pinky finger slowly depressed the humongous "enter" key and, like Godzilla flattening Mothra with a flying body slam, it made a thunderous noise. Immediately, the air all around me was filled with Matrix-like ones and zeros in millions of streaming rows as the digital firestorm of my search began. So, anyway, the central-nagging-eternal question in my now-historic internet poll is very simple: have John and Jane Q. Public finally expanded their amazingly narrow definition of Cheyenne people? Are we still animal, vegetable and/or wooden Indian, or have we become, finally, (gasp)

generations of Native peoples from the humiliation of these crushing stereotypes. This public will also have taken away the unholy power these denizens of the wayward media wield, an evil power that is slowly propelling our Native youth sideways into drug and alcohol abuse, depression, and, too often, suicide. Believe it or not, Native pride is not reflected in the blinding whiteness of Chief Wahoo's smile. Hey, maybe we can pick up a few jobs along the way, too, since now people will know we're alive. A bit utopian, but a fella can dream, can't he?

When the smoke from the digital firestorm of my landmark internet search cleared, one glorious number remained: 3,630,000. Hallelujah! I shouted quietly in my head. Why, this number of search results was significantly higher than any I had previously seen. Could our fortunes have finally turned? Surely this really big number is an indication of some forward progress of the awareness of Cheyenne culture by an otherwise lethargic public, right? After all, a similar search of the word "Lakota" netted only 1,080,000 results. The word "Arapaho" brought only 598,000 results, so on average, our numbers were pretty high. Then, out of curiosity, I plugged the misnomer "Sioux" into the search engine and up came 8,690,000 entries. Well, now we're not getting somewhere, I thought. My head swam with numbers. By the way, you'll notice I only did searches on the names of our allies. Did I mention my poll was subjective?

I shifted my attention away from the excessive totals (they reminded me too much of the unfathomable numbers that scientists bandy about when describing the age of our planet) and I began to examine the individual sites that made up my Cheyenne search results. The proof must surely be in the pudding, I thought. I couldn't have been more right. The number one-rated result, the one with the most hits, the one with the most searches and attention and visits, which made it the most representative of the public's, nay, the world's, view of Cheyenne people, was a man (or should I say, "dude") who had built a site specifically to celebrate,

honor, and ultimately sell, his beloved 1975 Chevy Cheyenne pickup.[1] It was a devastating blow, like a rusty dagger through my heart. As I looked to my immediate left, I could see that my miniscule anthropologist was now doubled over with laughter, tears streaming down his tiny face. It took everything I had to not pluck him off my shoulder and put him in the cupboard where he belonged.

I pushed on. The number two-rated site was no less disappointing. It was a classic truck site that gave directions on how to lower the rear end on a '75 Chevy Cheyenne pickup (again with the Cheyenne pickup). A quote on the site said, "Being that the Cheyenne was at stock height before all this even started, you'd be correct to assume that we had to address the rear end sooner or later . . . well, now is later!"[2] Well, I thought, the Cheyenne rear end may be a little flat, but that's certainly no reason to tinker with it. Weary of the incessant laughter emanating from my upper right side, I cocked my finger and flicked the tiny anthropologist off my shoulder. He landed with a tiny thud on the floor.

My hopes almost completely dashed, I endeavored to persevere. Site number three was the most promising of all. It actually talked about Cheyenne people, but, as is so often the case, it did so only in the past tense. It was an excerpt from Lewis and Clark's journals, or, as the pair has been irreverently referred to in Indian country, "Lois and Clark."[3] Lois or Clark, or whomever wrote the journals, referred to Cheyenne men as "portly" and Cheyenne women as "homely." They forgot to add "tolerant" and "generous," since my relatives could have just as easily terminated them as fed them. Had they known of Lois and Clark's true intentions, to subjugate Indian people with gifts of alcohol and peace medals (a plan devised by none other than founding father Thomas Jefferson) in exchange for surrendering their lands to their new "great father" in the east, they would have scorched the earth on which L & C stood.[4]

The journal went on to describe their Cheyenne hosts' "characteristics" and

"ways" in minute detail, just as thousands of documents by thousands of non-Natives have done since contact. These tireless, khaki-clad individuals loved nothing better than to dissect, document, tag, and accession every inch and iota of Cheyenne people and our way of life. I am convinced their "findings" were really meant to be a set of directions to be included in an anthropological kit, secretly devised in the late 1800s, with which they could, upon our timely vanishing (i.e., extermination), make their "Very Own Indian."

Really, just think of the possibilities. . . . (FADE IN—DREAM SEQUENCE BEGINS—WE MOVE THROUGH THE EXACT SAME FOG TO REVEAL THE EXACT SAME YOUNG DOCTOR, THOUGH THIS TIME HE IS DRESSED IN A LAB COAT AND IS POURING BROWN LIQUID FROM ONE TEST TUBE INTO ANOTHER FILLED WITH GLASS BEADS.) "Eureka!" the ambitious young researcher shouts. "I've re-created, in a controlled laboratory setting, one of the greatest cultures of the past: the Cheyenne. They're alive, alive! And so my financial future is secure. For now I will patent my secret process, start a theme park on a remote island in the Pacific, and populate it with my newly created friends and minions, the Cheyenne." Staring off into space, chin in hand, the young researcher continues, "I'll erect huge electric fences to keep them from escaping and then I'll re-create one of their mortal enemies and they will fight fiercely, day after day, to the delight of high paying customers the world over. It will be bigger than Crazy Horse Mountain, I just know it. What can go wrong with my plan, you ask? Nothing, why it's fool-proof! Think of it, just think of it!" (FADE TO WHITE—EXIT DREAM SEQUENCE—FADE IN ON THE SAME BLINDINGLY CHARISMATIC AND HUMOROUS CHEYENNE MAN MENTIONED EARLIER WHO IS NOW FINISHING THIS ESSAY.)

And now, thanks to the Human Genome Diversity Project (HGDP), which has unethically gathered the DNA from thousands of indigenous peoples around the world in the last fourteen years (often without informing donors of the potential commercial uses for their genetic material), this scenario is now absolutely possible. Headed by the Department of Energy (DOE) and the National Institutes of Health (NIH), the project has gathered DNA from some 722 indigenous groups. "One of the principal goals of the consortium has been to obtain blood, tissue and hair samples from genetically-distinct populations, many of whom are considered 'endangered', i.e., populations which may either shortly vanish from the human family or become genetically assimilated into other ethnic groups." And the NIH, in 1995, managed to secure a patent on the DNA of an indigenous man from the Hagahai peoples of New Guinea.[5] Anybody smell theme park? And don't forget folks, when you're mixing the recipe for "Cheyenne," it's shaken, not stirred.

Finally, both shaken and stirred by my experience, I abandoned my internet search and did the only thing I could—I turned to Native art. I took the mass of catalogues of little known but significant exhibitions of living, contemporary Native artists that I have accumulated over the years, put them on the floor, and bathed myself in them like Scrooge McDuck swimming in his money pit. It was the only way I could get the stench of the search off me. Feeling better, I picked up my favorite exhibition catalogues and randomly flipped through the pages. Powerful artwork from every Indian nation on this continent bathed my damaged psyche with relief. Unflinching art works in every medium imaginable leapt off the page, telling the real stories of Native peoples on this continent. The words of Native curators and critical writers ran off the pages like cups of cold, clear spring water on a hot day. Expressions of truth emanated from these paper vessels, the actions and expressions of Native peoples reclaiming their identities and the identities of their cultures. I felt as though I were standing on a high peak, deep in the high country of my reservation homeland, eyes closed, a cool wind caressing my face. Satiated and restored, I searched for and found my little anthropologist, picked him up by the scruff of his neck, and put him in the cupboard, where he belongs.

1. http://www.cars-on-line.com/18633.html
2. Fortier, R. (2005). http://www.classictrucksweb.com/tech/0504cl_bell/
3. Excerpt from an interview by author on March 27, 2005, with Dyani Bingham, director of the Montana Tribal Tourism Alliance.
4. Lois Red Elk, "Guest Opinion: Corps of Discovery Part of U.S. Plan to Subdue Indians," Billings Gazette, May 3, 2005.
5. Hilary Cunningham and Stephen Scharper, 1996, http://www.dartmouth.edu/%7Ecbbc/courses/bio4/bio4-1996/HumanGenome3rdWorld.html. Courtesy of Third World Network Features.

EMMA I. HANSEN joined the Buffalo Bill Historical Center in 1991 as Curator of the Plains Indian Museum. A member of the Pawnee Nation, Hansen holds a Master of Arts degree in anthropology and a Master of Arts degree in sociology from the University of Oklahoma. Hansen's early professional experiences include university teaching and museum positions in Oklahoma, where she also consulted with many tribes as they developed cultural centers and cultural preservation programs. At the Historical Center, Hansen has developed several exhibitions and programs related to Plains Indian arts and cultures. She co-curated *Powerful Images: Portrayals of Native America,* which traveled to eight museums in the United States and Canada in 1998–2000. In 2000, Hansen also directed the award-winning reinterpretation of the Plains Indian Museum and curated several exhibitions on Plains Indians arts and cultures. In 1997, she was Visiting Curator at the Hood Museum and Assistant Professor of Native American Studies at Dartmouth College. She has written numerous articles and conference papers and lectured at museums and other educational institutions in the United States, Canada, and Great Britain.

BEATRICE MEDICINE was born on the Standing Rock Reservation, Wakpala, South Dakota. She held a Bachelor of Science degree in education and art history from South Dakota State University, a Master of Arts degree in sociology and anthropology from Michigan State University, and a Ph.D. in cultural anthropology from the University of Wisconsin-Madison. She co-authored a book with Patricia Albers, *The Hidden Half: Studies of Indian Women in the Northern Plains* that is a standard title in the field. After teaching in the anthropology department at California State University for many years, Medicine took early retirement in 1988 and moved back to the Standing Rock Reservation. She traveled extensively and continued to teach, lecture, and write. Her most recent publications are *Learning to be an Anthropologist* and *Remaining Native: Selected Writings*, published in 2001, and *Drinking and Sobriety Among the Lakota Sioux*, published posthumously in 2006. She was the recipient of the Distinguished Service Award from the American Anthropology Association and the Society for Applied Anthropology's Malinowski Award, among many other honors.

GERARD BAKER is the Superintendent of Mount Rushmore National Memorial. A member of the Mandan-Hidatsa Tribe of the Fort Berthold Indian Reservation from Mandaree, North Dakota, Baker grew up on the reservation on his father's cattle ranch in western North Dakota. He holds degrees in criminology and sociology from Southern Oregon State University in Ashland, Oregon, and has worked as a deputy sheriff, a campground ranger, law enforcement ranger, wilderness ranger, park ranger-historian, and a park superintendent. He also served as superintendent of the Little Bighorn Battlefield National Monument, where he worked to establish the Indian Memorial, and at the Chickasaw National Recreation Area. As superintendent of Lewis and Clark National Historic Trail, Baker was responsible for trail management and the traveling exhibition *Corps of Discovery II: 200 Years to the Future*. On that exhibition, Baker worked with approximately fifty-eight American Indian tribes and nineteen states from Monticello, Virginia, to Fort Clatsop, Oregon. In May 2004, Gerard became superintendent of the Mount Rushmore National Memorial, responsible for more than 1,200 acres and the carvings representing four presidents of the United States.

JOSEPH MEDICINE CROW was born on the Crow reservation in Montana. His grandfather, White Man Runs Him, was a respected Crow warrior, military scout, and diplomat for the tribe. As the first male Crow tribal member to graduate from college, Medicine Crow earned a Master of Arts degree in anthropology from the University of Southern California in 1939. In 2003, he received an honorary doctorate from the University of Southern California, in recognition of the fact that he had nearly completed work on his Ph.D. in anthropology there when he was called to service in World War II. On the battlefields of Germany, he earned the status of War Chief by completing the four war deeds required of the Crow warrior. Crow tribal historian for the past sixty years, he has written several books including *Crow Migration Story, Medicine Crow*, the *Handbook of the Crow Indians Law and Treaties, Crow Indian Buffalo Jump Techniques, From the Heart of Crow Country, Counting Coup: Becoming a Crow Chief on the Reservation and Beyond,* and a children's book titled *Brave Wolf and the Thunderbird.* Medicine Crow is a founding member of the Plains Indian Museum Advisory Board.

ARTHUR AMIOTTE is also a founding member of the Plains Indian Museum Advisory Board and an Oglala Lakota artist and scholar. He is the descendant of Standing Bear, who fought at the Battle of Little Bighorn and later toured with Buffalo Bill's Wild West. Amiotte holds a Bachelor of Science degree in education from Northern State University, Aberdeen, South Dakota, and a Master of Arts degree in Interdisciplinary Studies in anthropology, religion, and art from the University of Montana, Missoula, and has studied with prominent Lakota artists and religious leaders. He also holds honorary doctorates from Oglala Lakota College, Brandon University in Manitoba, Canada, and South Dakota State University. Amiotte is the recipient of an Arts International; Lila Wallace Readers Digest Artists at Giverny, France, Fellowship; a Getty Foundation Grant; a Bush Leadership Fellowship; the South Dakota Governor's Award for Outstanding Creative Achievement in Arts; and the Lifetime Achievement Award as Artist and Scholar from the Native American Art Studies Association. His work is included in twenty-six public and nearly 200 private collections.

BENTLY SPANG is a multi-disciplinary visual artist who works in mixed media sculpture, video, performance, and installation. A member of the Northern Cheyenne Nation in Montana, he grew up both on and off the Northern Cheyenne reservation in places as diverse as Sitka, Alaska, and Portland, Oregon. Spang's work focuses on his experience as a contemporary Cheyenne. He combines many media to create his tableaus, which confront the intricacies of Native existence with pragmatism, humor, and deep introspection. His work is in museum and private collections in the United States and Europe, and he has exhibited widely in the U.S., Europe, Mexico, Canada, and South America. Spang is also a freelance curator and writer who has published many articles and essays on current trends in contemporary Native art, as well as two children's books. Spang holds a Bachelor's degree in art and business from Montana State University-Billings, and a Masters of Fine Art degree in sculpture from the University of Wisconsin-Madison.

Afton, Jean, David Fridtjof Halaas, and Andrew E. Masich. *Cheyenne Dog Soldiers: A Ledgerbook History of Coups and Combat.* Denver: Colorado Historical Society, 1996.

Albers, Patricia and Beatrice Medicine. "The Role of Sioux Women in the Production of Ceremonial Objects: The Case of the Star Quilt." In *The Hidden Half: Studies of Plains Indian Women.* Eds. Patricia Albers and Beatrice Medicine. Washington, D.C.: University Press of America, Inc., 1983. 123–142.

Amiotte, Arthur. "Artist's Statement." In *Arthur Amiotte Retrospective Exhibition: Continuity and Diversity.* Ed. John A. Day. Pine Ridge, S.D.: The Heritage Center, Inc., Red Cloud Indian School, 2001. 5–6.

_____. "The Lakota Sun Dance." *Sioux Indian Religion.* Eds. Raymond J. DeMallie and Douglas R. Parks. Norman and London: University of Oklahoma Press, 1987. 75–90.

_____. *This Path We Travel: Celebrations of Contemporary Native American Creativity.* Golden, Colorado: Fulcrum Publishing and the Smithsonian Institution, 1994. 24–29.

_____. "The Sun Dance." In Charlotte Heth, *Native American Dance: Ceremonies and Social Traditions.* Washington, D.C.: National Museum of the American Indian, Smithsonian Institution, 1992. 135–137.

Amiotte, Arthur, Janette k. Murray, and Lynn F. Huenemann. "Dakota/Lakota Arts Resources." *The Arts in South Dakota: A Selective Annotated Bibliography.* Eds. Ron MacIntyre and Rebecca L. Bell. Sioux Falls: Augustana College, Center for Western Studies, 1988. 131–215.

Archambault, JoAllyn. "Sun Dance." *Handbook of North American Indians.* 13 (2) *Plains.* Washington, D.C.: Smithsonian Institution, 2001. 983–995.

Archuleta, Margaret L., Brenda J. Child, and K. Tsarina Lomawaima, eds. *Away From Home: American Indian Boarding School Experiences, 1978–2000.* Phoenix: Heard Museum 2000.

Bad Heart Bull, Amos and Helen Blish. *A Pictographic History of the Oglala Sioux.* Lincoln: University of Nebraska Press, 1967.

Baillargeon, Morgan and Leslie Tepper. *Legends of Our Times: Native Cowboy Life.* Vancouver, British Columbia, Canada and Seattle, Washington, U.S.A.: UBC Press and University of Washington Press, 1998.

Bass, Althea. *The Arapaho Way: A Memoir of an Indian Boyhood.* New York: Clarkson N. Potter, 1966.

Batkin, Jonathan. "Mail-Order Catalogs as Artifacts of the Early Native American Curio Trade." *American Indian Art Magazine.* 29: 2 (Spring 2004): 40–49.

Bennett, Kathy. "Navajo Chief Blanket: A Trade Item Among Non-Navajo Groups." *American Indian Art Magazine.* 7: 1 (Winter 1981): 62–69.

Berlo, Janet Catherine, ed. *Plains Indian Drawings 1865–1935: Pages from a Visual History.* New York: Harry N. Abrams, Inc., 1996.

Berthong, Donald J. *The Southern Cheyennes.* Norman: University of Oklahoma Press, 1963.

Black Elk. *The Sixth Grandfather: Black Elk's Teachings Given to John C. Neihardt.* Raymond J. DeMallie, ed. Lincoln and London: University of Nebraska Press, 1984.

Botsford, James and Walter B. Echo-Hawk. "The Legal Tango: The Native American Church and the United States of America." In *One Nation Under God: The Triumph of the Native American Church.* Eds. Huston Smith and Reuben Snake. Santa Fe: Clear Light Publishers, 1996. 123–142.

Bowers, Alfred W. *Hidatsa Social and Ceremonial Organization.* Bureau of American Ethnology Bulletin 194. Washington: Smithsonian Institution; U.S. Government Printing Office, 1965; reprint, Lincoln and London: University of Nebraska Press, 1992.

_____. *Mandan Social and Ceremonial Organization.* Chicago: University of Chicago Press, 1950; reprint, Moscow, Idaho: University of Idaho Press, 1991.

Bruised Head, Mike. "The Impact and Effects of the Lewis and Clark Expedition from the Eyes of the Blackfoot." Presented at the Plains Indian Museum Seminar, *Native Perspectives on the Lewis and Clark Expedition,* Buffalo Bill Historical Center, Cody, Wyoming, October 4, 2003.

Catlin, George. *Indian Art in Pipestone: George Catlin's Portfolio in the British Museum.* John C. Ewers, ed. Washington, D.C.: Smithsonian Institution Press, 1979.

_____. *Letters and Notes on the Manners, Customs, and Conditions of the North American Indians: Written During Eight Years' Travel (1832–1839) Amongst the Wildest Tribes of Indians in North America,* 2 vols. New York: Wiley and Putnam, 1844; reprint, New York: Dover Publications, 1973.

_____. *O-kee-pa, A Religious Ceremony, and Other Customs of the Mandans.* London: Trubner and Company, 1867; reprint, New Haven, Conn.: Yale University Press, 1967.

Chardon, Francis A. *Journal at Fort Clark, 1834–39.* Pierre, S.D.: State of South Dakota, 1932.

Coe, Ralph T. *Sacred Circles: Two Thousand Years of North American Indian Art.* Kansas City: Nelson Gallery Foundation, 1977.

Conn, Richard. *Circles of the World: Traditional Art of the Plains Indians.* Denver: Denver Art Museum, 1982.

_____. *Native American Art in the Denver Art Museum.* Denver: Denver Art Museum, 1979.

Cunningham, Don. "Pahuk Place." *NEBRASKA land* (June, 1985): 27–31.

Deloria, Ella C. *Speaking of Indians.* New York: Friendship Press, 1944; rep., Vermillion: Dakota Books, 1992.

Deloria, Vine Jr. *God is Red: A Native View of Religion.* Golden, Colorado: Fulcrum Publishing, 1994.

DeMallie, Raymond J. and John C. Ewers. "History of Ethnological and Ethnohistorical Research." *Handbook of North American Indians* 13 (1), *Plains.* Washington, D.C.: Smithsonian Institution, 2001. 23–43.

Dempsey, Hugh A. "Blackfoot." *Handbook of North American Indians* 13 (1) *Plains.* Washington, D.C.: Smithsonian Institution, 2001. 604–628.

Densmore, Frances. *Pawnee Music.* Smithsonian Institution Bureau of American Ethnology Bulletin 93. Washington, D.C.: U.S. Government Printing Office, 1929.

_____. *Teton Sioux Music.* Bulletin of American Ethnology 61. Washington, D.C.: U.S. Government Printing Office, 1918.

Dunbar, John and Samuel Allis. "Letters Concerning the Presbyterian Mission in the Pawnee Country, Near Bellevue, Nebraska, 1821–1849." *Collections of the Kansas State Historical Society* 14 (1915–1918). 570–741.

Echohawk, John. "Justice." *Native American Rights Fund Newsletter* (Winter 1997): 2.

Ellis, Clyde. *A Dancing People: Powwow Culture on the Southern Plains.* Lawrence: University Press of Kansas, 2003.

Ellison, Rosemary. *Contemporary Southern Plains Indian Metalwork.* Anadarko, Oklahoma. Southern Plains Indian Museum and Crafts Center, 1976.

Ewers, John C. *The Blackfeet: Raiders on the Northwestern Plains.* Norman: University of Oklahoma Press, 1958.

_____. *The Horse in Blackfoot Indian Culture: With Comparative Material from Other Western Tribes.* Bureau of American Ethnology Bulletin 159. Washington D.C.: U.S. Government Printing Office, 1955.

_____. "The Humble Digging Stick: Symbol of Women's Contributions to Plains Indian Culture." Presentation at the Plains Indian Museum Seminar, Buffalo Bill Historical Center, Cody, Wyo., September 28, 1996.

_____. *Plains Indian History and Culture: Essays on Continuity and Change.* Norman: University of Oklahoma Press, 1997.

_____. *Plains Indian Sculpture: A Traditional Art from America's Heartland.* Washington D.C.: Smithsonian Institution Press, 1986.

Fletcher, Alice C. and Francis La Flesche. *A Study of Omaha Indian Music.* Archaeological and Ethnological Papers of the Peabody Museum 1 (5). Cambridge, Mass.: Harvard University, 1893; reprint, Lincoln: University of Nebraska Press, 1994.

Fletcher, Alice C., assisted by James R. Murie. *The Hako: Song, Pipe, and Unity in a Pawnee Calumet Ceremony.* Twenty-second Annual Report of the Bureau of American Ethnology. Washington, DC: U.S. Government Printing Office, 1904; reprint, Lincoln and London: University of Nebraska Press, 1996.

Fowler, Loretta. "Arapaho." *Handbook of North American Indians.* 13 (2) *Plains.* Washington, D.C.: Smithsonian Institution, 2001. 840–872.

_____. *Arapahoe Politics, 1851–1978: Symbols in Crises of Authority.* Lincoln and London: University of Nebraska Press, 1982.

Francis, Julie E. and Lawrence L. Loendorf. *Ancient Visions: Petroglyphs and Pictographs of the Wind River and Bighorn Country, Wyoming and Montana.* Salt Lake City: University of Utah Press, 2002.

Geist, Valerius. *Buffalo Nation: History and Legend of the North American Bison.* Stillwater, Minnesota: Voyageur Press, 1996.

Gillette, Jane Brown. "Sweetgrass Saga." *Historic Preservation* (September–October 1994): 28–33, 90–92.

Gilman, Carolyn. *Lewis and Clark: Across the Divide.* Washington, D.C.: Smithsonian Books, 2003.

Gilman, Carolyn and Mary Jane Schneider. *The Way to Independence: Memories of a Hidatsa Indian Family, 1840–1920.* St. Paul: Minnesota Historical Society, 1987.

Gilmore, Melvin R. "The Legend of Pahuk." Nebraska State Historical Society MS 231 Series 1, Folder 1, 1914.

_____. *Prairie Smoke.* New York: Columbia University Press, 1929.

_____. "Trip with White Eagle Determining Pawnee Sites, August 27–29, 1914." Nebraska State Historical Society, MS 231 Series 1, Folder 1, 1914.

Gonzalez, Mario. "The Black Hills: The Sacred Land of the Lakota and Tsistsistas." *Cultural Survival Quarterly,* 19, no. 4 (Winter 1996): 63–67.

Gonzalez, Mario and Elizabeth Cook-Lynn. *The Politics of Hallowed Ground: Wounded Knee and the Struggle for Indian Sovereignty.* Urbana and Chicago: University of Illinois Press, 1999.

Grinnell, Calvin. "The Oral Tradition of the Mandan and Hidatsa on Lewis and Clark." Presentation at Plains Indian Museum Seminar, Buffalo Bill Historical Center, Cody, Wyo., October 3, 2003.

Grinnell, George Bird. *The Cheyenne Indians: Their History and Ways of Life.* Vols. 1, 2. New Haven: Yale University Press, 1923.

Gulliford, Andrew. *Sacred Objects and Sacred Places: Preserving Tribal Traditions.* Boulder: University Press of Colorado, 2000.

Hail, Barbara A. *Gifts of Pride and Love: Kiowa and Comanche Cradles.* Bristol, R.I.: Haffenreffer Museum of Anthropology, Brown University, 2000.

_____. *Hau, Kóla! The Plains Collection of the Haffenreffer Museum of Anthropology.* Bristol, R.I.: Haffenreffer Museum of Anthropology, Brown University, 1980.

Hansen, Emma I. "Powerful Images: Art of the Plains and Southwest." *Powerful Images: Portrayals of Native America.* Seattle: University of Washington Press, 1997. 3–34.

Hansen, Emma I. With contributions by Rebecca T. Menlove, Anne Marie Shriver, and Rebecca S. West. *Plains Indian Museum Curator's Notes.* Cody, Wyo.: Buffalo Bill Historical Center, 2004.

Hassrick, Royal B. *The Sioux: Life and Customs of a Warrior Society.* Norman: University of Oklahoma, 1969, reprint, 1988.

Hebard, Grace Raymond. *Washakie: Chief of the Shoshones.* Cleveland: A.H. Clark Co., 1930; reprint, Lincoln and London: University of Nebraska Press, 1995.

Herbst, Tony and Kopp, Joel. *The Flag in American Indian Art.* Seattle: University of Washington Press, 1993.

Hill, John Sr. "The Medicine Wheel of Wyoming." Presentation at Plains Indian Museum Seminar, Buffalo Bill Historical Center, Cody, Wyo., September 14, 2000.

Hill, Rick. *Creativity Is our Tradition: Three Decades of Contemporary Indian Art at the Institute of American Indian Arts.* Santa Fe: Institute of American Indian and Alaska Native Culture and Arts Development, 1992.

Hoebel, E. Adamson. *The Cheyennes: Indians of the Great Plains.* New York: Holt, Rinehart and Winston, 1960.

Holder, Preston. *Hoe and the Horse on the Plains: A Study of Cultural Development Among North American Indians.* Lincoln and London: University of Nebraska Press, 1970.

Hoxie, Frederick E. *Parading Through History: The Making of the Crow Nation in America 1805–1935.* Cambridge, United Kingdom: Cambridge University Press, 1995.

Hudson, Marilyn. " 'We Are Not Here to Sell Our Land': The Mandan, Hidatsa, and Arikara People and the Flood Control Act of 1944." Presentation at Plains Indian Museum Seminar, Buffalo Bill Historical Center, Cody, Wyo., October 1, 2005.

Hyde, George E. *The Pawnee Indians.* Denver: University of Denver Press, 1951; reprint, Norman: University of Oklahoma Press, 1974.

Inter Tribal Bison Cooperative. *Annual Report.* Rapid City, South Dakota, 1998.

Irving, Washington. *The Adventures of Captain Bonneville, U.S.A., in the Rocky Mountains and the Far West.* 1837; reprint, Norman: University of Oklahoma Press, 1961.

Isenberg, Andrew C. *The Destruction of the Bison: An Environmental History, 1750–1920.* Cambridge: Cambridge University Press, 2000.

Jackson, Helen Hunt. *A Century of Dishonor.* Boston: Roberts Brothers, 1893.

James, Edwin. "Account of an expedition from Pittsburgh to the Rocky Mountains, Performed in the Years 1829, 1820, under the command of Major S. H. Long." *In Early Western Travels, 1748–1846.* Cleveland: Arthur II. Clark Company, 1905.

Kroeber, Alfred L. *The Arapaho, Bulletin of the American Museum of Natural History* 18. 1902, 1904, 1907; reprint, Lincoln: University of Nebraska Press, 1983.

Lame Deer, John Fire and Richard Erdoes. *Lame Deer: Seeker of Visions.* New York: Simon & Schuster, 1972.

Liberty, Margo W., Raymond Wood, and Lee Irwin. "Omaha." *Handbook of North American Indians.* 13 (1) *Plains.* Washington, D.C.: Smithsonian Institution, 2001. 399–415.

Linderman, Frank B. *American: The Life Story of a Great Indian, Plenty-coups, Chief of the Crows.* Rathway, New Jersey: The John Day Company, 1930; reprinted as *Plenty-coups, Chief of the Crows,* Lincoln: University of Nebraska Press, 1962.

_____. *Red Mother: The Life Story of Pretty-Shield, Medicine Woman of the Crows.* Rathway, New Jersey: The John Day Company, 1932; reprinted as *Pretty Shield; Medicine Woman of the Crows.* Lincoln: University of Nebraska Press, 1972.

Lomawaima, K. Tsianina. *They Called It Prairie Light: The Story of Chilocco Indian School.* Lincoln and London: University of Nebraska Press, 1994.

Lowie, Robert H. *The Crow Indians.* New York: Farrar and Rinehart, 1935; reprint, Lincoln and London: University of Nebraska Press, 1983.

Mallery, Garrick. *A Calendar of the Dakota Nation.* Bulletin of the United States Geological and Geographical Survey of the Territories 3 (1). Washington D.C.: U.S. Government Printing Office. 3–25.

_____. *Picture Writing of the American Indians.* 10th Annual Report of the Bureau of Ethnology for 1888–89. Reprint, New York: Dover Publications, 1972.

Marriott, Alice Lee and Carol K. Rachlin. *American Indian Mythology.* New York: New American Library, 1968.

Marquis, Thomas B. "Iron Teeth, A Cheyenne Old Woman." *Cheyenne and Sioux: The Reminiscences of Four Indians and a White Soldier.* Stockton, Calif.: University of the Pacific, Center for Western Historical Studies, 1973.

_____. *A Warrior Who Fought Custer.* Minneapolis: Midwest Company, 1931; reprinted as Wooden Leg: A Warrior Who Fought Custer; Lincoln: University of Nebraska Press, 1957.

Maurer, Evan M. *Visions of the People: A Pictorial History of Plains Indian Live.* Minneapolis: Minneapolis Institute of Art, 1992.

McCleary, Timothy P. *The Stars We Know: Crow Indian Astronomy and Lifeways.* Prospect Heights, Ill.: Waveland Press, Inc., 1997.

McFadden, David Revere and Ellen Naipiura Taubman. *Changing Hands: Art Without Reservations 2: Contemporary Native North American Art from the West, Northwest, & Plains.* New York: Museum of Arts & Design, 2005.

Medicine, Beatrice. "Indian Women and Traditional Religion." *Sioux Indian Religion.* Eds. Raymond J. DeMallie and Douglas R. Parks. Norman and London: University of Oklahoma Press, 1987. 159–172.

_____. "Lakota Star Quilts: Commodity, Ceremony and Economic Development." *To Honor and Comfort: Native Quilting Traditions*. Marsha L. MacDowell and C. Kurt Dewhurst eds. Santa Fe: Museum of New Mexico Press and Michigan State University, 1997. 111–118.

_____. " 'Warrior Women'—Sex Role Alternatives for Plains Indian Women." Eds. Patricia Albers and Beatrice Medicine. In *The Hidden Half: Studies of Plains Indian Women*. Washington, D.C.: University Press of America, Inc., 1983. 267–278.

Medicine Crow, Joseph. *From The Heart of The Crow Country; The Crow Indians' Own Stories*. New York: Orion Books, 1992.

Momaday, N. Scott. *The Names: A Memoir*. Tucson and London: University of Arizona Press, 1976; reprint, 1987.

_____. *The Way to Rainy Mountain*. Albuquerque: University of New Mexico Press, 1969.

Mooney, James. *The Ghost-Dance Religion and the Sioux Outbreak of 1890*. Fourteenth Annual Report of the Bureau of Ethnology, 1892–93, Part 2. Washington, D.C.: U.S. Government Printing Office, 1896; reprint, Lincoln and London: University of Nebraska Press, 1991.

Moore, John H. *The Cheyenne Nation: A Social and Demographic History*. Lincoln and London: University of Nebraska Press, 1987.

Murie, James R. *Ceremonies of the Pawnee*. Douglas R. Parks, ed. Washington D.C.: Smithsonian Institution, 1981.

_____. "Pawnee Indian Societies." *American Museum of Natural History Anthropological Papers* 11 (7), 1914, 543–644.

Nabokov, Peter. *Two Leggings: The Making of a Crow Warrior*. New York: Thomas Y. Crowell, Publishers, 1964.

Nabokov, Peter and Lawrence Loendorf. *American Indians and Yellowstone National Park: A Documentary Overview*. Yellowstone National Park: National Park Service, 2002.

Nabokov, Peter, ed. *Native American Testimony: A Chronicle of Indian-White Relations From Prophecy to the Present, 1492–1992*. New York: Penguin Books, 1978; reprint, 1992.

_____. *Restoring a Presence: American Indians and Yellowstone National Park*. Norman: University of Oklahoma Press, 2004.

Neihardt, John G. *Black Elk Speaks: Being the Life Story of a Holy Man of the Oglala Sioux*. Lincoln and London: University of Nebraska Press, 1932; reprint, 1979.

Parks, Douglas R. *Traditional Narratives of the Arikara Indians*. 4 vols. Lincoln and London: University of Nebraska Press, 1991.

Parks, Douglas R. and Waldo R. Wedel. "Pawnee Geography: Historical and Sacred." *Great Plains Quarterly* 5 (3) (1985): 143–176.

Penney, David W. *Art of the American Indian Frontier: The Chandler-Pohrt Collection*. Seattle and London: University of Washington Press, 1992.

Peters, Virginia Bergman. *Women of the Earth Lodges: Tribal Life on the Plains*. New Haven, Conn.: Archon Books, 1995.

Peterson, Karen Daniels. *Plains Indian Art from Fort Marion*. Norman: University of Oklahoma Press, 1971.

Pike, Zebulon Montgomery. *The Expeditions of Zebulon Montgomery Pike to headwaters of the Mississippi River through Louisiana Territory, and in New Spain, during the years 1805–1807*. Minneapolis: Ross & Haines, 1965.

Powers, Marla N. *Oglala Women: Myth, Ritual, and Power*. Chicago and London: The University of Chicago Press, 1986.

Powers, William K. *Oglala Religion*. Lincoln and London: University of Nebraska Press, 1977.

Prucha, Francis Paul. *The Great Father: The United States Government and the American Indians*. Lincoln: University of Nebraska Press, 1986.

Red Shirt, Delphine. *Turtle Lung Woman's Granddaughter*. Lincoln and Nebraska: University of Nebraska Press, 2002.

Red Star, Kevin. "A History of the Contemporary Artist." Presented at Plains Indian Museum Seminar, Buffalo Bill Historical Center, Cody, Wyo., September 28, 1995.

Reid, Gordon. *Head-Smashed-In Buffalo Jump*. Calgary, Alberta: Fifth House Press, 2002.

Schneider, Mary Jane. "Three Affiliated Tribes." *Handbook of North American Indians* 13 (1) *Plains*. Washington, D.C.: Smithsonian Institution, 2001. 391–398.

_____. "Women's Work: An Examination of the Women's Roles in Plains Indian Arts and Crafts." Eds. Patricia Albers and Beatrice

Medicine. *In The Hidden Half: Studies of Plains Indian Women*. Washington, D.C.: University Press of America, Inc., 1983. 101–122.

Snell, Alma Hogan. *Grandmother's Grandchild: My Crow Indian Life*. Ed. Becky Matthews. Lincoln and London: University of Nebraska Press, 2000.

Stamm, Henry E., IV. *People of the Wind River: The Eastern Shoshones 1825–1900*. Norman: University of Oklahoma Press, 1999.

Standing Bear, Luther. *My Indian Boyhood*. Boston: Houghton Mifflin, 1931; reprint, Lincoln and London: University of Nebraska Press, 1988.

_____. *My People the Sioux*. Ed. E.A. Brininstool. New York: Houghton-Mifflin, 1928; reprint, Lincoln and London: University of Nebraska Press, 1975.

Stands In Timber, John and Margot Liberty, with the assistance of Robert M. Utley. *Cheyenne Memories*. New Haven: Yale University, 1967; reprint, Lincoln and London: University of Nebraska Press, 1972.

Stewart, Omer. *Peyote Religion: A History*. Norman: University of Oklahoma Press, 1987.

Thomas, David Hurst. *Exploring Ancient Native America: An Archaeological Guide*. New York: Macmillan, 1994.

_____. *Skull Wars: Kennewick Man, Archaeology, and the Battle for Native American Identity*. New York: Basic Books, 2001.

Thornton, Russell. *American Indian Holocaust and Survival: A Population History Since 1492*. Norman: University of Oklahoma Press, 1987; reprint, 1990.

Tsatoke, Monroe. *The Peyote Ritual: Visions and Descriptions*. San Francisco: The Grabhorn Press, 1957.

Utley, Robert M. *The Last Days of the Sioux Nation*. New Haven: Yale University Press, 1963.

VanDevelder, Paul. *Coyote Warrior: One Man, Three Tribes and the Trial That Forged a Nation*. Boston: Little, Brown and Company, 2004.

Viola, Herman J. *After Columbus: The Smithsonian Chronicle of the North American Indian*. Washington, DC: Smithsonian Institution, 1990.

_____. *Diplomats in Buckskins: A History of Indian Delegations in Washington City*. Bluffton, S. C.: Rivilo Books, 1995.

Voget, Fred W. *The Shoshoni-Crow Sun Dance*. Norman: University of Oklahoma Press, 1984.

Voget, Fred W., assisted by Mary K. Mee. *They Call Me Agnes: A Crow Narrative Based on the Life of Agnes Yellowtail Deernose*. Norman and London: University of Oklahoma Press, 1995.

Walker, James R. *Lakota Society*. Raymond J. Demallie, ed. Lincoln and London: University of Nebraska Press, 1992.

Weidman, Dennis and Candace Greene. "Early Kiowa Peyote Ritual and Symbolism: The 1891 Drawing Books of Silverhorn (Haungooah)." *American Indian Art Magazine* (Autumn 1988): 32–41.

Weist, Katherine. "Beasts of Burden and Menial Slaves: Nineteenth Century Observation of Northern Plains Indian Women." Eds. Patricia Albers and Beatrice Medicine. *The Hidden Half: Studies of Plains Indian Women*. Washington, D.C.: University Press of America, Inc., 1983. 29–62.

Welch, James. *Fools Crow*. New York: Penguin Books, 1986.

Welch, James with Paul Stekler. *Killing Custer: The Battle of the Little Bighorn and the Fate of the Plains Indian*. New York and London: W.W. Norton & Company, 1994.

Weltfish, Gene. *The Lost Universe: Pawnee Life and Culture*. Lincoln: University of Nebraska Press, 1965.

Will, George F. and George E. Hyde. *Corn Among the Indians of the Upper Missouri*. Lincoln: University of Nebraska Press, 1964.

Wilson, Gilbert L. *Agriculture of the Hidatsa Indians; An Indian Interpretation*. University of Minnesota Studies in the Social Sciences 9. St. Paul: Minnesota Historical Society Press, 1987; reprinted as *Buffalo Bird Woman's Garden: Agriculture of the Hidatsa Indians*.

_____. *Waheenee: An Indian Girl's Story: Told by Herself to Gilbert L. Wilson*. St. Paul Minnesota: Webb Publishing Company, 1927; reprint, Lincoln and London: University of Nebraska Press, 1981.

Winship, George Parker. *The Coronado Expedition, 1540–1542*. 14th Annual Report of Bureau of American Ethnology, 1892–1893. Washington, D.C: Smithsonian Institution, 1896.

Wishart, David J. *An Unspeakable Sadness: The Dispossession of the Nebraska Indians*. Lincoln and London: University of Nebraska Press, 1994.

Wood, Raymond J. and Lee Irwin. "Mandan." *Handbook of North American Indians*. 13 (1) *Plains*. Washington, D.C.: Smithsonian Institution, 2001. 349–364.

Wroth, William, Ed. *Ute Indian Arts & Culture: From Prehistory to the New Millennium*. Colorado Springs: Colorado Springs Fine Arts Center, 2000.

YellowHair, Gordon Sr. "Nooha-Vose--Hoxehe?Eohe?E." Presentation at Plains Indian Museum Seminar, Buffalo Bill Historical Center, Cody, Wyo., September 15, 2000.

Yellowtail, Thomas. *Yellowtail: Crow Medicine Man and Sun Dance Chief, An Autobiography as told to Michael Oren Fitzgerald*. Norman and London: University of Oklahoma Press, 1991.

Young, Gloria A. and Erik D. Gooding. "Celebrations and Giveaways." *Handbook of North American Indians*. 13 (2) *Plains*. Washington, D.C.: Smithsonian Institution, 2001. 1011–1025.

Zephier, Mitchell. "Taking the Best of the White Man's Road: New Traditions in Northern Plains Metalwork." Presented at Plains Indian Museum Seminar, Buffalo Bill Historical Center, Cody, Wyo., September 30, 1995.

Note: Page numbers in *italics* refer to photographs and captions; those followed by "n" indicate footnotes.

abortion, 95
adoption, *163*, 195
"aesthetic of mobility," 70
age-graded societies, 146, 155–162, 182–183
agriculture, 15–16, 58–62
Âiya´äka, 121–122, 129–133
akí´cita (Lakota soldier society), 129–133, 153–155
American flag motif, 37, 236
American Fur Company, 213, 218
American Horse, 43, *150*, 221–222
American Indian Movement, 261
American Indian Religious Freedom Act, 31
American War Mothers, Pawnee Chapter, 269
Amiotte, Arthur
   on arts, 273
   banner (with Rose Gibbons), *283*
   inspirations and training, 283–284
   "A New and Different Life on a Small Part of a Very Old Place," 246–251
   on Sun Dance, 185–186, 260–261
   The Visit, *283*
Amoskapi Pikuni. *See* Blackfeet (Amoskapi Pikuni)
animal spirits, 147, 164–166, *206*, *207*
Apache
   Coronado and, 14–15
   Drama on the Plains (Houser), *254*
   hide processing, art of, 77
   Jennings and, 279
Apsáalooke or Apsaroke. *See* Crow (Apsáalooke or Apsaroke)
Arapaho (Hinono'ei)
   age-graded societies, 155, 160–162

buffalo dances, women's, 181–182
buffalo hunting and, 17
cattle hunting, 225
Crow and, 205
eagle wing fans, 169
Ghost Dance clothing, *202*, *207*, *208*
Ghost Dance songs, 209–210
guilds, 86
horses and, 116
Indian Memorial and, *258*
on Internet, 296
ledger drawings, 140
Little Bighorn and, 220
pipe bag, *37*
quillwork vs. beadwork, 181
sacred places, 25, 27, 28, 31
Shoshone battles against, 150
Sun Dance, 185
Yellowman, 29
Arapaho, Northern
   beadwork (Dewey), *277*, 277
   Buffalo Society woman's headdress, *182*
   cradle, *178*
   language and culture classes, 254
   leadership, 149, 151–152
   powwows, *264*, 265
   quillwork apprenticeships, 179
   song for Ghost Dance, 210
Arapaho, Southern, 151, 225
   Arapooish (Rotten Belly), 19, 199
Arikara (Sahnish)
   baskets, *53*
   beads and, 74, 77

buffalo and, 147
Garrison Dam and, 19–20, 29–30
historical development of, 15
horses and, 118
horticulture, 58, 60–61
Indian Memorial and, *258*
Memorial at Old Scouts Cemetery (Hansen), *259*
sacred places, 25
shields, *108*
shirt, 79
smallpox and, 44
Three Affiliated Tribes, 19–20, 46n9
tipis and lodges, 66
women's societies, 182, 183
arm bands, Oglala Lakota, 274
artistic styles and specialization, 77, 86
arts programs at boarding schools, 231–232
assimilation program, 225, 259
Assiniboine
   buffalo hunts and, 16
   buffalo restoration, 257–258
   Chief Wets It, Assiniboine (Rinehart), *110*
   Coyote Legend (Hyde), *252*
   horses and, 117
   sacred places, 28

babies, 88, 95–96
bags
   mirror bag, Crow, *161*
   storage bags, Blackfeet, 76
   storage bags, Cheyenne, *105*
   storage bags, Crow, *76*

storage bags, Lakota, *243, 249*

See also hide containers and parfleches; pipe bags

Baker, Cora (Sweet Grass), 146

Baker, Gerard, 146–147

Baker, Paige, Sr. (Sacred Horse), 146

banner (Amiotte and Gibbons), *283*

Bannock, 149, 270

basket, Mandan, *53*

beadwork

about, 74–77

belt and bag (McAdams), *278*

blanket strips, *75*

contemporary artists, 274–280

cradle (Jennings), *278*

dresses, *81, 229, 231, 233, 275*

dress yoke, Kiowa, *84*

floral designs, *237*

hair pipes, *132, 247*

knives with cases, Lakota, *77*

Lakota, *233,* 236–237

man's leggings, *130*

moccasins, *80, 85, 275*

on Native American Church ritual objects, *262*

pipe bags, 36–37

quillwork vs., 181

saddle (Dewey), *277*

shirts, *78, 177*

vests, *276, 277*

beans, 60, 62

Bear Butte (*Mato Paha*), 26

bear claw necklaces, 172, *172*

Bear Lodge (Devil's Tower), 27–28

Bear Lodge (Devil's Tower) (Hansen), *29*

bears

Arikara shield and covers, *108–109*

claw necklaces, 172, *172*

Crow shield covers, *140, 141, 142*

Hidatsa shield cover, *143*

belt, woman's (*maípsuka´sa*), *181*

belt and bag, Eastern Shoshone (McAdams), *278*

berries, 55–56

berry cakes, *57*

Bies, Michael T.

Petroglyph in Bighorn Basin of Wyoming, *21*

Big Crow, 95

Big Day, William, 259

Big Foot, 219, 221

Bighorn Medicine Wheel, 26, *27*

Bíiluuke ("Our Side"), 39

See also Crow (Apsáalooke or Apsaroke)

bison. See buffalo

Biss, Earl, 285

General Custer in Blue and Green, 285

Blackbirds (Crow Tobacco Society chapter), 41–42

Black Coal, 151–152, 169

Black Elk, 26, 32, 154–155, 203, 222

Black Elk Speaks, 283

Blackfeet (Amoskapi Pikuni)

buffalo horn bonnet, *114*

butchering, 133

conflicts with U.S. military, 219

Crow Fair and, 270

dress, 229

eagle feather bonnet, *165*

A Grandmother's Lodge (Parsons), *288*

hair ornament, men's, *133*

horse riding equipment, *194*

land, reverence for, 21

leggings, 86, 237

moccasins, 85, *107*

pipe bags, 38

powwows, 266

prairie turnips and, 55

quillwork, 179

sacred places, 28

shirt, *238*

Shoshone battles against, 150

storage bags, 76

Blackfoot

beadwork, 237

buffalo hunts and, 16, 111

buffalo jumps (*pisskan or pisská-ni*), 107, 109

horses and, 117, 122

iniskin (buffalo amulet), 106

quillwork, 86, 179

smallpox epidemic, 218

Sun Dance, 185

See also Blood (Kanai); Piegan

Black Foot (Sits In The Middle Of The Land), 199–201

Black Hills (*Paha Sapa*) as sacred place, 25–26

Black Kettle, 219, 220

Black Mouth Society, 158–160

blankets

Lakota, 251

Otoe, 241

quilts, 250, 251, 280–282, 282

Tobacco Society, Apsáalooke (Crow), 40

wool, 74

See also saddle blankets

blanket strips, 75

blessing of lodges, 66

Blood (Kanai), 111, 218

blood drinking, 133

boarding schools, 225–235, 248–249

Girls Dormitory, Crow Boarding School (Miller), 220

boat (bullboat), Mandan, 20

Bodmer, Karl, 218

bonnets and headdresses, 169–172

buffalo horn and eagle feather bonnet, Cheyenne, *111*

buffalo horn bonnet, Blackfeet, *114*

buffalo horn bonnet, Crow, *112*

buffalo horn bonnet, Lakota, *114*

Buffalo Society woman's headdress, Northern Arapaho, *182*

Cheyenne Chief Two Moon, at Fort Keogh (Huffman), *153*

Chief Rocky Bear, Sioux (Rinehart), *33*

eagle feather bonnet, Blackfeet, *165*

eagle feather bonnet, Crow, *168*

eagle feather bonnet and trailer, Eastern Shoshone, *167*

eagle feather bonnet and trailer, Lakota, *167*

eagle headdress, Crow, *164*

feather bonnet of rooster hackles, *170*

on Lakota pipe bag, *36*

Spies on the Enemy, Crow (Rinehart), *113*

top hat, *261*

turban, Meskwaki, *241*

bow cases, *126*

bowls

feast bowl, Eastern Sioux, *58*

Lakota rawhide bowl, *106*

Box, Austin, 280

boxes, peyote, *262*

boxes and containers, hide. See hide containers and parfleches

bracelets, 179–181

Brady, Matthew, 285

Brave Buffalo, 105–106

breadroot, Indian (prairie turnip), 53–55

breastplate, Lakota, *132*

Bridgeman, John, 150

bridle, Blackfeet, *194*

Bright Wings, 188

Bright Wings, Amy, 284

brucellosis, 256, 257

Bruised Head, Mike, 218

Brule Lakota dance shield, *157*

Brunot Treaty (1872), 149

buffalo

beliefs and traditions, 99–103, 147

blood drinking, 133

brucellosis and, 256, 257

Buffalo Grazing the Big Open, Northern Montana (Huffman), *15*

butchering of, 133, 255

ceremonies, 106–107, 146–147

decline and demise of, 141–142, 143, 205–206, 211–215, 213, 255, 257

hunting methods, 107–111 (See also hunting)

images of, 105

on Lakota pipe bag, 36

life after, 49

Mandan-Hidatsa way of life and, 146–147

restoration of, 147, 201, 255–258

sacred power of, 105–106

sustenance from, 103–104

Texas legislature and, 244n21

traditions, development of, 58

in vision quest, 162–164

Buffalo Bill's Wild West, 172, 203, 247, 248

Buffalo Bird Woman, 56, 62, 66, 70, 115, 179–181, 218

Buffalo Bull, 147
Buffalo Bull society, 146
Buffalo Calling Ceremony, 106–107, 146–147
buffalo dances, 107, 147, 160, 181–182
buffalo horns
    bonnet, Blackfeet, 114
    bonnet, Crow, 112
    bonnet, Lakota, 114
    eagle feather and buffalo horn bonnet,
        Cheyenne, 111
    scraper handles, Sioux, 93n42
    spoons, 59
buffalo jumps, 107–111
buffalo mask, Mandan, 147
Buffalo Medicine Keeper (Cannon), 286
buffalo robes, 70–74
    commercial demand for, 212
    Hidatsa, 72, 101
    Lakota, 72, 73, 136
    Mandan, 103
    quilling societies and, 177–178
Buffalo Sing (*Tatanka Olowanpi*) ceremony, 95–96
Buffalo Song, 133
Buffalo Spirit Places, 146
Buffalo Woman. *See* White Buffalo Calf Woman
Buffalo Woman Society, 182
bullboat, Mandan, 20
Bull Society, 160
burden basket, Mandan, 53
Bureau of Indian Affairs, 30
bustle, dance (Dakota), 264
butchering, 133, 255
buttes as Buffalo Spirit Places, 146

Caddo
    artists of, 285
    Buffalo Medicine Keeper (Cannon), 286
    Native American Church and, 210
    Sun Dance, 262
Caesar, Bruce, 263
Caesar, Julius, 263
California Trail, 212
Calumet Ceremony (*Hako*), 99
calumets, 34, 34–35
camp, moving, 63, 63–66
Campbell, Robert, 19, 199
Cannon, T.C. (Tommy Wayne), 285, 286–288
    Buffalo Medicine Keeper, 286
canvas used for tipis, 100
Carlisle Indian School, 226–228, 232
cartoonish stereotypes, 295–296
cases, rawhide. *See* hide containers and parfleches
Castle Gardens, 25
Catches, Pete, 25
Catlin, George, 35, 147, 218
catlinite, 35
cattle, 212, 225
Cayuse, 194
celebrations. *See* ceremonies, rituals, and celebra-

tions
Cemetery, Old Scouts, 259
ceremonies, rituals, and celebrations
    and Buffalo, return of, 258
    Buffalo Calling ceremony, 106–107, 146–147
    Buffalo Sing (*Tatanka Olowanpi*) ceremony,
        95–96
    children's life events, 89
    Dancing Through the Camp ceremony, 272–273
    Earth Naming Ceremony, 146
    government restrictions on, 187–191
    hand drum, Lakota, 185
    horses and, 124, 125
    hunting and, 133–134
    Okipa ceremony, 106–107, 146–147, 147, 160
    Pawnee, 186
    pipe ceremonies, 34–35, 258
    powwows and homecomings, 263–269
    puberty, 95–96
    reservation life and, 250–251, 258
    seasonal cycle of, 183
    surrogate leader ceremonies (Lakota), 250–251
    women's life cycle and, 95–96
    of women's societies, 182–183
    See also Crow Fair (*Uhba'asaxpiluua*); dance
        equipment and regalia; dances; Sun Dance
Chardon, Francis A., 244n34
Charging, Shelley, 265
Chased By Bears (Mato-Kuwapi), 32, 185
chastity, 95
Cherokee, 216, 286
Cheyenne (Tsististas)
    beadwork, 181
    blanket strips, 75
    bonnets, 111, 169–172
    bow case and quiver, 126
    buffalo hunting and, 17
    cattle hunting, 225
    Cheyenne Boy (Huffman), 19
    child's tipi cover, 88
    counting coups, 136
    cradles, 90
    Crow and, 205
    Crow Fair and, 270
    Custer and, 285
    in cyber space, 294–297
    dresses, 81, 230
    elk teeth, use of, 227
    families, 95
    food trading, 62
    guilds, 86
    hide processing, art of, 77
    horses and, 116, 118, 122
    horticulture, 58–60
    Indian Memorial and, 258
    leadership, 155
    ledger drawings, 120, 140
    Little Bighorn and, 220
    marriage, 95

    moccasins, 175, 239
    name of, 294
    parfleches, 68
    pipe bag, 37
    'Pretty Nose,' Cheyenne Girl (Huffman), 52
    quilling society, 175–176
    quillwork, 235
    rawhide case, 64
    sacred places, 24–28, 31
    'Spotted Fawn'—Cheyenne Girl of 13
        (Huffman), 12
    Spotted Horse, self-portrait, 139
    storage bags, 105
    Sun Dance, 184–185, 259, 292n8
    White Hawk—Cheyenne (Huffman), 123
Cheyenne, Northern
    alliance with Lakota and Northern Arapaho,
        151
    artists of, 288–289
    Cheyenne Chief Two Moon, at Fort Keogh
        (Huffman), 153
    eagles, 169
    horticulture, 58–60
    name of, 294
    Northern Cheyenne Women Gathering Wood
        (Grinnell), 54
    Pevah (Spang), 295
    women's rankings, 176
    *Wooden Leg Drawing Events from Battle of
        Little Big Horn* (Marquis), 139
    See also Northern Cheyenne Reservation
Cheyenne, Southern
    Galloping, Little Man, Kiowa, and Sweetwater
        drawings, 139, 140
    sacred sites, responsibility to protect, 28–29
Cheyenne and Arapaho Reservation, Oklahoma,
    225
Cheyenne Boy (Huffman), 19
Cheyenne Chief Two Moon, at Fort Keogh
    (Huffman), 153
Cheyenne River Lakota
    Tatanka Wan, A Buffalo Bull (Yellow), 256
chickadees, 164
chief, role of, 153
    See also leadership
Chief Mountain, 28
Chief Rocky Bear, Sioux (Rinehart), 33
Chief Society (Lakota), 155
Chief Wets It, Assiniboine (Rinehart), 110
Chien, Pierre, 200
childbirth, 95
children
    buffalo robe, Lakota, 72
    Cheyenne Boy (Huffman), 19
    A Child's Lodge—Piegan (Curtis), 17
    Girls Dormitory, Crow Boarding School
        (Miller), 220
    girl's saddle, Crow, 187
    horses and, 122–124

hunting and boys, 125–128
lives of, 87–91, 95
Mother and Child—Apsaroke (Curtis), 50
moving camp and, 64
naming of, 95–96
removal of, 187
renaming of, 226–228
Spotted Fawn (Cheyenne), 12
Two Crow Children (Petzoldt), 217
warfare and boys, 134–136
See also boarding schools; clothing, children's;
cradles
A Child's Lodge—Piegan (Curtis), 17
Chilocco Indian Agricultural School, 228–231
Chippewa
Coyote Legend (Hyde), 252
Chippewa Cree, 28
Chiricahua Apache
Drama on the Plains (Houser), 254
Chivington, John M., 220
chokecherry cakes, 56
clans, Mandan-Hidatsa, 146
Clark, William, 46n2, 53, 60, 74, 147, 198, 296
Clinton, William Jefferson, 31
clothing, adult
dress yoke, Kiowa, 84
for Ghost Dance, 202, 206, 207–209
for hunting, 138
missionary impacts on, 249
in reservation period, 235–237, 246
sewing machines, 221, 235, 249
See also buffalo robes; dresses; leggings; moccasins; shirts
clothing, children's
boy's pants, Lakota, 234
boy's shirt, Crow, 174
boy's vest, Lakota, 234
child's moccasins, Cheyenne, 175
Crow, girl's dress, 83
girl's dress, Crow, 83
girl's dress, Lakota/Cheyenne, 230
girl's leggings, Crow, 226
Cody, Cadzi (Codsiogo), 98, 256
Cody, William F. (Buffalo Bill), 247, 248
See also Buffalo Bill's Wild West
Cold Wind, 39–40
collages
A Grandmother's Lodge (Parsons), 288
The Visit (Amiotte), 283
Colleges, 254
Collier, John, 201, 256, 259
Collier, Richard
Medicine Wheel, 26
Comanche
alliance with Kiowa, 24
buffalo hunting and, 17
hide processing, art of, 77
Native American Church and, 210
Sun Dance, 262

commercial hide hunting, 212–214
containers, rawhide. *See* hide containers and
parfleches
corn, 60, 61, 186
Cornhusk Earrings, 60
Corn Woman, 60
Coronado, Francisco Vásquez de, 14–15, 73
corrals, 111
Council of Forty-four (Cheyenne), 155
coups, counting, 136–138, 152, 267
Court of Indian Offenses, 292n7
courtship, 55, 95
cowrie shells
breastplate, Lakota, 132
dress, Cheyenne, 81
Coyote, 109
Coyote Legend (Hyde), 252
Cradleboard Pendant (Knife Chief), 290
cradles
Cheyenne, 90
Crow, 50, 51, 89, 90
Kiowa, 224, 278
Lakota, 88–89, 176
making of, 88–89, 197n46
Northern Arapaho, 178, 179
Salish, 242
Crazies lodge, 161
Crazy Horse, 246
Creator, 20, 22, 109
Cree
horses and, 116–117
Painted Pony Series: Games People Play (Quick-
to-See Smith), 289
sacred places, Chippewa Cree, 28
saddle, 193
cross (Zephier), 263
Crow (Apsáalooke or Apsaroke)
ankle trailers, 158
Arapooish on Crow country, 19
artists of, 284–285
battle with Hunkpapa, 44
beadwork, 237
blanket strips, 75
bow case and quiver, 126
and buffalo, loss of, 204–205, 206, 212
buffalo emblems, 105
buffalo horn bonnet, 112
buffalo hunts and, 16, 109, 111
counting coups, 137–138
cradles, 50, 51
Crow Riders at Indian Memorial Dedication
(Hansen), 258
Crow Winter Camp in Teepees (Red Star), 284
Crow women working on hides (Rau), 102
cylinder cases, rawhide, 71
dances and gatherings, 191–195
division of labor, 53
dresses, 83, 227
eagle feather bonnet, 168

eagle headdress, 164
families, 95
General Custer in Blue and Green (Biss), 285
Girls Dormitory, Crow Boarding School
(Miller), 220
girl's leggings, 226
horse riding equipment, 187, 189, 190, 192
horses and, 117, 121
horse stealing charm, 116
jacket, 228
lance case, 191
leadership, 198–201
life after buffalo, 49
Mashed berries made into berry cakes (Petzoldt),
57
mirror bag, 161
moccasins, 96, 239
Mother and Child—Apsaroke (Curtis), 50
moving camp, 64, 65
name of, 39, 124
Northern Arapaho and, 151
origins of, 198
parfleche, 104
petroglyphs and, 25
pipe bag, 37
plant collecting, 55
powwows, 266, 268
*Pretty Shell and Pretty Beads in Doorway of
Tipi*, 23
rawhide art, 67
sacred places, 27, 28, 31
seasonal circle, 258
shield covers, 140, 141, 142
shirts, 128, 174, 200
Shoshone battles against, 150
Sitting Bull Killing a Crow Indian (Sitting Bull),
120
smallpox and, 44, 218, 244n30
Spotted Horse and, 120
storage bags, 76
Sun Dance, 259–260
toy cradle, 90
*In Traditional Dress, Bright Wings, Beth Iron
Horse, Annie Talking Pipe and Nellie
Scratches Face*, 188
Two Crow Children (Petzoldt), 217
"two spirit" males, 95
vision quests, 162–169
White Man Runs Him—Apsaroke (Curtis), 135
Crow Arrow Throw, 195, 195
Crow Fair (*Uhba'asaxpiluua*), 270–273
Crow Indian Parade Rider (Red Star), 270
Crow Tipi Village, Riverside (Sharp), 186
Kiowa at, 24
lance case, 191
parade tradition, 193
Riders in Crow Fair Parade (Hansen), 270
Crow Indian Parade Rider (Red Star), 270
Crow-Owners Society (Lakota), 138

Crow Reservation
    buffalo restoration, 256–257
    ceremonies, 191
    Collier's rehabilitation plan, 201
    Crow women working on hides (Rau), 102
    "fasting beds," 166
    Green hides showing geometric design for parfleches (Rau), 67
    Mashed berries made into berry cakes (Petzoldt), 57
    Medicine Crow—Apsaroke (Curtis), 199
    Men throwing arrows in winter (Petzoldt), 195
    Moving camp (Petzoldt), 63
    Plenty Coups with Adopted Daughter, 163
    Pretty Shell and Pretty Beads in Doorway of Tipi, 23
    Senate bill to open to white settlers, 201
    Tobacco Society Ceremony and Field, 41
    In Traditional Dress, Bright Wings, Beth Iron Horse, Annie Talking Pipe and Nellie Scratches Face, 188
    White Man Runs Him—Apsaroke (Curtis), 135
    Woman using a sewing machine (Petzoldt), 221
Crow Riders at Indian Memorial Dedication (Hansen), 258
crows, 210
Crow Tipi Village, Riverside (Sharp), 186
Crow Tobacco Ceremony, 193–195
Crow Tobacco Society, 39–42
    blanket, 40
    Tobacco Society Ceremony and Field, 41
Crow Winter Camp in Teepees (Red Star), 284
crupper, Crow, 190
cuffs, Oglala Lakota, 274
Curtis, Edward S.
    A Child's Lodge—Piegan, 17
    Long-time Dog—Hidatsa, 128
    Mandan Earthen Lodge, 20
    Mother and Child—Apsaroke, 50
    White Man Runs Him—Apsaroke, 135
Custer, George Armstrong, 137, 219, 220
    General Custer in Blue and Green (Biss), 285
Custer Battlefield National Monument. *See* Little Bighorn Battlefield National Monument

Dakota
    Black Hills and, 25
    dance bustle, 264
    division of labor, 53
    guns, first use of, 44
    Lone Dog's Winter Count, 43
    pipes, 32
    sacred sites, 21–22
    women, role of, 51
    See also Sioux, Eastern (Santee Dakota)
dance equipment and regalia
    ankle trailers, Crow, 158
    dance bustle, Dakota, 264
    dance shields and covers, Lakota, 156, 157

dance stick, Otoe, 160
    feather bonnet of rooster hackles, 170
    horse dance stick, Lakota, 160
    mirror bag, Crow, 161
dances
    Buffalo Dance, 107, 147, 160, 181–182
    Grass Dance (Omaha Dance), 159, 162, 191, 265
    horses and, 124
    Hot Dance, 191–193
    Owl Dance, 191
    Victory Dances, 267, 269
    See also Ghost Dance; Sun Dance
"Dancing Through the Camp" ceremony, 272–273
Dawes Act (1887), 246, 247, 259
death, 96
Deernose, Agnes, 95
Delaware, 87, 262
Deloria, Ella, 51
Deloria, Vine, Jr., 21–22, 28, 294
Densmore, Frances, 105–106, 134
dentalium shells, 94
Devil's Lake, 39, 40, 198
Devil's Tower. *See* Bear Lodge
Dewey, Marcus, 277, 277
disease, 30, 44, 217–219
divorce, 95
DNA, 296–297
Dodge, Richard I., 27
dogs, 115
Dogs lodge, 161
dolls, 89–91
    Crow, 89
    Lakota, 48, 89
Double Woman, 179
Drama on the Plains (Houser), 254
drawings, 139–140
    ledger drawing (Galloping, Little Man, Kiowa, and Sweetwater), 139
    ledger drawing (Spotted Horse), 120
    Sitting Bull Killing a Crow Indian (Sitting Bull), 120
    Spotted Horse, self-portrait, 139
    Wooden Leg Drawing Events from Battle of Little Big Horn (Marquis), 139
dreams, 105–106, 140
dresses
    Arapaho Ghost Dance dresses, 202, 208
    Blackfeet, 229
    Cheyenne, 81
    Crow, 83, 227
    Eastern Shoshone (Swallow family), 275
    Kiowa, 240
    Lakota, 94, 232, 233
    Lakota/Cheyenne girl's dress, 230
    Lakota girls, South Dakota, late 1800s, 231
    Oglala Lakota ribbon dress (Amiotte and Gibbons), 283
    Shoshone, 82

dress yokes
    Kiowa, 84
    nursing and, 96
Drinks Water, 203
droughts, 211–212
drum, Lakota, 185
Dunbar, John, 50–51, 54–55

eagle feather bonnets. *See* bonnets and headdresses
eagle feathers, 169, 267
Eagle Shield, 138
eagle wing fans, 169
Earthen Lodges tribe. *See* Hidatsa
earth lodges, 20, 66
Earth Naming Ceremony, 146
Eastern Shoshone. *See* Shoshone, Eastern
Eastern Sioux. *See* Sioux, Eastern (Santee Dakota)
Echohawk, John, 31
eclipse of the sun, 44
elders, 161
Elk, 60
elk teeth, 84, 227
Enemy Society, 183
ethnographers, 95
Ewers, John, 55

fairs, 251
    See also Crow Fair (*Ubba'asaxpiluua*)
families, 95
fans
    eagle wing, 169
    feather, 262
    Native American Church Set (Her Many Horses), 261
    Omaha, 210
farming, 250
fasting, 146, 166
"fasting beds," 166
feasts and hunting, 133–134
feather bonnets. *See* bonnets and headdresses
feather or peyote boxes, 262
feathers, eagle, 169, 267
Fighting Bear, 108
Firewood, 179
First Maker, 198
flag motif, 37, 236
Flood Control Act, 29
floral designs, 237
    cradle, Kiowa, 278
    cradle, Salish, 242
    dress, Kiowa, 240
    rose pattern, Shoshone, 275, 276, 276
food
    buffalo meat, 102, 104
    horticulture, 15–16, 58–62
    plant gathering, 53–58
    on reservations, 250
Fort Belknap, 258
Fort Berthold Reservation

buffalo at, 147

legislation for compensation of, 47n35

Long-time Dog—Hidatsa (Curtis), 128

Mandan Earthen Lodge (Curtis), 20

shield and covers, 108–109

shirt, Hidatsa or Mandan, 223

Fort Bridger Treaty (1868), 149

Fort Keogh

    Cheyenne Chief Two Moon, at Fort Keogh (Huffman), 153

Fort Laramie, Treaty of (1868), 199–201

Fort Marion, Florida, 140

Fort Randall, South Dakota, 36, 120, 125, 155

Fort Supply, Oklahoma, 140

Fort Union, 218

Four Bears, 218

Four Robes, 155

Fourth of July, 191, 249

Fox, Mike, 257

Friday, 152

fringes

    dress, Kiowa, 240

    dress yoke, Kiowa, 84

    of hair, 155, 196n13

    impenetrability from, 206

    moccasins, Kiowa, 239

    shirt, Hidatsa or Mandan, 223

funerals, 96, 282

Gaigwa. *See* Kiowa (Gaigwa)

Galloping, 139, 140

game, "wild horses," 124

gardening. *See* horticulture

Garrison Dam, 19–20, 29–30

German silver, 262–263

Geronimo, 234

Ghost Dance

    Arapaho pipe bag symbolism, 37

    freedom of religion and, 30

    origin of, 206

    sacred clothing for, 202, 206, 207–209

    songs for, 209–210

    The Visit (Amiotte), 283

    Wounded Knee and, 221–222

Gilmore, Melvin, 22

Girls Dormitory, Crow Boarding School (Miller), 220

giveaways, 246

glass beads. *See* beadwork

God is Red (Deloria), 21–22

Goes Ahead, 49, 95

Goggles, Gloria, 255

Going Without Water, 166

Good Furred Robe, 60

Goodsell, Freda Mesteth, 282–283

    star quilt, 282

Goose Society, 183

gourd rattles, 261, 262

government, federal

assimilation policy, 225, 259

battle with military, 219–222

negotiations with, 149–152, 201, 222–225

restrictions on ceremonies, 187–191

See also treaties

Grand Entry ceremonies, 268

grandmothers, 88, 89, 91, 234

A Grandmother's Lodge (Parsons), 288

Grass Dance (Omaha Dance), 159, 162, 191, 265

Great American Desert, 14

Great Plains Region, description of, 14

Great Spirit, 19, 35

Green hides showing geometric design for parfleches (Rau), 67

Grey Horn Butte (Bear Lodge), 27, 29

Grinnell, Calvin, 66

Grinnell, George Bird, 24–25, 95, 176, 178

Grinnell, Mrs. George Bird "Elizabeth"

    Northern Cheyenne Women Gathering Wood, 54

    Woman Using Smoother in Applying Porcupine Quills, 79

grizzly bears

    bear claw necklaces, 172

    Crow shield cover, 141

    Hidatsa shield cover, 143

    See also bears

Gros Ventre

    buffalo hunts and, 16

    buffalo restoration and, 257–258

    conflicts with U.S. military, 219

    sacred places, 28

Guadal-tseyu, 211

guilds. *See* societies

gun case, Lakota, 127

guns, first use of, 44

Hail, Barbara, 197n46

hair ornaments, men's

    Blackfeet, 133

    Lakota, 132

    Oglala Lakota, 267

hair pipes, 132, 247

Hako (Calumet Ceremony), 99

half leggings, Eastern Sioux, 222

Hampton Normal and Agricultural Institute, 225

hanbleceya ("crying for a vision"), 166

hand drum, Lakota, 185

Hansen, Emma I.

    Bear Lodge (Devil's Tower), 29

    Crow Riders at Indian Memorial Dedication, 258

    Memorial at Old Scouts Cemetery, 259

Harney Peak, 26

Haskell Institute, 228–231

Hassrick, Royal, 93n42, 95, 96, 155

Hawk Chief Run, 269

Hayes, Rutherford B., 151

Head-Smashed-In Buffalo Jump (Alberta), 111

headwear. *See* bonnets and headdresses

health, impact of buffalo loss on, 257

Heart Mountain, 199

Heavy Runner, 220

herbalists, 96

Her Holy Door, 155

Her Many Horses, Emil

    Native American Church Set, 261

Hethuska Dance, 265

Hidatsa

    age-graded societies, 155–160, 162, 182–183

    baskets, 53

    beads and, 74, 77

    Black Hills and, 25

    blanket strips, 75

    buffalo and, 146–147

    buffalo calling ceremonies, 106

    buffalo emblems, 105

    buffalo robes, 72, 101

    Crow and, 40

    dogs, role of, 115

    Fort Berthold Reservation and, 108

    Garrison Dam and, 19–20, 29–30

    historical development of, 15, 39

    horses and, 118

    horticulture, 58, 60–61, 62

    leggings, 180

    Long-time Dog—Hidatsa (Curtis), 128

    migration and origin story, 39–40, 198

    moccasins, 223

    plant gathering, 56

    quillwork, 79

    relocation, 215

    rings and bracelets, 179

    shirts, 223

    smallpox epidemic, 30, 218

    Three Affiliated Tribes, 19–20, 46n9

    tipis and lodges, 66

hide containers and parfleches, 67–70

    box, Lakota, 65

    case, Cheyenne, 64

    cylinder cases, Crow, 71

    Green hides showing geometric design for parfleches (Rau), 67

    knives with cases, Lakota, 77

    parfleche, Crow, 104

    parfleches, Cheyenne, 68

    parfleches, Lakota, 69

    storage bags, Blackfeet, 76

    storage bags, Cheyenne, 105

    storage bags, Crow, 76

    storage bags, Lakota, 243, 249

hide hunting, commercial, 212–214

hide robes. *See* buffalo robes

hide scrapers, 86–87, 93n42

hide tanning, 70–71, 77, 181

Hill, Rick, 290

Hinono'ei. *See* Arapaho (Hinono'ei)

Hoebel, Adamson E., 95

holidays, Euro-American, 191, 249
homecomings, 266–269
homes. *See* lodges and tipis
horns. *See* buffalo horns
horse dance stick, Lakota, 160
horse mask, Nez Perce, 194
horse medicine, 124
horse riding equipment, 124
  bridle, Blackfeet, 194
  crupper, Crow, 190
  horse mask, Nez Perce, 194
  martingales, Crow, 189, 192
  quirt, Osage, 116
  saddlebags, 105, 119
  See also saddle blankets; saddles
horses
  buffalo hunting and, 111
  children and, 122–124
  first encounters and acquisition of, 16, 95,
    115–116, 198
  horse stealing charm, 116
  images of, 120, 124, 139
  on Lakota pipe bag, 36
  marriage and, 94, 95
  Moving camp (Petzoldt), 63
  names for, 117
  parades and, 193
  Plateau people and, 194
  raids for, 121, 136
  spiritual significance, 124–125
  value of, 118–120
  war horses, 121–122
  *Woman and Children Traveling with Horse and
    Travois*, 16
horticulture, 15–16, 58–62
Hot Dance, 191–193
Houser, Allan C., 285, 285
  Drama on the Plains, 254
houses, log, 214
  See also lodges and tipis
Howe, Oscar, 283–284
Hoyt, John W., 149, 151, 152
Hudson, Marilyn, 19–20, 29
Huffman, L.A.
  Cheyenne Boy, 19
  Cheyenne Chief Two Moon, at Fort Keogh, 153
  'Pretty Nose,' Cheyenne Girl, 52
  Sioux Chief Hump with his wives, 204
  'Spotted Fawn'—Cheyenne Girl of 13, 12
  In the track of the skin hunters, 1878, 213
  Two Moon's Children, 53
  White Hawk—Cheyenne, 123
Human Genome Diversity Project (HGDP),
    296–297
Hump, Chief, 204
Hunkpapa Lakota, 44, 246
  See also Sitting Bull
hunting
  boys and, 125–128
  butchering, 133
    of cattle, 225
    communal hunt and soldier societies, 128–133
    demise of buffalo and, 141–142
    equipment, 126
    hide hunting, commercial, 212–214
    horses and, 121
    methods of, 107–111
    spiritual aspects, 133–134
    traveling for, 16–17
Hyde, Doug, 285
  Coyote Legend, 252

Ichi-chay (sacred seeds), 198
Iktomi (trickster), 35
Indian breadroot (prairie turnip), 53–55
Indian Memorial, Little Bighorn Battlefield, 258
"Indian offenses," 259, 292n7
Indian Reorganization Act, 30, 46n9, 201
Indian Territory, 216–217, 237
iniskin (buffalo amulet, Blackfoot), 106
initiations for quill and bead work, 86
Institute of American Indian Arts (IAIA), 284–286
  Biss at, 285
  Cannon at, 286
  Houser at, 254
  Hyde at, 253
Internet, 294–297
Inter Tribal Bison Cooperative, 257
In the track of the skin hunters, 1878 (Huffman),
    213
*In Traditional Dress, Bright Wings, Beth Iron
    Horse, Annie Talking Pipe and Nellie
    Scratches Face*, 188
Iowa tribe, 44
Iron Cloud, Sandra, 267
Iron Horse, Beth, 188
Iron Tail, 235
Iron Teeth, 64, 115, 122–124
Iruska ("the fire is in me"), 265

jackets
  Crow, 228
  Lakota, 236
  Oglala Lakota, 235
Jackson, Charles Thomas, 35
Jay, Debra Lee Stone, 276–277
  vest, 276
Jefferson, Thomas, 14, 296
Jennings, Vanessa Paukeigope, 277–280
  cradle, 278
jewelry, 179–181
Joe, Oreland C.
  Star Blanket, 287
Johnson, Louella, 55
Jones Berry, Anna E., 279
Joseph, Chief, 118, 246
June berries, 55–56

Kanai (Blood), 111, 218
Kansa (Kaw), 15
Keintaddle, 278
Kicked In the Bellies, 39
Kicking Bear, 221
Kills-good, 67
Kiowa (Cheyenne artist), 139, 140
Kiowa (Gaigwa)
  artists of, 263, 277–280, 285
  beadwork, 237
  buffalo demise and, 214–215
  buffalo emblems, 105
  buffalo hunting and, 17
  Buffalo Medicine Keeper (Cannon), 286
  cradle, 224
  disease and, 217
  dress, 240
  dress yoke, 84
  hide processing, art of, 77
  ledger drawings, 140
  migration journey, 24
  moccasins, 85, 239
  Omaha Dance, 265
  sacred places, 25, 28, 31
  Spotted Horse and, 120
  Sun Dance, 262
  winter counts, 42
Kit Foxes lodge, 161
Knife Chief, Charles, 22, 24
Knife Chief, Kim
  Cradleboard Pendant, 290
knives and cases, Lakota, 77
Kootenai, 28
Kroeber, Alfred, 161

La Framboise, 45
Lakota
  akí'cita (soldier societies), 129–133, 153–155
  alliance with Northern Arapaho and Northern
    Cheyenne, 151
  artists of, 263, 282–284
  beadwork, 74, 236–237
  blanket, 251
  blanket strips, 75
  boarding schools and, 226
  bow case and quiver, 126
  bowl, 106
  boy's pants, Lakota, 234
  boy's vest, 234
  breastplate, 132
  buffalo, spiritual beliefs about, 101–103,
    105–106
  buffalo horn bonnet, 114
  buffalo hunting and, 17
  buffalo robes, 72, 73, 136
  Buffalo Sing (*Tatanka Olowanpi*) ceremony,
    95–96
  Cheyenne River Lakota, 256
  childbirth, 95–96

code of conduct, 87
courtship, 95
cradles, 88–89, *176*
Crow and, 205
Crow-Owners Society, 138
Custer and, 285
dance shield, Brule Lakota, *157*
dance shield cover, *156*
dolls, *48*, 89
dresses, *94, 230, 232, 233*
eagle feather bonnet and trailer, *167*
eagle feather bonnets and, 169, *170–172*
elk teeth, use of, 227
families, 95
food trading, 62
freedom of religion and, 30
Ghost Dance and, 206, 210
guilds, 86
gun case, *127*
hair ornament, men's, *132*
hand drum, *185*
horn spoon, *59*
horse dance stick, *160*
horses and, 116, 117, 121, 122
Hunkpapa Lakota, 44, 246
hunting, 127–128
Indian Memorial and, *258*
on Internet, 296
jacket, *236*
knives with cases, 77
Lakota girls, South Dakota, late 1800s, *231*
leadership, 155
leggings, *130*
Little Bighorn and, 220
Little Bighorn hide painting, *137*
moccasins, *80, 180*
Native American Church Cross (Zephier), *263*
necklaces, *247*
Omaha Dance, 265
parfleches, *69*
pipe bags, *36–37*
pipes, 32, *32*, 35
powwows, 266
prairie turnips and, 53
quillwork, *179*, 235–236
quilting, 280–281
rawhide box, *65*
sacred places, 25, 26, 27, 28, 31
saddle blanket, *119*
shirts, *148*, 154, *171, 177, 209*
Sioux as misnomer for, 294
storage bags, *243, 249*
Sun Dance, 184, *185*, 260–261
Tatanka Wan, A Buffalo Bull (Yellow), *256*
tomahawk, *125*
traditional arts in early reservation period,
    246–251
"two spirit" males, 95
utensils, *61*

vision quests (*hanbleceya*), 166
warrior role, 134
winter counts, 42–45
women's role, 173
See also Oglala Lakota; Sioux; Sitting Bull;
    Wounded Knee
lance case, Crow, *191*
Lance Society, 267, 269
land. *See* sacred places
language preservation, 254
leadership
    clothing and regalia, 169–173
    Crow leaders, 198–201
    honors and accomplishments and, 152–153
    reservation chiefs and negotiations with
    Washington, 149–152
    on reservations, 246
    shirts and, *200*
    surrogate leader ceremonies, 250–251
    vision quests and, 162–169
    warrior societies and, 153–155
ledger drawings, 139–140
    Galloping, Little Man, Kiowa, and Sweetwater
    drawings, *139*
    Spotted Horse, *120*, 139
    *Wooden Leg Drawing Events from Battle of
    Little Big Horn* (Marquis), *139*
Left Hand, 95
Legend Rock, 25
leggings
    girl's leggings, Crow, *226*
    half leggings, Eastern Sioux, *222*
    man's leggings (Upper Missouri Region), *222*
    man's leggings, Blackfeet, *237*
    man's leggings, Hidatsa, *180*
    man's leggings, Lakota, *130*
    man's leggings, Oglala Lakota, *131*
    woman's leggings, Blackfeet, *86*
    woman's moccasins with leggings, Crow, *239*
Leonid meteor storm (1833), 44
Lewis, Meriwether, 53, 60, 74, 147, 296
Like-a-Fishhook village, 60–61, 62, 160, 259
Linderman, Frank B., 49, 95, 205
Little Bighorn, Battle of, 219, 220
    hide painting, *137*
    Sitting Bull and, *155*
    Two Moon and, *153*
    *Wooden Leg Drawing Events from Battle of
    Little Big Horn* (Marquis), *139*
Little Bighorn Battlefield National Monument, *258*
Little Man, *139*, 140
Little Wound, 149, 150
Llewellyn, Karl N., 95
lodges, age-graded, 161
    See also societies
lodges and tipis
    buffalo hide tipi, Nez Perce, *100*
    A Child's Lodge—Piegan (Curtis), *17*
    child's tipi cover, Cheyenne, *88*

earth lodges, 66
Mandan Earthen Lodge (Curtis), *20*
moving camp and, 63, *63*–66
Pretty Shell and Pretty Beads with tipi (Crow),
    23
Loloma, Charles, *285*
Lone Dog, 44
Lone Man, 20
Lone Woman, 91, 93n43
Long, Stephen H., 46n2
Long Hair, Chief (Red Feather at His Temple),
    198–199
Long-time Dog—Hidatsa (Curtis), *128*
Lower Brule Reservation, 263
Lowie, Robert, 41

maípsuka'sa (woman's belt), *181*
males, "two spirit," 95
Mallery, Garrick, 44
Mandan (Nueta)
    age-graded societies, 155, 160
    beads and, 74, 77
    Black Hills and, 25
    buffalo and, 146–147
    buffalo mask, *147*
    buffalo robe, *103*
    burden basket, *53*
    Crow and, 40
    Fort Berthold Reservation and, *108*
    Garrison Dam and, 19–20, 29–30
    historical development of, 15
    horses and, 118
    horticulture, 58, 60–61, 62
    Mandan Earthen Lodge (Curtis), *20*
    Okipa ceremony, 106–107, 146–147, *147*
    origin story, 20
    quillwork, 79
    shirts, *223*
    smallpox and, 44, 218
    smallpox epidemic, 30
    Three Affiliated Tribes, 19–20, 46n9
    tipis and lodges, 66
    women's societies, *182, 183*
Mandan Earthen Lodge (Curtis), *20*
Man with a Beard, Mary, 163
Many Tail Feathers, *165*
Marias River massacre, 28, 219, 220
Marquis, Thomas
    Plenty of Drying Meat, *214*
    Sun Dance Lodge (Medicine Lodge), *184*
    *Wooden Leg Drawing Events from Battle of
    Little Big Horn*, *139*
Marquis, Thomas B., 59, 139
marriage, *94*, 95, 250
    See also courtship
marriage of metals technique, 263
martingales, Crow, *189, 192*
mascot stereotypes, 295–296
Mashed berries made into berry cakes (Petzoldt), *57*

mask
    buffalo mask, Mandan, *147*
    horse mask, Nez Perce, *194*
Mato-Kuwapi (Chased By Bears), 32, 185
Mato Paha (Bear Butte), 26
Maximilian, Prince of Wied, *103*
McAdams-Swallow, Wilma Jean, 274–276, *275*
McCleary, Timothy, 42
McClellan military saddles, 277
measles, 44
meat, buffalo, *102*, *104*, 133
Medicine, Beatrice, 94–97, 173, 261
medicine bags, sacred, 179
Medicine Crow ("Sacred Raven")
    Medicine Crow—Apsaroke (Curtis), *199*
    negotiation in Washington, 201, 225
    Plenty Coups and, 164
    vision quests, 166
    as warrior, 137–138
Medicine Crow, Joseph
    on buffalo jumps, 109
    counting coup, 137–138
    on Crow Fair, 272–273
    Crow Tribal Leaders, 198–201
    on horse medicine, 124
    on origins of Crow and Hidatsa, 39–40
    on vision quests, 164–166
    White Man Runs Him and, *135*
Medicine Lodge, 184
    See also Sun Dance
medicine men, 22
Medicine Tipi Ceremony, 185, 197n67
    See also Sun Dance
Medicine Wheel (Collier), 26
Medicine Wheel Alliance, 27
medicine women, 96
Memorial at Old Scouts Cemetery (Hansen), *259*
memorials, 219
men and division of labor, 53
    See also hunting; warriors and war
menstruation, 95
Men throwing arrows in winter (Petzoldt), *195*
"mescal beans" (peyote), 262
Meskwaki
    bear claw necklaces, 172, *172*
    moccasins, *87*
    turban, *241*
Mesteth, Christina Standing Bear, 282
metalwork, 262–263
    Cradleboard Pendant (Knife Chief), *290*
Métis
    clothing, impact of missionaries on, 249
    half leggings, *222*
    hide trade and, 214
Michelson, Truman, 95
migrations and travel
    buffalo hunts, 16–17
    Crow and Hidatsa, 39–41
    horses and, *118*

Kiowa, 24
    memories of the land and, 13
    moving camp, 63–66, 91
    observation during, 99
    political divisions, 39
    relocations, 216–217, 237, 246
military service, 267–269
Miller, Fred E.
    Girls Dormitory, Crow Boarding School, *220*
mirror bag, Crow, *161*
missionaries, 247, 248, 249, 259
Missionary Education Movement, 44
Missouria, 216
Missouri River, 19–20
mixed blood families, 250
moccasins
    Arapaho, *85*
    Blackfeet, *85*, *107*
    Cheyenne, *175*, *239*
    Crow, *96*, *239*
    Eastern Shoshone (Swallow family), *275*
    Eastern Sioux, *80*
    girls learning to make, 91
    Hidatsa, *223*
    Kiowa, *85*, *239*
    Lakota, *80*, *180*
    Meskwaki, *87*
    Pawnee, *131*
    Shoshone, *104*
Momaday, N. Scott, 13, 24, 211
Mopope, Etta (Paukeigope), 278, 279
Mopope, Jeanette Berry, 278, 279
Mopope, Stephen, 278, 279
Mother and Child—Apsaroke (Curtis), *50*
Mother Corn, 60, 186
Mountain Crows, 39, 42
Mount Scott, 215
mourning, 96
moving. *See* migrations and travel
Moving camp (Petzoldt), *63*
museums, 205

Nakota, 25
names, 124, 226–228
National Bison Range, 256
National Trust for Historical Preservation, 31
Native American Church
    fan, Omaha, *210*
    origins of, 210
    persecutions and prohibitions, 31, 261–262
    ritual objects, 261, 262–263, *263*
Native American Church Cross (Zephier), *263*
Native American Church Set (Her Many Horses),
    261
Native American Graves Protection and
    Repatriation Act (1990), 254–255
Native American Rights Fund, 31
Navajo, 287
necklaces

bear claw, 172, *172*
    hair pipe, Lakota, *247*
Neihardt, John, 26, 203
New, Lloyd, 273, 286, 288
New Holy, Sophie, 274
New Holy Blue Legs, Alice, 267, *274*
New Life Lodge, 185
    See also Sun Dance
Nez Perce (Nimíipu)
    artists of, 285
    buffalo hide tipi, *100*
    Coyote Legend (Hyde), *252*
    Crow Fair and, 270
    horse mask, *194*
    resistance to relocation, 246
    saddle blanket, *118*
Nicotiana mutivalvis, 41
Nimíipu. *See* Nez Perce (Nimíipu)
"noble savage," 94
Northern Arapaho. *See* Arapaho, Northern
Northern Cheyenne. *See* Cheyenne, Northern
Northern Cheyenne Reservation
    Cheyenne Boy (Huffman), *19*
    Northern Cheyenne Women Gathering Wood
        (Grinnell), *54*
    Painted Rocks site, 24–25
    Plenty of Drying Meat (Marquis), *214*
    'Pretty Nose,' Cheyenne Girl (Huffman), *52*
    Spang and, 288
    'Spotted Fawn'—Cheyenne Girl of 13
        (Huffman), *47*n35
    Sun Dance Lodge (Medicine Lodge) (Marquis),
        184
    Two Moon's Children (Huffman), *53*
    *Woman Using Smoother in Applying Porcupine
        Quills* (Grinnell), *79*
Northern Cheyenne Women Gathering Wood
    (Grinnell), *54*
No Vitals (No Intestines or No Insides), 39–41,
    198
Nueta. *See* Mandan (Nueta)
nursing, 96

Offerings Lodge, 185
    See also Sun Dance
Oglala Lakota
    American Horse, 43
    artists of, 282–283
    banner (Amiotte and Gibbons), *283*
    jacket, *235*
    man's hair ornament (New Holy Blue Legs), *267*
    man's leggings, *131*
    Native American Church Set (Her Many
        Horses), *261*
    resistance to relocation, 246
    shirt, Oglala Teton Lakota, *129*
    shirt of Red Cloud, *148*
    star quilt (Goodsell), *282*
    transitions and struggles, 203

The Visit (Amiotte), 283
Washington conferences, 225
Okipa (O-Kee-Pa) ceremony, 106–107, 146–147, 147, 160
Old Men's lodge, 161
Old Scouts Cemetery, 259
Omaha
    beadwork and, 87
    bear claw necklaces, 172
    fan, 210
    Grass Dance, 162
    Hethuska Dance, 265
    historical development of, 15
    horticulture, 58
    Major Long and, 46n2
    Ponca and, 216
    wáwa ceremony, 34–35
Omaha Dance (Grass Dance), 159, 162, 191, 265
Omaha Reservation, 216
oral traditions, 45, 147, 214–215
Oregon Trail, 212
Osage
    beadwork and, 87
    historical development of, 15
    in ledger drawing by Spotted Horse, 120
    Omaha Dance, 265
    quirt (riding whip), 116
    roach headdress and spreader, 159
Otoe
    beadwork, 87, 237
    bear claw necklaces, 172
    blanket, 241
    dance stick, 160
    historical development of, 15
    horticulture, 58
    Major Long and, 46n2
    relocation, 216
    smallpox and, 44
otters, 172
Owl Dance, 191

Paha Sapa (Black Hills), 25–26
Pahuk (Pahaku), 22–24
Painted Rocks, 24–25
painting on hides, 73–74
    Battle of Little Bighorn, 137
    buffalo robes, 72, 103
    by Codsiogo, 98
paintings
    Buffalo Medicine Keeper (Cannon), 286
    Crow Winter Camp in Teepees, 284
    General Custer in Blue and Green (Biss), 285
Paiute, 206, 221
pants, boy's, Lakota, 234
    See also leggings
parades
    Crow Fair and, 186, 193
    Crow Indian Parade Rider (Red Star), 270
    Riders in Crow Fair Parade (Hansen), 270

In Traditional Dress, Bright Wings, Beth Iron
    Horse, Annie Talking Pipe and Nellie
    Scratches Face, 188
parfleches. See hide containers and parfleches
Parker, Quanah, 210
Parsons, Neil
    A Grandmother's Lodge, 288
patchwork quilts, 250, 280
    See also quilts
Pawnee (Chaticks si Chaticks)
    artists of, 263
    beadwork and, 87
    bear claw necklaces, 172
    ceremonies, 186
    Cradleboard Pendant (Knife Chief), 290
    division of labor, 53
    Ghost Dance and, 210
    historical development of, 15
    Homecoming, 267–269
    horticulture, 58, 60, 62
    Iruska ("the fire is in me"), 265
    moccasins, 131
    relocation, 216–217
    sacred places, 22–24, 31
    Skidi band of, 22
    song, 99
    Spotted Horse and, 120
    in Wild West Show, 248
    women, role of, 50–51
Pawnee Chapter of the American War Mothers,
    269
Pawnee Indian Veterans Association, 269
pemmican, 56
Petroglyph in Bighorn Basin of Wyoming (Bies), 21
petroglyphs, 24–25
Petzoldt, William A.
    eagle feather bonnet given to, 168
    Mashed berries made into berry cakes, 57
    Men throwing arrows in winter, 195
    Moving camp, 63
    Two Crow Children, 217
    Woman using a sewing machine, 221
Pevah (Spang), 295
peyote, 262
peyote boxes, 262
Picking Bones Woman, 197n51
Pictograph Cave, 25
pictographs, 24–25
Piegan
    A Child's Lodge—Piegan (Curtis), 17
    Crow and, 204
    Head-Smashed-In Buffalo Jump, 111
    horses and, 116–117
    smallpox epidemic, 218
    warfare and, 135–136
pigments, 73–74, 81
Pike, Zebulon, 46n2
Pine Ridge Reservation, 248
pipe bags

Arapaho, 37
Blackfeet, 38
Cheyenne, 37
Crow, 37
Lakota, 36–37
Northern Plains, 38
Sioux, 33
pipe ceremony, 258
pipes, 32–39
    Buffalo Woman and, 101–103
    calumets, 34, 34–35
    Lakota, 32, 35
    Sioux, 33
Pipestone National Monument, 35
pipe tomahawks, 172–173, 173
Plains Indian Museum Powwow, Cody, Wyoming,
    265, 268
plant gathering, 53–58
Plays With His Face, 198
Pleiades, the, 25
Plenty Coups
    chief, role of, 153
    on counting coup, 137, 152
    on loss of buffalo, 205, 211
    negotiations in Washington, 201
    Plenty Coups with Adopted Daughter, 163
    vision quests, 162–164, 166, 169
Plenty of Drying Meat (Marquis), 214
Pollock, William, 268
Pompey's Pillar (Where the Mountain Lion Sits),
    198, 199
Ponca
    beadwork and, 87
    bear claw necklaces, 172
    Black Hills and, 25
    blanket strips, 75
    historical development of, 15
    horticulture, 58
    Omaha Dance, 265
    Prairie style of beadwork among, 87
    relocation, 216
    smallpox and, 44
population decline, 216–217
portraits
    Cheyenne Boy (Huffman), 19
    Cheyenne Chief Two Moon, at Fort Keogh
        (Huffman), 153
    Chief Rocky Bear, Sioux (Rinehart), 33
    Chief Wets It, Assiniboine (Rinehart), 110
    Lakota girls, South Dakota, late 1800s, 231
    Long-time Dog—Hidatsa (Curtis), 128
    Medicine Crow—Apsaroke (Curtis), 199
    Mother and Child—Apsaroke (Curtis), 50
    Plenty Coups with Adopted Daughter, 163
    'Pretty Nose,' Cheyenne Girl (Huffman), 52
    Sioux Chief Hump with his wives (Huffman),
        204
    Sioux Delegation in Washington, Red Dog,
        Little Wound, Red Cloud, American Horse,

Red Shirt, John Bridgeman, *150*
Sitting Bull (Tatanka Iyotake) and Family
    (Spooner), *155*
Spies on the Enemy, Crow (Rinehart), *113*
'Spotted Fawn'—Cheyenne Girl of 13
    (Huffman), *12*
Spotted Horse, self-portrait, *139*
White Hawk—Cheyenne (Huffman), *123*
White Man Runs Him—Apsaroke (Curtis), *135*
potato, prairie (prairie turnip), *53–55*
Potawatomi, *87*
power, from buffalo, *105–106*
Powers, Marla, *96*
Powers, William, *95–96*
powwows, *263–267*
    Plains Indian Museum Powwow, *265, 268*
    Shoshone rose design and, *275, 276*
prairie turnip (*Psoralea esculenta*), *53–55*
Pratt, D. L., *36*
Pratt, Richard Henry, *226*
Pretty Beads, *23*
Pretty Eagle, *201*
'Pretty Nose,' Cheyenne Girl (Huffman), *52*
Pretty Shell, *23*
Pretty Shell and Pretty Beads in Doorway of Tipi,
    23
Pretty Shield
    on buffalo jumps, *111*
    on digging prairie turnips, *56*
    on family, *95*
    on hide painting, *73*
    Linderman interview with, *49*
    on loss of buffalo, *205–206, 212*
    on marriage, *95*
    on moving camp, *64–65*
    Snell on, *71, 77*
Pretty Voice Hawk (Mitchell Zephier), *263, 263*
    Native American Church Cross, 263
Psoralea esculenta (prairie turnip), *53–55*
Pté Oyáte (Buffalo People), *183, 256*
puberty, *95–96*
Pursh, Frederick, *53*

Quick-to-See Smith, Jaune
    Painted Pony Series: Games People Play, 289
quillwork
    about, *74*
    blanket strips, *75*
    man's cuffs and arm band, Oglala Lakota (New
        Holy), *274*
    man's hair ornament, Oglala Lakota (New Holy
        Blue Legs), *267*
    moccasins, *80*
    Northern Arapaho, *179*
    in reservation period, *235–236*
    shirts, *78, 79, 177*
    societies for, *175–179, 197n51*
    Woman Using Smoother in Applying Porcupine
        Quills (Grinnell), *79*

quilts, *250, 251, 280–282*
    star quilt, Oglala Lakota (Goodsell), *282*
quirt (riding whip), Osage, *116*
quivers, *126*
Quivira, people of, *15*

railroad lines, *213*
ranching, *250*
rattles, gourd, *261, 262*
Rau, William H.
    Green hides showing geometric design for
        parfleches, 67
rawhide. *See* hide containers and parfleches
Red Cloud, *149, 150, 225, 246*
Red Dog, *150*
Red Feather at His Temple (Chief Long Hair),
    198–199
Red Scout, *39–40*
Red Shirt, *150*
Red Shirt, Delphine, *87, 93n43, 183*
Red Star, Kevin, *284–285*
    Crow Indian Parade Rider, 270
    Crow Winter Camp in Teepees, 284
Reed, High, *44*
religion
    earth lodges and, *66*
    freedom of, *30–31*
    organized, *147*
    See also ceremonies, rituals, and celebrations;
        Ghost Dance; Native American Church
relocations, *216–217, 237, 246*
reservation chiefs, *150–151*
Reynolds, Samuel C., *271–272*
riding equipment. *See* horse riding equipment
Rinehart, F.A.
    Chief Rocky Bear, Sioux, 33
    Chief Wets It, Assiniboine, 110
    Spies on the Enemy, Crow, 113
rings, *179*
rituals. *See* ceremonies, rituals, and celebrations
River Crows, *39, 42*
roach headdress and spreader, Osage, *159*
Roan Horse, *95*
robes. *See* buffalo robes
Rocky Bear, Chief, *33*
rodeos, *251*
rooster hackles, *170*
Rosebud, Battle of, *155*
Rosebud Sioux Reservation, *263*
rose design, Shoshone, *275, 276, 276*
Rotten Belly (Arapooish), *19, 199*
Rotten Tail (Twines His Tail), *199*
Rough Riders, *268*
Running Coyote, *41, 198*

sacred places
    Bear Butte (*Mato Paha*), *26*
    Bear Lodge (Devil's Tower), *27–28, 29*
    Bighorn Medicine Wheel, *26, 27*

Black Hills (*Paha Sapa*), *25–26*
    freedom of religion and, *30–31*
    Harney Peak, *26*
    as memorials of struggles, *28–29*
    Pahuk (Pahaku), *22–24*
    petroglyphs and pictographs and, *21, 24–25*
    protection of, *29–31*
    significance of, *20–22*
    Sweetgrass Hills, *28, 31*
    tribal identities and, *31*
Sacrifice Lodge, *185*
    See also Sun Dance
saddlebags, *105, 119*
    See also hide containers and parfleches
saddle blankets, *124*
    Lakota, *119*
    Nez Perce, *118*
    Upper Missouri Region, *117*
saddles, *124*
    beaded saddle, Northern Arapaho (Dewey), *277*
    Cree, *193*
    girl's saddle, Crow, *187*
    McClellan military saddles, *277*
    See also horse riding equipment
Sahnish. *See* Arikara (Sahnish)
Salish (Squelix'u)
    buffalo horn spoon, *59*
    cradle, *242*
    Painted Pony Series: Games People Play (Quick-
        to-See Smith), *289*
    sacred places, *28*
Salt Fork River, *216*
Sandall, Derek, *255*
Sand Creek massacre, *28, 219, 220*
San Francisco Art Institute, *253, 285, 285*
Santa Fe Trail, *212*
Santee Dakota. *See* Sioux, Eastern (Santee Dakota)
Saukamaupee, *116–117*
Scholder, Fritz, *285*
schools
boarding schools, *225–235, 248–249*
    Girls Dormitory, Crow Boarding School
        (Miller), *220*
    Wind River Tribal College, *254*
    Wyoming Indian School, *254*
    See also Institute of American Indian Arts (IAIA)
Scratches Face, Nellie, *188*
sculpture
    Coyote Legend (Hyde), *252*
    Cradleboard Pendant (Knife Chief), *290*
    Drama on the Plains (Houser), *254*
    Pevah (Spang), *295*
    Star Blanket (Joe), *287*
    Tatanka Wan, A Buffalo Bull (Yellow), *256*
Secretary's Orders (1887), *201*
Seen by the Nation, *155*
Sees the Living Bull, *42*
sewing machines, *221, 235, 249*
Sharp, Joseph Henry

Crow Tipi Village, Riverside, 186
Sharp Nose, 152
Sheridan, Philip, 214, 244n21
shield covers
    Arikara, *109*
    Crow, *140, 141, 142*
    dance shield cover, Lakota, *156*
    Hidatsa, *143*
shields
    Arikara, *108*
    dance shield, Brule Lakota, *156*
shirts, 172
    Arikara, *79*
    Blackfeet, *238*
    Crow, *128, 174, 200*
    fringes of hair on, 155, 196n13
    Ghost Dance shirt, Arapaho, *207*
    Ghost Dance shirt, Lakota, *209*
    Hidatsa and Mandan, *223*
    Lakota, *148, 154, 171, 177*
    Oglala Teton Lakota, *129*
    Southern Ute (Box), *280*
    Upper Missouri region, *78*
    war honors on, *129*
Shirt Wearers (wicaŝayatanpi), 155, 172
shoes. *See* moccasins
Shooter, 134
Short Bull, 221
Shoshone (So-soreh)
    Bighorn Medicine Wheel and, 27
    Crow Fair and, 270
    dress, *82*
    Ghost Dance and, 210
    horses and, 116–117
    man's winter moccasins, *104*
    Painted Pony Series: Games People Play (Quick-to-See Smith), *289*
Shoshone, Eastern
    artists of, 256
    dress and moccasins, (Swallow family), *275*
    eagle feather bonnet and trailer, *167*
    language and culture classes, 254
    painted hide (Codsiogo), *98*
    petroglyphs and, 25
    powwows, 265
    reservation treaties and, 149–151
    Sun Dance, 259
    Swallow family beadworkers, 274–276
Shoshone-Bannock Reservation, 276
Shoshone-Bannock vest (Jay), *276*
silver, German, 262–263
Singer, Richard, 266
Sioux
    buffalo hunting and, 17
    buffalo restoration, 257–258
    Chief Rocky Bear, Sioux (Rinehart), *33*
    Crow and, 204
    Crow Fair and, 270
    horn scraper handles, 93n42

hunting, 125
    on Internet, 296
    Little Bighorn and, 220
    as name, 294
    prairie turnips and, 55
    smallpox and, 44
    winter counts, 42–45, *43*
    Yankton Sioux, 55
    See also Dakota; Lakota; Oglala Lakota
Sioux, Eastern (Santee Dakota)
    feast bowl, *58*
    half leggings, 222
    moccasins, *80*
    pipestone and, 35
    See also Dakota
Sioux Chief Hump with his wives (Huffman), *204*
Sioux Delegation in Washington, *150*
Sits In The Middle Of The Land (Black Foot), 199–201
Sitting Bull
    drawings by, *120*
    items traded by, 36, 59, 61
    resistance to relocation, 246
    second coming of, 201
    as spokesman, 246
    tomahawk of, 125
    in Wild West Show, 248
    Wounded Knee and, 221
Sitting Bull (Tatanka Iyotake) and Family (Spooner), *155*
Sitting Bull Killing a Crow Indian (Sitting Bull), *120*
Skidi band of Pawnee, 22
Skunk Society, 182–183
smallpox epidemics, 30, 44, 147, 217–218, 244n30
Snakes, 151
Snell, Alma Hogan, 56, 64–65, 71, 77
social units, 95
societies
    age-graded, 146, 155–162, 182–183
    women's, 175–179, 182–183, 197n51
    See also warrior societies
soldier societies. *See* warrior societies
Soldier Wolf, Cassie, 263–264
Soldier Wolf, Fay Ann, 265
songs
    about horses, 121, 122, 124, 125
    Buffalo Song, 133
    for Ghost Dance, 209–210
    hand drum, Lakota, *185*
    Pawnee, 99
So-soreh. *See* Shoshone (So-soreh)
Southern Arapaho, 151, 225
Southern Cheyenne. *See* Cheyenne, Southern
Spang, Bently, 288–289, 294–297
    Pevah, *295*
Spanish American War, 268
Spears lodge, 161
Spies on the Enemy, Crow (Rinehart), *113*

spirits
    of buffalo, 147
    Ghost Dance and, 206, 207
    sacred places and, 22
    vision quests and, 164–166
Spooner, John Pitcher
    Sitting Bull (Tatanka Iyotake) and Family, *155*
spoons, horn, 59
sports mascots, 295–296
Spotted Bird, Trent, 258
'Spotted Fawn'—Cheyenne Girl of 13 (Huffman), *12*
Spotted Horse
    ledger drawing, *120*
    self-portrait, *139*
Spotted Tail, 246
squash, 60, 62
Squelix'u. *See* Salish (Squelix'u)
St. Clair, Eloise, 279
staffs, 262
    Native American Church Set (Her Many Horses), *261*
Standing Bear, 216, 282–283, *284*
Standing Bear, Luther, 125, 127, 226–228, 231
Stands in Timber, John, 169, 259
star quilts, 281–282, *282*
Stars lodge, 161
stereotypes, cartoonish, 295–296
Stone Hammer Society, 155–158, 182
stories, teaching, 147
    See also oral traditions
Strikes-with-an-axe, 95
sun, eclipse of, 44
Sun Dance, 183–186
    Buffalo Medicine Keeper (Cannon), *286*
    chastity and, 95
    horses and, 95
    prohibition of, 30, 259, 292n7, 292n8
    revitalization of, 259–261
Sun Dance Lodge (Medicine Lodge) (Marquis), *184*
sunflowers, 60, 62
Sun Gazing Dance, 185
    See also Sun Dance
Swallow, Vivian, 274–276, *275*
Swallow-Hunter, Sandra, 274–276, *275*
sweet grass, 265
Sweetgrass Hills, 28, 31
Sweetwater, 139, 140
Sweezy, Carl, 225

Talking Pipe, Annie, *188*
Tallbull, Bill, 27
tanning, 70–71, 77, 181
    See also hide containers and parfleches
Tatanka Wan, A Buffalo Bull (Yellow), *256*
teeth, elk, 84, 227
Teton Sioux, 184
    See also Oglala Teton Lakota, shirt

Thompson, David, 116–117
Three Affiliated Tribes (Hidatsa, Mandan, and Arikara), 19–20, 46n9
    See also Arikara (Sahnish); Hidatsa; Mandan (Nueta)
thunderbird, 169
tipi cover, child's (Cheyenne), 88
Tirawahat ("the one above"), 22
tobacco, 32, 39–42
    See also pipes
Tobacco Society Ceremony and Field, 41
tomahawks
    Lakota, 125
    pipe tomahawks, 172–173, 173
Tomahawks lodge, 161
Tongue River Reservation, 153
tools for women's art, 86–87
top hat, 261
Tossitisie, Renee, 265
toys, 89–91
    cradles and dolls, Crow, 89, 90
    doll, Lakota, 89
trade with Europeans
    in buffalo hides, 214
    drastic changes from, 198
    goods acquired in, 16
    leadership symbols, 172–173
Trail of Tears, 216
travel. See migrations and travel
travois
    drawn by dogs, 115
    horses and, 118
    moving camp and, 64
    Woman and Children Traveling with Horse and Travois, 16
treaties
    Brunot Treaty (1872), 149
    Fort Bridger Treaty (1868), 149
    Fort Laramie (1868), 199–201
    reservation chiefs and, 150–152
Trehero, John, 259
tribal fairs, annual, 251
Trickster, 35, 147
Trosper, Phyllis, 255
Tsatoke, Monroe, 263
Tsististas. See Cheyenne (Tsististas)
Tung Sa'u Dah ("the place of hot water"), 24
turban, Meskwaki, 241
turnips, prairie, 53–55
Turtle Lung Woman, 87, 91, 93n43, 133
Twines His Tail (Rotten Tail), 199
Two Crow Children (Petzoldt), 217
Two Leggings, 42, 121, 135, 166, 204–205
Two Moon, 153
Two Moon's Children (Huffman), 53
"two spirit" males, 95

Uhba'asaxpiluua. See Crow Fair
Umatilla, 194

universe, depiction of, 208
U.S. government. See government, federal
Uses His Head for Rattle, 60
Ute
    Northern Arapaho and, 151
    Shoshone battles against, 150
    Spotted Horse and, 120
    Star Blanket (Joe), 287
Ute, Southern
    artists of, 280
    shirt (Box), 280
utensils
    horn spoons, 59
    Lakota, 61

vests, 277
    beaded vest, Northern Arapaho (Dewey), 277
    boy's vest, Lakota, 234
    Shoshone-Bannock (Jay), 276
veterans and homecomings, 266–269
Victory Dances, 267, 269
villages, summer and winter, 146
vision quests, 162–169
visions, 140, 146

Wagner, Curly Bear, 21, 28, 39, 133, 134, 267
Wakan (latent power), 95
Walker River Reservation, 206
Walla Walla, 194
wall tents, 246
Warm Springs Chiricahua Apache
    Drama on the Plains (Houser), 254
warriors and war
    art of, 138–141
    boys and, 134–136
    clothing and preparations, 138
    counting coup, 136–138, 152, 267
    eagle feather bonnets and, 170
    equipment, 126, 127, 140, 141, 141, 142, 143
    horse raids, 121, 136
    horses and, 116–117, 121–122
    level of warfare, 134
    men, role of, 134
    militarism after Euro-American contact, 198
    reservation life and end of warfare, 204–205
    U.S. military, battles with, 219–222
    war honors on shirt, 129
warrior societies
    akí'cita (Lakota soldier society), 129–133, 153–155
    battle preparations and, 138
    roach headdress and spreader, Osage, 159
    veterans and homecomings, 266–269
Washakie, 149–151, 151, 152, 169, 196n3
Washakie, Mary, 279
Washita River massacre, 28, 219, 220
Water-Pouring Old Men, 161
Waving Corn Stalk, 60
wáwa ("to sing for someone") ceremony, 34–35

weapons
    bow cases and quivers, 126
    gun case, Lakota, 127
    guns, first use of, 44
    lance case, Crow, 191
    pipe tomahawks, 172–173, 173
    tomahawk, Lakota, 125
weasel hides, 142
Welch, James, 219, 253
Wets It, Chief, 110
Where the Mountain Lion Sits (Pompey's Pillar), 198, 199
White Antelope, 220
White Buffalo Calf Woman, 32, 95–96, 101–103
White Buffalo Cow Society, 183
White Eagle (Pawnee), 22
White Hawk—Cheyenne (Huffman), 123
White Man Runs Him, 168, 285
White Man Runs Him—Apsaroke (Curtis), 135
whooping cough, 44
wicaŝayatanpi ("praiseworthy men" or Shirt Wearers), 155, 172
wicaŝitancan ("leaders of men"), 155
Wichita
    cradles, 88
    Ghost Dance and, 210
    historical development of, 15
    horticulture, 58, 60
    Sun Dance, 262
Wild West Shows, 172, 203, 247, 248
Wiles, Sara
    Wind River High School Students Butchering Buffalo, 255
Wilson, John, 210
Wind River Reservation
    artists of, 256
    language preservation, 254
    painted hide by Codsiogo, 98
    petroglyphs and, 25
    Swallow family beadworkers, 274–276
    treaties and negotiations, 149–151
    Wind River High School Students Butchering Buffalo (Wiles), 255
Wind River Tribal College, 254
Winnebago, 87
winter counts
    about, 42–45
    and buffalo, disappearance of, 214
    Kiowa epidemic and, 217
    Lone Dog's Winter Count, 43
Witkowins ("Crazy Women"), 95
Wolf Chief, 158–160
Woman and Children Traveling with Horse and Travois, 16
Woman using a sewing machine (Petzoldt), 221
Woman Using Smoother in Applying Porcupine Quills (Grinnell), 79
women
    age-graded societies, 182–183

Buffalo Dance, 181–182
  division of labor, 53
  horses and, 122–124
  horticulture, 58–62
  lodges and moving camp, 63–66
  pipes and, 39
  plant gathering, 53–58
  at powwows, 265, 266–267
  roles of, 49–53, 94–97
women's arts
  beadwork, 74–77
  buffalo robes, 70–74
  honors from, 173–175, 179–181, 197n51
  parfleches and other containers, 67–70
  quillwork, 175–179
  societies or guilds for, 175–179
  styles and creative skills, 77–86

  tools of, 86–87
  See also specific items
Wooden Leg, 118, 169–170, 220
Wooden Leg Drawing Events from Battle of Little
  Big Horn (Marquis), 139
World War I, 268–269
World War II, 269
Wounded Knee
  freedom of religion and, 30
  and Ghost Dance, suppression of, 210
  impact of, 219, 221–222
  as sacred place, 28
Wovoka, 206, 209, 209, 221
Wraps Up His Tail, 201
Writing-on-Stone (Alberta, Canada), 28
Wyoming Indian School, 254

Yanktonai, 44, 283–284
Yankton Sioux, 55
"Year the Stars Fell," 44
Yellow, Francis G.
  Tatanka Wan, A Buffalo Bull, 256
Yellowman, Gordon, Sr., 29
Yellowstone Lake region, 24
Yellowstone National Park, 214, 256
Yellowtail, Robert, 201, 256, 272
Yellowtail, Thomas, 259–260
Yellowtail Deernose, Agnes, 258, 270
Young Bear, John, 173, 241
Young Man Afraid of His Horses, 225
Young White Buffalo, 198

Zephier, Mitchell (Pretty Voice Hawk), 263, 263
  Native American Church Cross, 263